SHIROICHI AMAUI &
KONEKONEKO PRESENTS

CHARACTER DESIGN
TAMAGONOKIMI

# The HERO LIFE
## of a (Self-Proclaimed) "Mediocre"
# DEMON!

**7**

AUTHOR  **SHIROICHI AMAUI**

ARTIST **KONEKONEKO**

**CHARACTER
DESIGN** **TAMAGONOKIMI**

THE
HERO LIFE OF A
(SELF-PROCLAIMED)
"MEDIOCRE"
DEMON!

# CONTENTS

The HERO LIFE
of a (Self-Proclaimed) "Mediocre"
DEMON!

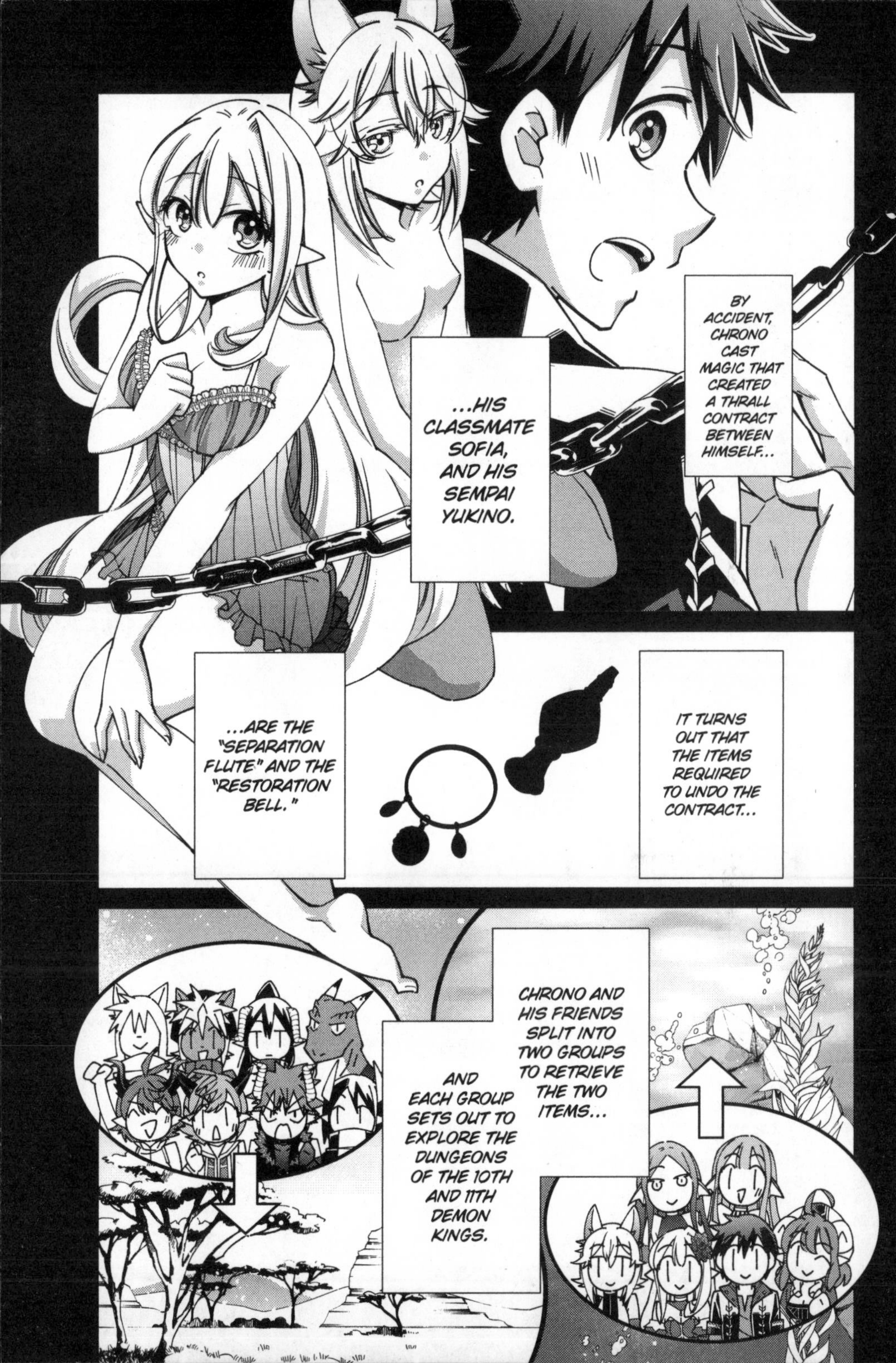
BY ACCIDENT, CHRONO CAST MAGIC THAT CREATED A THRALL CONTRACT BETWEEN HIMSELF...
...HIS CLASSMATE SOFIA, AND HIS SEMPAI YUKINO.
IT TURNS OUT THAT THE ITEMS REQUIRED TO UNDO THE CONTRACT...
...ARE THE "SEPARATION FLUTE" AND THE "RESTORATION BELL."
CHRONO AND HIS FRIENDS SPLIT INTO TWO GROUPS TO RETRIEVE THE TWO ITEMS...
AND EACH GROUP SETS OUT TO EXPLORE THE DUNGEONS OF THE 10TH AND 11TH DEMON KINGS.

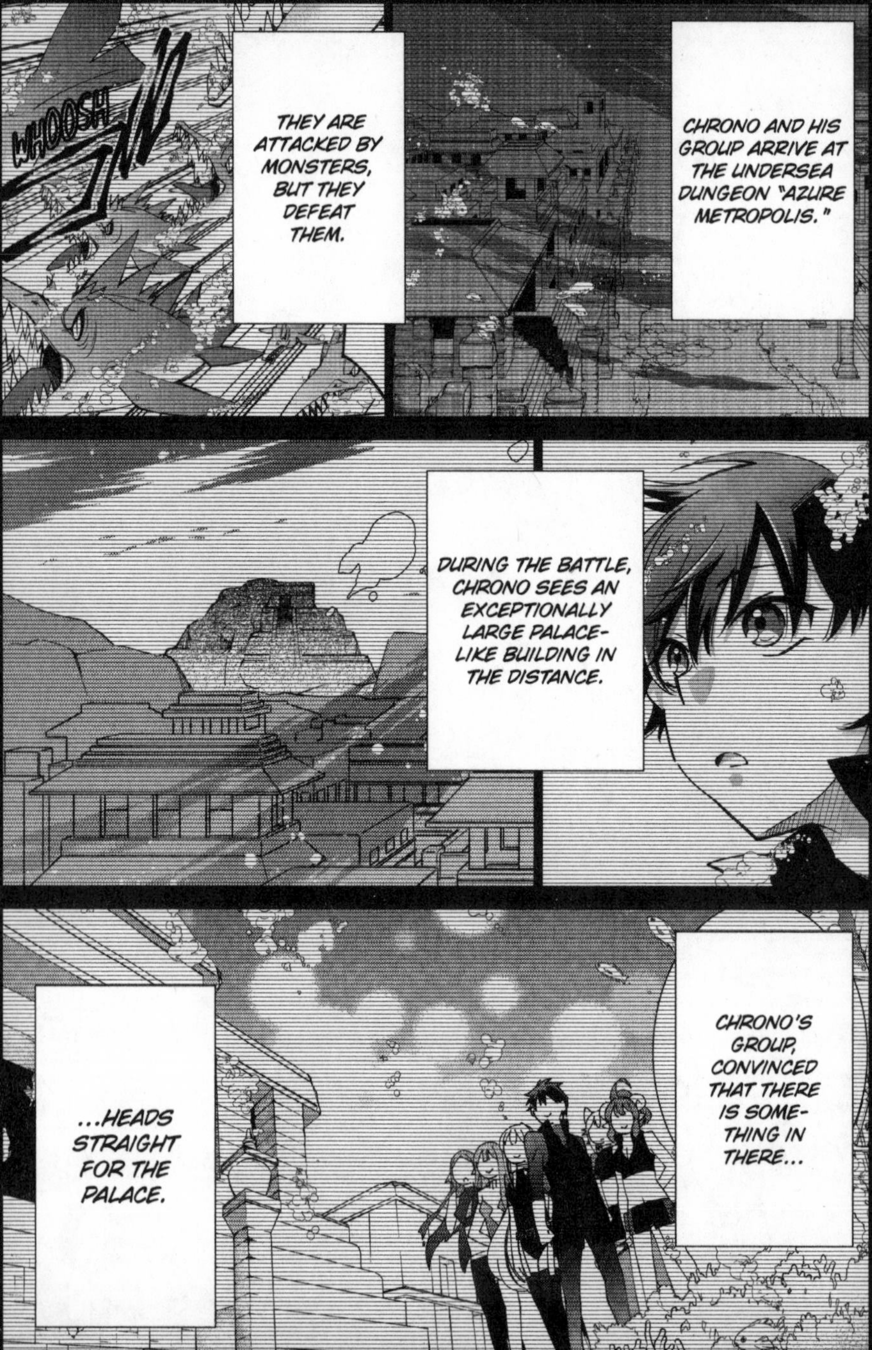
CHRONO AND HIS GROUP ARRIVE AT THE UNDERSEA DUNGEON "AZURE METROPOLIS."
THEY ARE ATTACKED BY MONSTERS, BUT THEY DEFEAT THEM.
WHOOSH
DURING THE BATTLE, CHRONO SEES AN EXCEPTIONALLY LARGE PALACE-LIKE BUILDING IN THE DISTANCE.
CHRONO'S GROUP, CONVINCED THAT THERE IS SOME-THING IN THERE...
...HEADS STRAIGHT FOR THE PALACE.

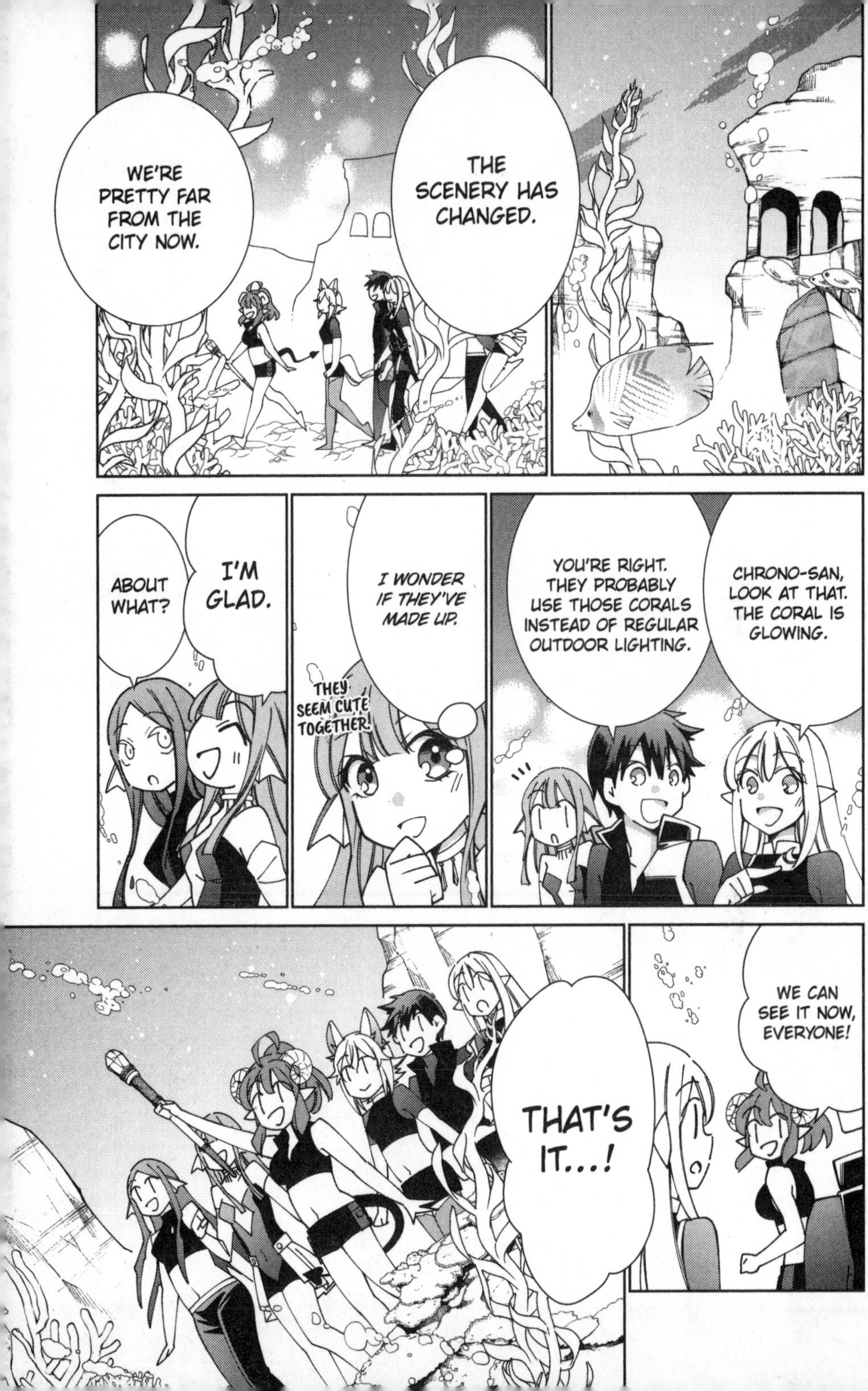
THE SCENERY HAS CHANGED.
WE'RE PRETTY FAR FROM THE CITY NOW.
CHRONO-SAN, LOOK AT THAT. THE CORAL IS GLOWING.
YOU'RE RIGHT. THEY PROBABLY USE THOSE CORALS INSTEAD OF REGULAR OUTDOOR LIGHTING.
I WONDER IF THEY'VE MADE UP.
THEY SEEM CUTE TOGETHER!
I'M GLAD.
ABOUT WHAT?
WE CAN SEE IT NOW, EVERYONE!
THAT'S IT...!

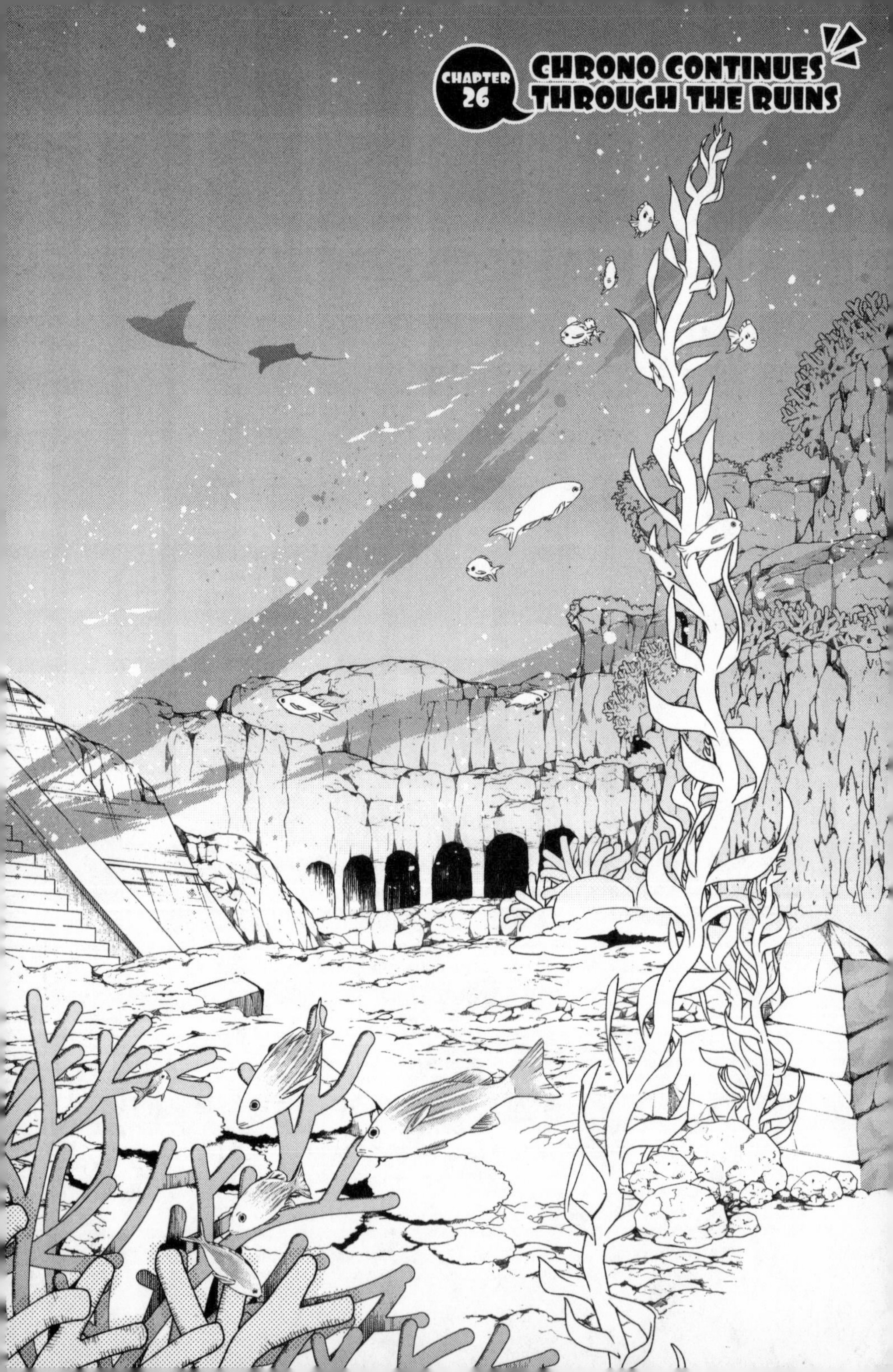
CHAPTER 26
CHRONO CONTINUES THROUGH THE RUINS

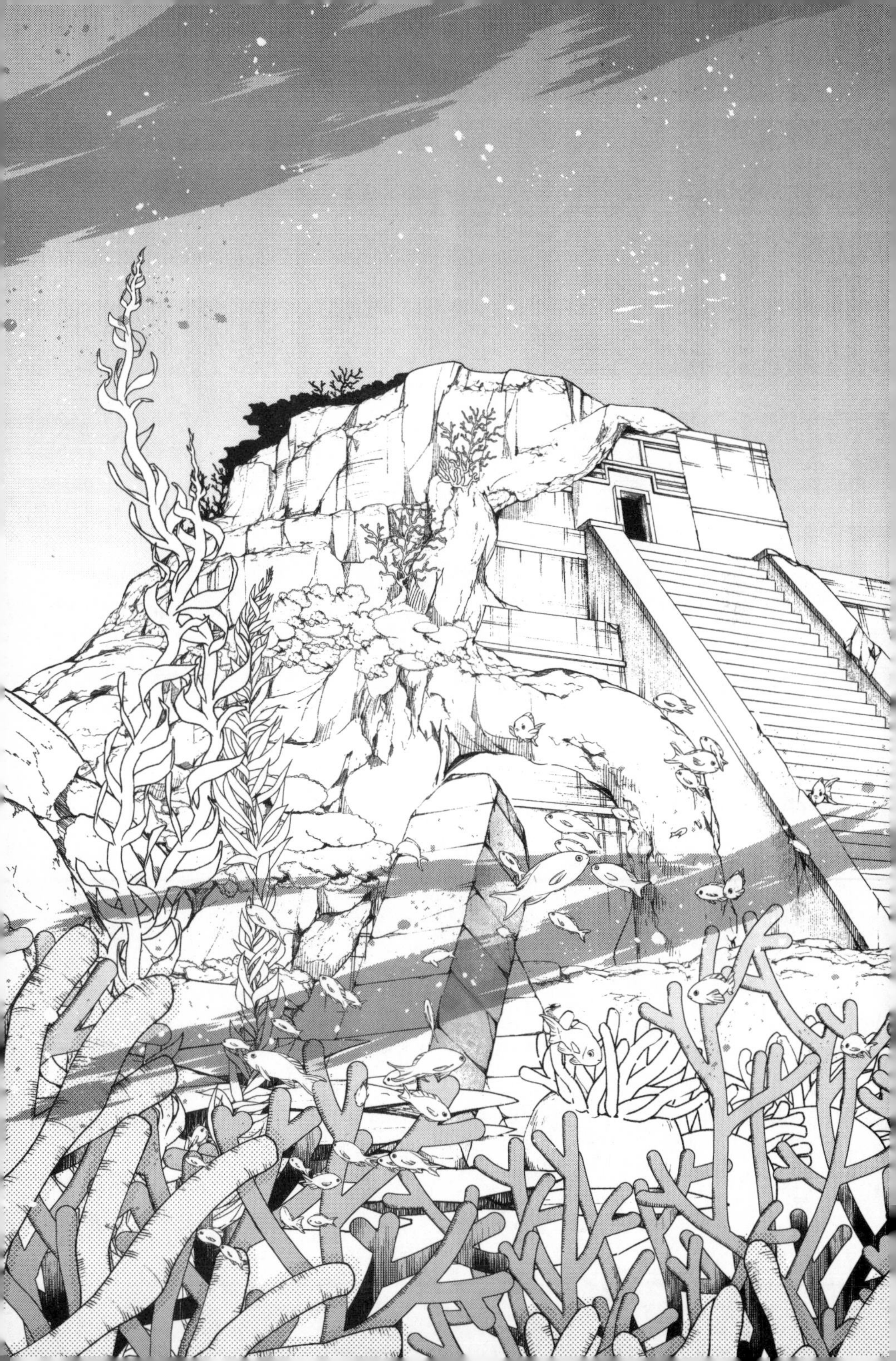

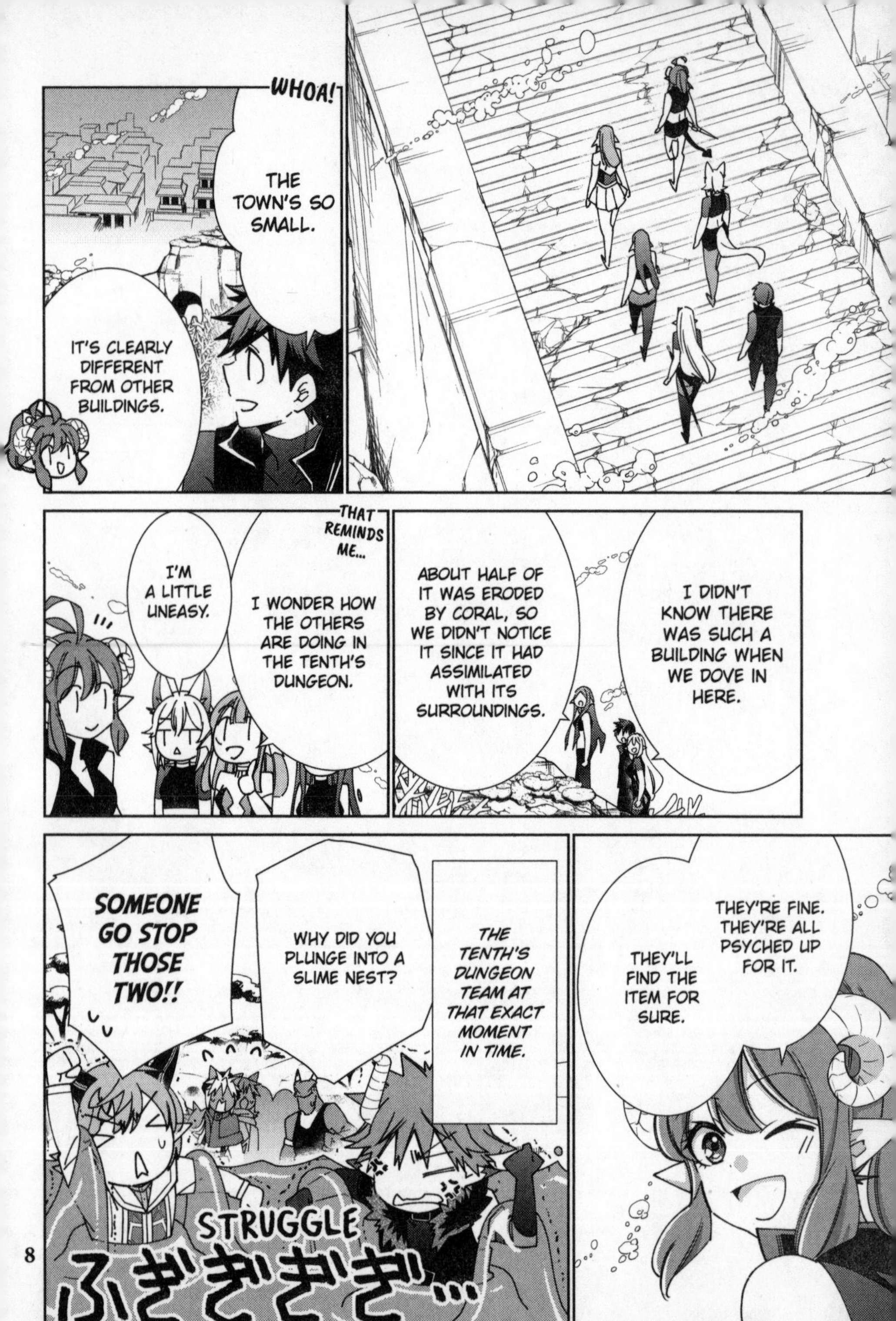
WHOA!
THE TOWN'S SO SMALL.
IT'S CLEARLY DIFFERENT FROM OTHER BUILDINGS.
I DIDN'T KNOW THERE WAS SUCH A BUILDING WHEN WE DOVE IN HERE.
ABOUT HALF OF IT WAS ERODED BY CORAL, SO WE DIDN'T NOTICE IT SINCE IT HAD ASSIMILATED WITH ITS SURROUNDINGS.
THAT REMINDS ME...
I WONDER HOW THE OTHERS ARE DOING IN THE TENTH'S DUNGEON.
I'M A LITTLE UNEASY.
THEY'RE FINE. THEY'RE ALL PSYCHED UP FOR IT.
THEY'LL FIND THE ITEM FOR SURE.
THE TENTH'S DUNGEON TEAM AT THAT EXACT MOMENT IN TIME.
WHY DID YOU PLUNGE INTO A SLIME NEST?
SOMEONE GO STOP THOSE TWO!!
STRUGGLE
ふぎぎぎぎ…

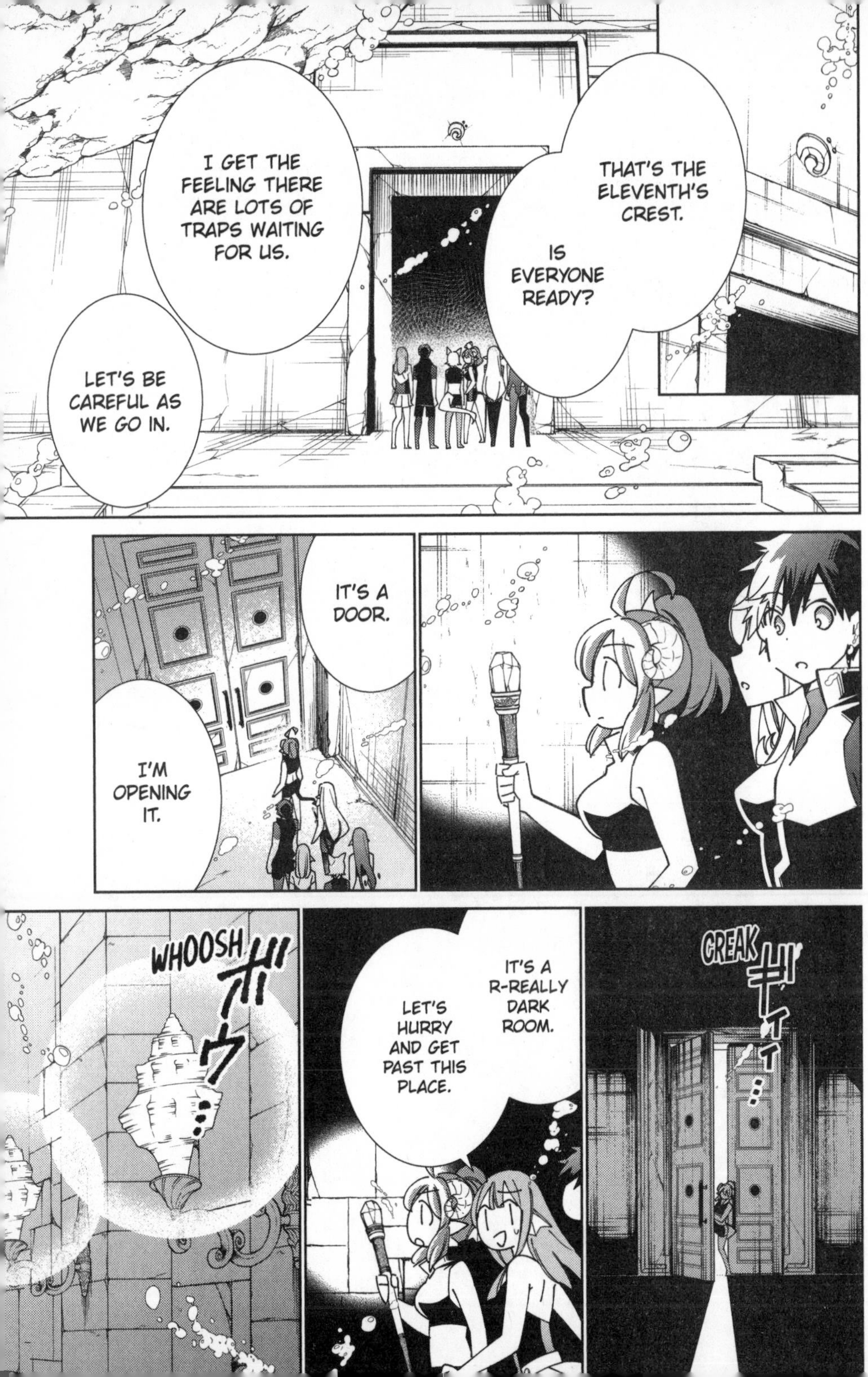
THAT'S THE ELEVENTH'S CREST.
IS EVERYONE READY?
I GET THE FEELING THERE ARE LOTS OF TRAPS WAITING FOR US.
LET'S BE CAREFUL AS WE GO IN.
IT'S A DOOR.
I'M OPENING IT.
CREAK
ギィィ…
IT'S A R-REALLY DARK ROOM.
LET'S HURRY AND GET PAST THIS PLACE.
WHOOSH
ボウ…

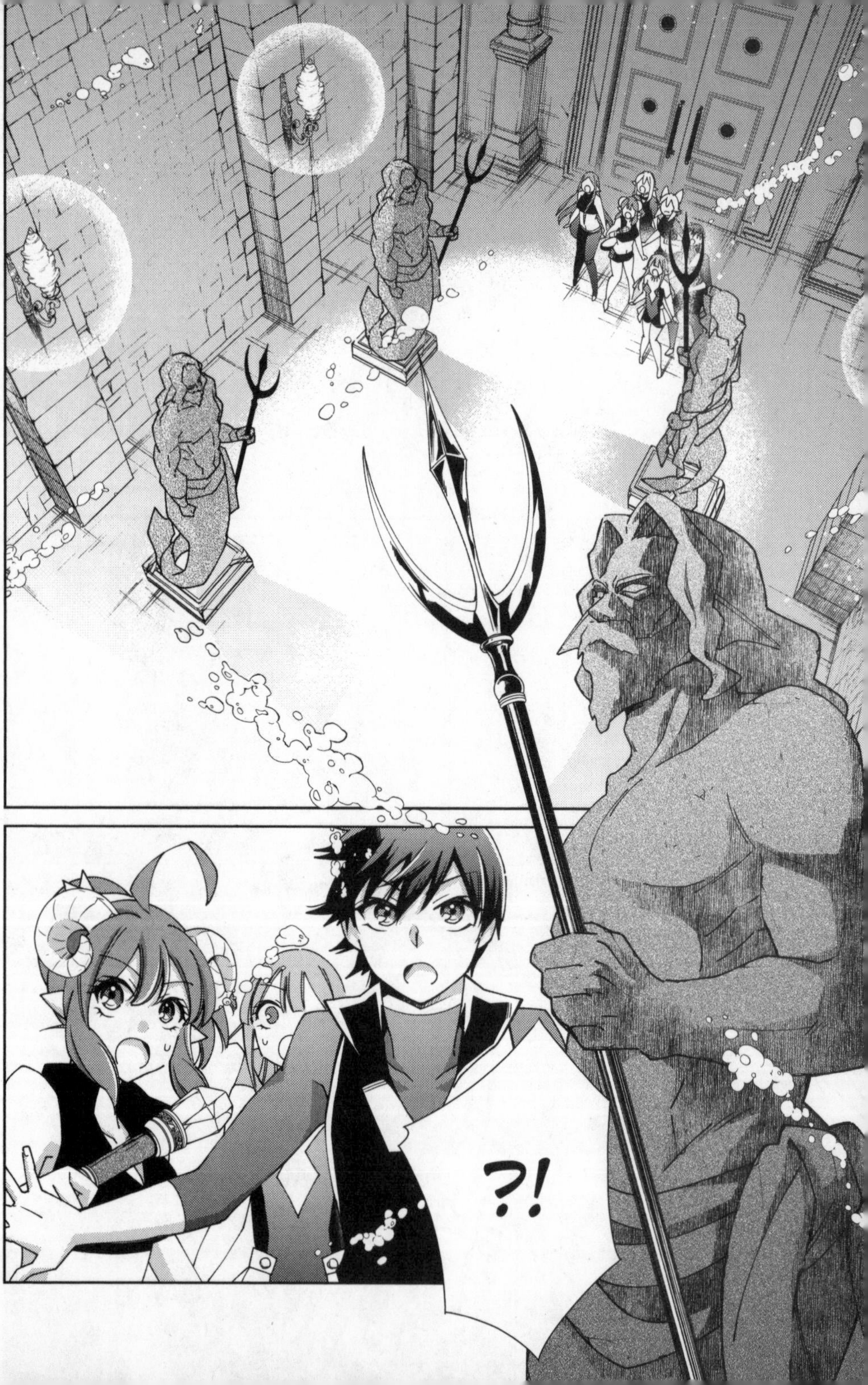
?!

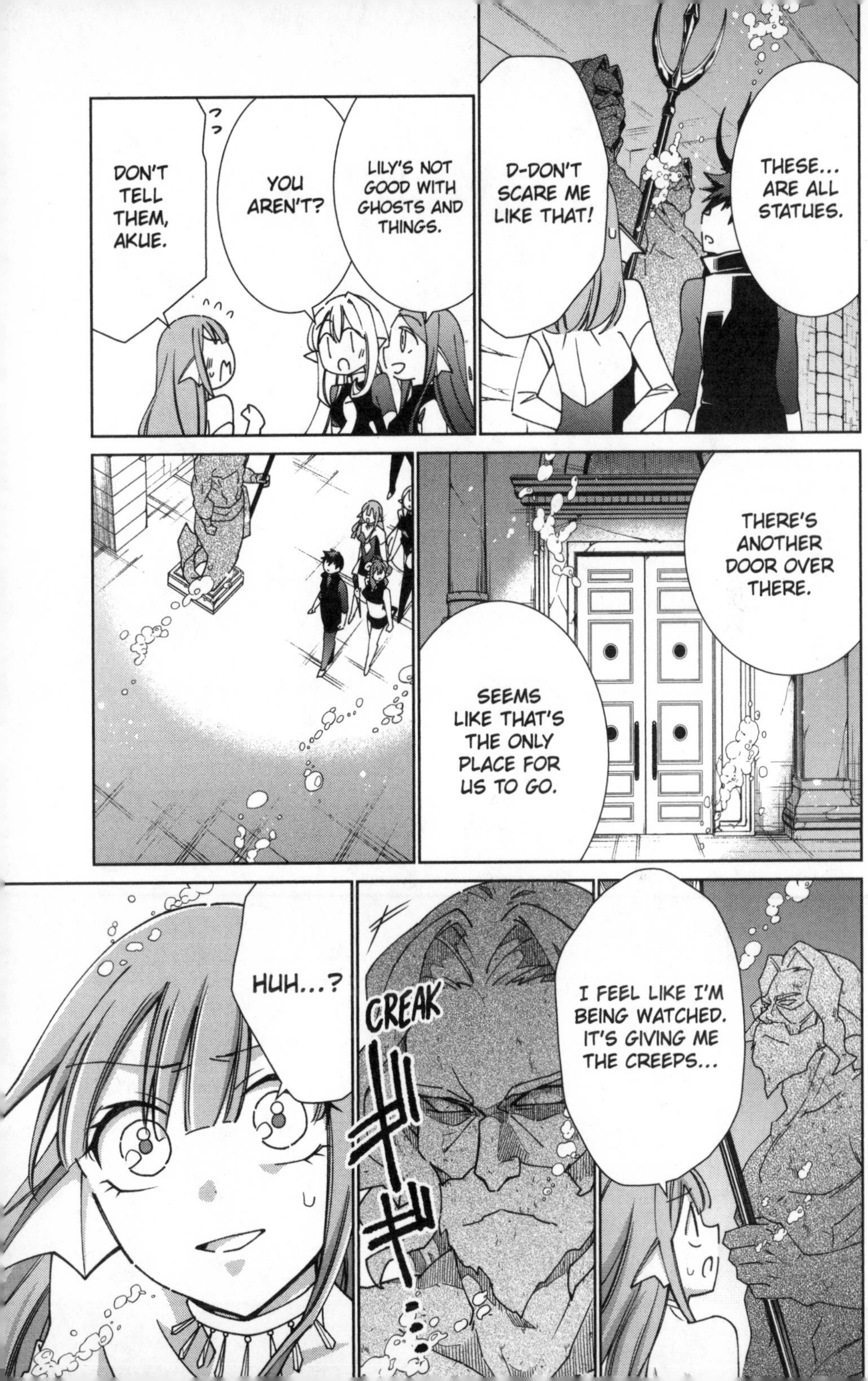
THESE... ARE ALL STATUES.
D-DON'T SCARE ME LIKE THAT!
LILY'S NOT GOOD WITH GHOSTS AND THINGS.
YOU AREN'T?
DON'T TELL THEM, AKUE.
THERE'S ANOTHER DOOR OVER THERE.
SEEMS LIKE THAT'S THE ONLY PLACE FOR US TO GO.
I FEEL LIKE I'M BEING WATCHED. IT'S GIVING ME THE CREEPS...
CREAK
HUH...?

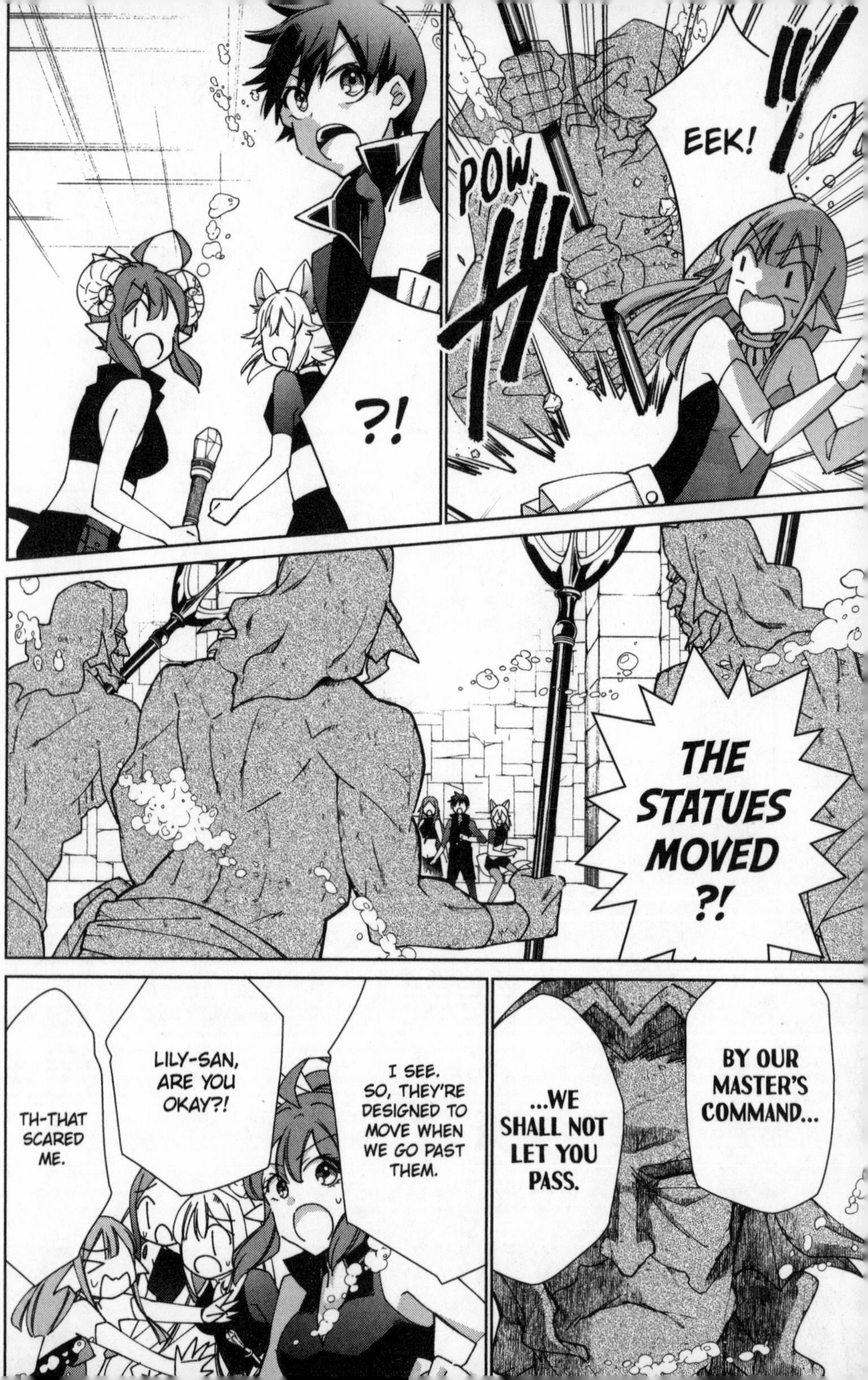
EEK!
POW
?!
THE STATUES MOVED ?!
BY OUR MASTER'S COMMAND...
...WE SHALL NOT LET YOU PASS.
I SEE. SO, THEY'RE DESIGNED TO MOVE WHEN WE GO PAST THEM.
LILY-SAN, ARE YOU OKAY?!
TH-THAT SCARED ME.

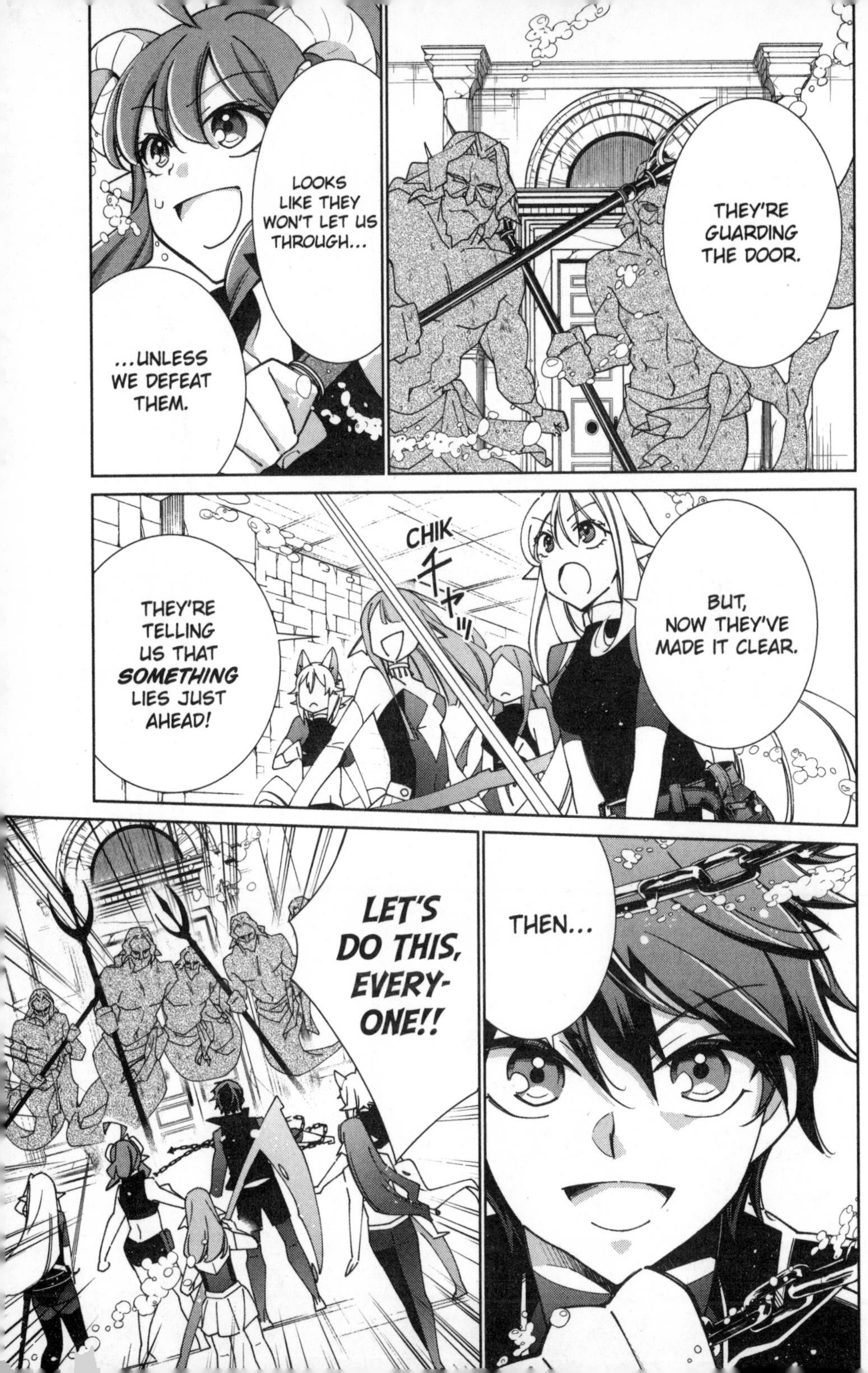

THEY'RE GUARDING THE DOOR.
LOOKS LIKE THEY WON'T LET US THROUGH...
...UNLESS WE DEFEAT THEM.
BUT, NOW THEY'VE MADE IT CLEAR.
CHIK
チャッ
THEY'RE TELLING US THAT *SOMETHING* LIES JUST AHEAD!
THEN...
LET'S DO THIS, EVERY-ONE!!

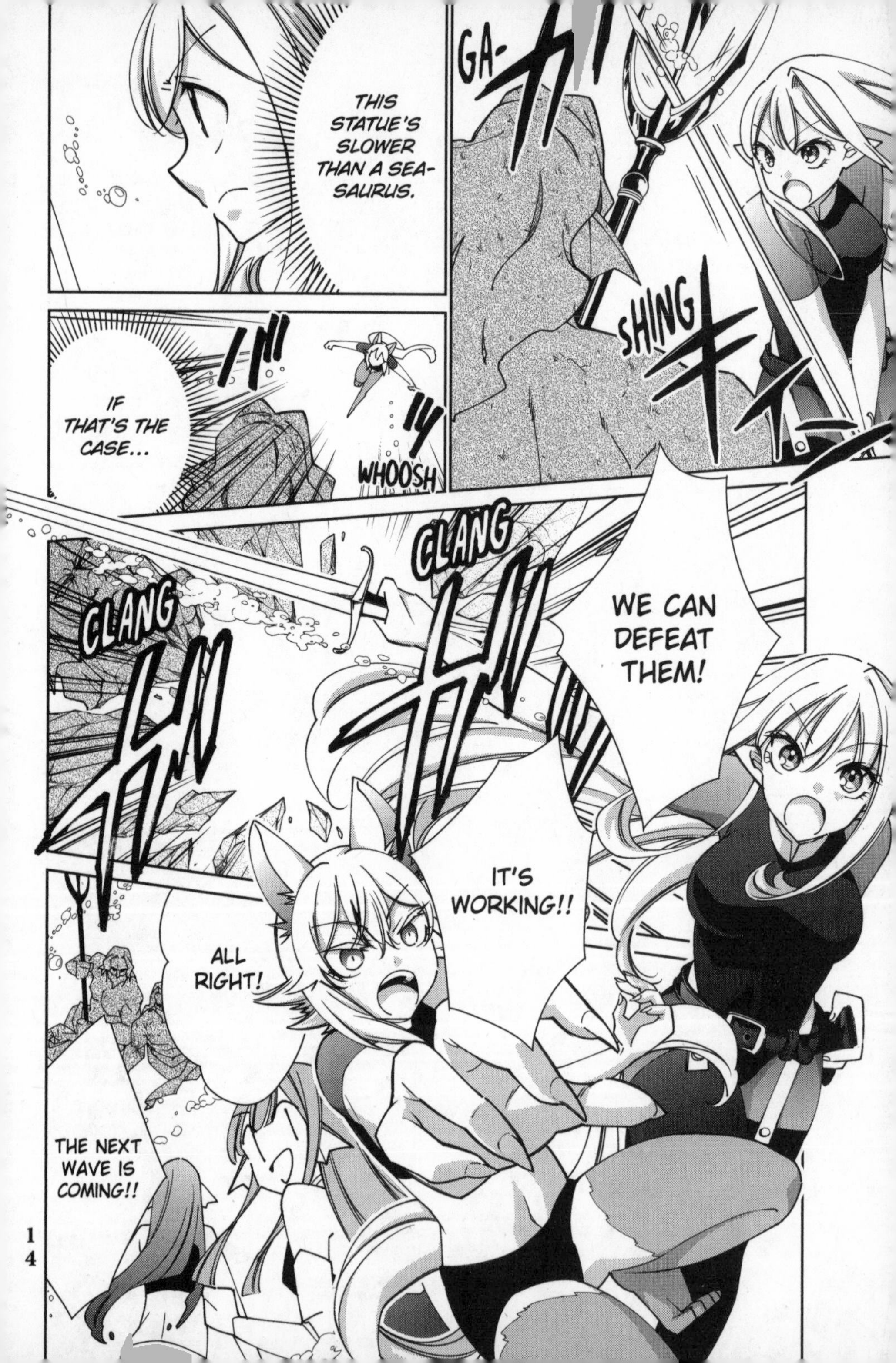
GA-
SHING
THIS STATUE'S SLOWER THAN A SEA-SAURUS.
IF THAT'S THE CASE...
WHOOSH
WE CAN DEFEAT THEM!
CLANG
CLANG
IT'S WORKING!!
ALL RIGHT!
THE NEXT WAVE IS COMING!!

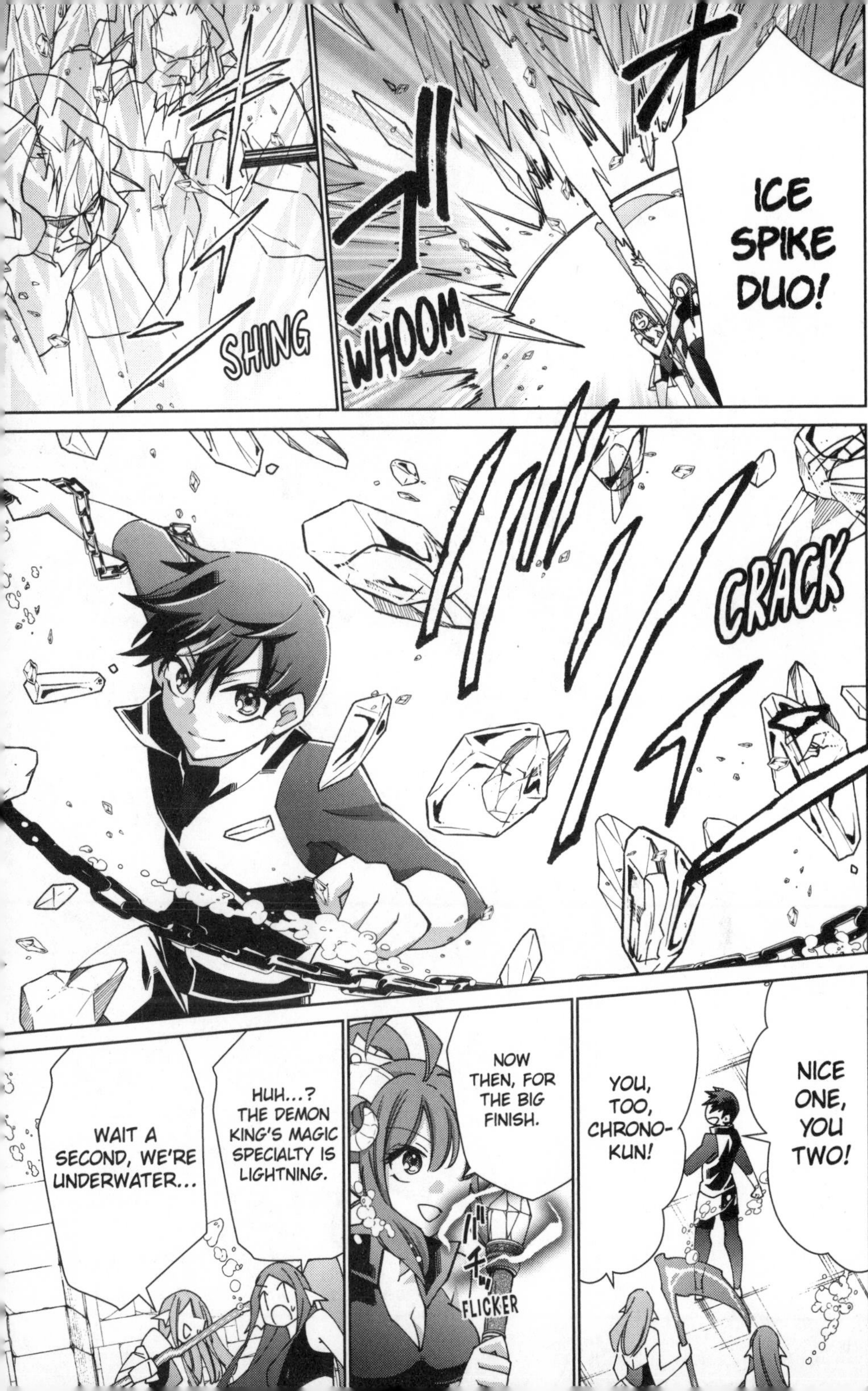
ICE SPIKE DUO!
WHOOM
SHING
CRACK
NICE ONE, YOU TWO!
YOU, TOO, CHRONO-KUN!
NOW THEN, FOR THE BIG FINISH.
FLICKER
HUH...? THE DEMON KING'S MAGIC SPECIALTY IS LIGHTNING.
WAIT A SECOND, WE'RE UNDERWATER...

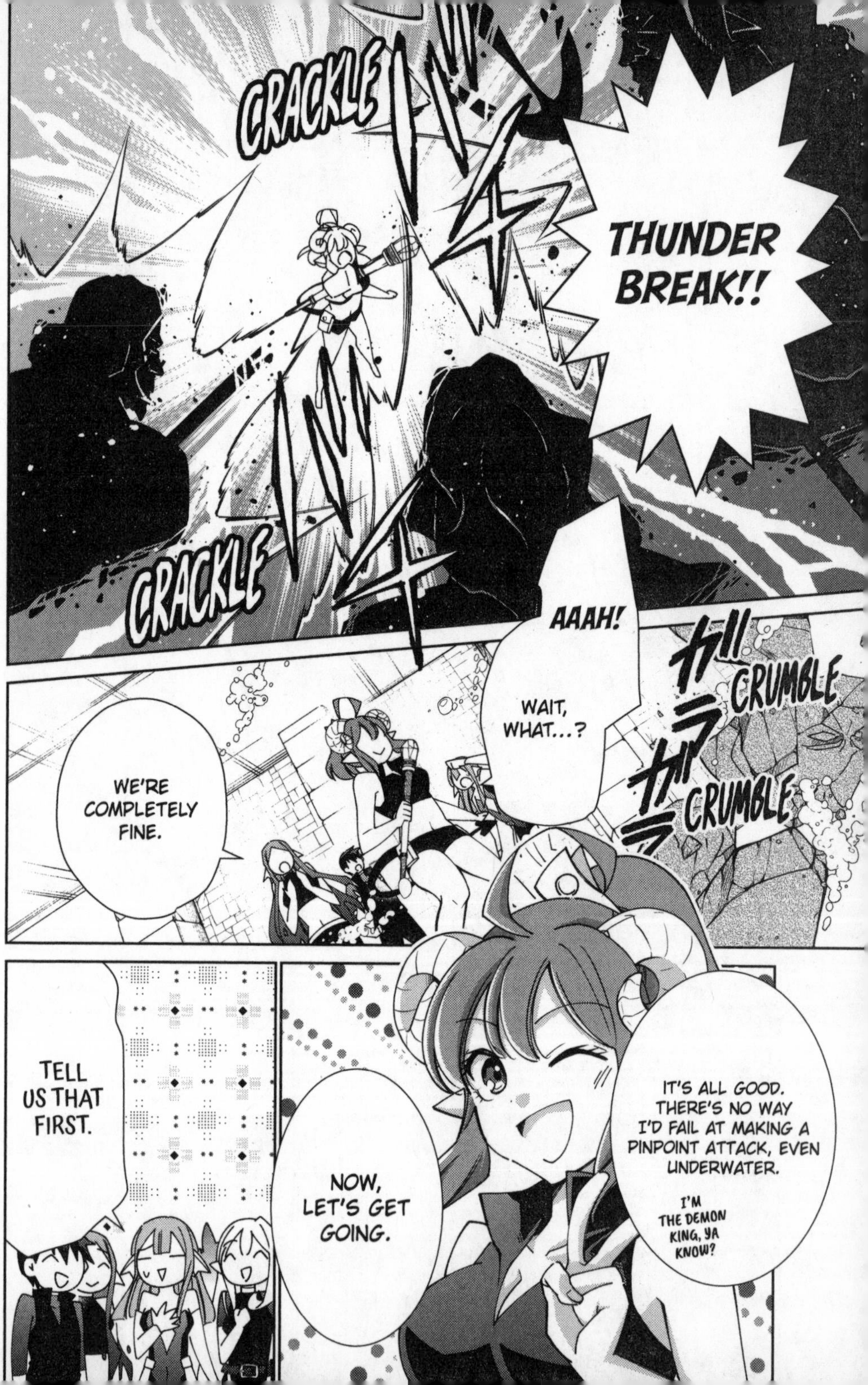
THUNDER BREAK!!
CRACKLE
CRACKLE
CRUMBLE
CRUMBLE
AAAH!
WAIT, WHAT...?
WE'RE COMPLETELY FINE.
IT'S ALL GOOD. THERE'S NO WAY I'D FAIL AT MAKING A PINPOINT ATTACK, EVEN UNDERWATER.
I'M THE DEMON KING, YA KNOW?
NOW, LET'S GET GOING.
TELL US THAT FIRST.

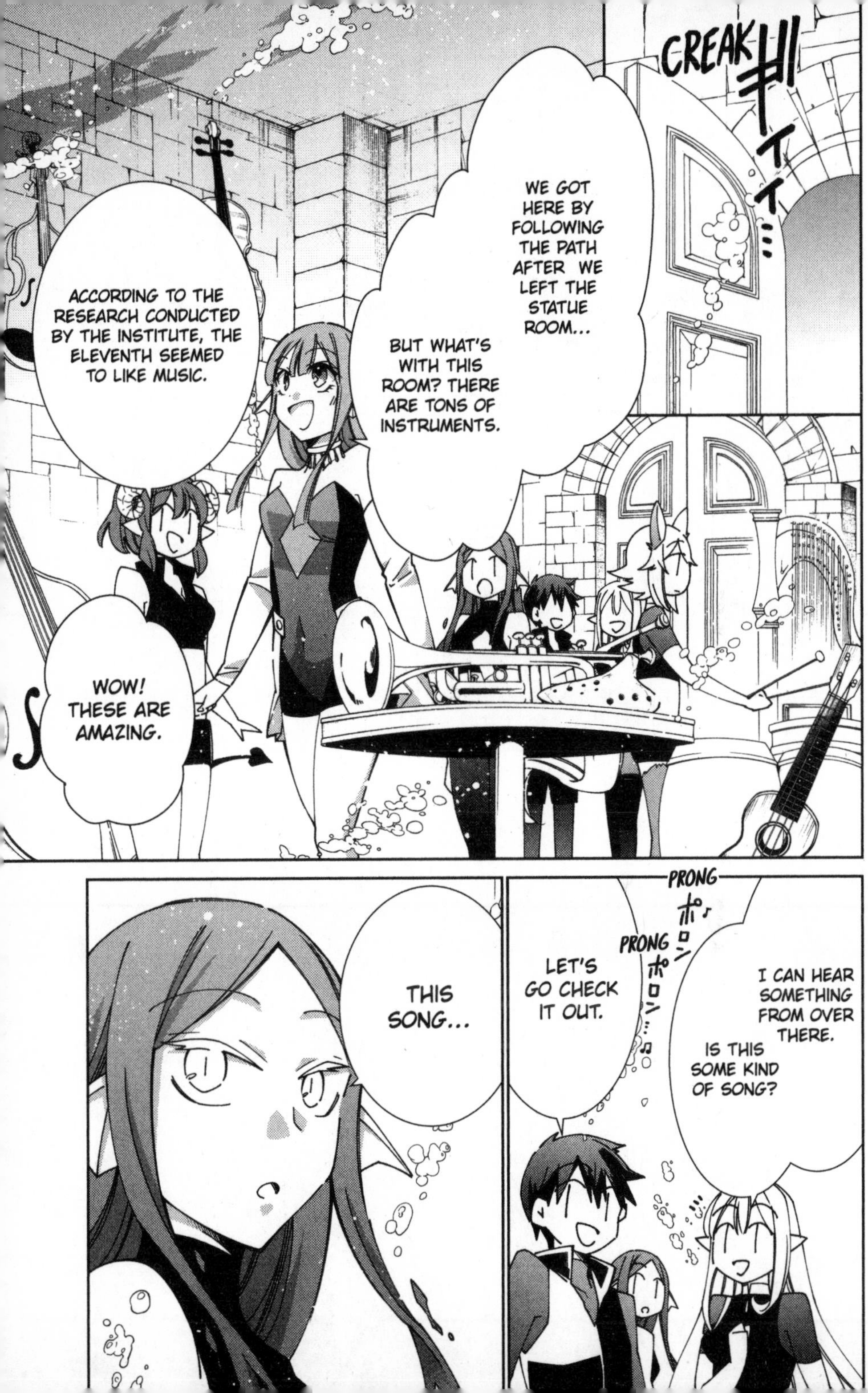
CREAK
WE GOT HERE BY FOLLOWING THE PATH AFTER WE LEFT THE STATUE ROOM...
BUT WHAT'S WITH THIS ROOM? THERE ARE TONS OF INSTRUMENTS.
ACCORDING TO THE RESEARCH CONDUCTED BY THE INSTITUTE, THE ELEVENTH SEEMED TO LIKE MUSIC.
WOW! THESE ARE AMAZING.
PRONG
ポロン
PRONG
ポロン…
I CAN HEAR SOMETHING FROM OVER THERE.
IS THIS SOME KIND OF SONG?
LET'S GO CHECK IT OUT.
THIS SONG...

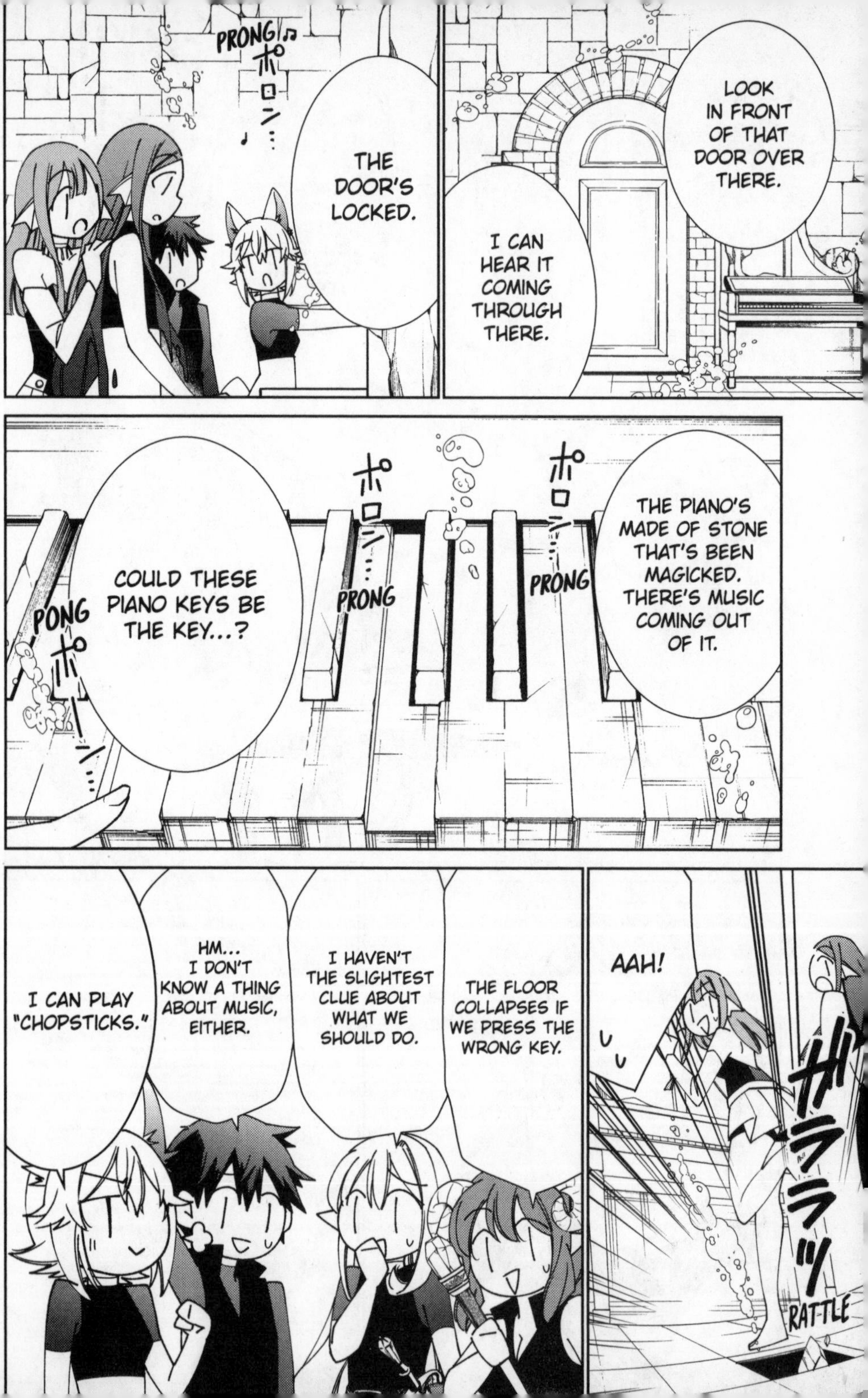
LOOK IN FRONT OF THAT DOOR OVER THERE.
I CAN HEAR IT COMING THROUGH THERE.
PRONG♫
ポロン…
THE DOOR'S LOCKED.
THE PIANO'S MADE OF STONE THAT'S BEEN MAGICKED. THERE'S MUSIC COMING OUT OF IT.
ポロン…
PRONG
ポロン…
PRONG
COULD THESE PIANO KEYS BE THE KEY...?
PONG
ポーン…
AAH!
ガララッ
RATTLE
THE FLOOR COLLAPSES IF WE PRESS THE WRONG KEY.
I HAVEN'T THE SLIGHTEST CLUE ABOUT WHAT WE SHOULD DO.
HM... I DON'T KNOW A THING ABOUT MUSIC, EITHER.
I CAN PLAY "CHOPSTICKS."

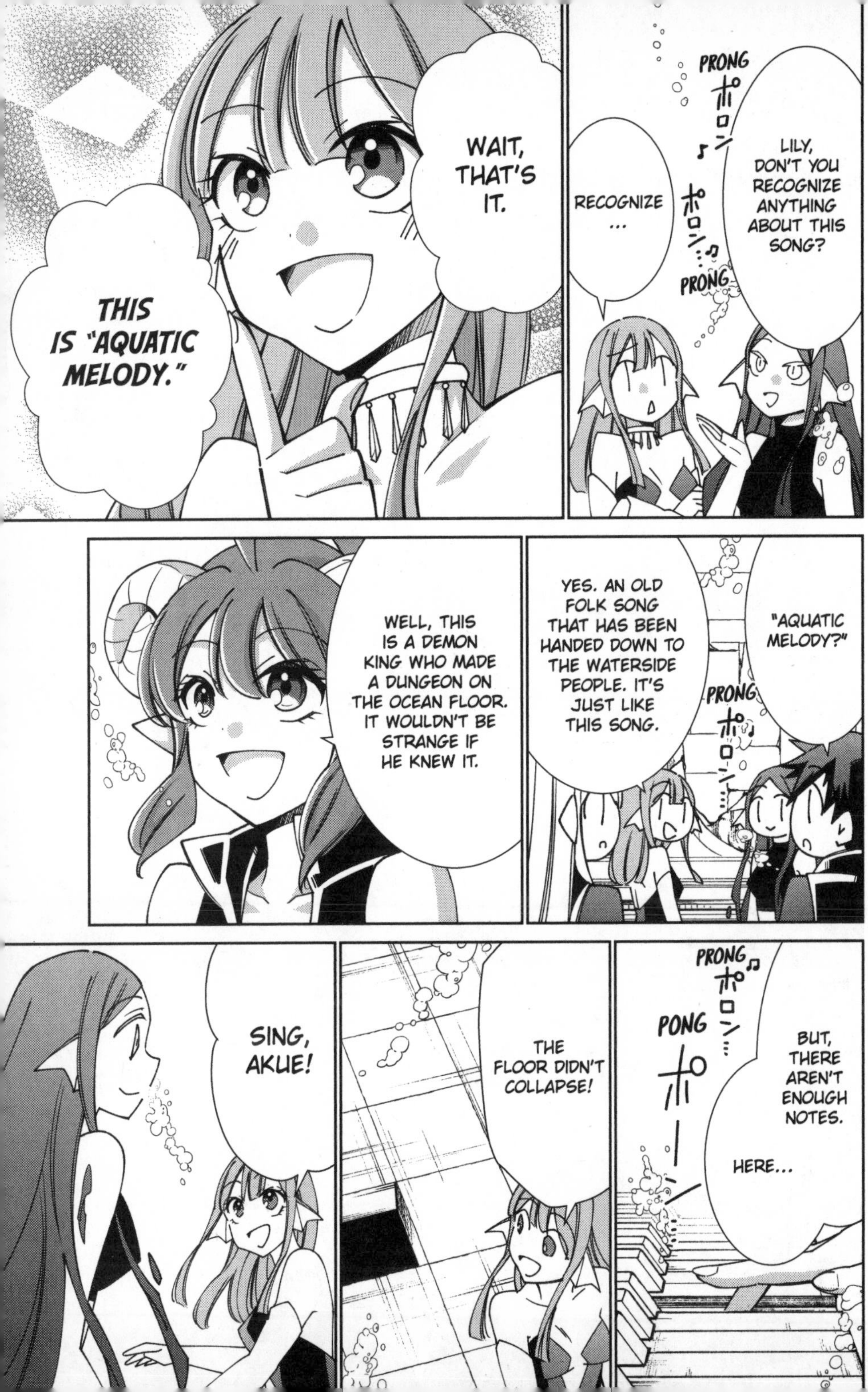
PRONG
ポロン
LILY, DON'T YOU RECOGNIZE ANYTHING ABOUT THIS SONG?
ポロン…
PRONG
RECOGNIZE …
WAIT, THAT'S IT.
THIS IS "AQUATIC MELODY."
"AQUATIC MELODY?"
YES. AN OLD FOLK SONG THAT HAS BEEN HANDED DOWN TO THE WATERSIDE PEOPLE. IT'S JUST LIKE THIS SONG.
PRONG
ポロン…
WELL, THIS IS A DEMON KING WHO MADE A DUNGEON ON THE OCEAN FLOOR. IT WOULDN'T BE STRANGE IF HE KNEW IT.
PRONG
ポロン…
BUT, THERE AREN'T ENOUGH NOTES.
PONG
ポー
HERE…
THE FLOOR DIDN'T COLLAPSE!
SING, AKUE!

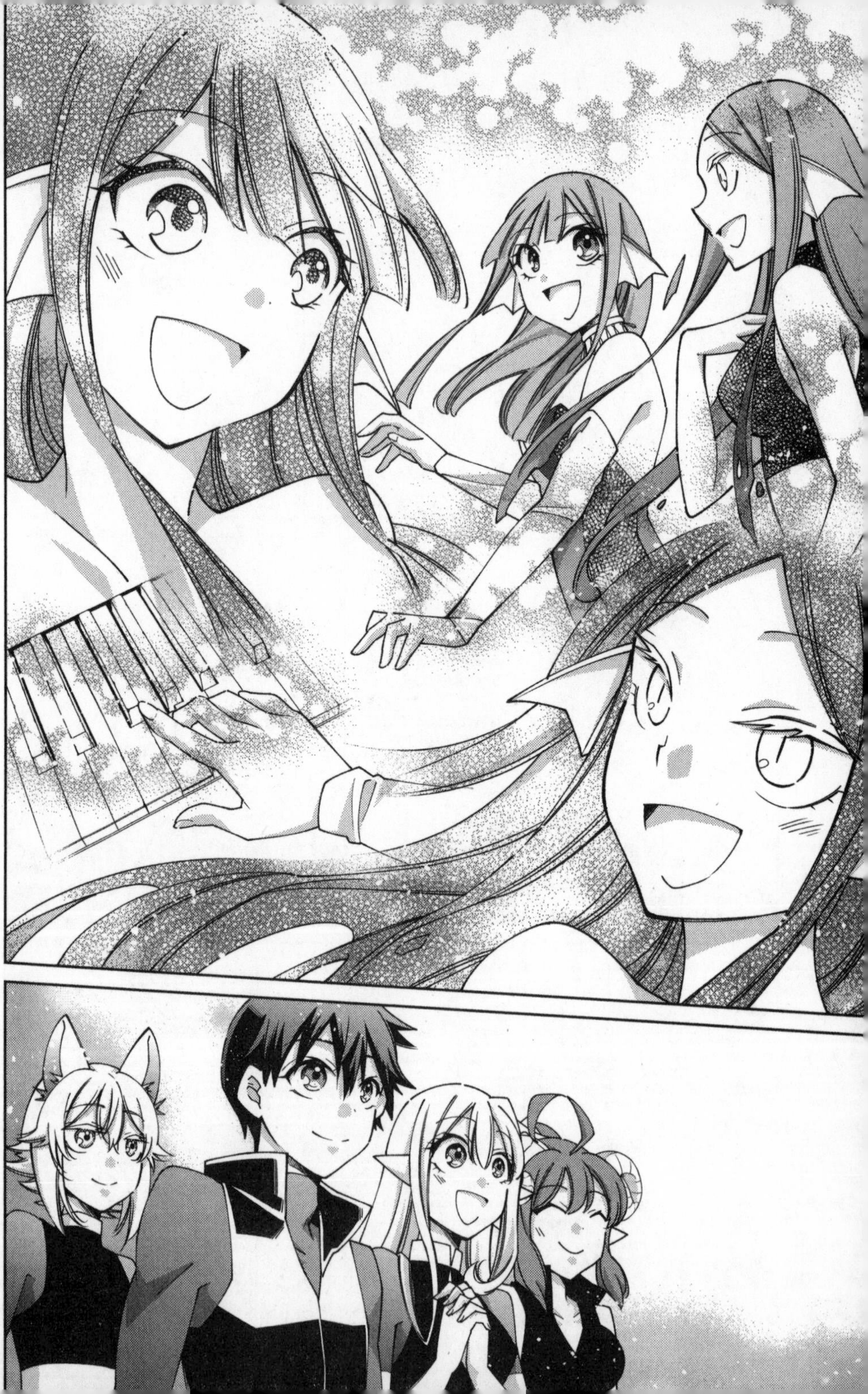

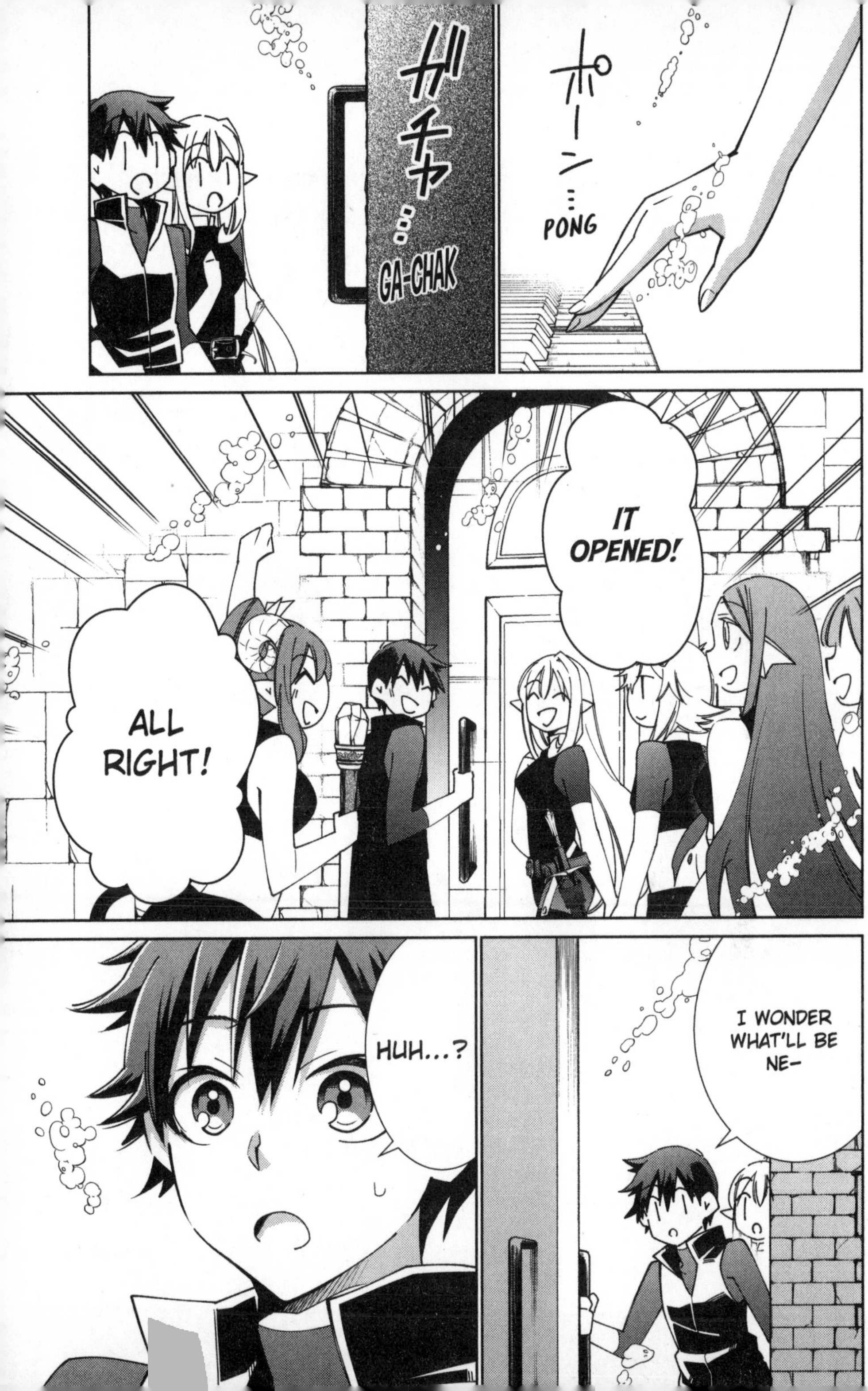
ポーン…
PONG
ガチャ…
GA-CHAK
IT OPENED!
ALL RIGHT!
I WONDER WHAT'LL BE NE–
HUH...?

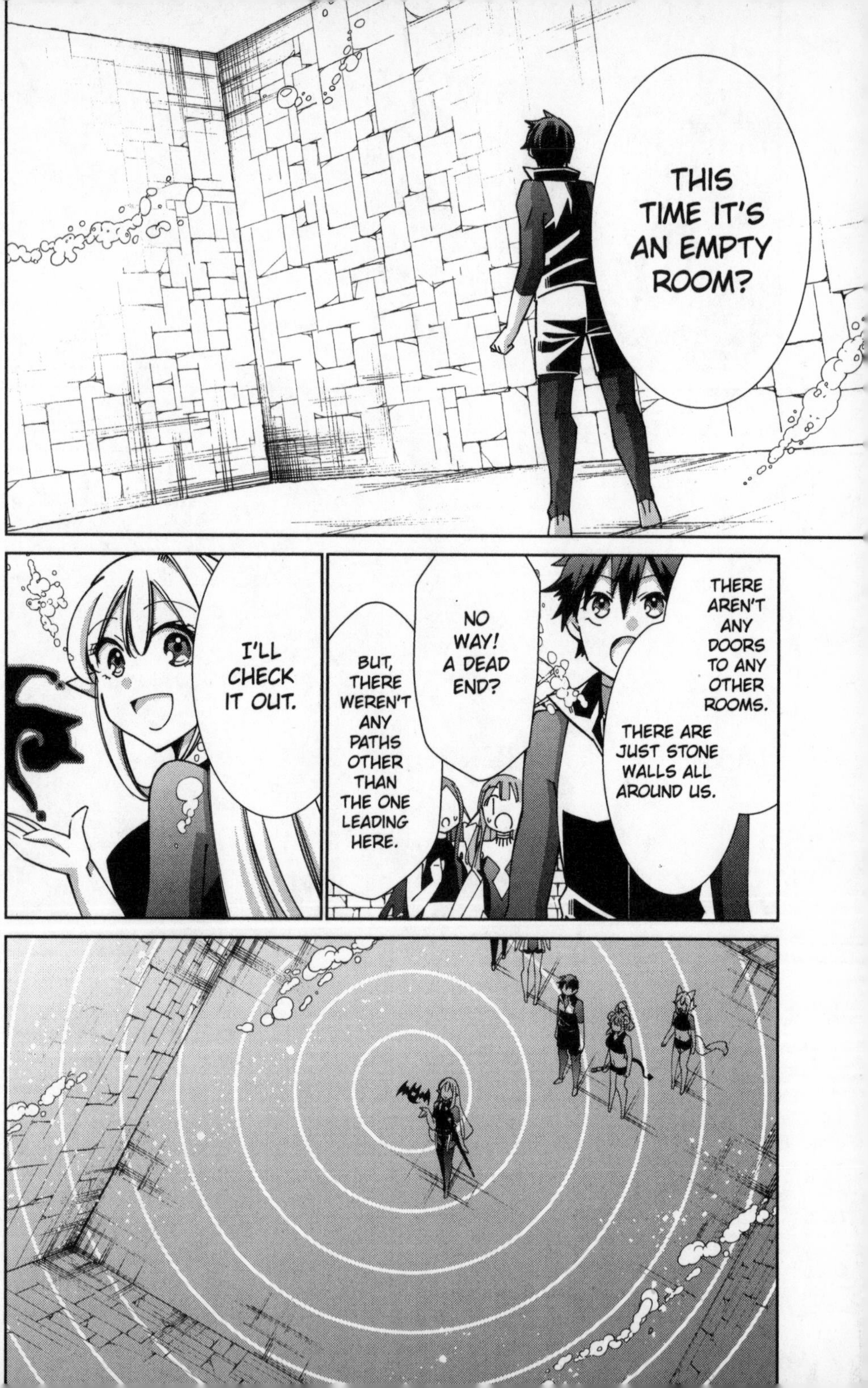
THIS TIME IT'S AN EMPTY ROOM?
THERE AREN'T ANY DOORS TO ANY OTHER ROOMS.
THERE ARE JUST STONE WALLS ALL AROUND US.
NO WAY! A DEAD END?
BUT, THERE WEREN'T ANY PATHS OTHER THAN THE ONE LEADING HERE.
I'LL CHECK IT OUT.

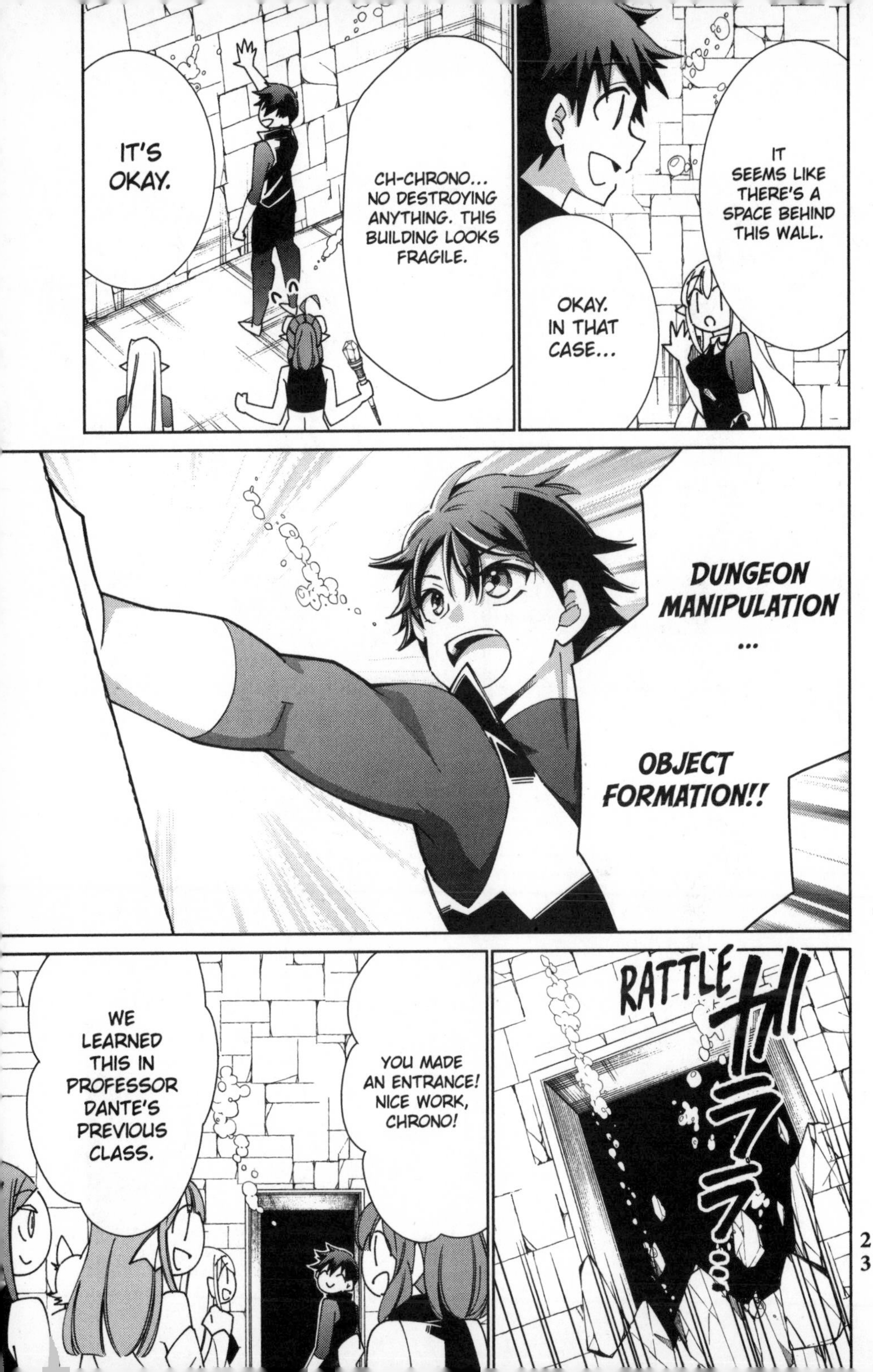
IT SEEMS LIKE THERE'S A SPACE BEHIND THIS WALL.
OKAY. IN THAT CASE...
CH-CHRONO... NO DESTROYING ANYTHING. THIS BUILDING LOOKS FRAGILE.
IT'S OKAY.
DUNGEON MANIPULATION ...
OBJECT FORMATION!!
RATTLE
YOU MADE AN ENTRANCE! NICE WORK, CHRONO!
WE LEARNED THIS IN PROFESSOR DANTE'S PREVIOUS CLASS.

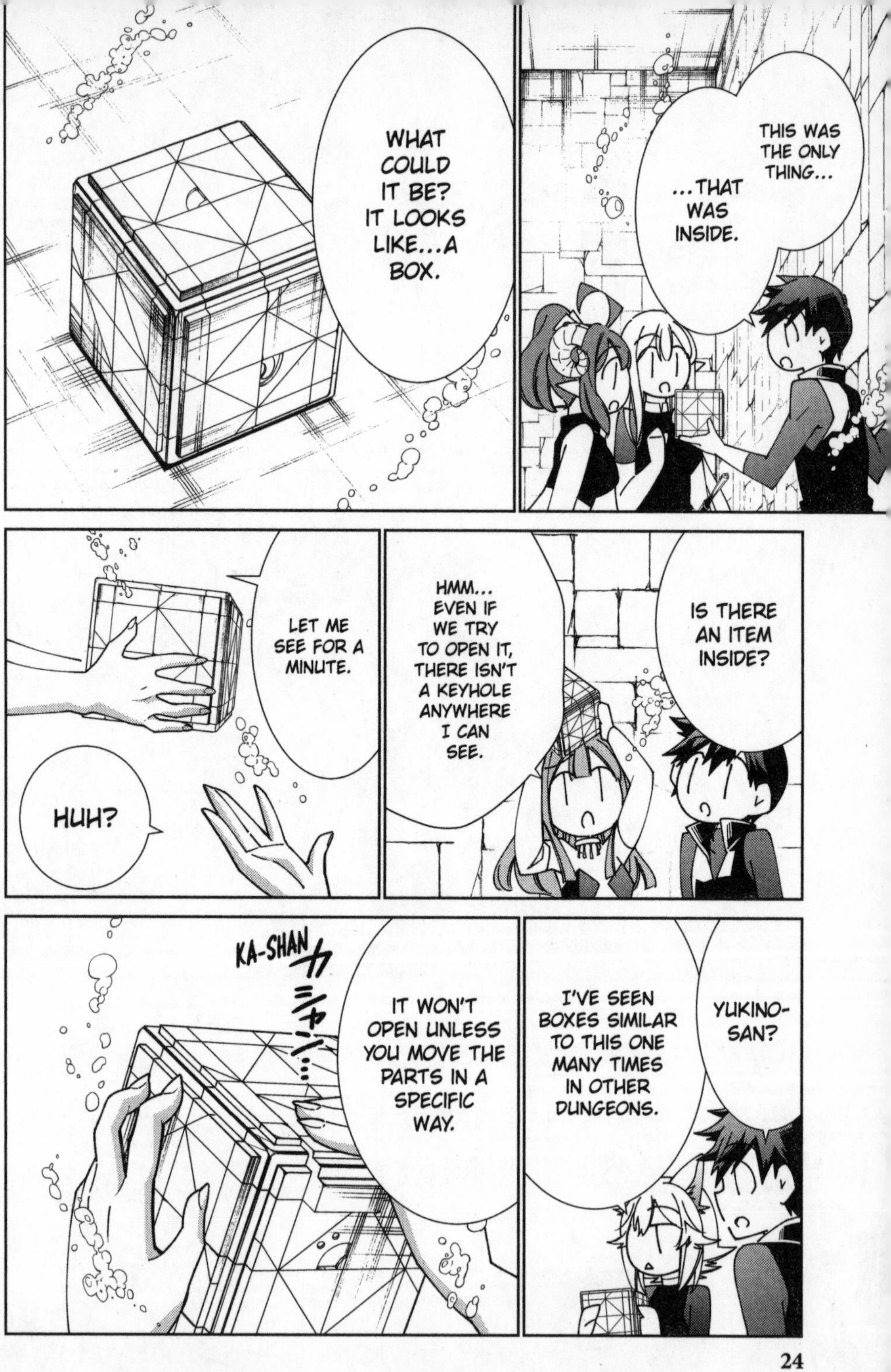
THIS WAS THE ONLY THING...
...THAT WAS INSIDE.
WHAT COULD IT BE? IT LOOKS LIKE...A BOX.
IS THERE AN ITEM INSIDE?
HMM... EVEN IF WE TRY TO OPEN IT, THERE ISN'T A KEYHOLE ANYWHERE I CAN SEE.
LET ME SEE FOR A MINUTE.
HUH?
YUKINO-SAN?
I'VE SEEN BOXES SIMILAR TO THIS ONE MANY TIMES IN OTHER DUNGEONS.
IT WON'T OPEN UNLESS YOU MOVE THE PARTS IN A SPECIFIC WAY.
KA-SHAN

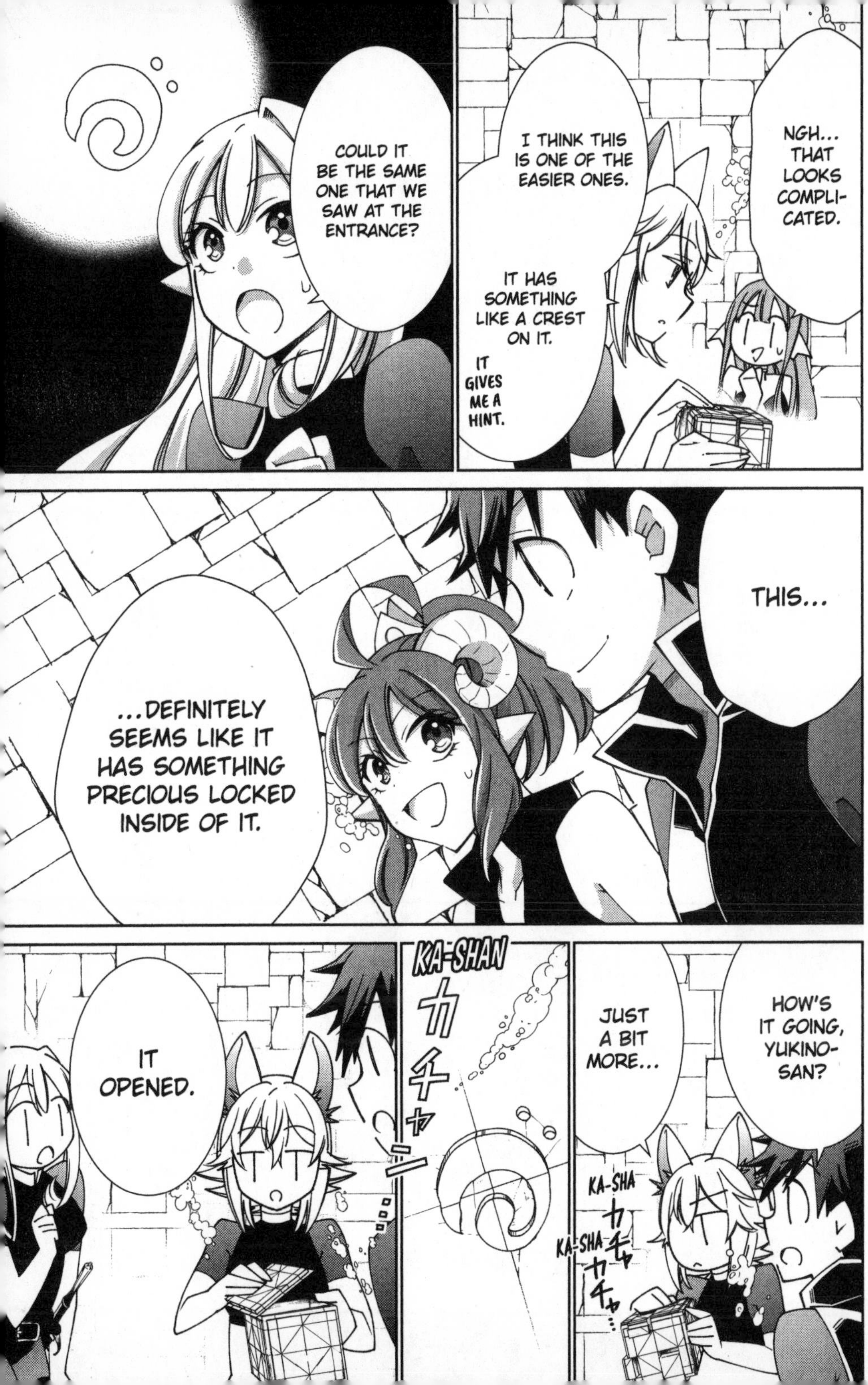
NGH... THAT LOOKS COMPLI-CATED.
I THINK THIS IS ONE OF THE EASIER ONES.
IT HAS SOMETHING LIKE A CREST ON IT.
IT GIVES ME A HINT.
COULD IT BE THE SAME ONE THAT WE SAW AT THE ENTRANCE?
THIS...
...DEFINITELY SEEMS LIKE IT HAS SOMETHING PRECIOUS LOCKED INSIDE OF IT.
HOW'S IT GOING, YUKINO-SAN?
JUST A BIT MORE...
KA-SHA カチャ
KA-SHA カチャ...
KA-SHAN カチャーン
IT OPENED.

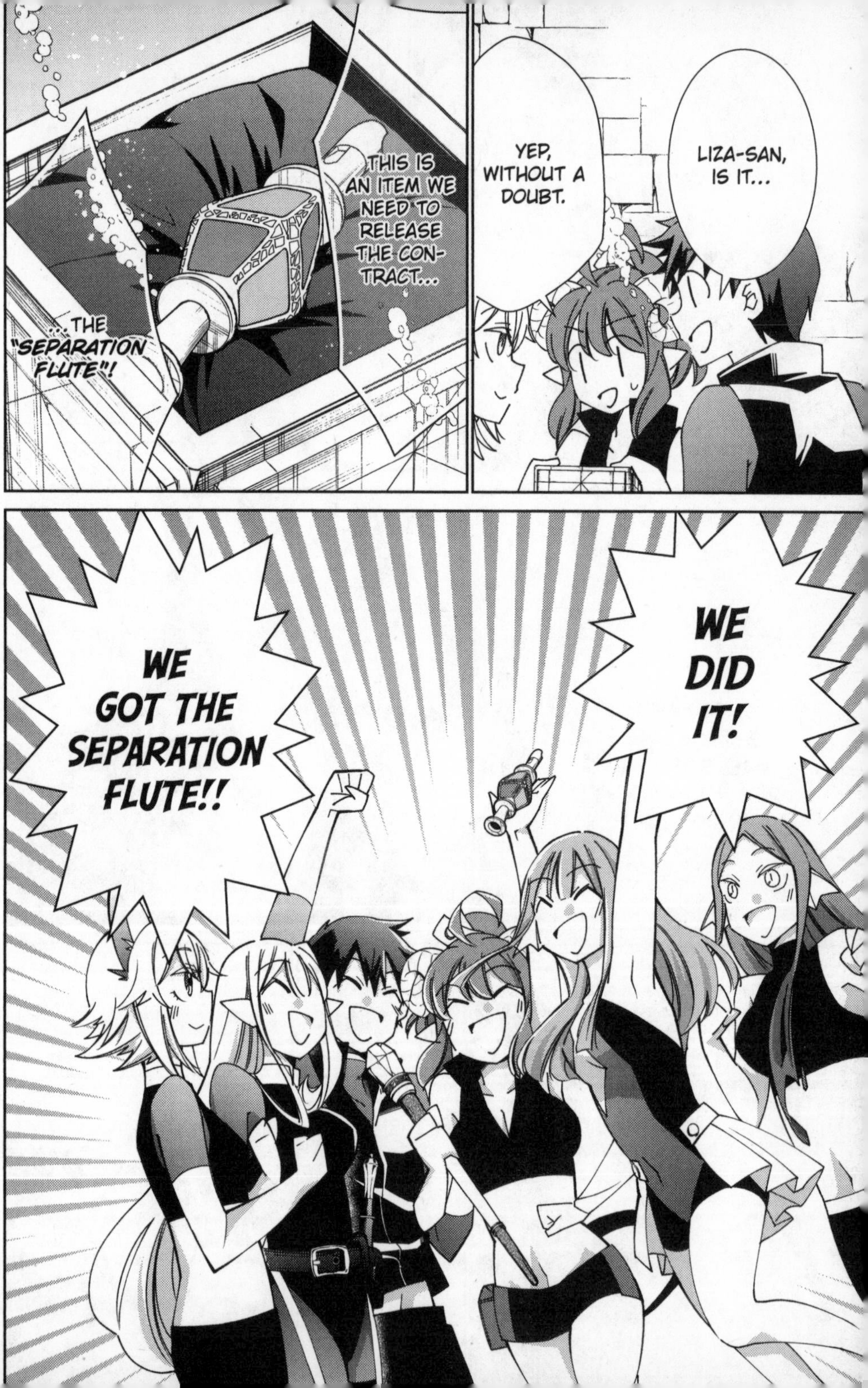
LIZA-SAN, IS IT...
YEP, WITHOUT A DOUBT.
THIS IS AN ITEM WE NEED TO RELEASE THE CON-TRACT...
...THE "SEPARATION FLUTE"!
WE DID IT!
WE GOT THE SEPARATION FLUTE!!

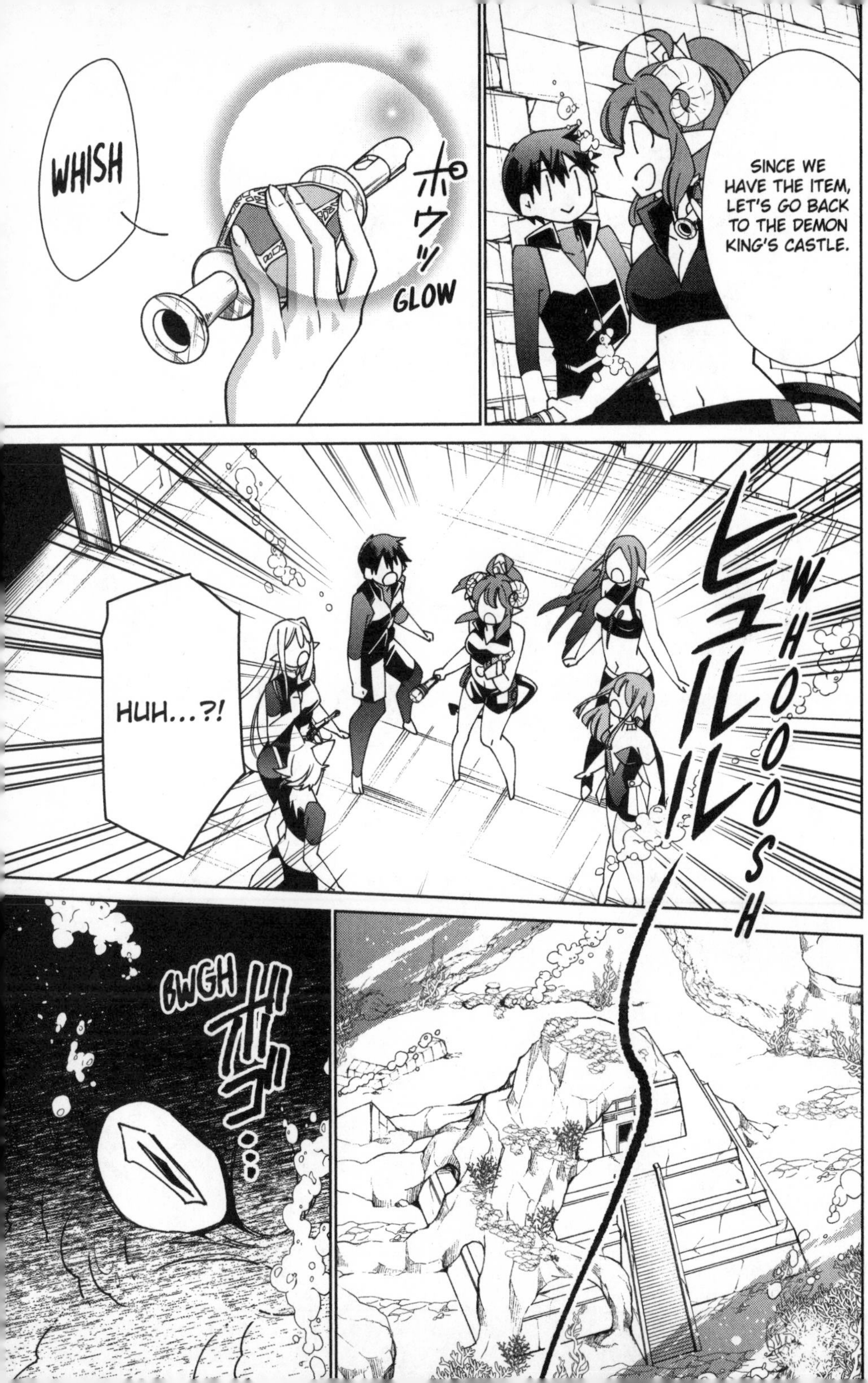
SINCE WE HAVE THE ITEM, LET'S GO BACK TO THE DEMON KING'S CASTLE.
WHISH
ホウッ
GLOW
ヒュルルル
WHOOOOOSH
HUH...?!
BWGH
ガボ…

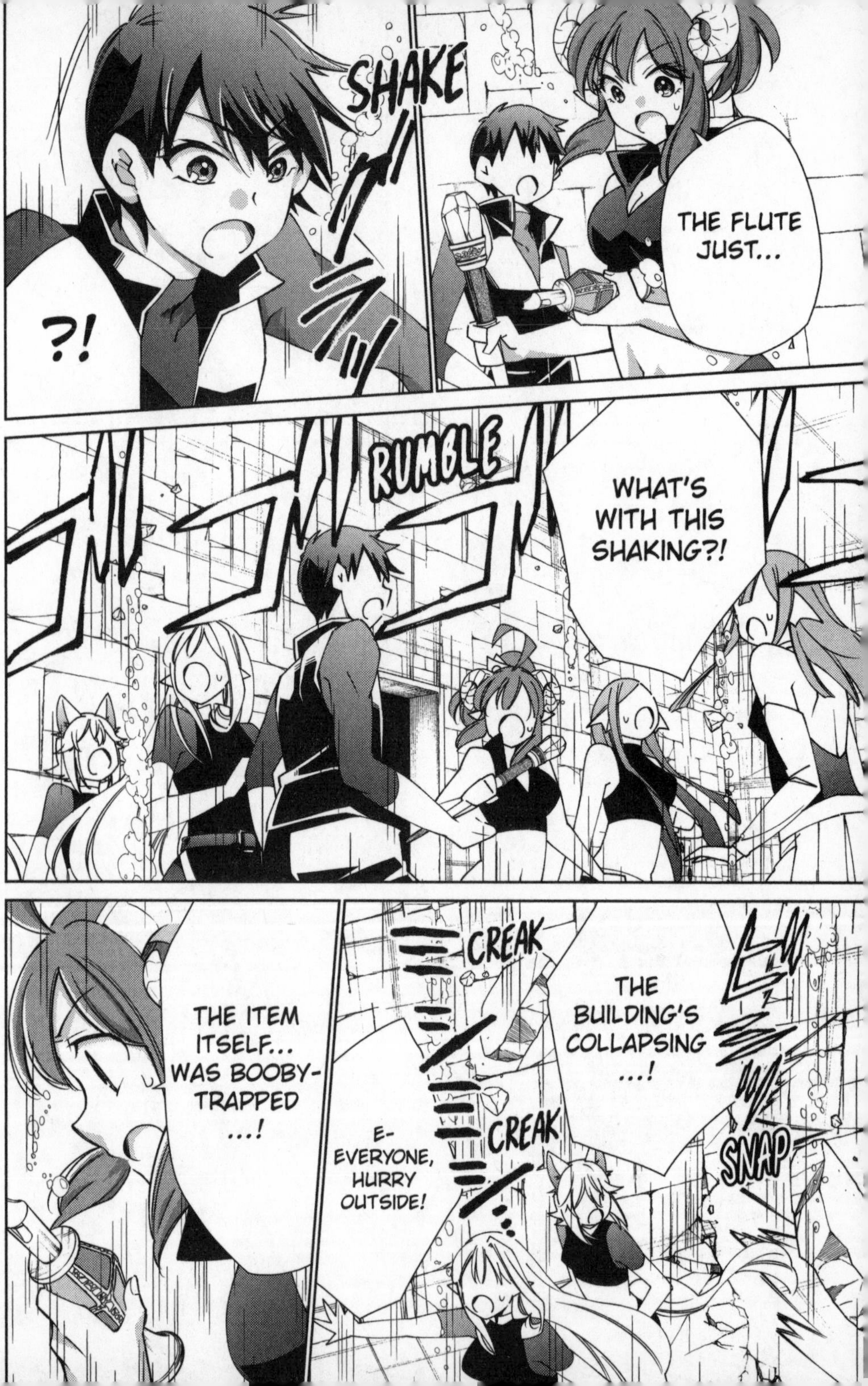
THE FLUTE JUST...
SHAKE
?!
WHAT'S WITH THIS SHAKING?!
RUMBLE
THE BUILDING'S COLLAPSING ...!
SNAP
CREAK
CREAK
E-EVERYONE, HURRY OUTSIDE!
THE ITEM ITSELF... WAS BOOBY-TRAPPED ...!

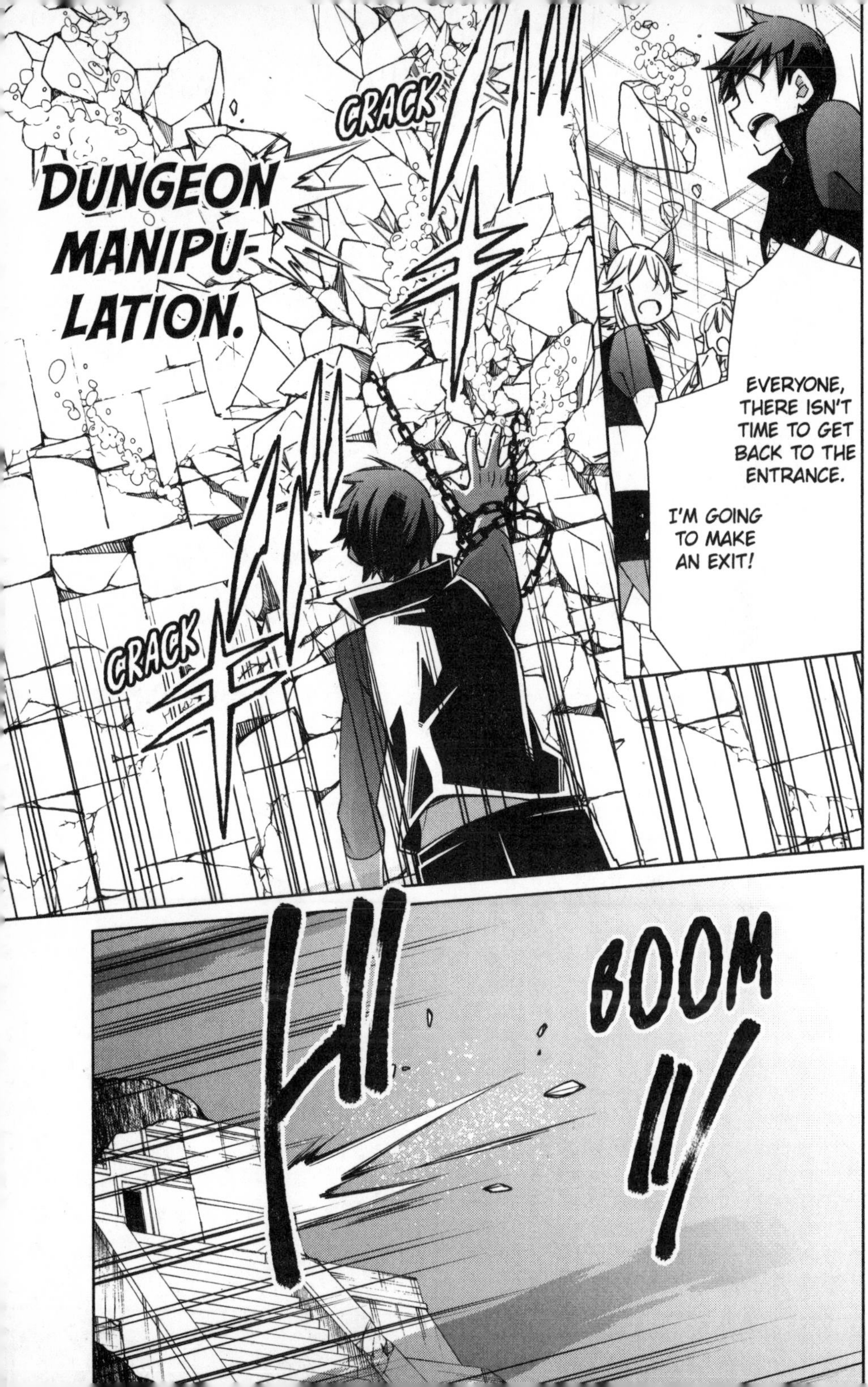
EVERYONE, THERE ISN'T TIME TO GET BACK TO THE ENTRANCE.
I'M GOING TO MAKE AN EXIT!
CRACK
DUNGEON MANIPU-LATION.
CRACK
BOOM

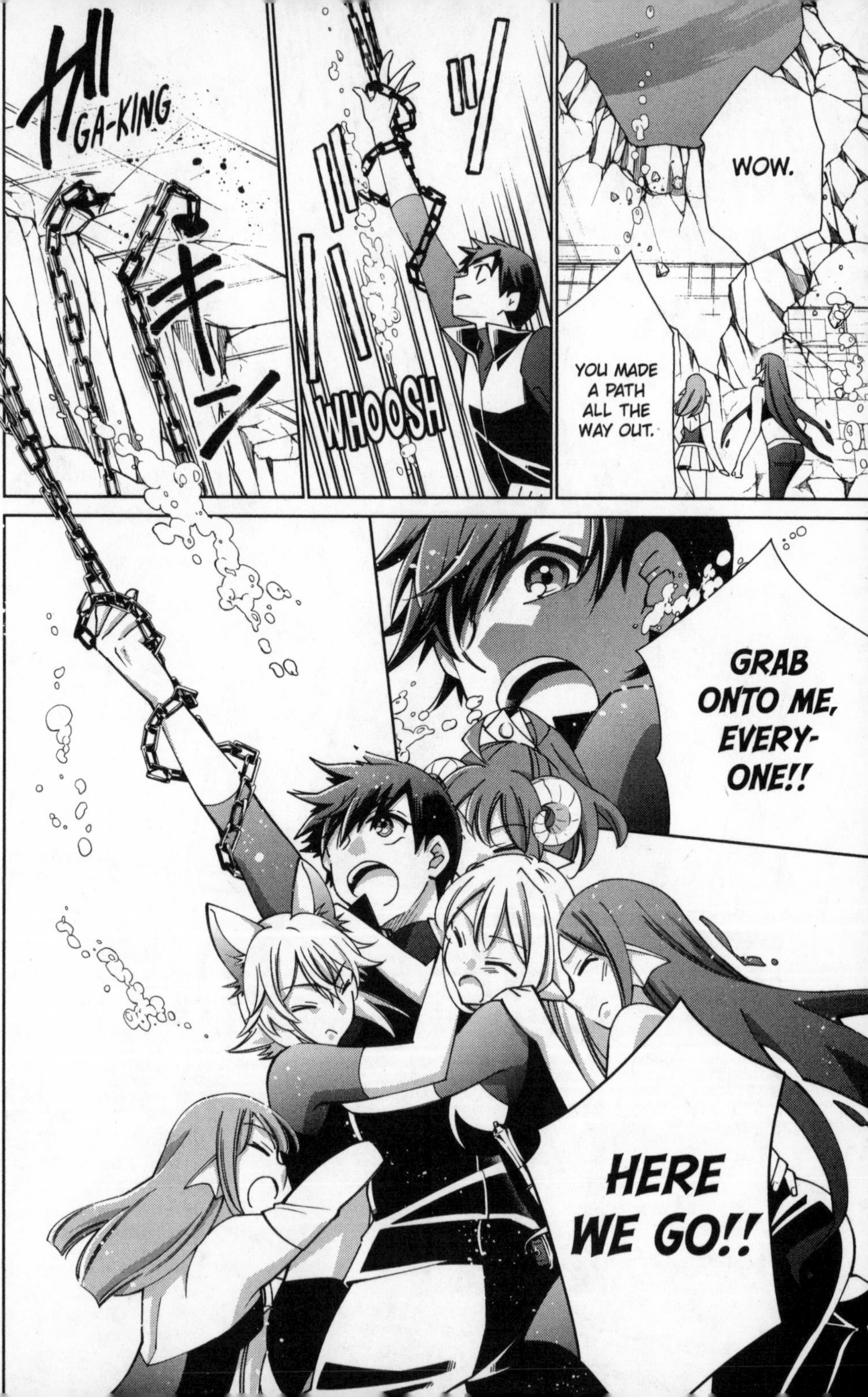
WOW.
YOU MADE A PATH ALL THE WAY OUT.
WHOOSH
GA-KING
GRAB ONTO ME, EVERY-ONE!!
HERE WE GO!!

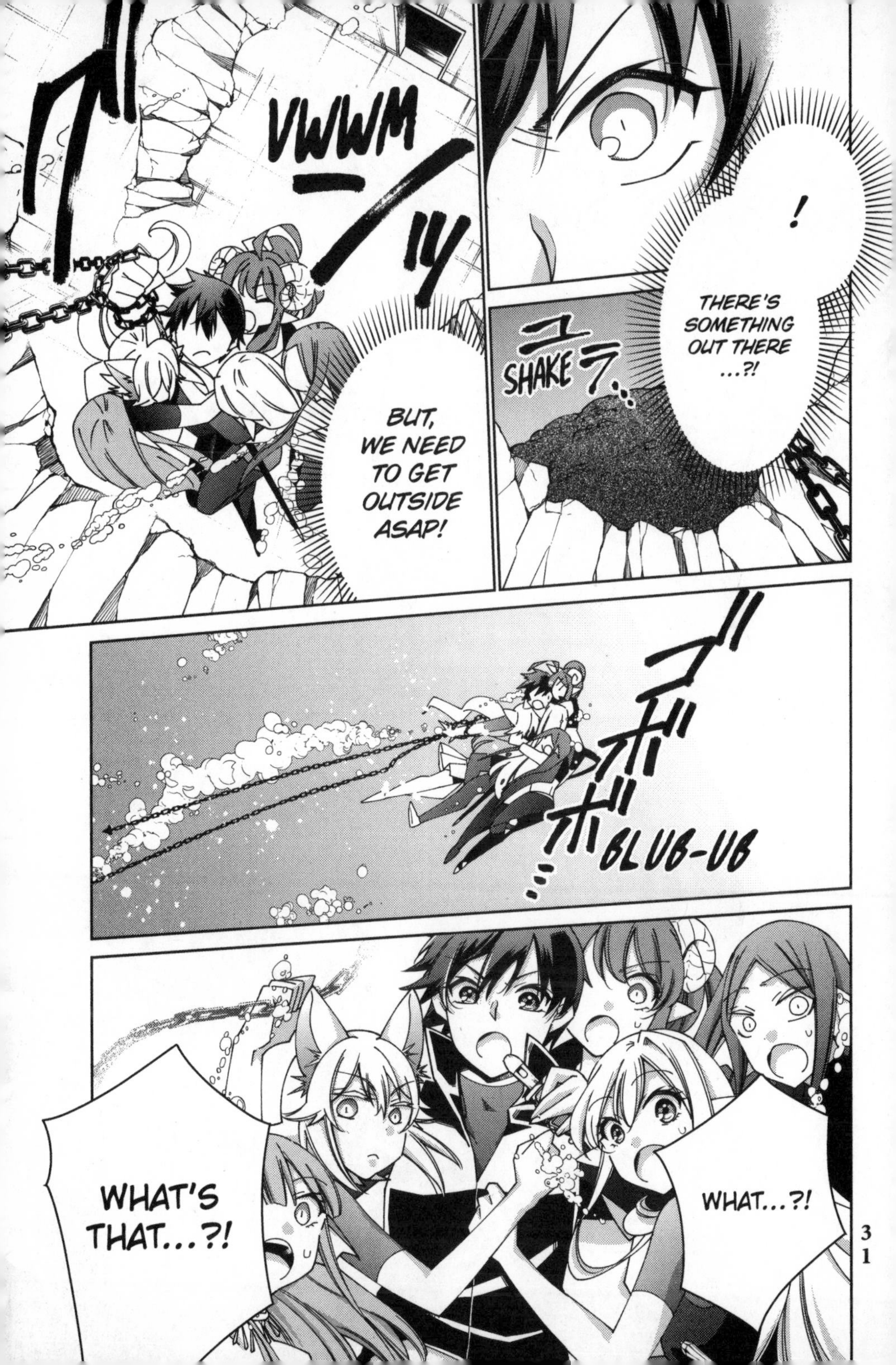
!
SHAKE
THERE'S SOMETHING OUT THERE ...?!
VWWM
BUT, WE NEED TO GET OUTSIDE ASAP!
BLUB-UB
WHAT...?!
WHAT'S THAT...?!

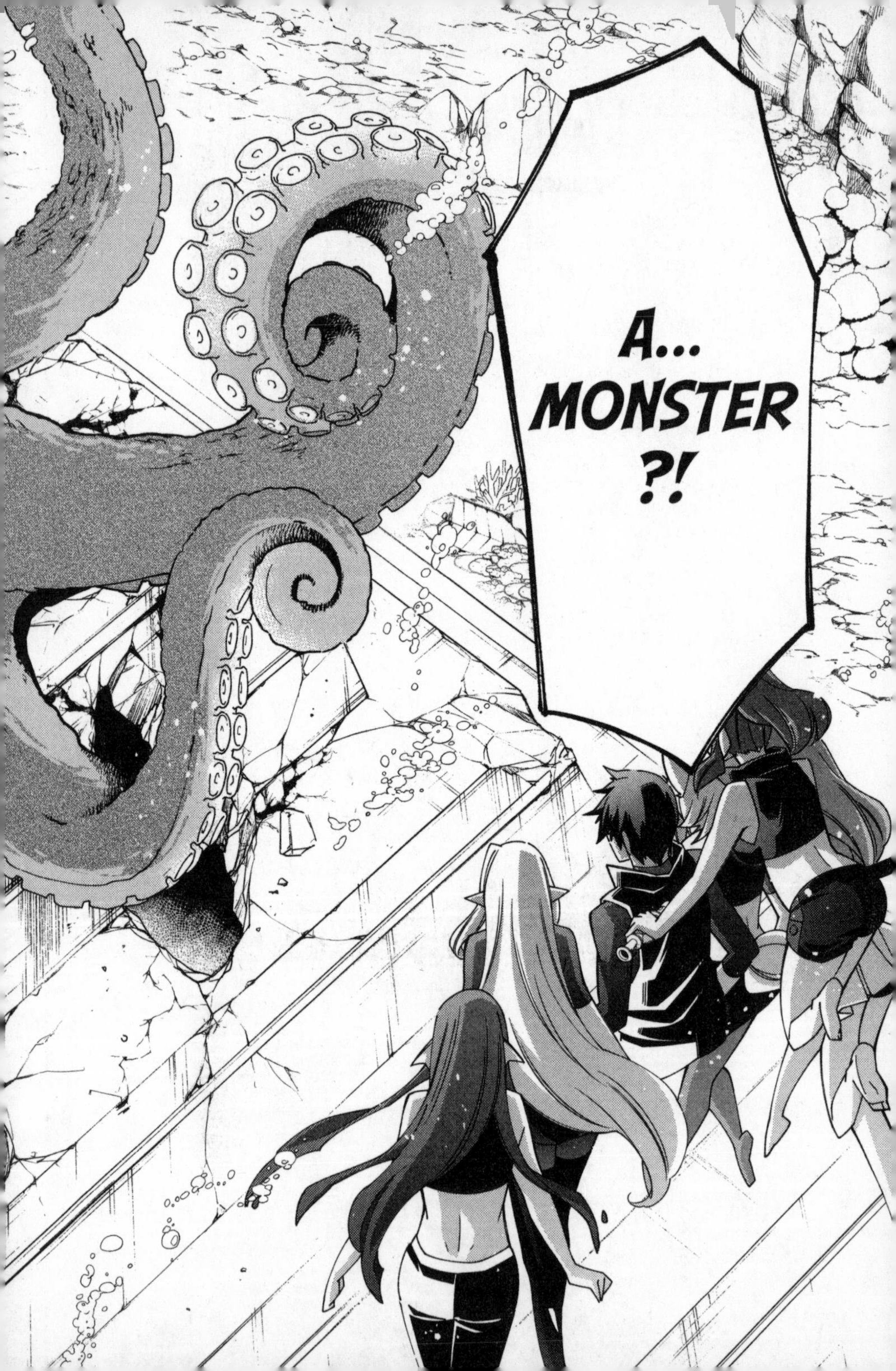
A... MONSTER ?!

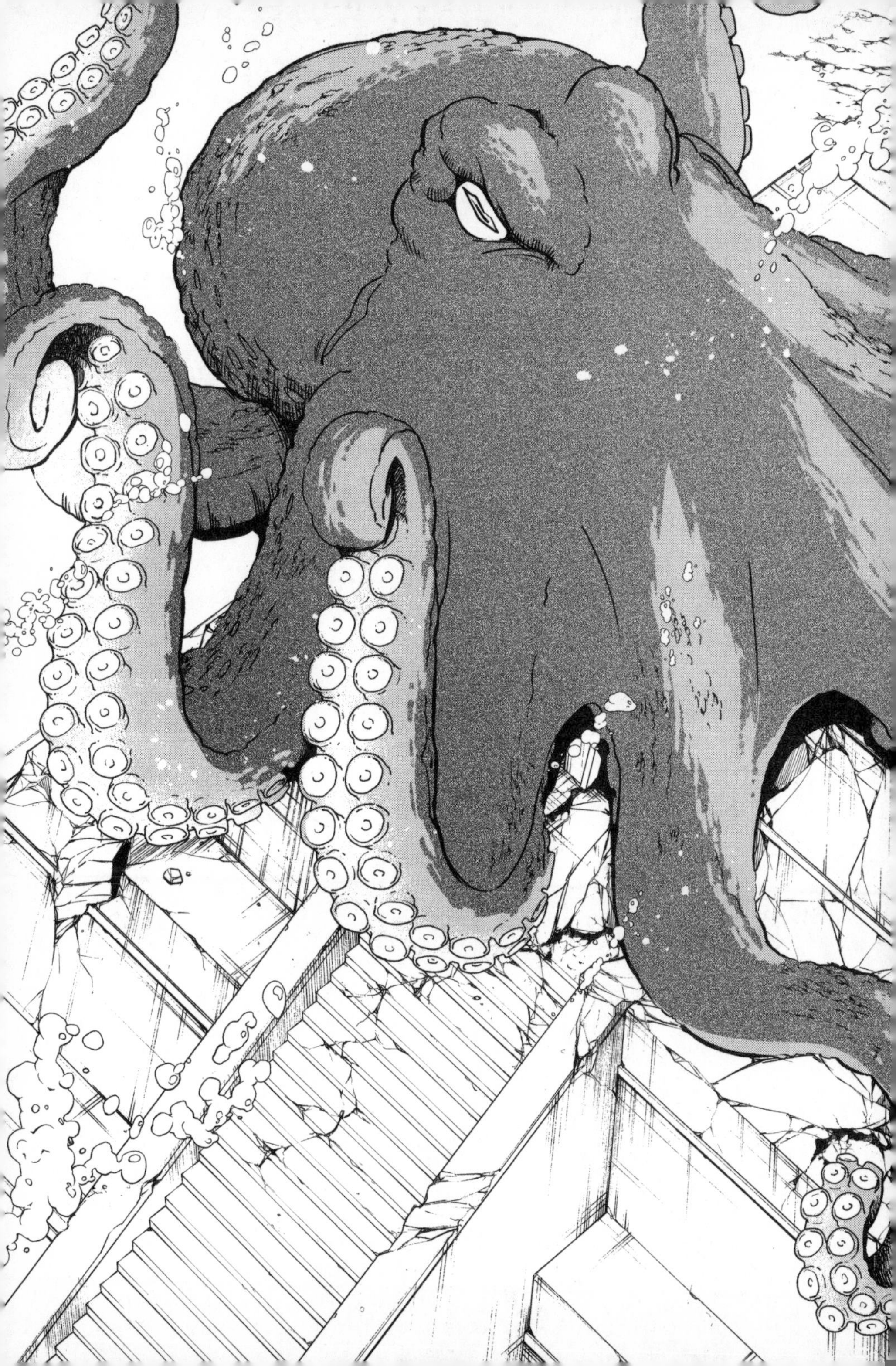

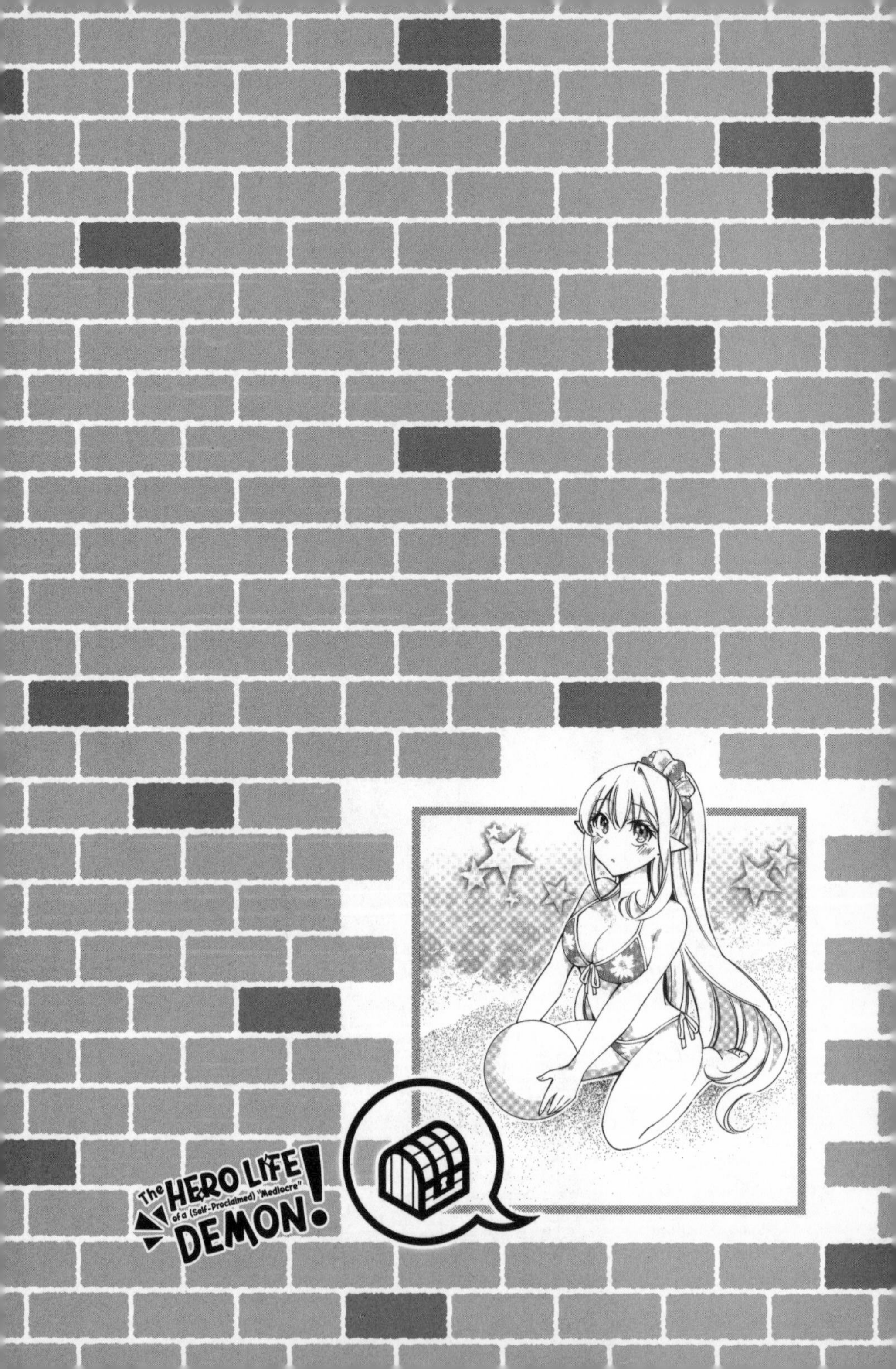
The HERO LIFE of a (Self-Proclaimed) "Mediocre" DEMON!

## CHAPTER 27 CHRONO CALLS FOR SOFIA

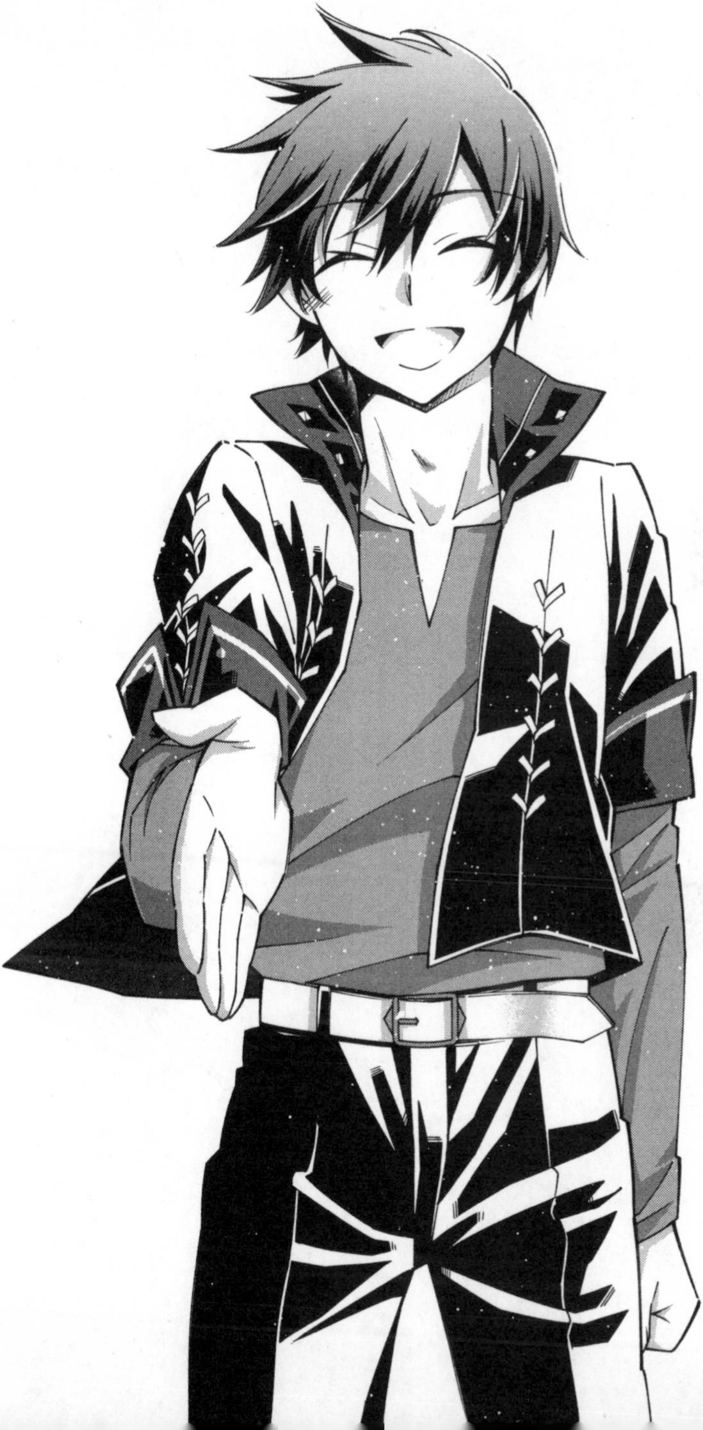

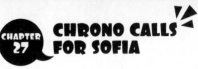

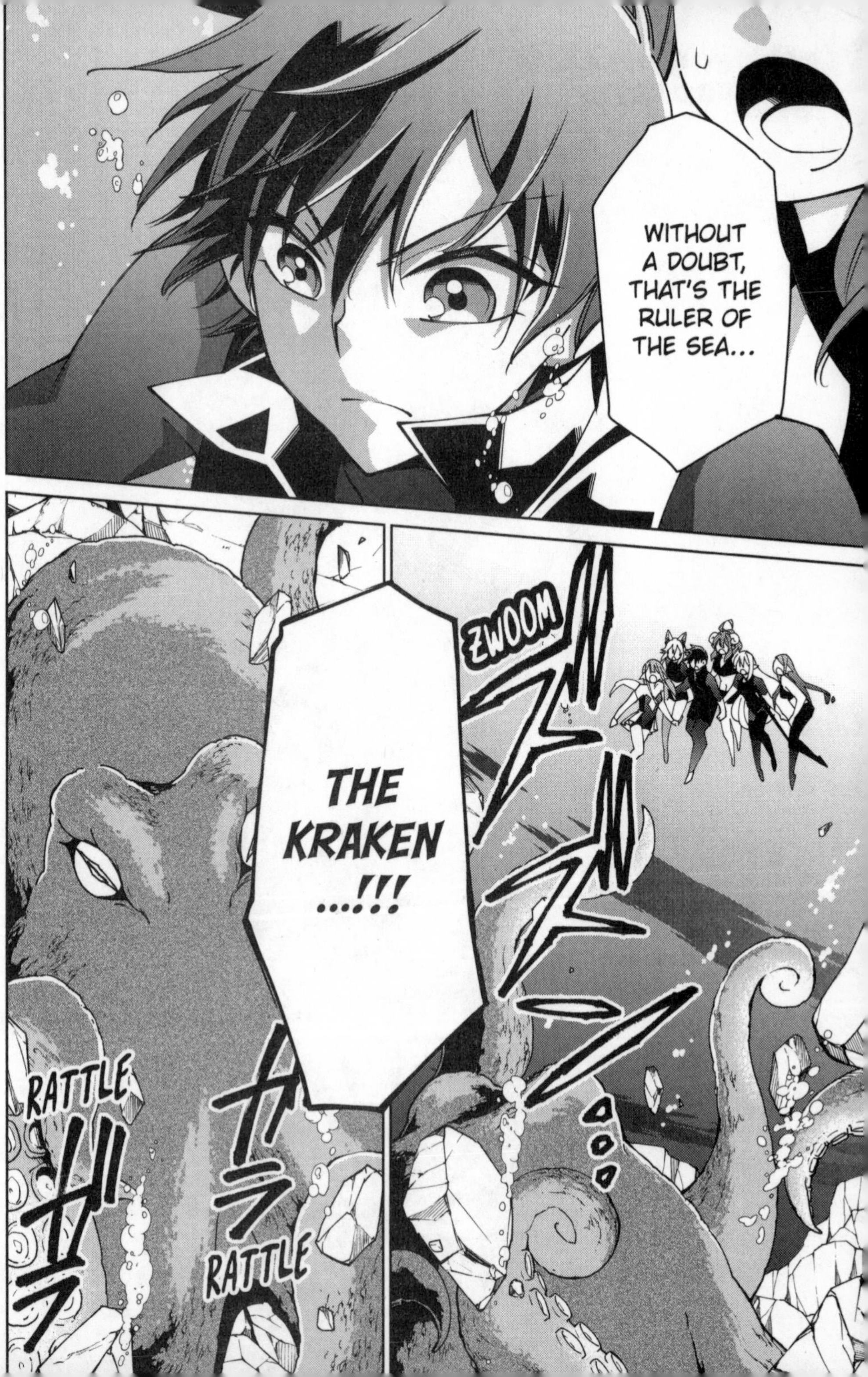
WITHOUT A DOUBT, THAT'S THE RULER OF THE SEA...
ZWOOM
THE KRAKEN ...!!!
RATTLE
RATTLE

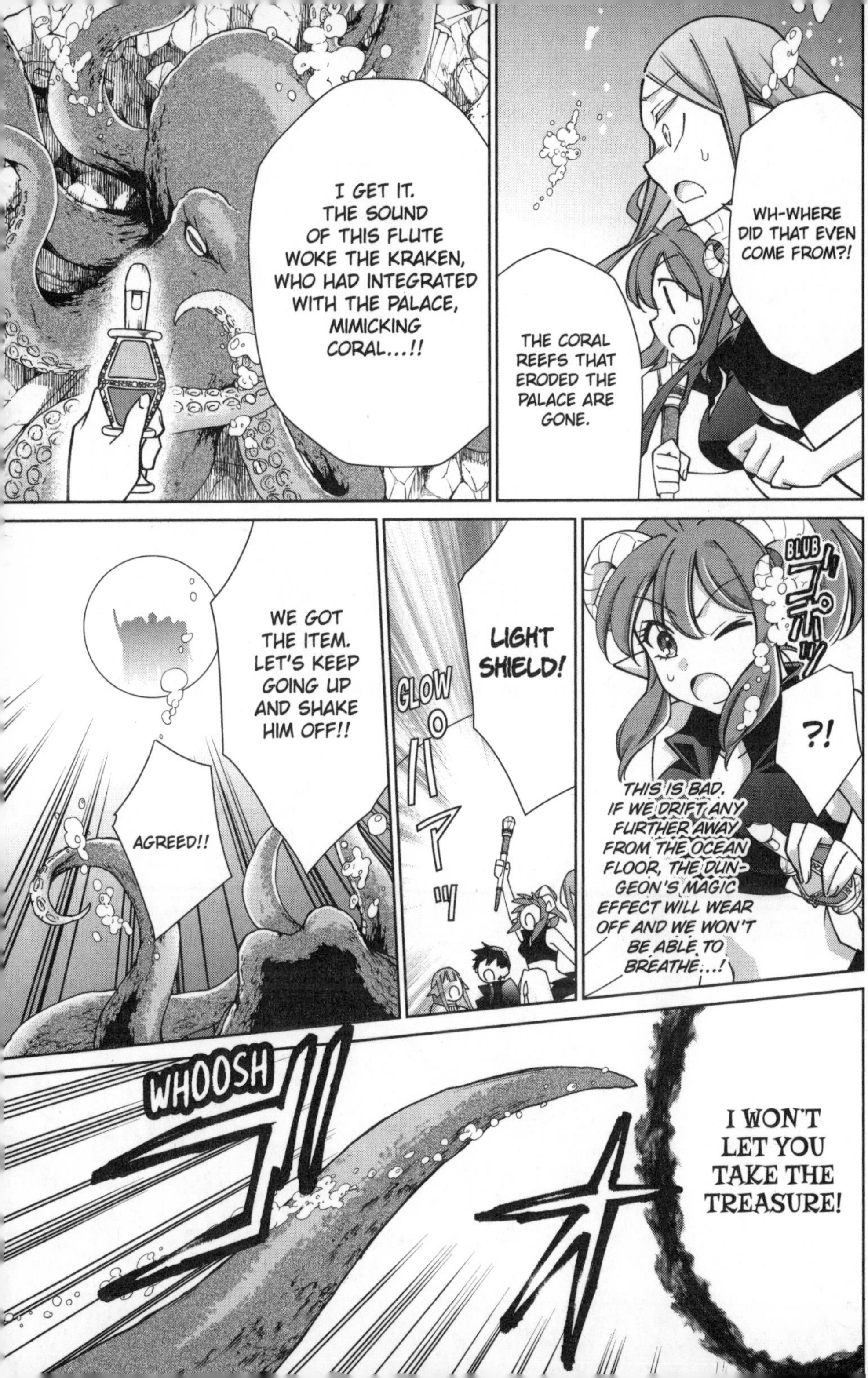
WH-WHERE DID THAT EVEN COME FROM?!
THE CORAL REEFS THAT ERODED THE PALACE ARE GONE.
I GET IT. THE SOUND OF THIS FLUTE WOKE THE KRAKEN, WHO HAD INTEGRATED WITH THE PALACE, MIMICKING CORAL...!!
BLUB
?!
THIS IS BAD. IF WE DRIFT ANY FURTHER AWAY FROM THE OCEAN FLOOR, THE DUN-GEON'S MAGIC EFFECT WILL WEAR OFF AND WE WON'T BE ABLE TO BREATHE...!
LIGHT SHIELD!
GLOW
WE GOT THE ITEM. LET'S KEEP GOING UP AND SHAKE HIM OFF!!
AGREED!!
I WON'T LET YOU TAKE THE TREASURE!
WHOOSH

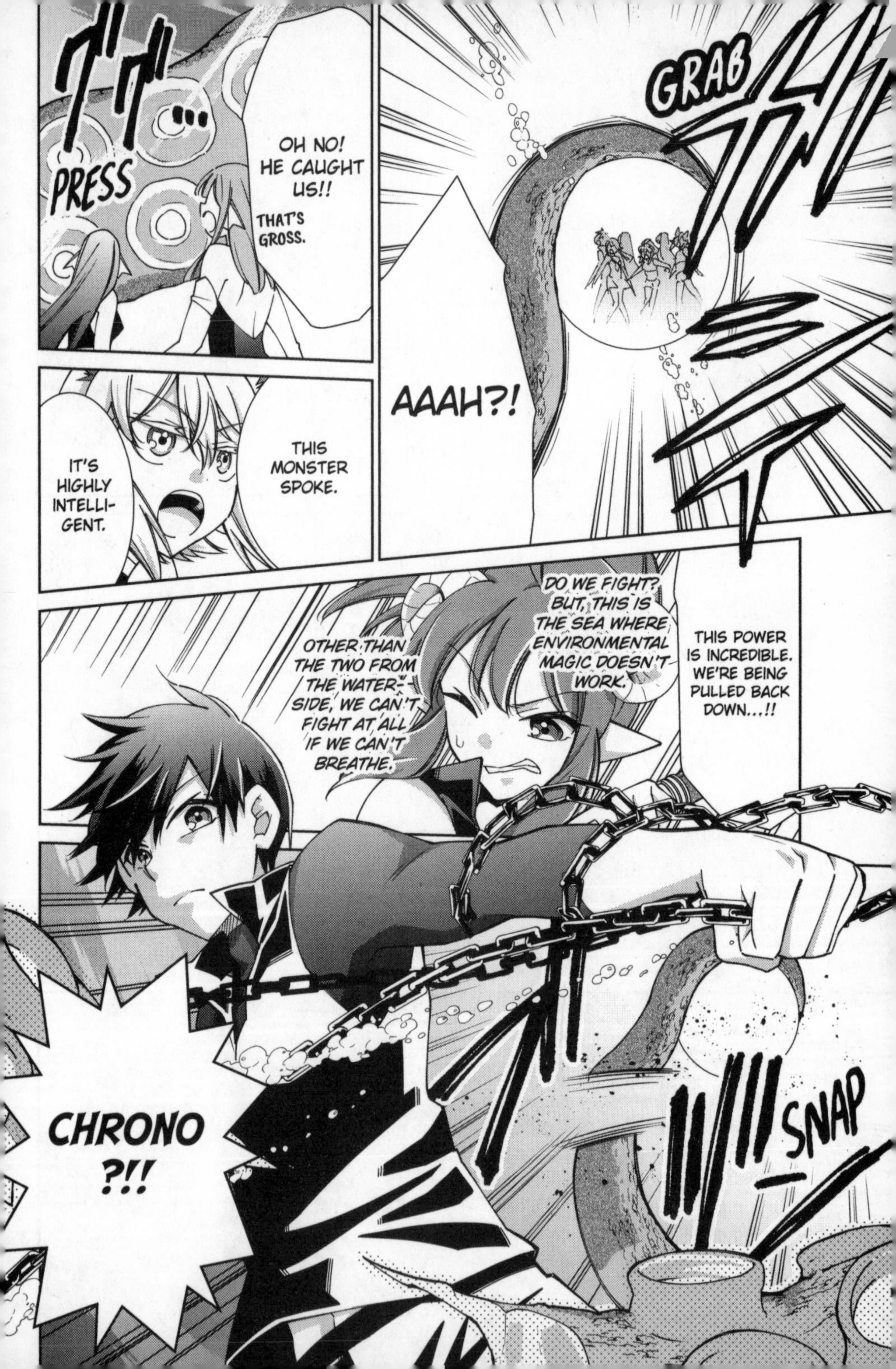
GRAB
AAAH?!
PRESS
...
OH NO! HE CAUGHT US!!
THAT'S GROSS.
THIS MONSTER SPOKE.
IT'S HIGHLY INTELLI-GENT.
THIS POWER IS INCREDIBLE. WE'RE BEING PULLED BACK DOWN...!!
DO WE FIGHT? BUT, THIS IS THE SEA WHERE ENVIRONMENTAL MAGIC DOESN'T WORK.
OTHER THAN THE TWO FROM THE WATER-SIDE, WE CAN'T FIGHT AT ALL IF WE CAN'T BREATHE.
SNAP
CHRONO ?!!

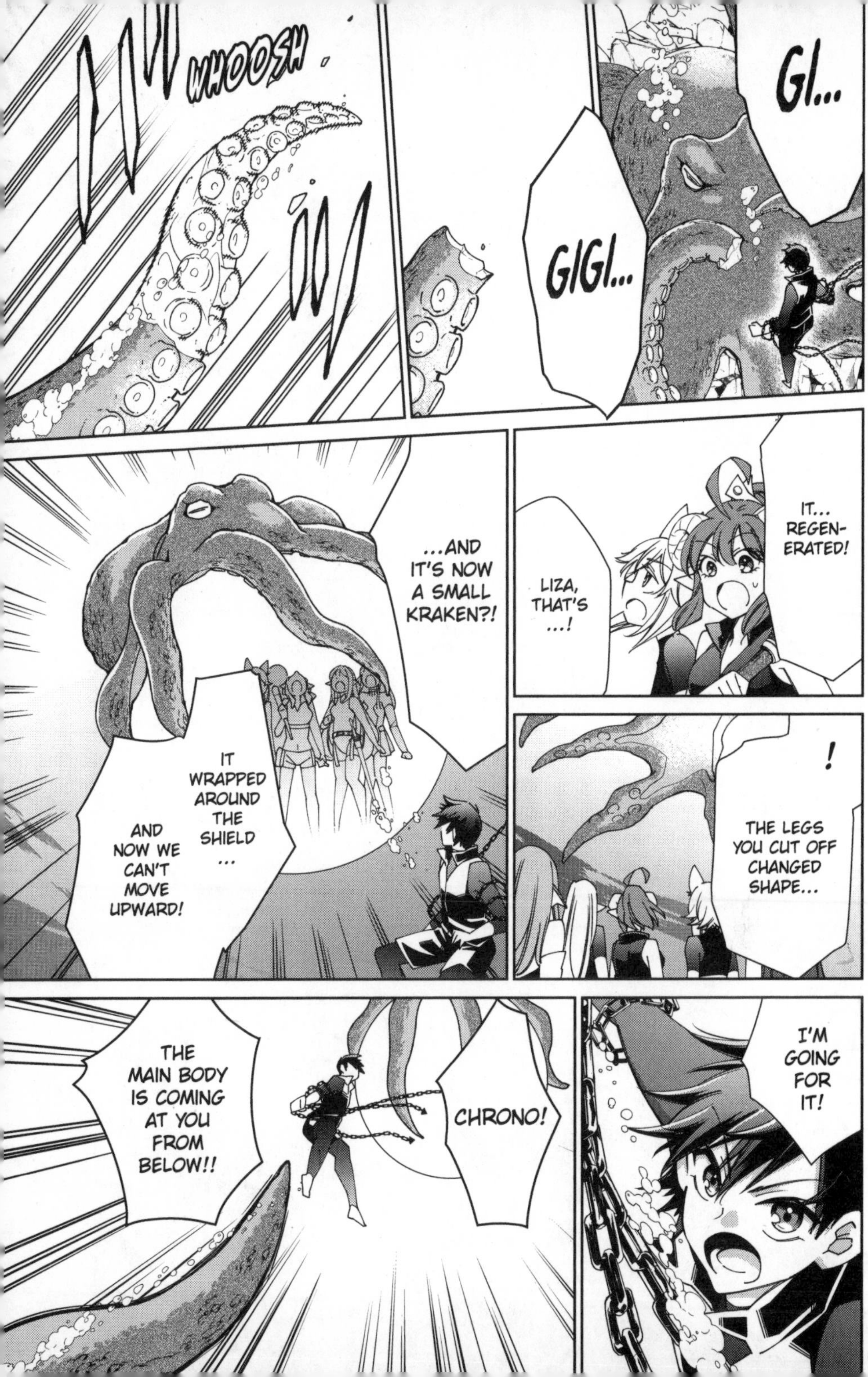
GI...
GIGI...
WHOOSH
IT... REGEN-ERATED!
LIZA, THAT'S ...!
!
THE LEGS YOU CUT OFF CHANGED SHAPE...
...AND IT'S NOW A SMALL KRAKEN?!
IT WRAPPED AROUND THE SHIELD ...
AND NOW WE CAN'T MOVE UPWARD!
I'M GOING FOR IT!
THE MAIN BODY IS COMING AT YOU FROM BELOW!!
CHRONO!

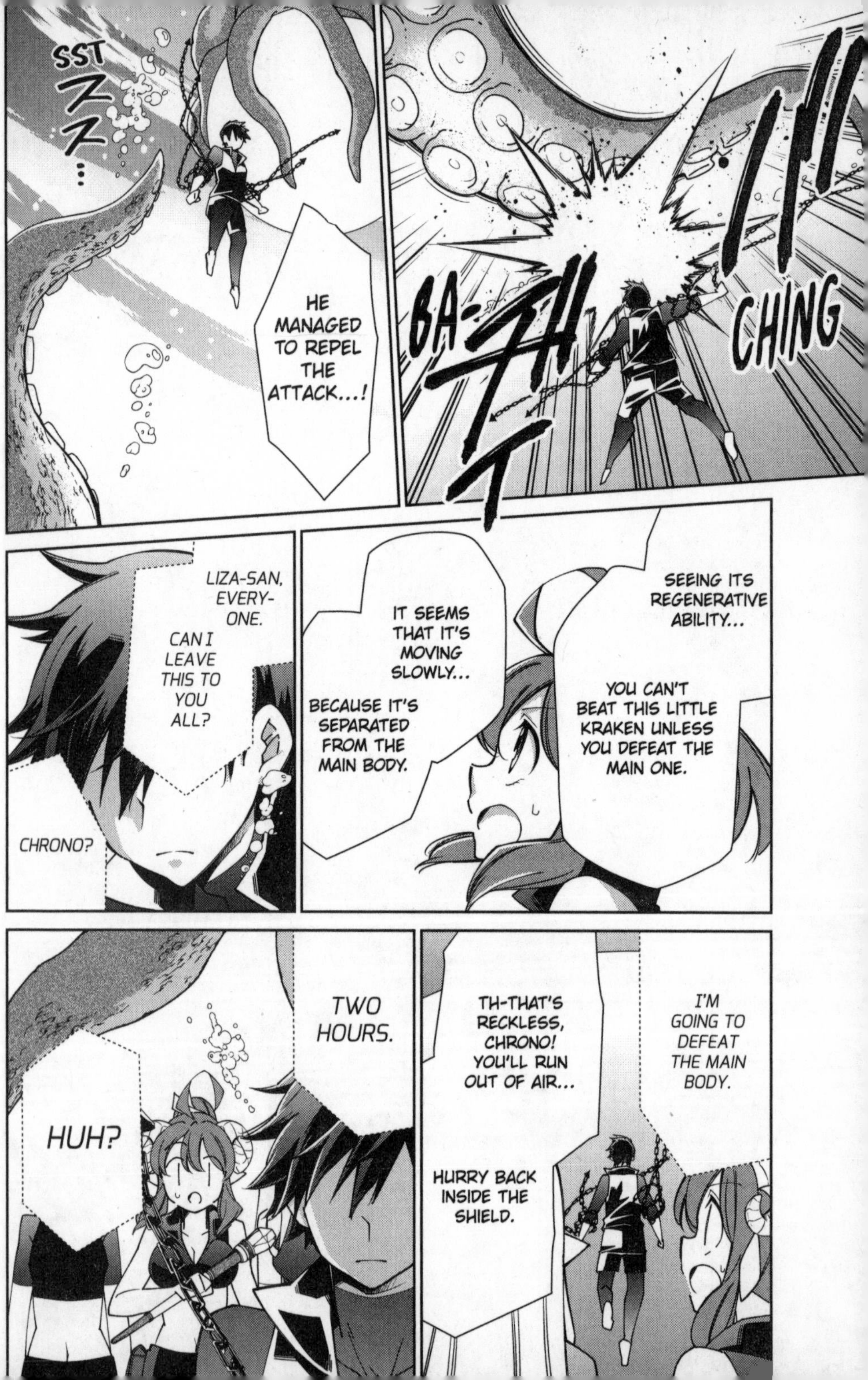
CHING
HE MANAGED TO REPEL THE ATTACK...!
SST
SEEING ITS REGENERATIVE ABILITY...
YOU CAN'T BEAT THIS LITTLE KRAKEN UNLESS YOU DEFEAT THE MAIN ONE.
IT SEEMS THAT IT'S MOVING SLOWLY...
BECAUSE IT'S SEPARATED FROM THE MAIN BODY.
LIZA-SAN, EVERY-ONE.
CAN I LEAVE THIS TO YOU ALL?
CHRONO?
I'M GOING TO DEFEAT THE MAIN BODY.
TH-THAT'S RECKLESS, CHRONO! YOU'LL RUN OUT OF AIR...
HURRY BACK INSIDE THE SHIELD.
TWO HOURS.
HUH?

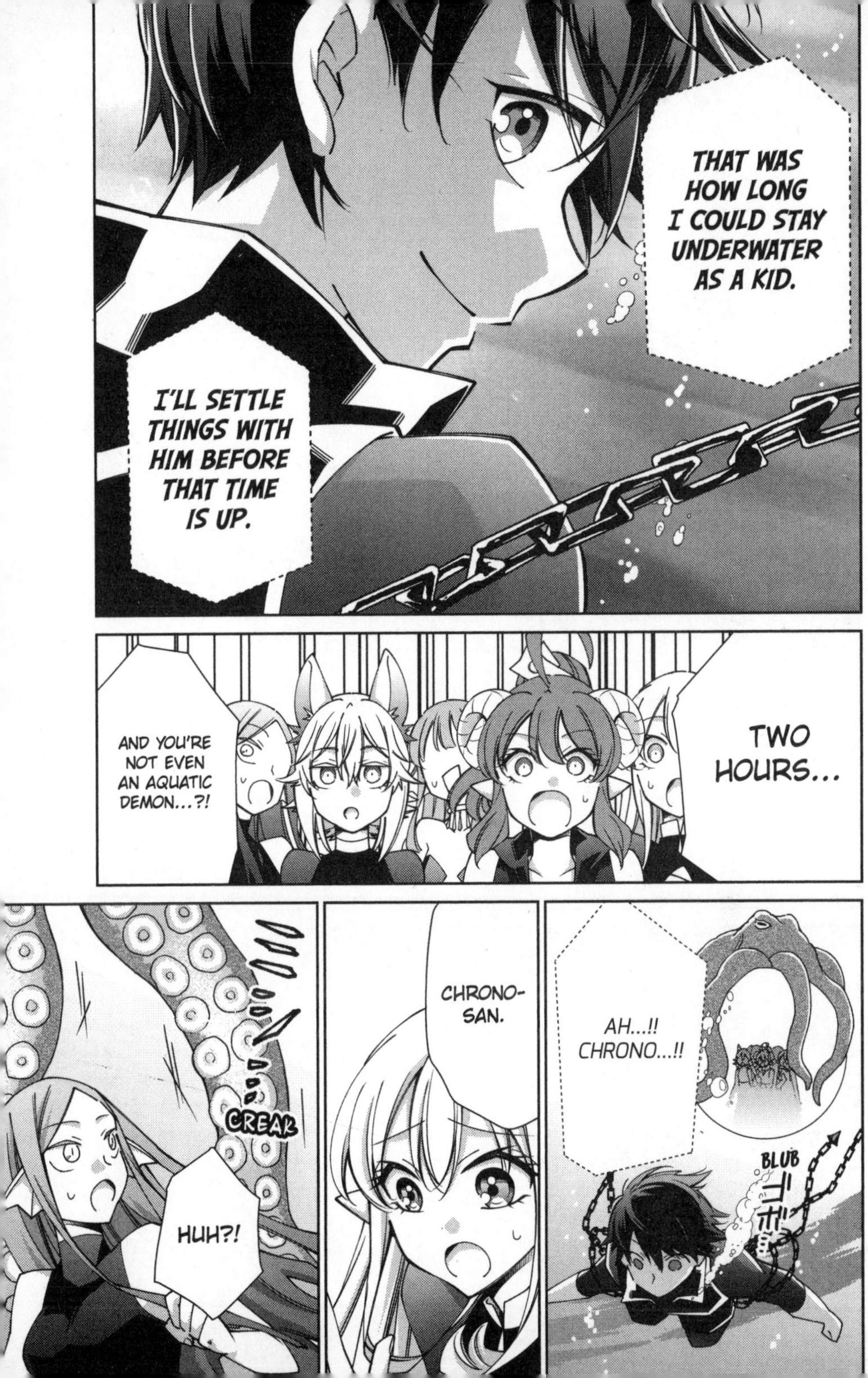

THAT WAS HOW LONG I COULD STAY UNDERWATER AS A KID.
I'LL SETTLE THINGS WITH HIM BEFORE THAT TIME IS UP.
TWO HOURS...
AND YOU'RE NOT EVEN AN AQUATIC DEMON...?!
AH...!! CHRONO...!!
BLUB
CHRONO-SAN.
CREAK
HUH?!

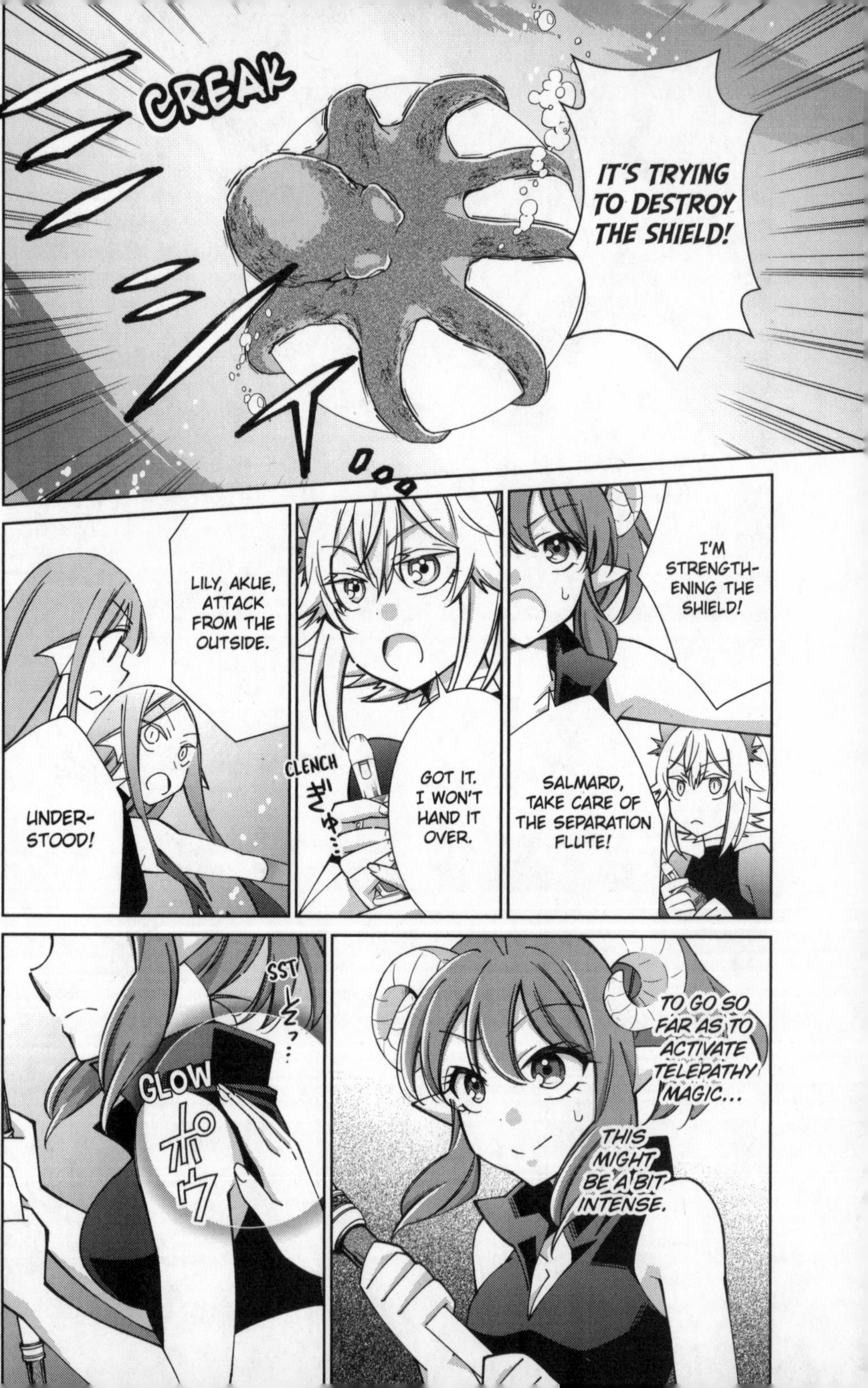
CREAK
IT'S TRYING TO DESTROY THE SHIELD!
I'M STRENGTH-ENING THE SHIELD!
SALMARD, TAKE CARE OF THE SEPARATION FLUTE!
CLENCH
GOT IT. I WON'T HAND IT OVER.
LILY, AKUE, ATTACK FROM THE OUTSIDE.
UNDER-STOOD!
TO GO SO FAR AS TO ACTIVATE TELEPATHY MAGIC...
THIS MIGHT BE A BIT INTENSE.
SST
GLOW

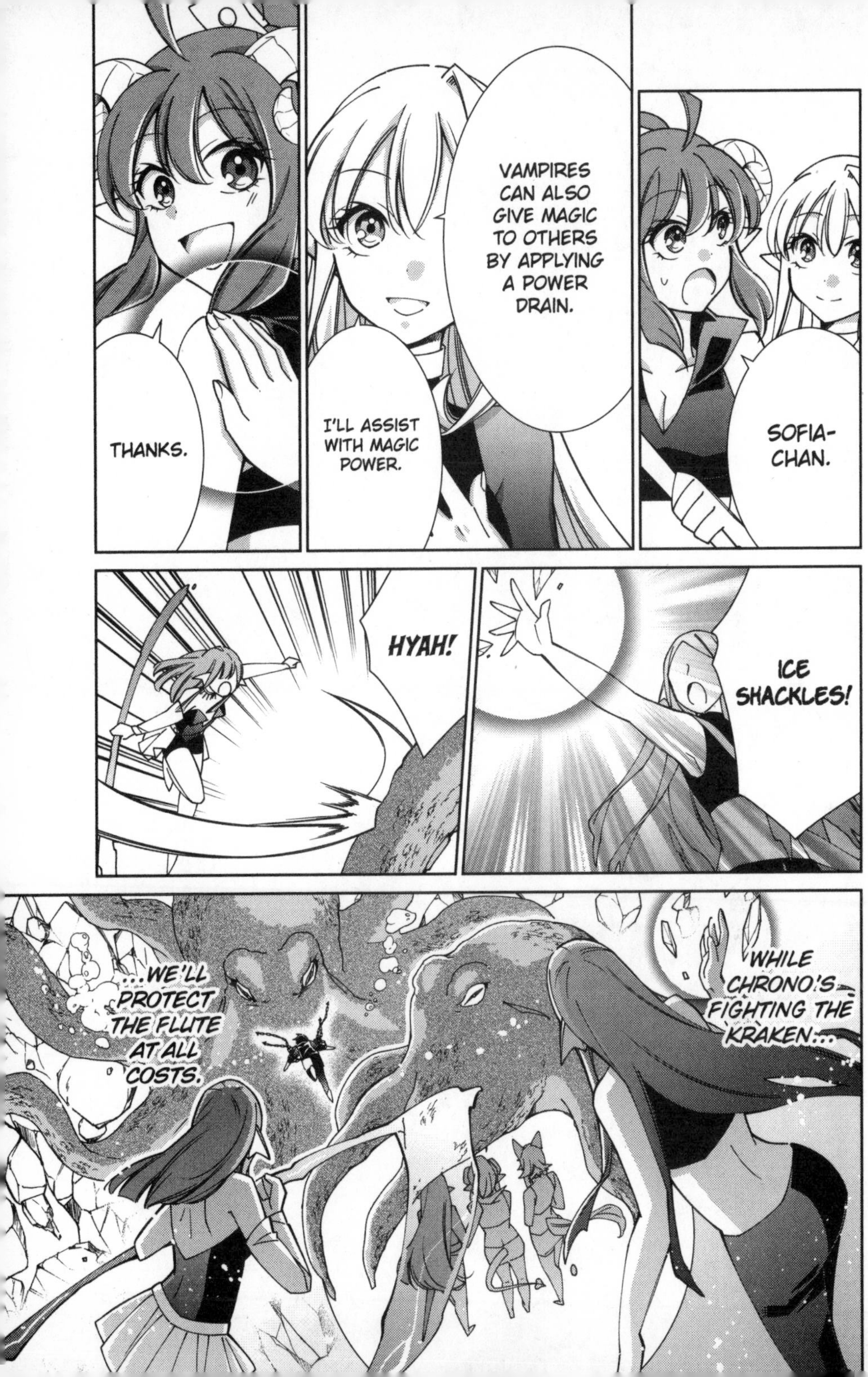
SOFIA-CHAN.
VAMPIRES CAN ALSO GIVE MAGIC TO OTHERS BY APPLYING A POWER DRAIN.
I'LL ASSIST WITH MAGIC POWER.
THANKS.
ICE SHACKLES!
HYAH!
WHILE CHRONO'S FIGHTING THE KRAKEN...
...WE'LL PROTECT THE FLUTE AT ALL COSTS.

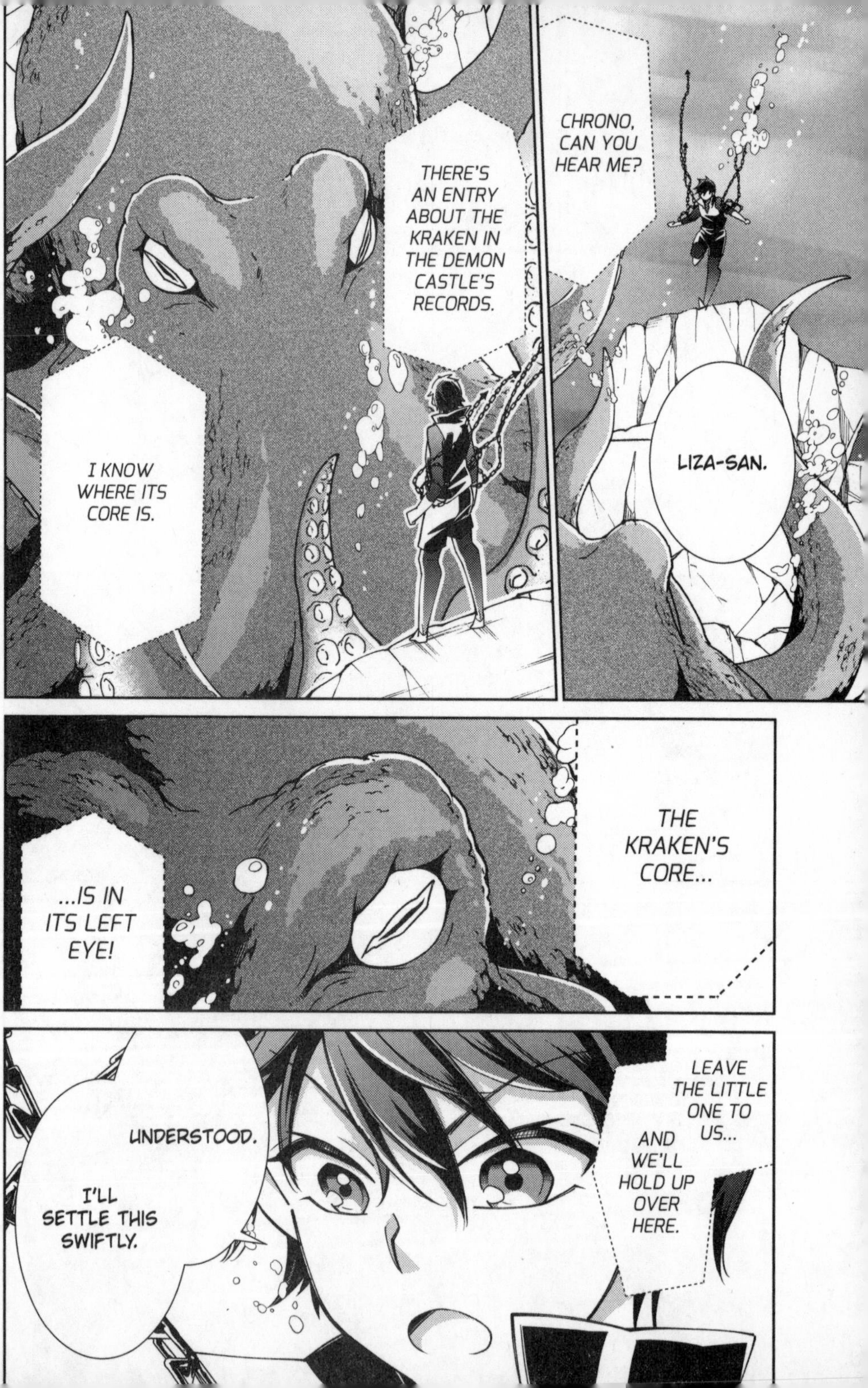
CHRONO, CAN YOU HEAR ME?
LIZA-SAN.
THERE'S AN ENTRY ABOUT THE KRAKEN IN THE DEMON CASTLE'S RECORDS.
I KNOW WHERE ITS CORE IS.
THE KRAKEN'S CORE...
...IS IN ITS LEFT EYE!
LEAVE THE LITTLE ONE TO US...
AND WE'LL HOLD UP OVER HERE.
UNDERSTOOD.
I'LL SETTLE THIS SWIFTLY.

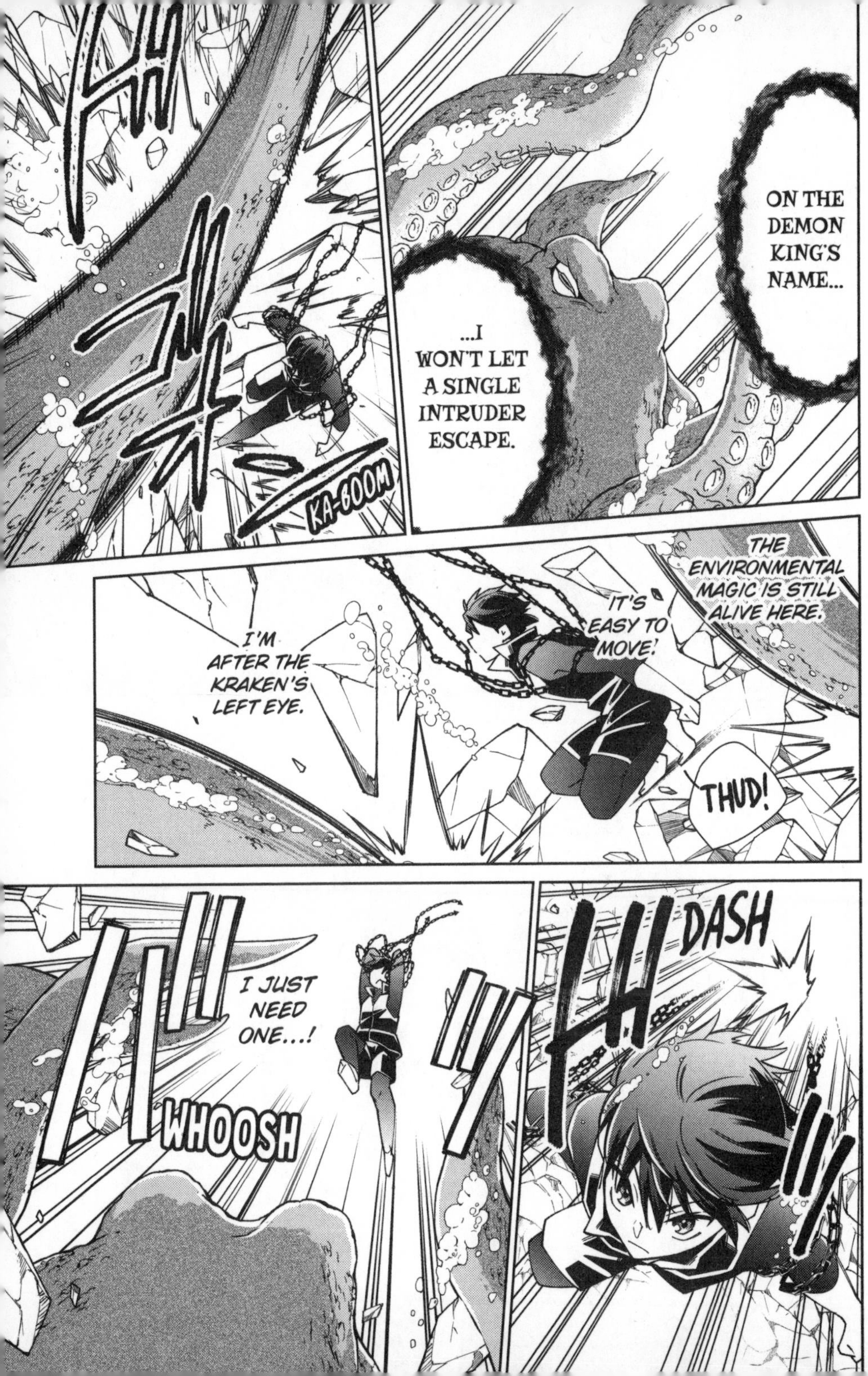
ON THE DEMON KING'S NAME...
...I WON'T LET A SINGLE INTRUDER ESCAPE.
KA-BOOM
THE ENVIRONMENTAL MAGIC IS STILL ALIVE HERE.
IT'S EASY TO MOVE!
I'M AFTER THE KRAKEN'S LEFT EYE.
THUD!
DASH
I JUST NEED ONE...!
WHOOSH

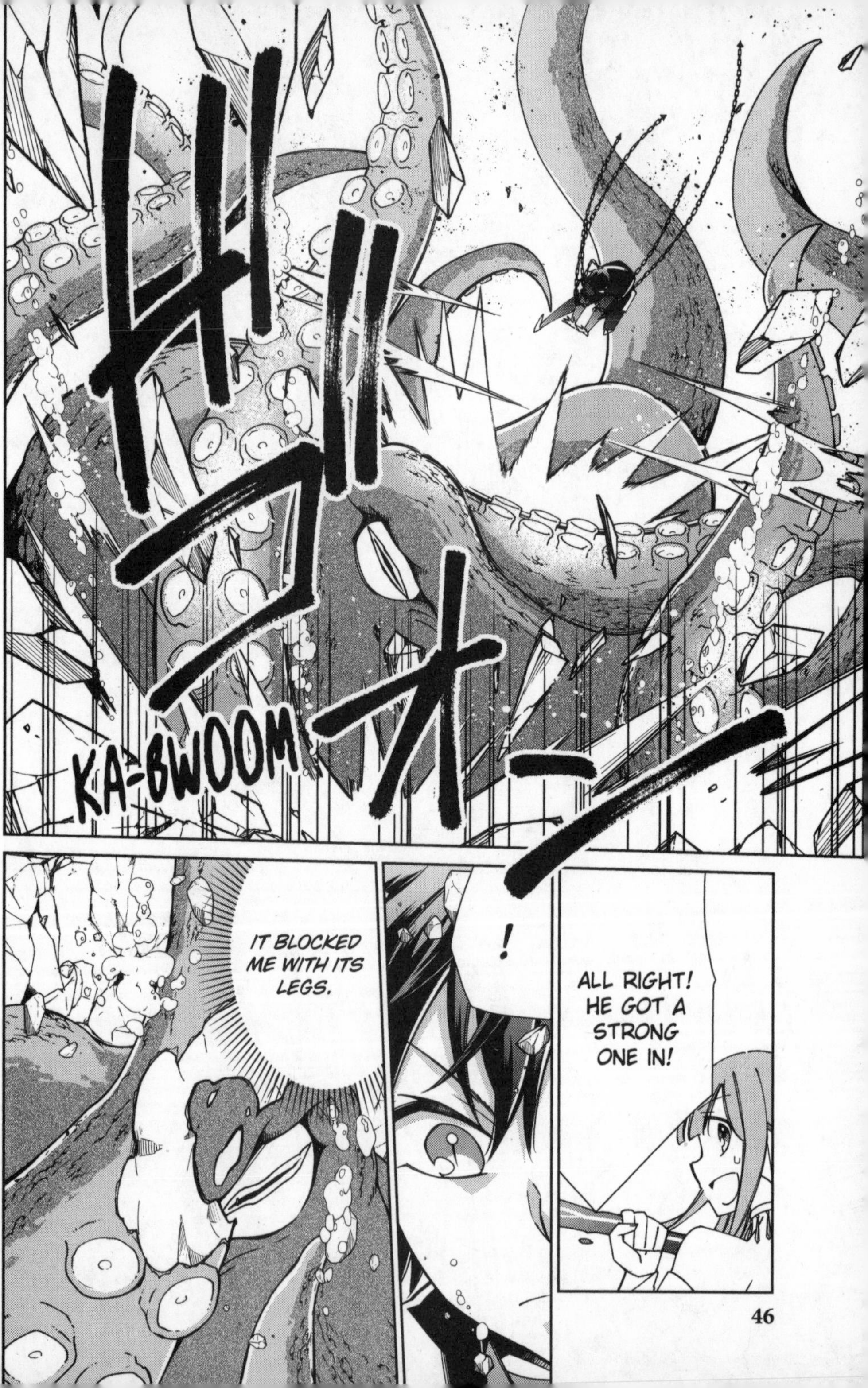
KA-BWOOM
ALL RIGHT! HE GOT A STRONG ONE IN!
!
IT BLOCKED ME WITH ITS LEGS.

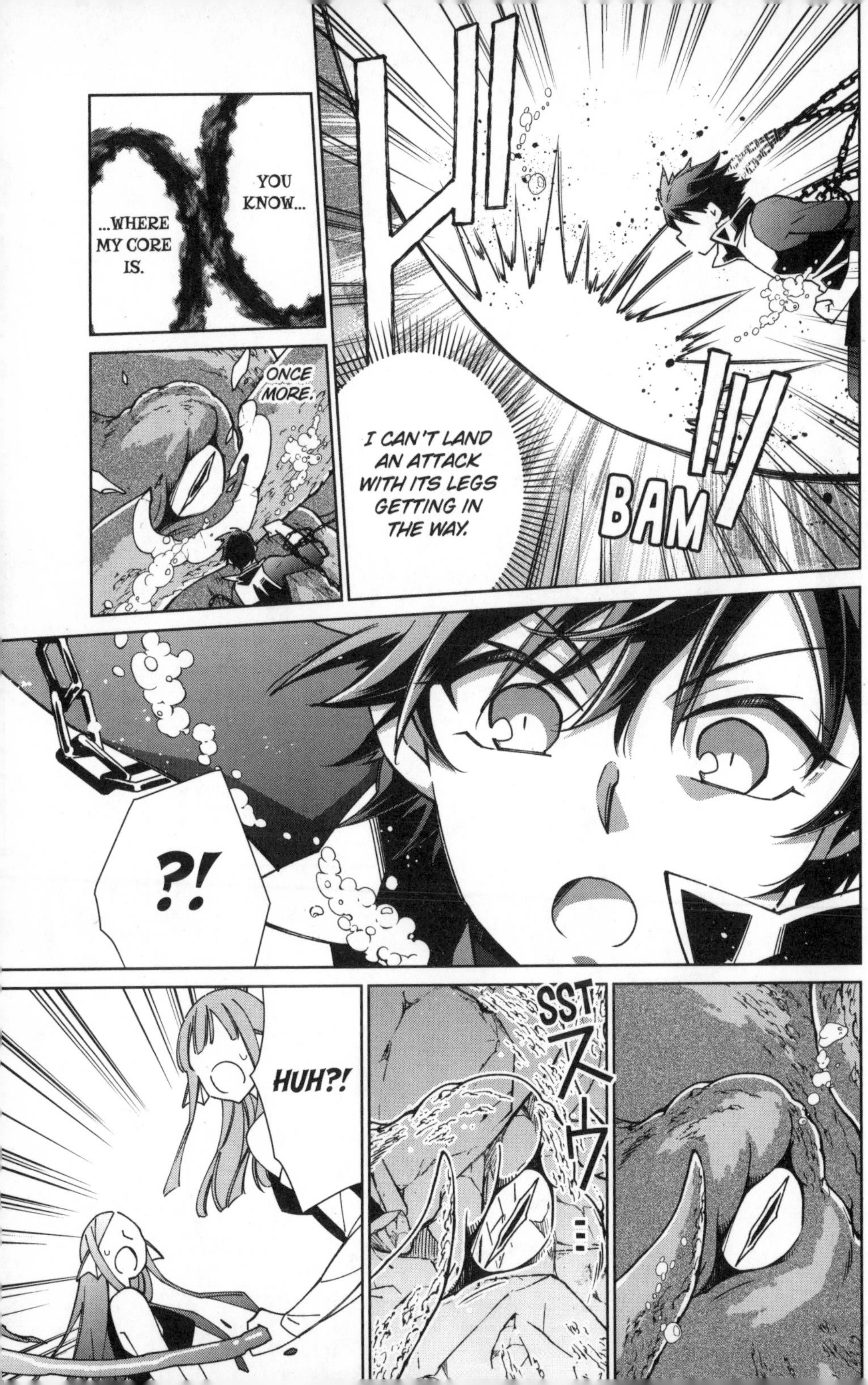
BAM
I CAN'T LAND AN ATTACK WITH ITS LEGS GETTING IN THE WAY.
YOU KNOW...
...WHERE MY CORE IS.
ONCE MORE.
?!
SST
...
HUH?!

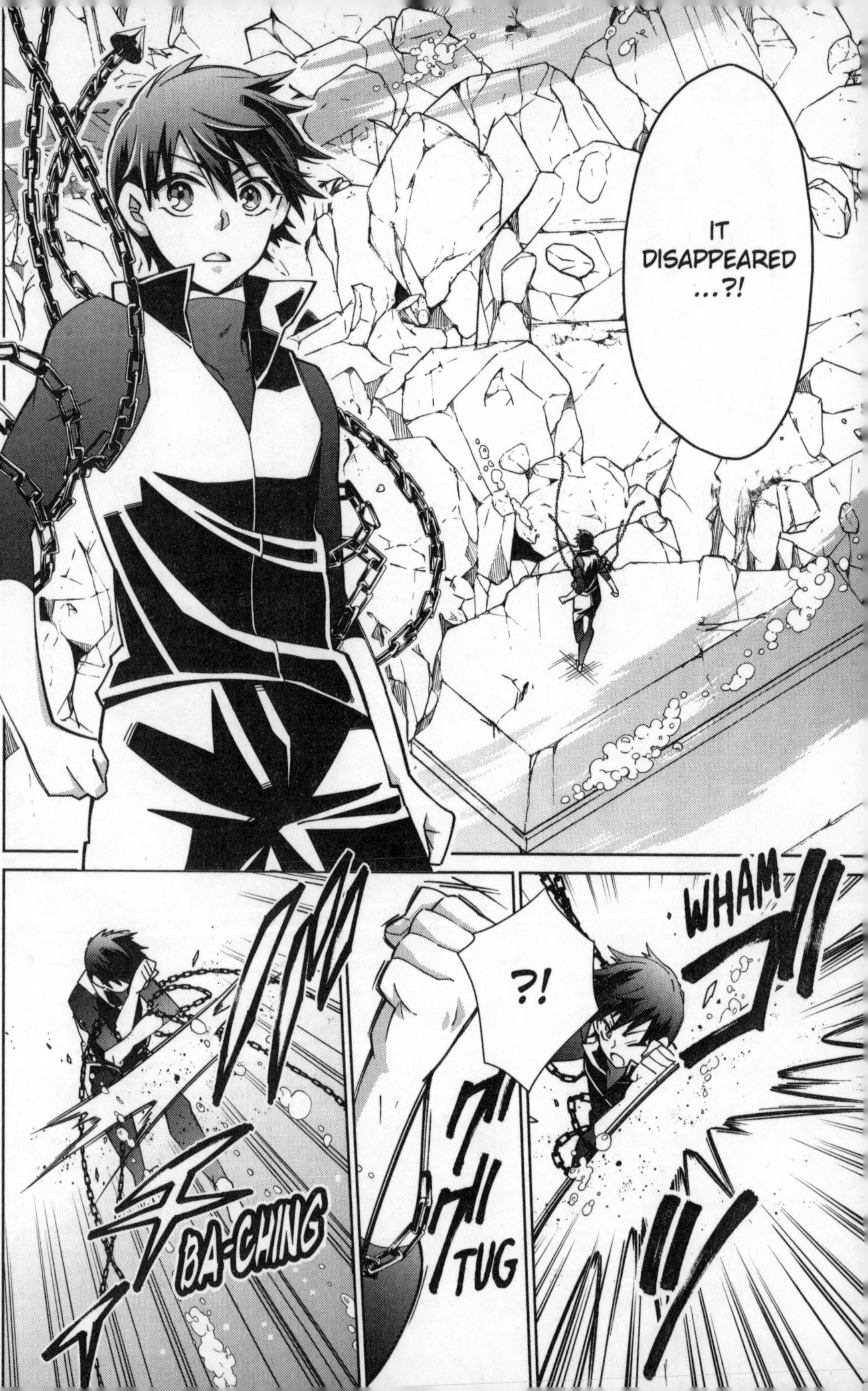
IT DISAPPEARED ...?!
WHAM
?!
TUG
BA-CHING

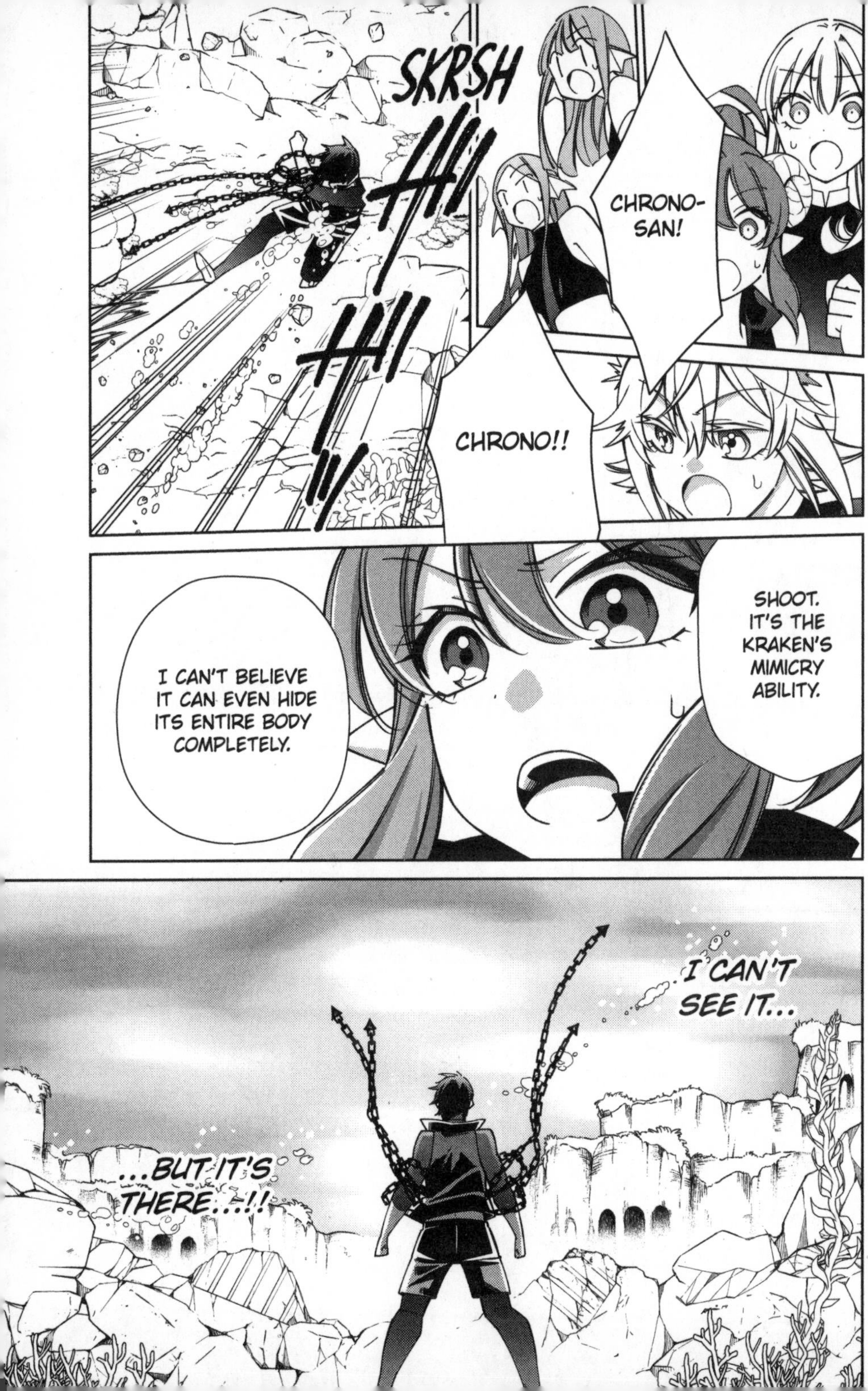
CHRONO-SAN!
CHRONO!!
SKRSH
SHOOT. IT'S THE KRAKEN'S MIMICRY ABILITY.
I CAN'T BELIEVE IT CAN EVEN HIDE ITS ENTIRE BODY COMPLETELY.
I CAN'T SEE IT...
...BUT IT'S THERE...!!

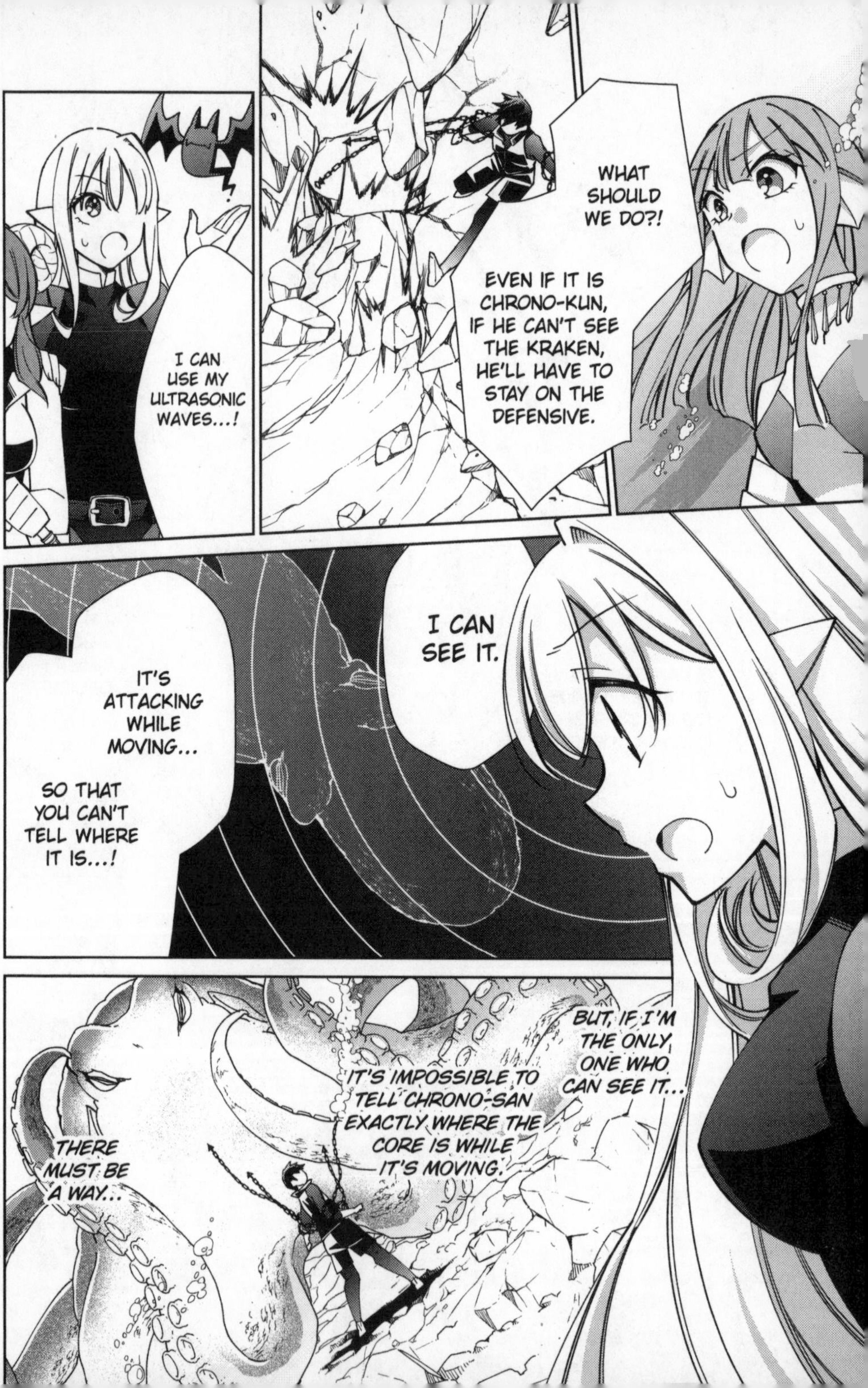
WHAT SHOULD WE DO?!
EVEN IF IT IS CHRONO-KUN, IF HE CAN'T SEE THE KRAKEN, HE'LL HAVE TO STAY ON THE DEFENSIVE.
I CAN USE MY ULTRASONIC WAVES...!
I CAN SEE IT.
IT'S ATTACKING WHILE MOVING...
SO THAT YOU CAN'T TELL WHERE IT IS...!
BUT, IF I'M THE ONLY ONE WHO CAN SEE IT...
IT'S IMPOSSIBLE TO TELL CHRONO-SAN EXACTLY WHERE THE CORE IS WHILE IT'S MOVING.
THERE MUST BE A WAY...

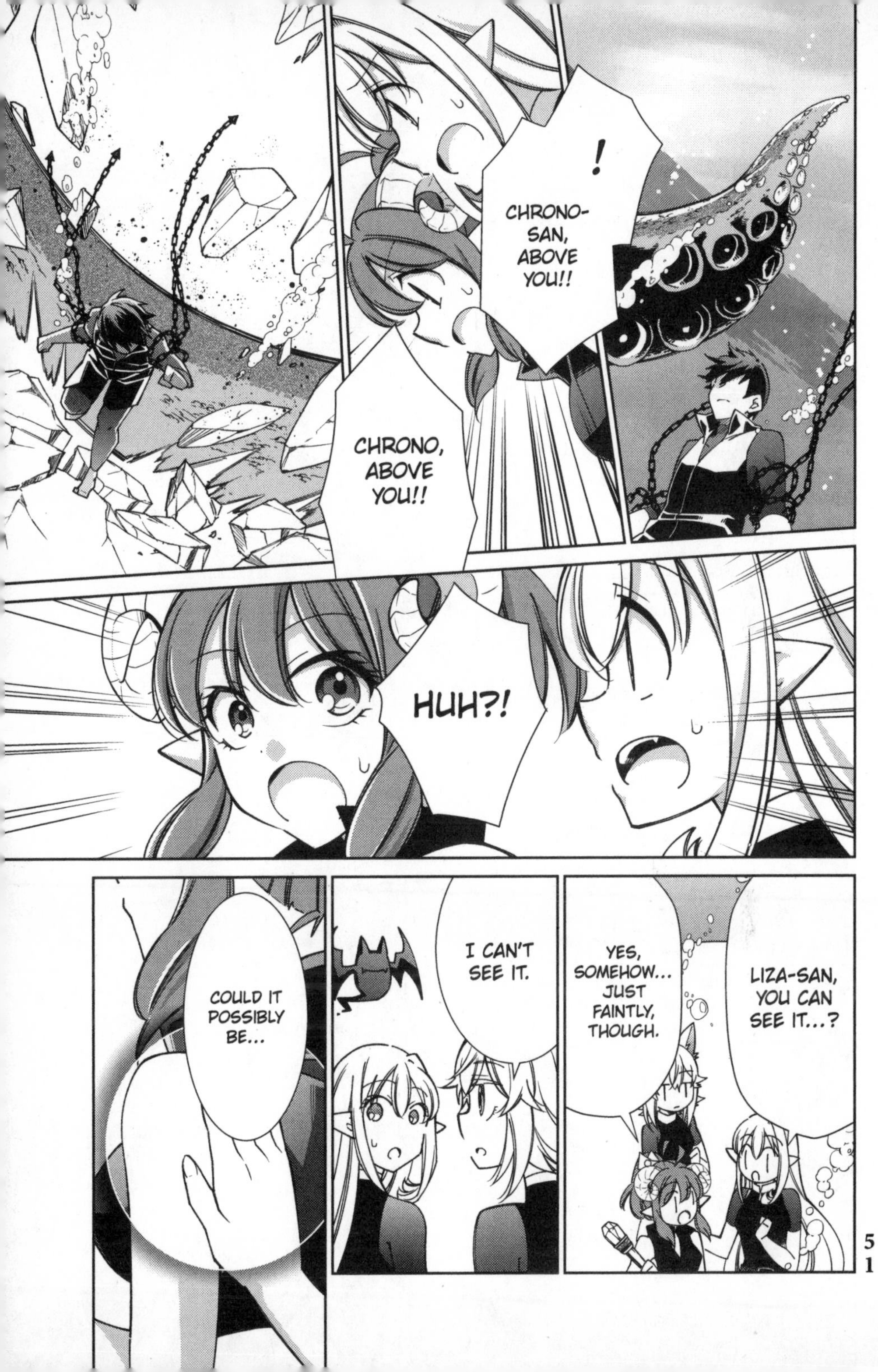
!
CHRONO-SAN, ABOVE YOU!!
CHRONO, ABOVE YOU!!
HUH?!
LIZA-SAN, YOU CAN SEE IT...?
YES, SOMEHOW... JUST FAINTLY, THOUGH.
I CAN'T SEE IT.
COULD IT POSSIBLY BE...

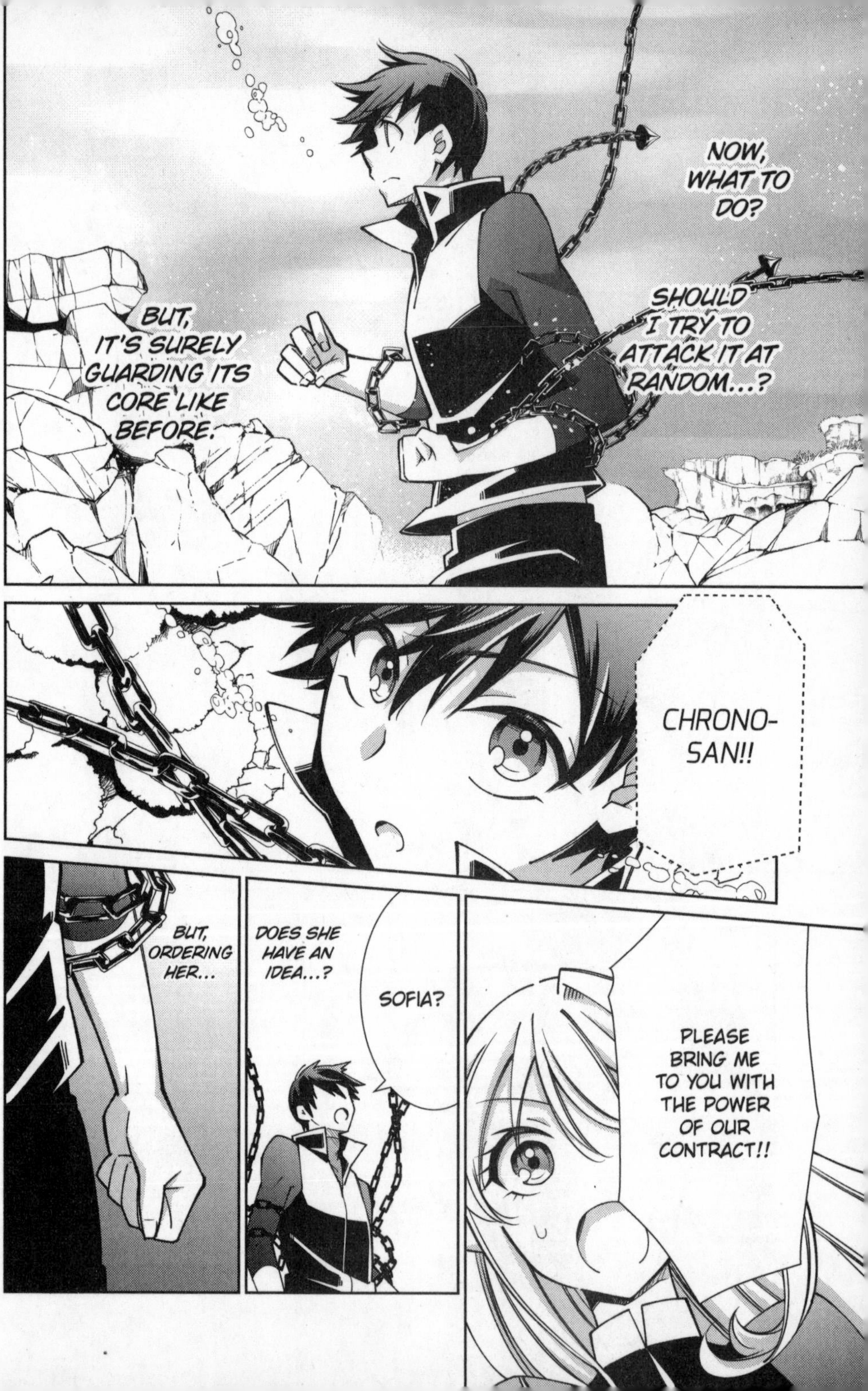
NOW, WHAT TO DO?
SHOULD I TRY TO ATTACK IT AT RANDOM...?
BUT, IT'S SURELY GUARDING ITS CORE LIKE BEFORE.
CHRONO-SAN!!
PLEASE BRING ME TO YOU WITH THE POWER OF OUR CONTRACT!!
SOFIA?
DOES SHE HAVE AN IDEA...?
BUT, ORDERING HER...

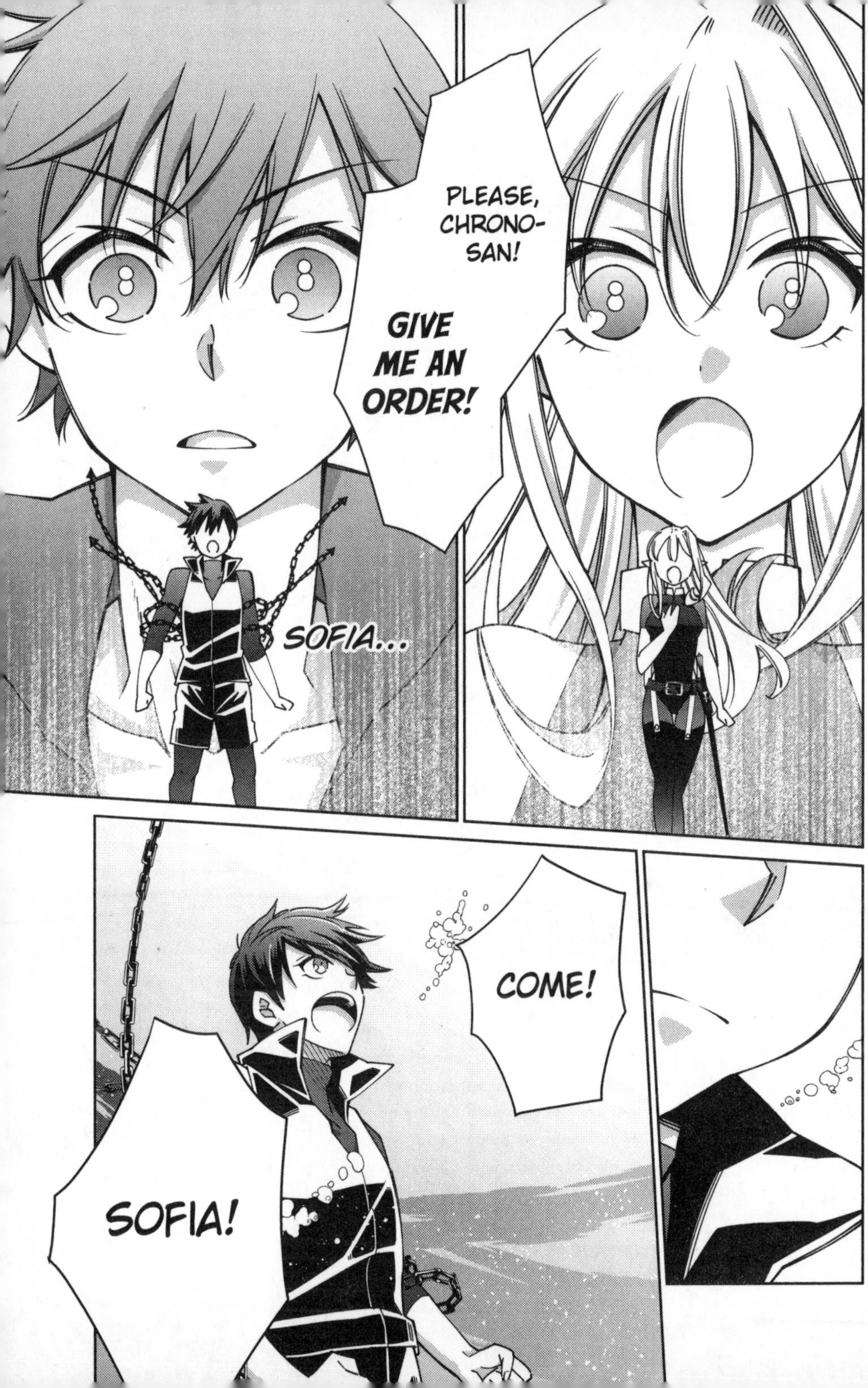
PLEASE, CHRONO-SAN!
GIVE ME AN ORDER!
SOFIA...
COME!
SOFIA!

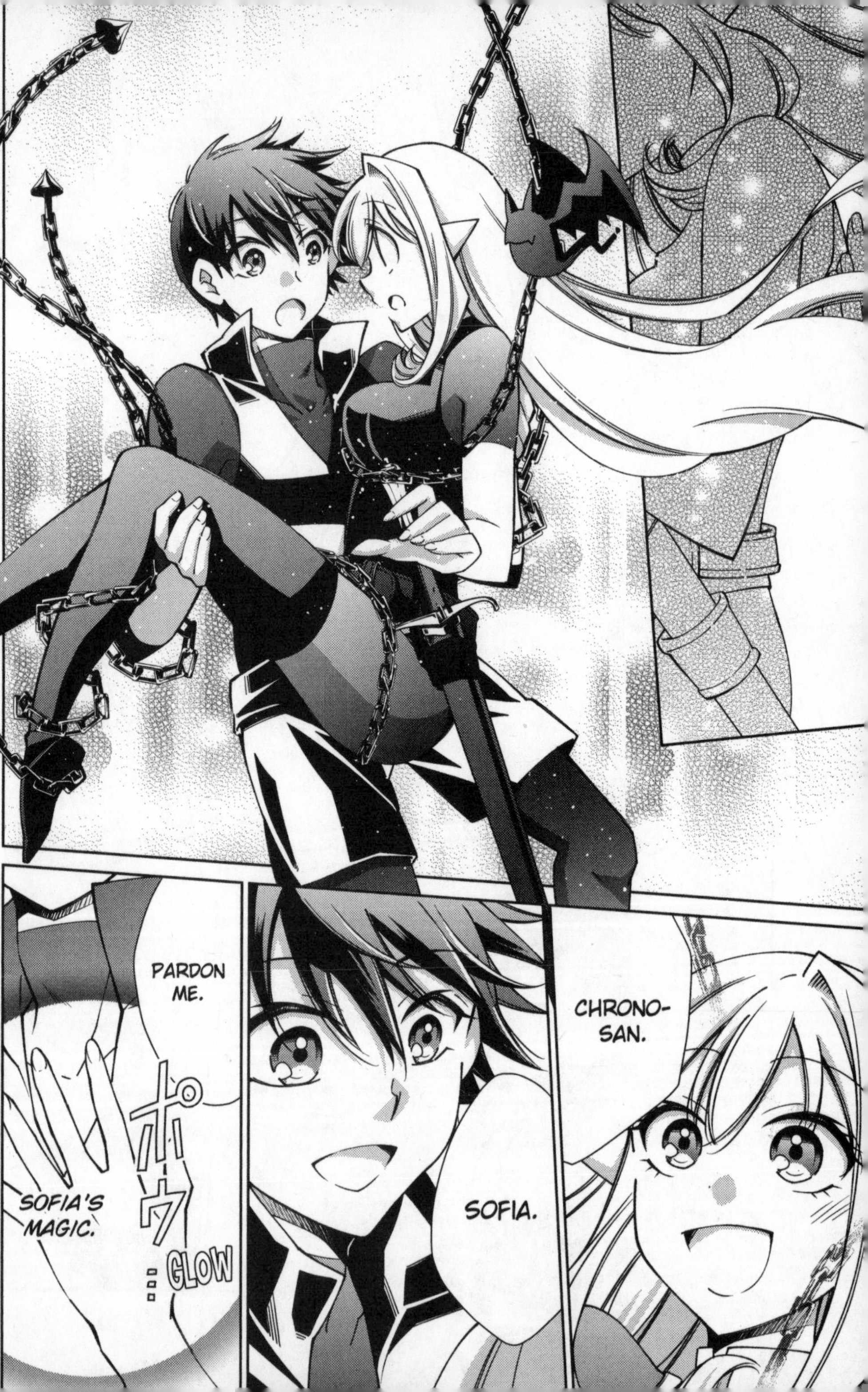
CHRONO-SAN.
SOFIA.
PARDON ME.
ポウ…
GLOW
SOFIA'S MAGIC.

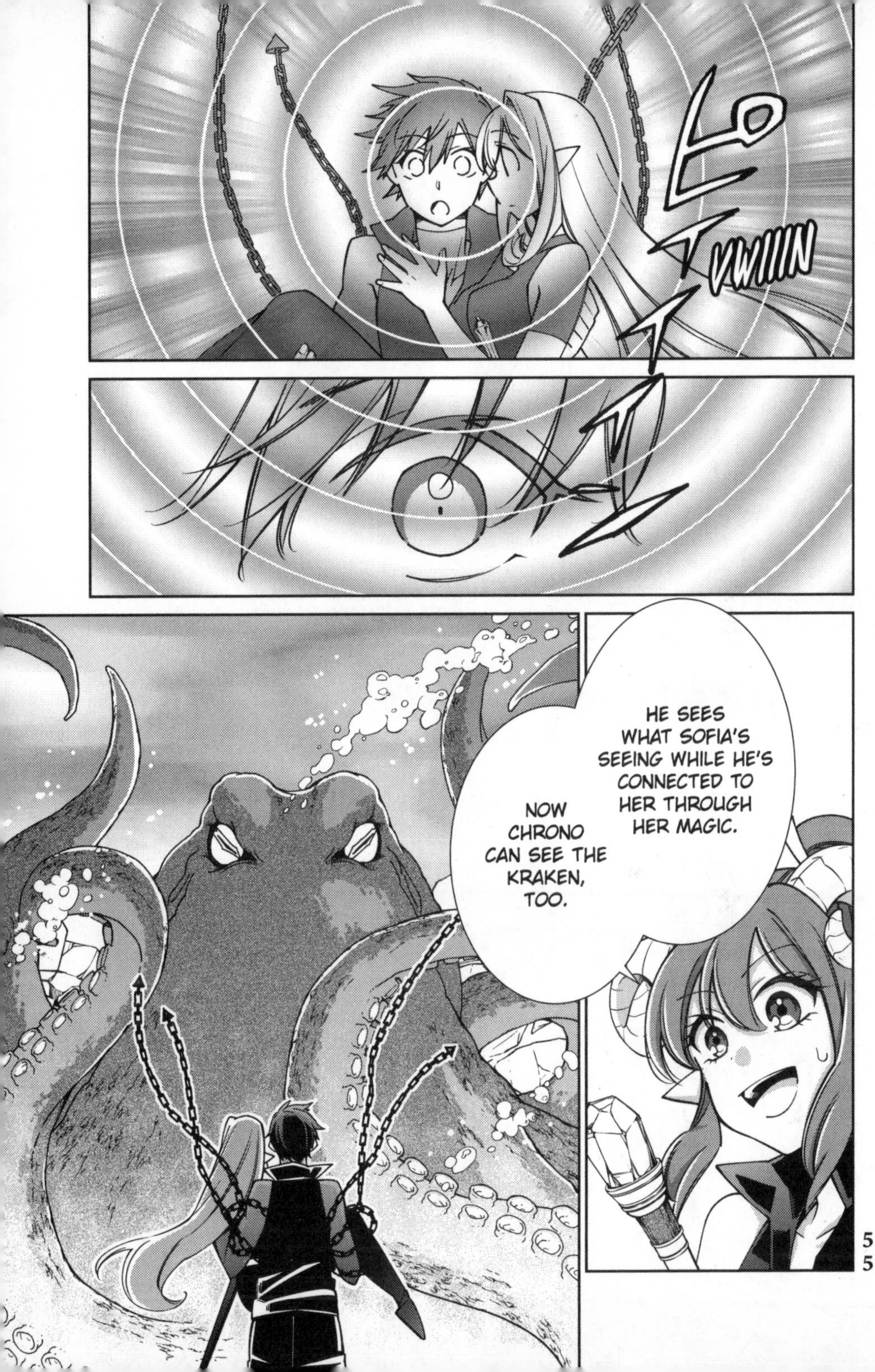
VWIIIN
HE SEES WHAT SOFIA'S SEEING WHILE HE'S CONNECTED TO HER THROUGH HER MAGIC.
NOW CHRONO CAN SEE THE KRAKEN, TOO.

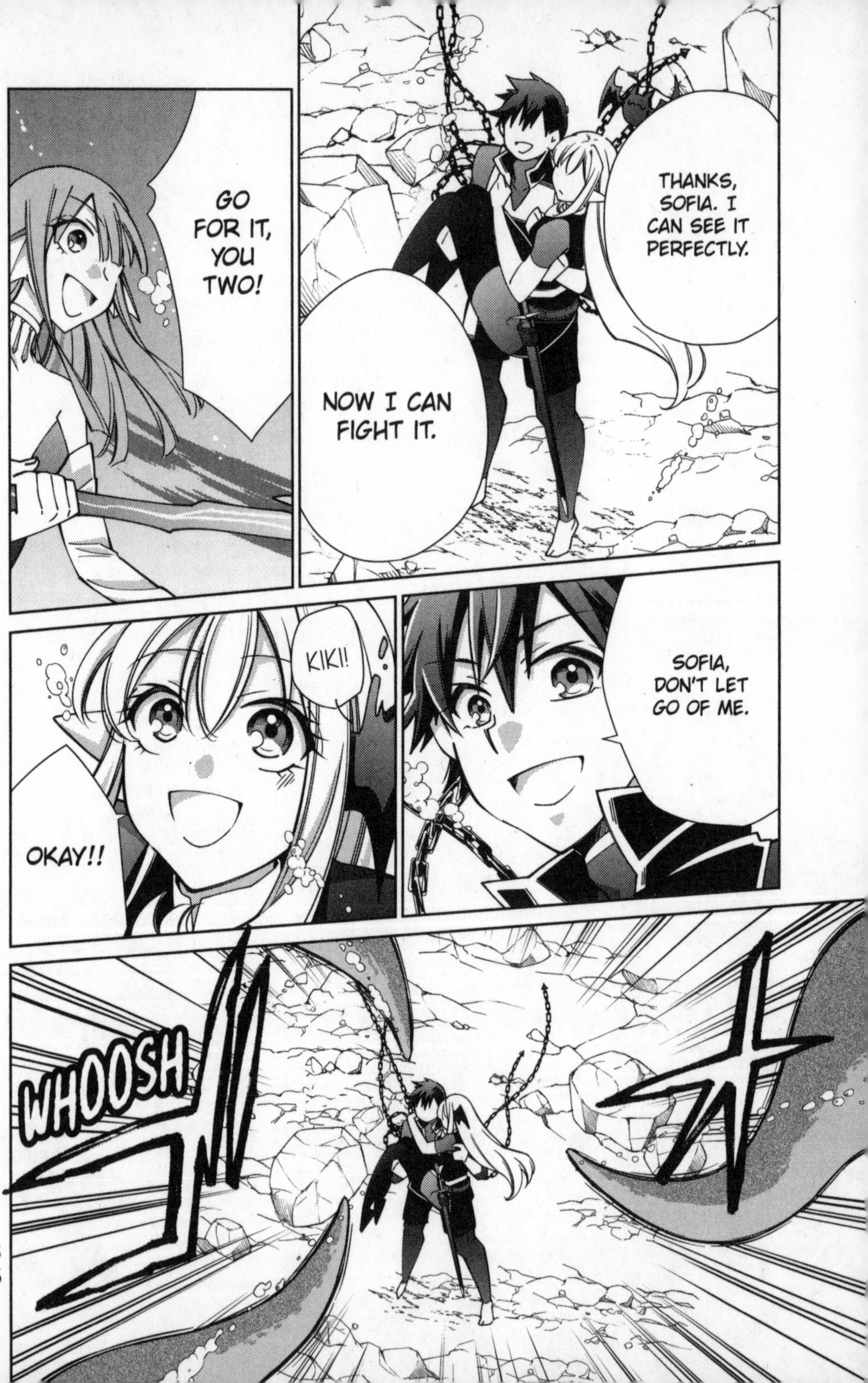
THANKS, SOFIA. I CAN SEE IT PERFECTLY.
NOW I CAN FIGHT IT.
GO FOR IT, YOU TWO!
SOFIA, DON'T LET GO OF ME.
KIKI!
OKAY!!
WHOOSH

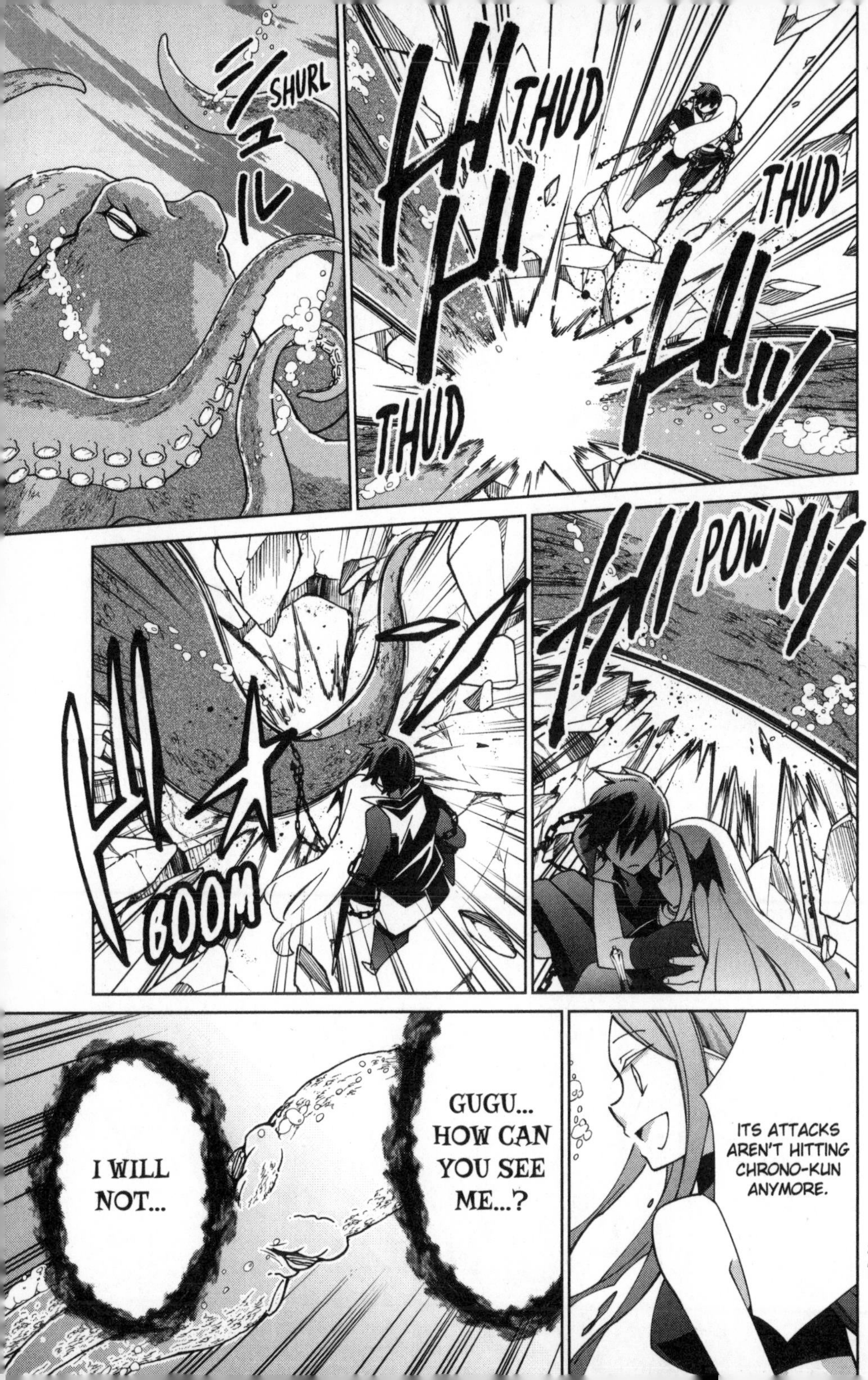
THUD
THUD
THUD
シュル
SHURL
POW
BOOM
ITS ATTACKS AREN'T HITTING CHRONO-KUN ANYMORE.
GUGU... HOW CAN YOU SEE ME...?
I WILL NOT...

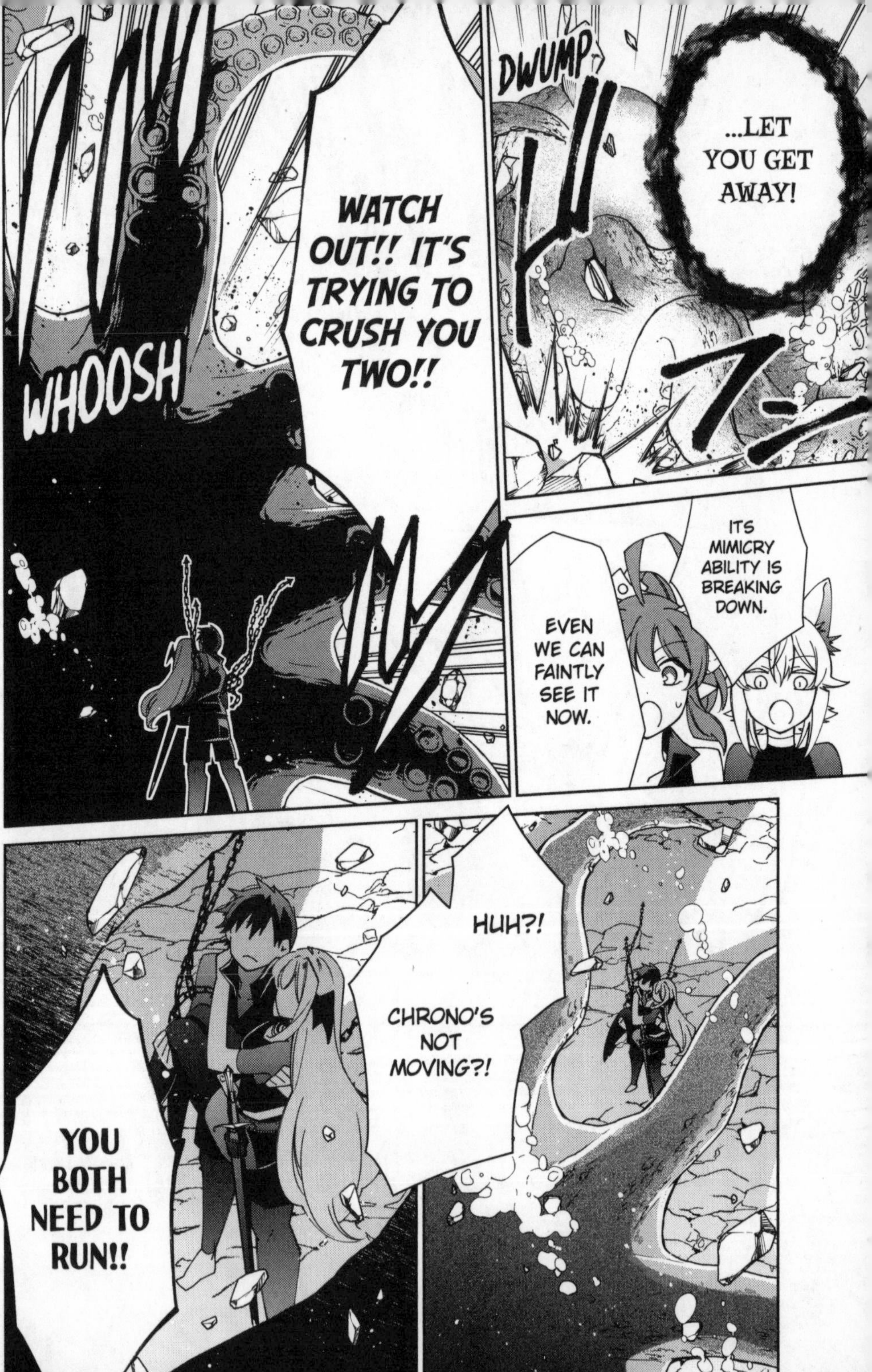
DWUMP
...LET YOU GET AWAY!
ITS MIMICRY ABILITY IS BREAKING DOWN.
EVEN WE CAN FAINTLY SEE IT NOW.
WHOOSH
WATCH OUT!! IT'S TRYING TO CRUSH YOU TWO!!
HUH?!
CHRONO'S NOT MOVING?!
YOU BOTH NEED TO RUN!!

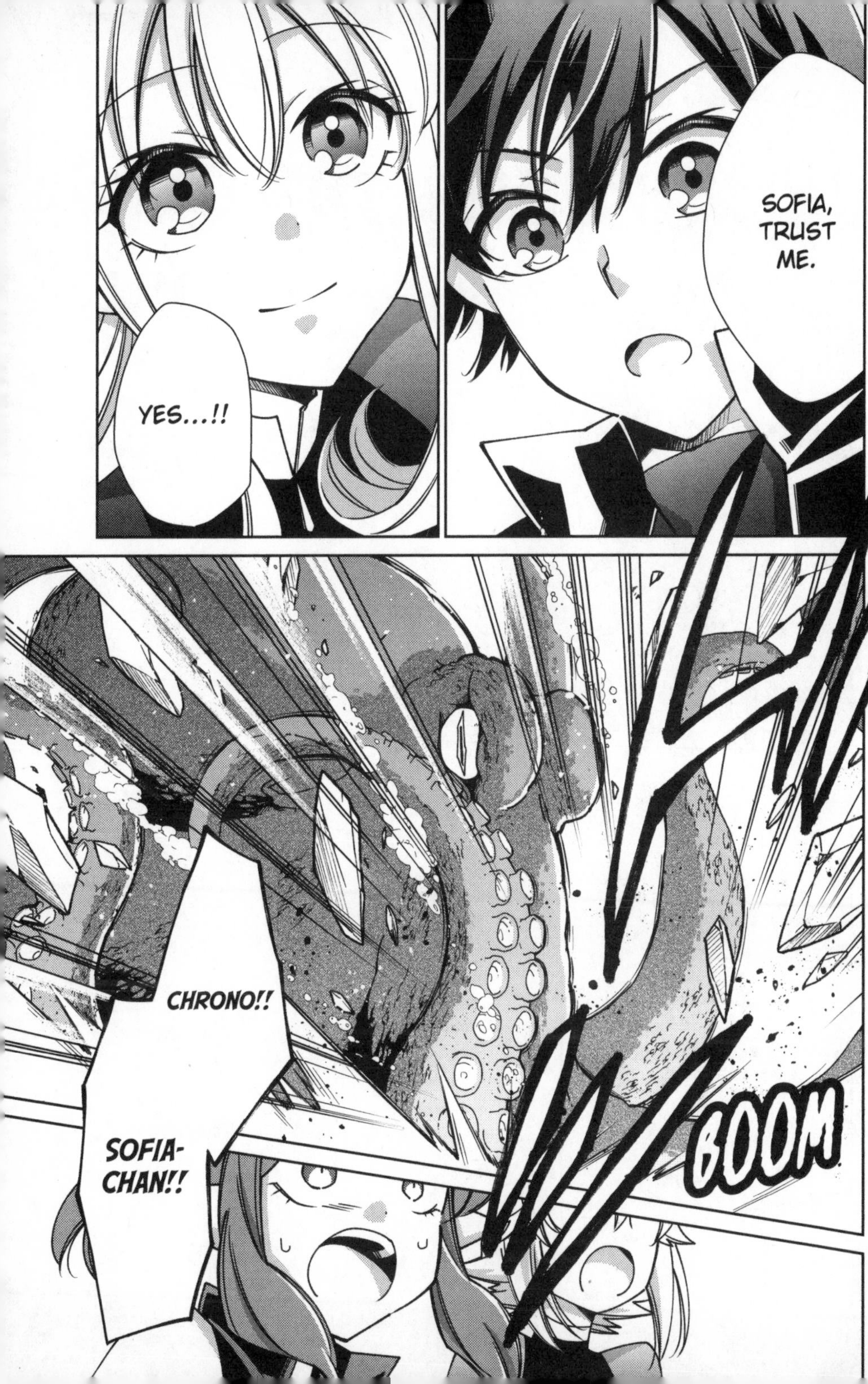
SOFIA, TRUST ME.
YES...!!
BOOM
CHRONO!!
SOFIA-CHAN!!

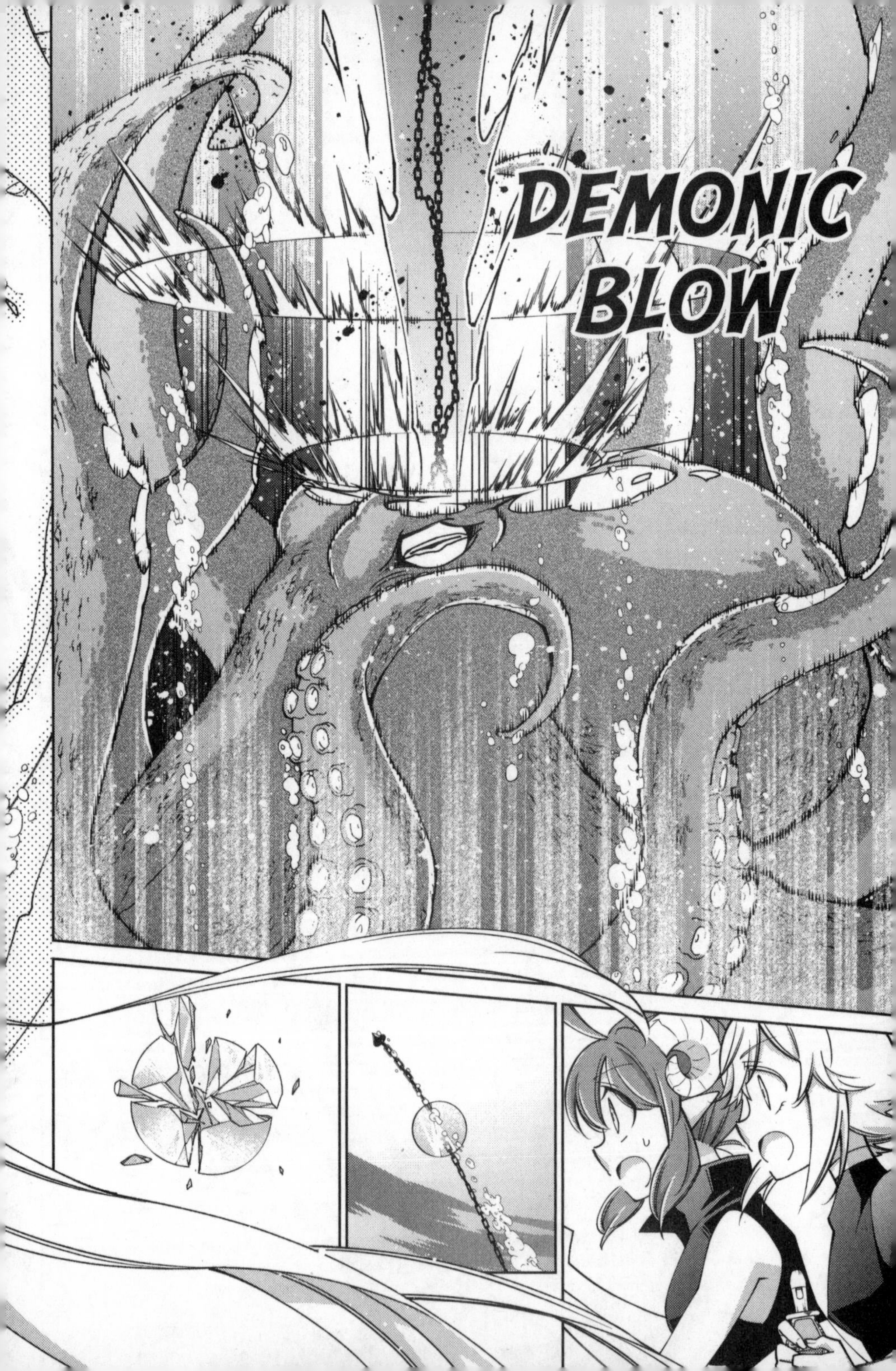
DEMONIC BLOW

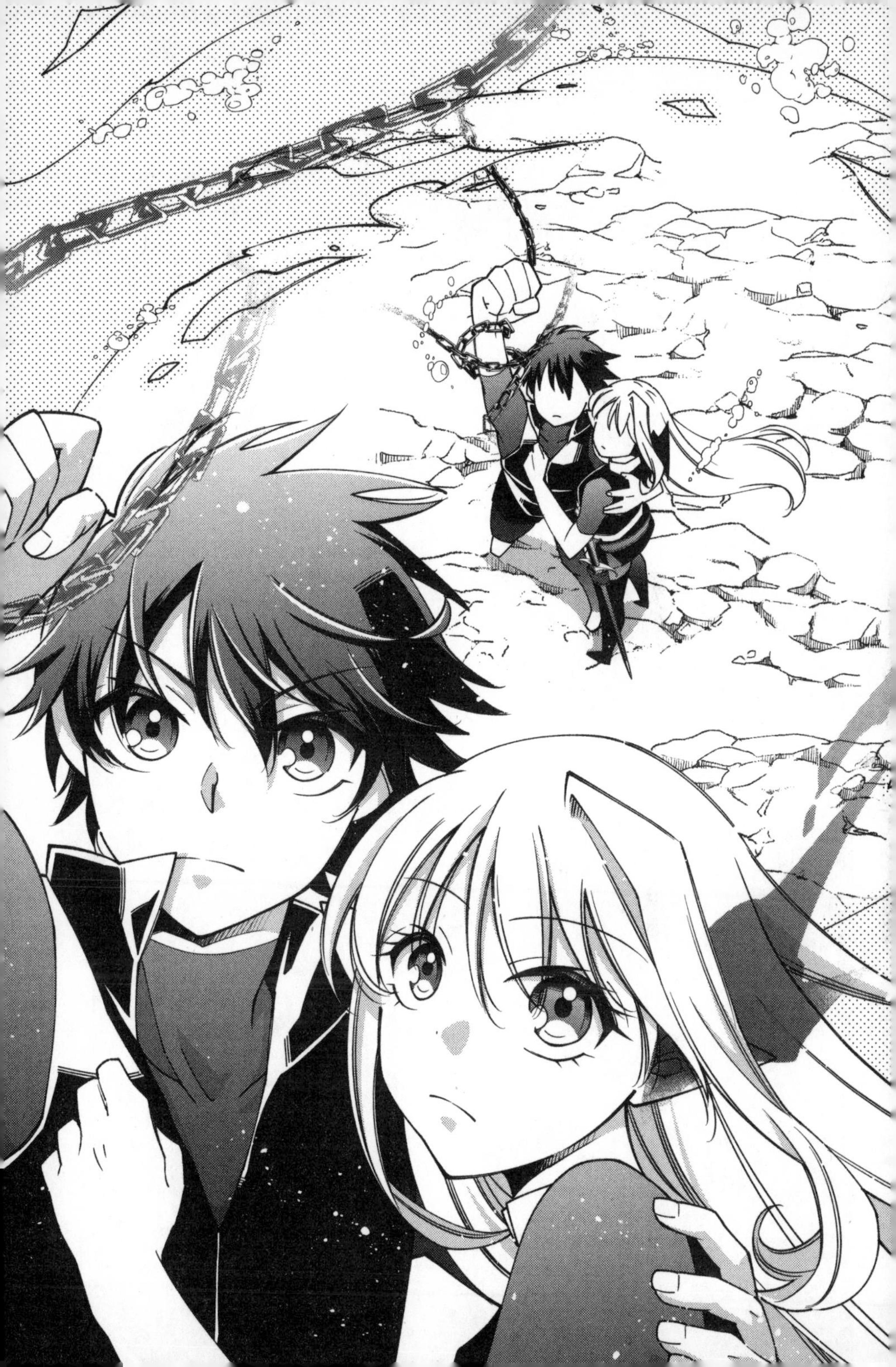

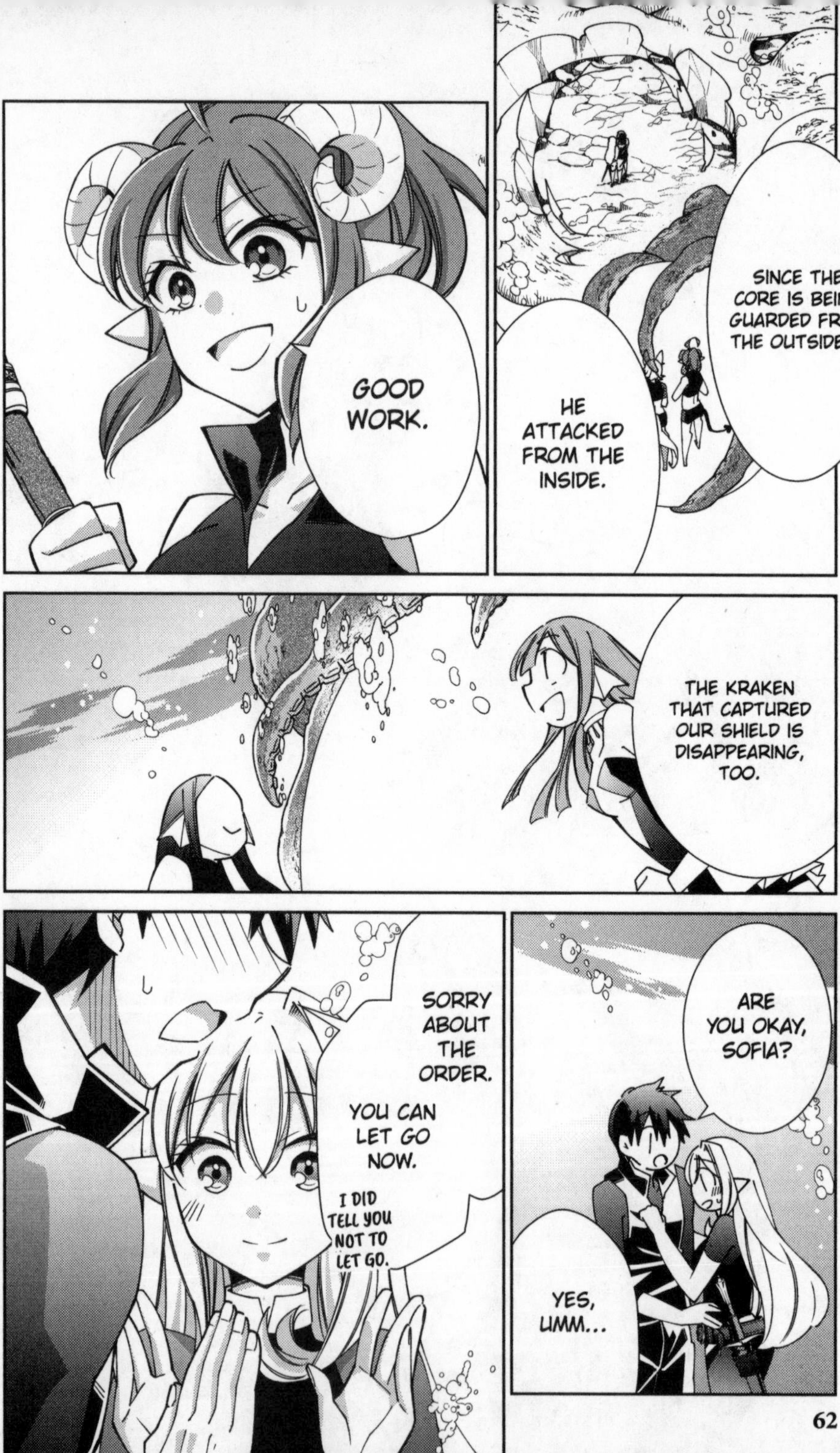
SINCE THE CORE IS BEING GUARDED FROM THE OUTSIDE...
HE ATTACKED FROM THE INSIDE.
GOOD WORK.
THE KRAKEN THAT CAPTURED OUR SHIELD IS DISAPPEARING, TOO.
ARE YOU OKAY, SOFIA?
YES, UMM...
SORRY ABOUT THE ORDER.
YOU CAN LET GO NOW.
I DID TELL YOU NOT TO LET GO.

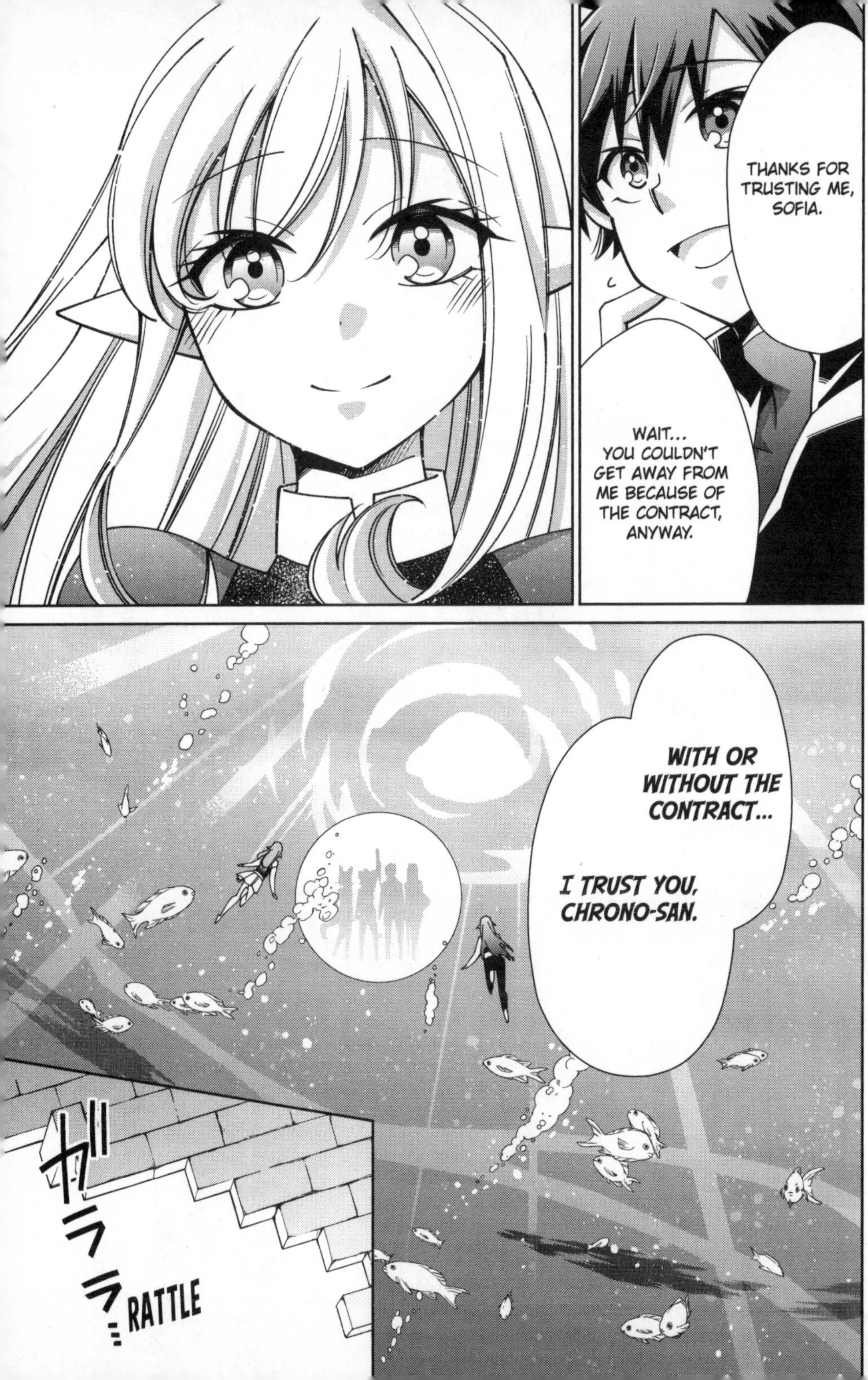
THANKS FOR TRUSTING ME, SOFIA.
WAIT... YOU COULDN'T GET AWAY FROM ME BECAUSE OF THE CONTRACT, ANYWAY.
WITH OR WITHOUT THE CONTRACT...
I TRUST YOU, CHRONO-SAN.
ガラ
RATTLE

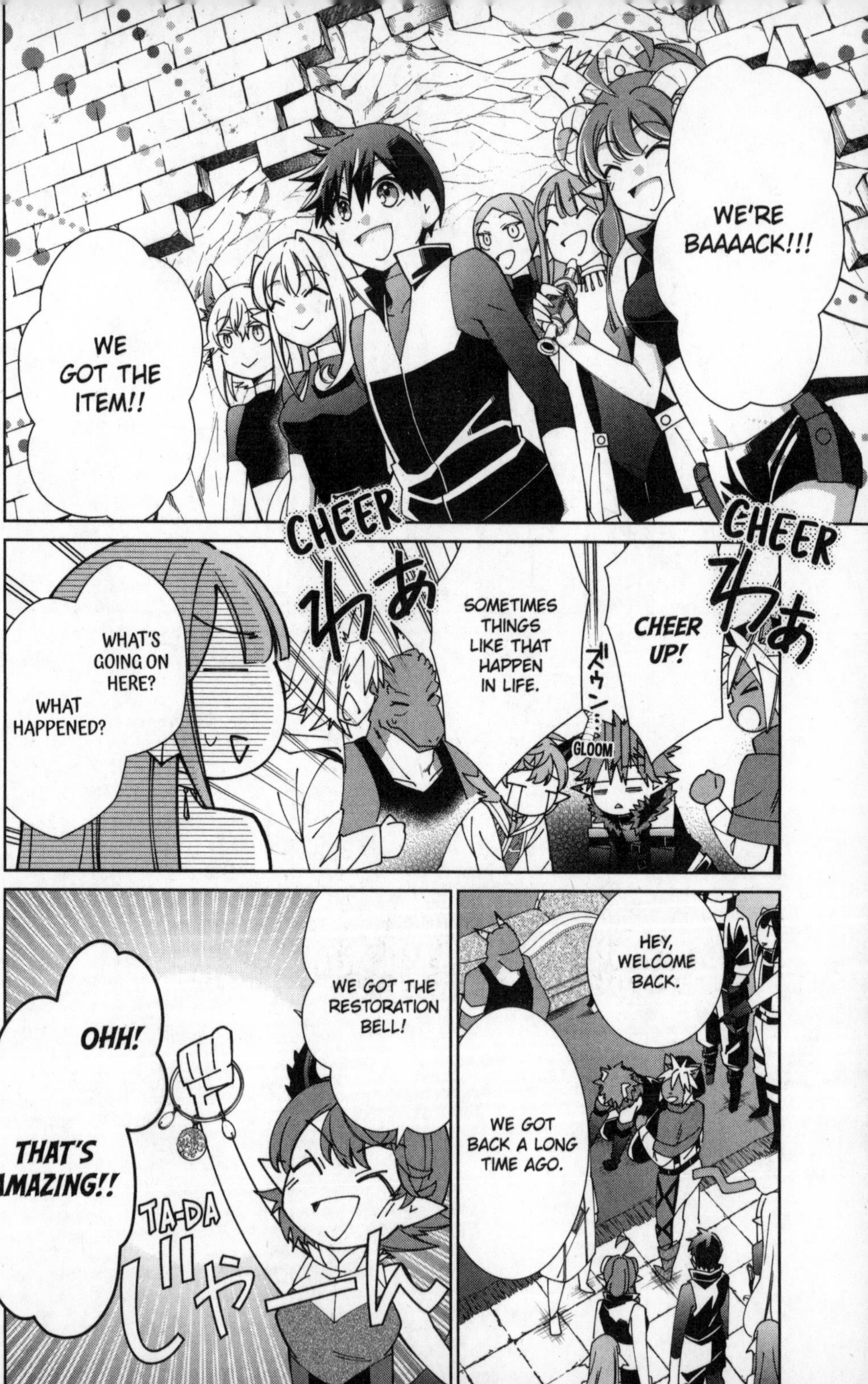
WE'RE BAAAACK!!!
WE GOT THE ITEM!!
CHEER
わあ
CHEER UP!
ズウン…
GLOOM
SOMETIMES THINGS LIKE THAT HAPPEN IN LIFE.
CHEER
わあ
WHAT'S GOING ON HERE?
WHAT HAPPENED?
HEY, WELCOME BACK.
WE GOT BACK A LONG TIME AGO.
WE GOT THE RESTORATION BELL!
OHH!
THAT'S AMAZING!!
TA-DA
じゃーん

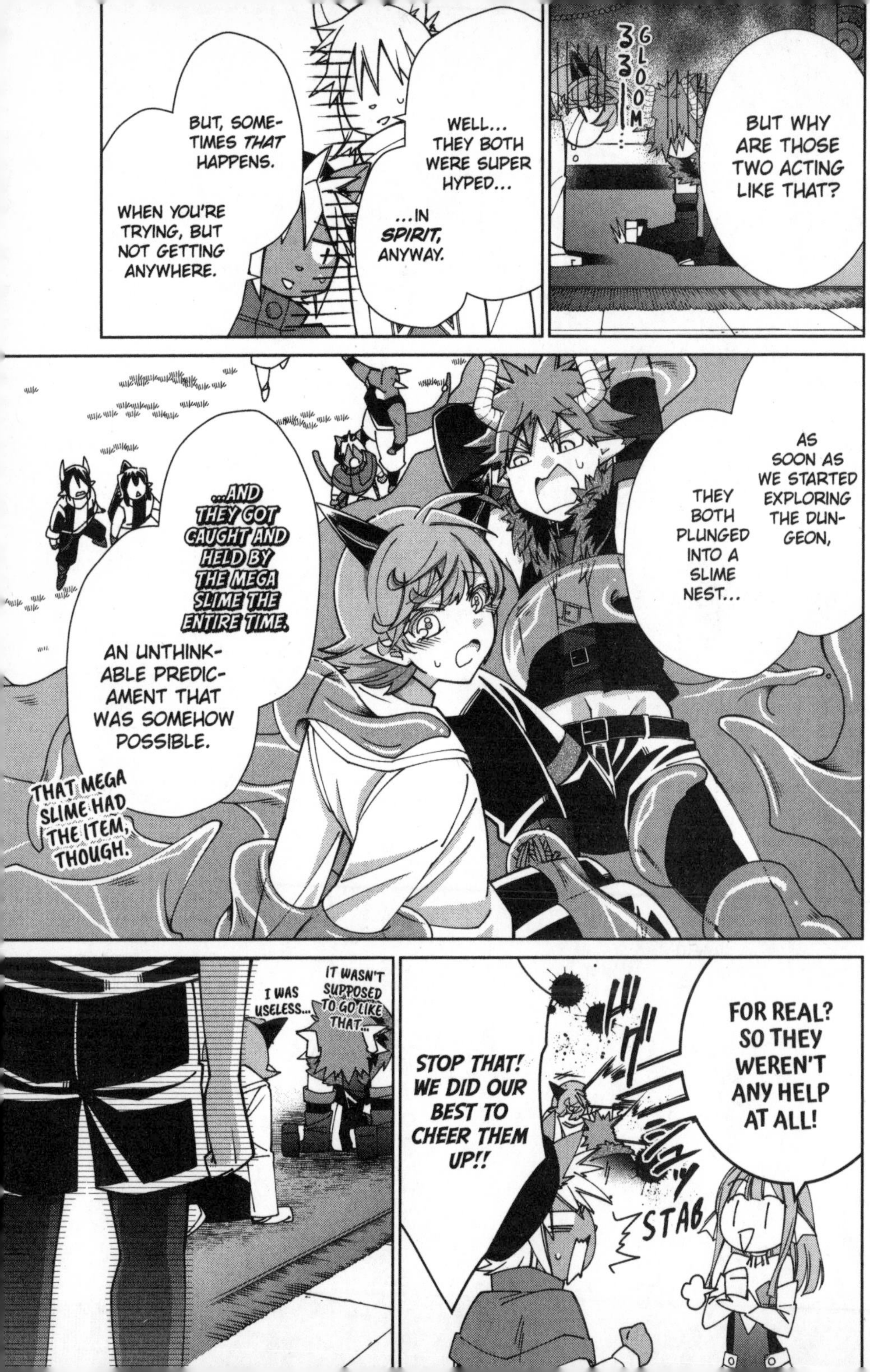
GLOOM
BUT WHY ARE THOSE TWO ACTING LIKE THAT?
WELL... THEY BOTH WERE SUPER HYPED...
...IN SPIRIT, ANYWAY.
BUT, SOME-TIMES THAT HAPPENS.
WHEN YOU'RE TRYING, BUT NOT GETTING ANYWHERE.
AS SOON AS WE STARTED EXPLORING THE DUN-GEON,
THEY BOTH PLUNGED INTO A SLIME NEST...
...AND THEY GOT CAUGHT AND HELD BY THE MEGA SLIME THE ENTIRE TIME.
AN UNTHINK-ABLE PREDIC-AMENT THAT WAS SOMEHOW POSSIBLE.
THAT MEGA SLIME HAD THE ITEM, THOUGH.
FOR REAL? SO THEY WEREN'T ANY HELP AT ALL!
STOP THAT! WE DID OUR BEST TO CHEER THEM UP!!
STAB
IT WASN'T SUPPOSED TO GO LIKE THAT...
I WAS USELESS...

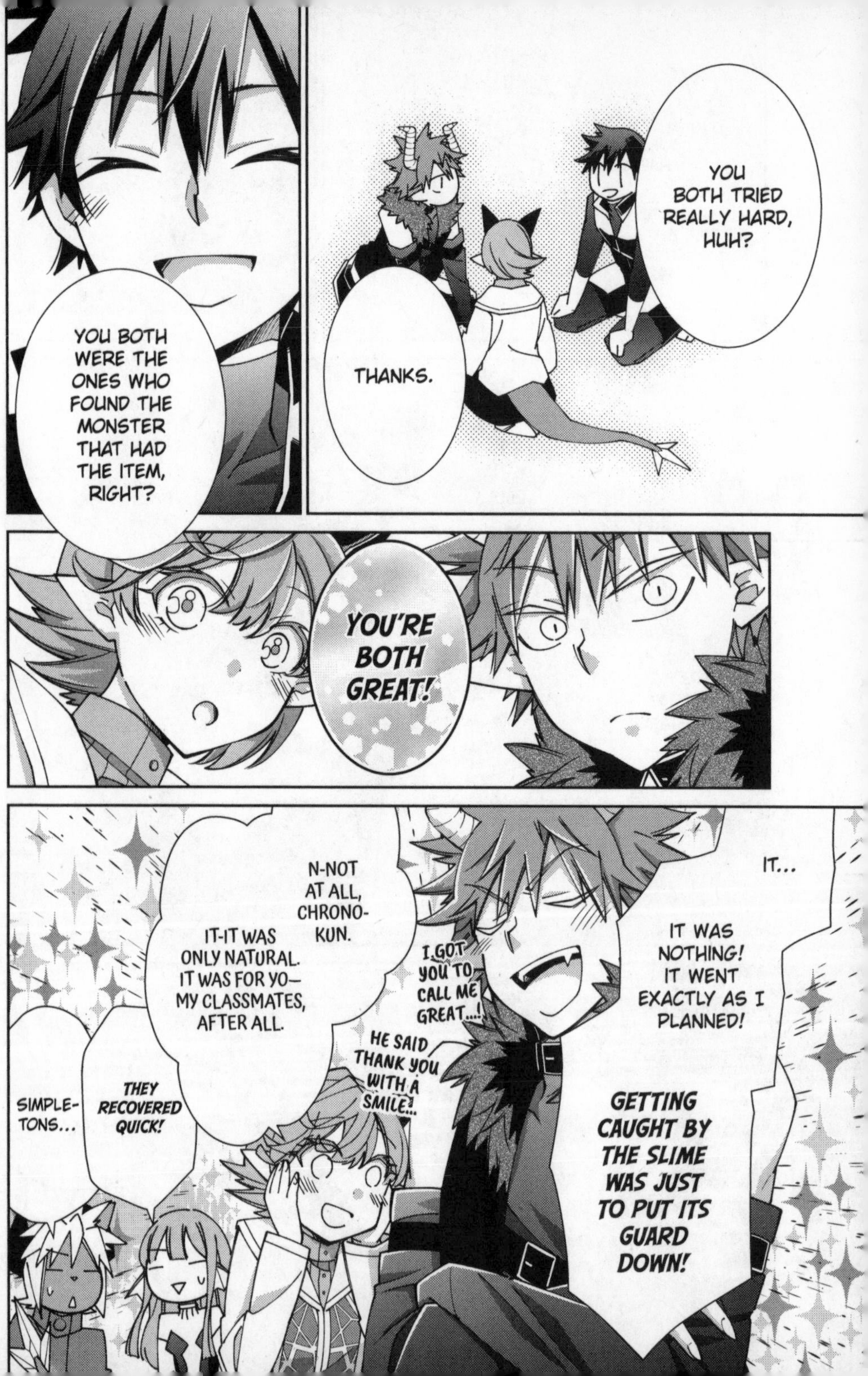
YOU BOTH TRIED REALLY HARD, HUH?
THANKS.
YOU BOTH WERE THE ONES WHO FOUND THE MONSTER THAT HAD THE ITEM, RIGHT?
YOU'RE BOTH GREAT!
IT...
IT WAS NOTHING! IT WENT EXACTLY AS I PLANNED!
GETTING CAUGHT BY THE SLIME WAS JUST TO PUT ITS GUARD DOWN!
I GOT YOU TO CALL ME GREAT...!
N-NOT AT ALL, CHRONO-KUN.
IT-IT WAS ONLY NATURAL. IT WAS FOR YO— MY CLASSMATES, AFTER ALL.
HE SAID THANK YOU WITH A SMILE...
THEY RECOVERED QUICK!
SIMPLE-TONS...

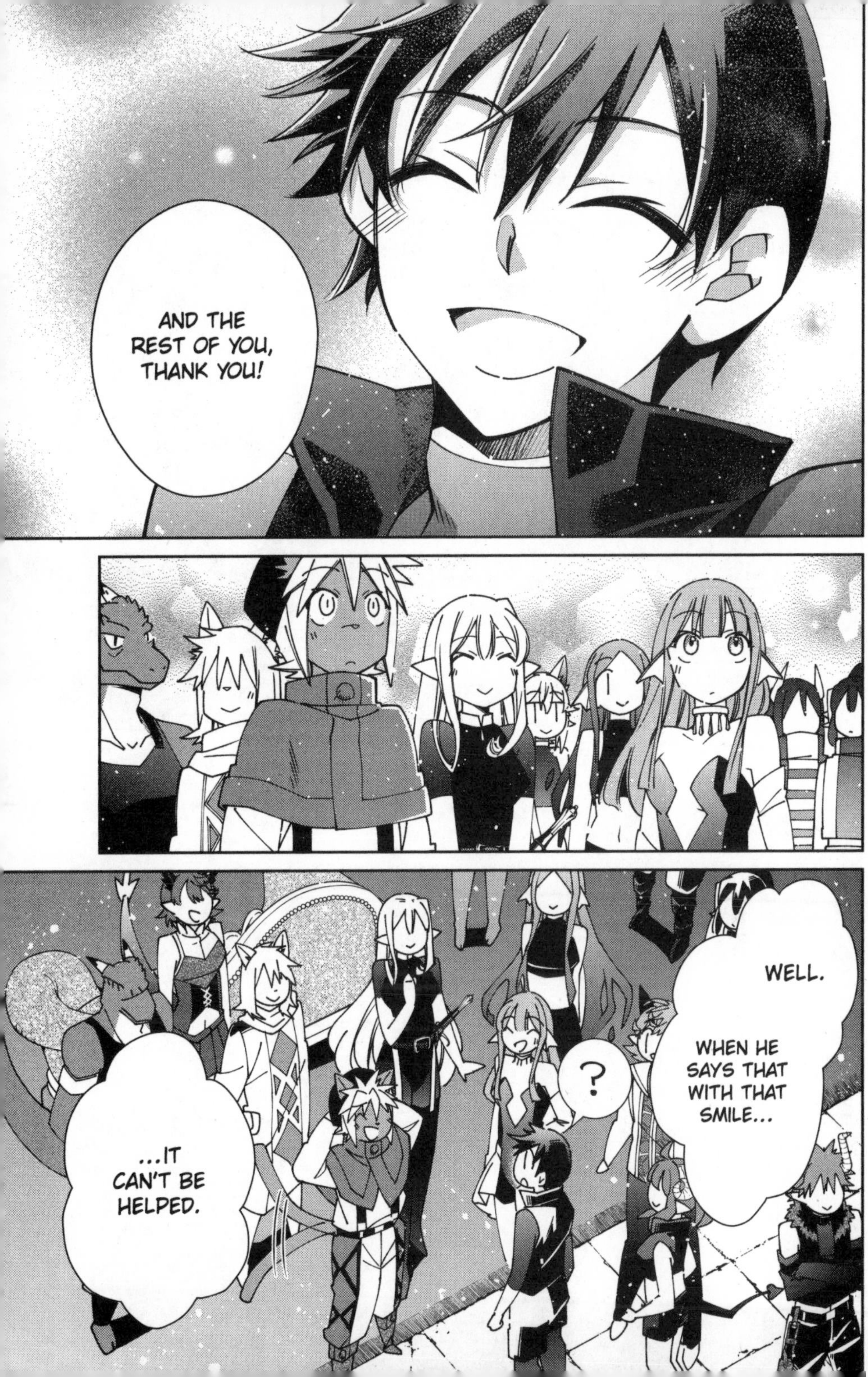
AND THE REST OF YOU, THANK YOU!
WELL.
WHEN HE SAYS THAT WITH THAT SMILE...
?
...IT CAN'T BE HELPED.

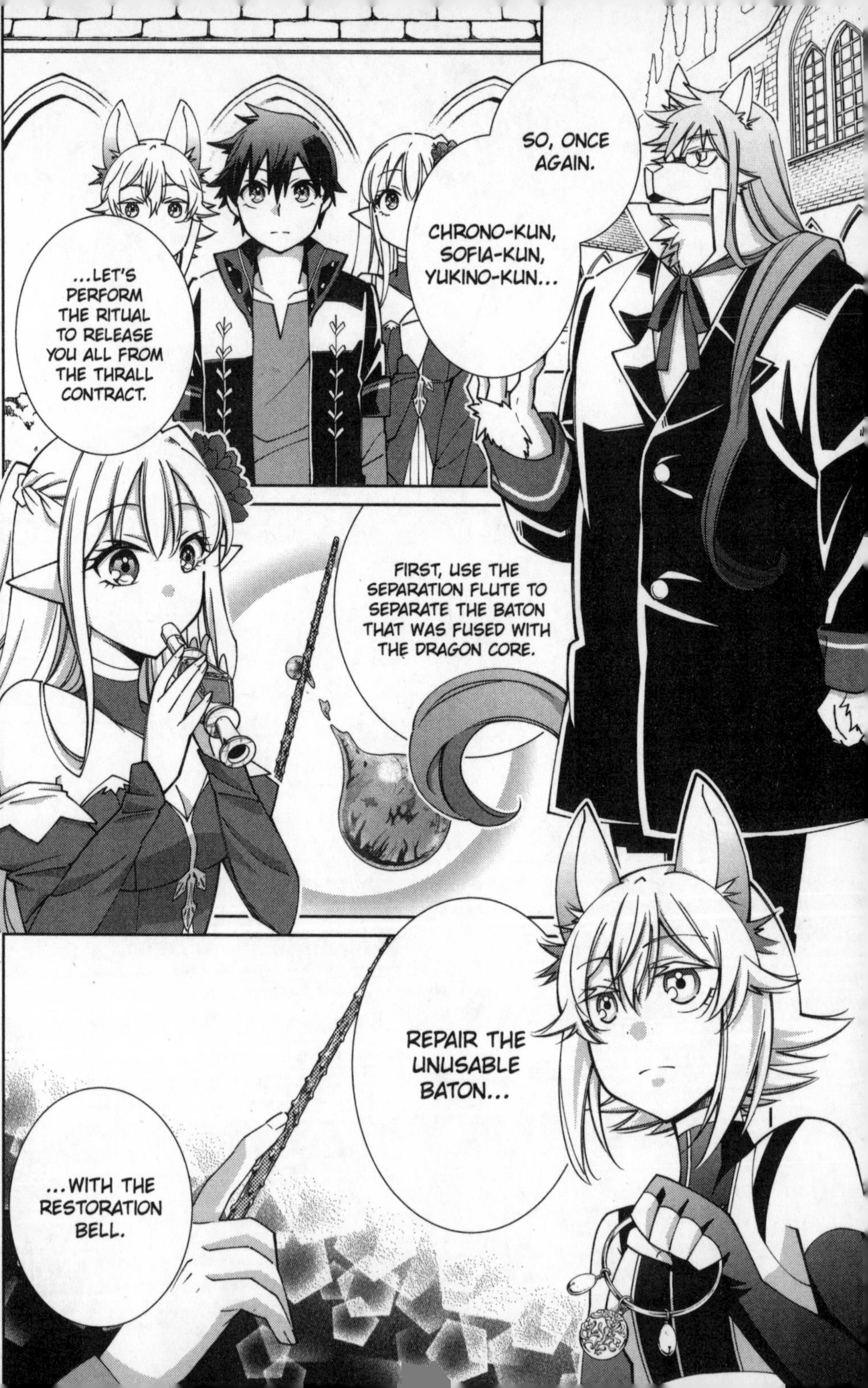
SO, ONCE AGAIN.
CHRONO-KUN, SOFIA-KUN, YUKINO-KUN...
...LET'S PERFORM THE RITUAL TO RELEASE YOU ALL FROM THE THRALL CONTRACT.
FIRST, USE THE SEPARATION FLUTE TO SEPARATE THE BATON THAT WAS FUSED WITH THE DRAGON CORE.
REPAIR THE UNUSABLE BATON...
...WITH THE RESTORATION BELL.

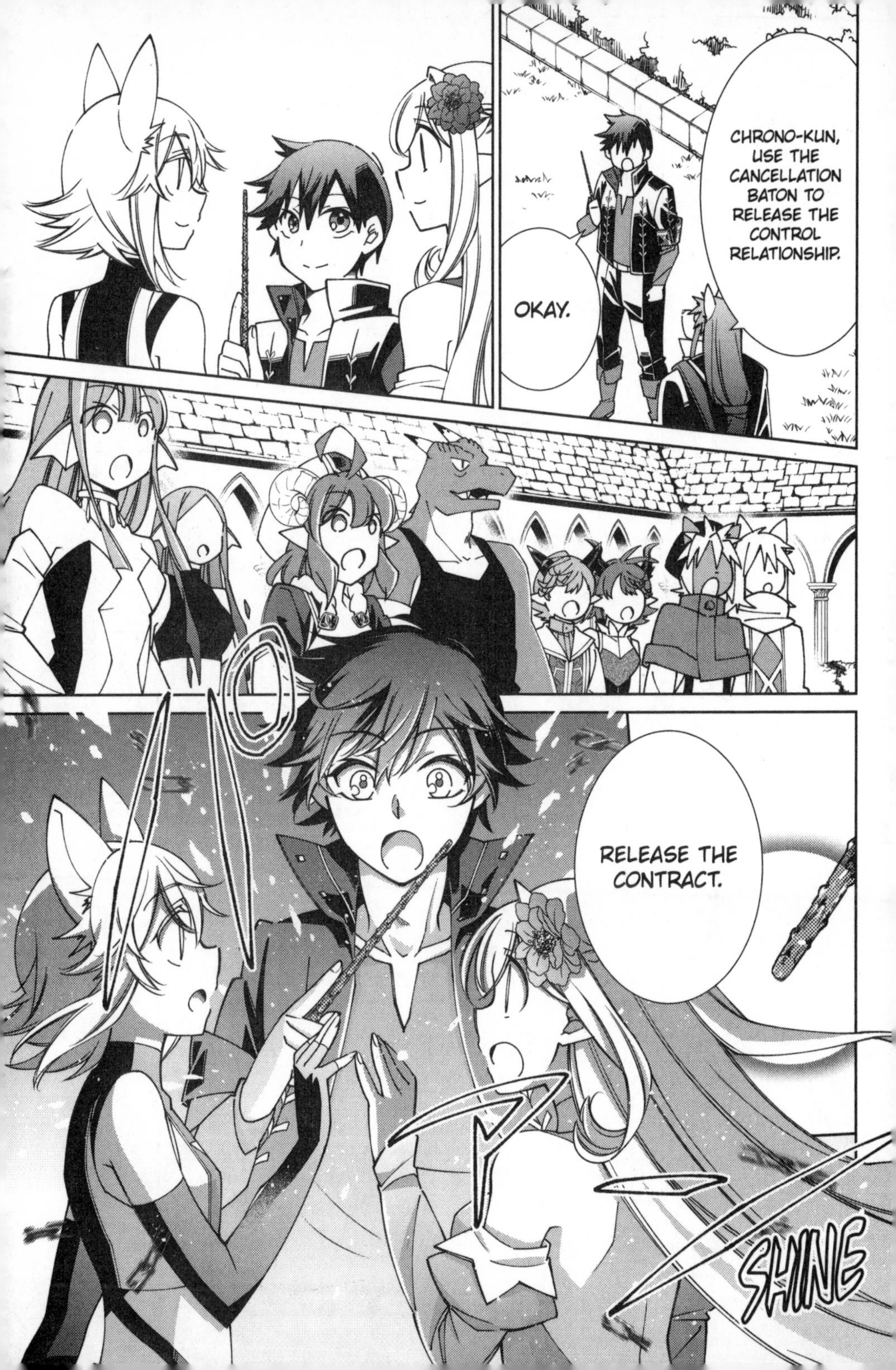
CHRONO-KUN, USE THE CANCELLATION BATON TO RELEASE THE CONTROL RELATIONSHIP.
OKAY.
RELEASE THE CONTRACT.
SHINE

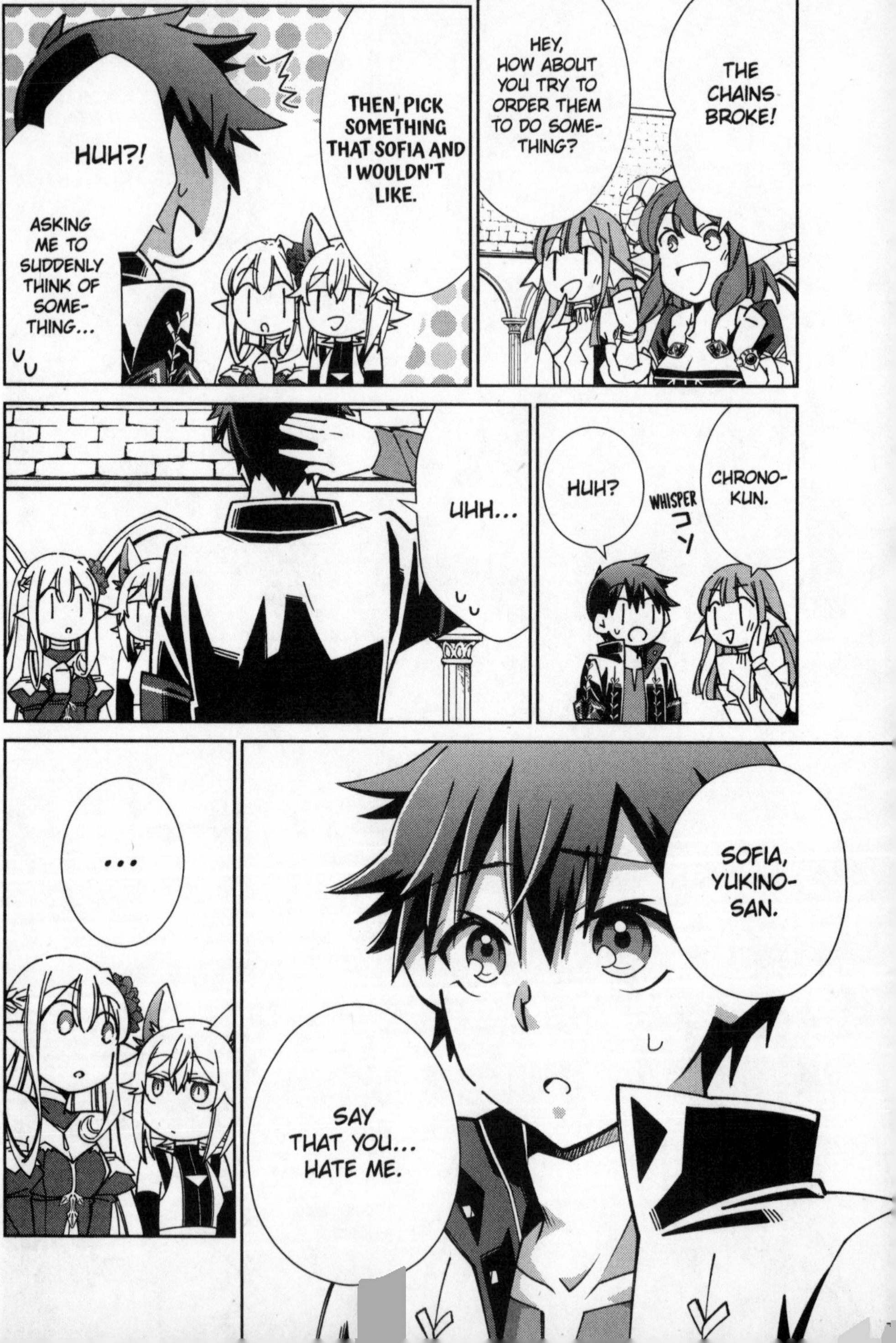
THE CHAINS BROKE!
HEY, HOW ABOUT YOU TRY TO ORDER THEM TO DO SOME-THING?
THEN, PICK SOMETHING THAT SOFIA AND I WOULDN'T LIKE.
HUH?!
ASKING ME TO SUDDENLY THINK OF SOME-THING...
CHRONO-KUN.
WHISPER
HUH?
UHH...
SOFIA, YUKINO-SAN.
SAY THAT YOU... HATE ME.
...

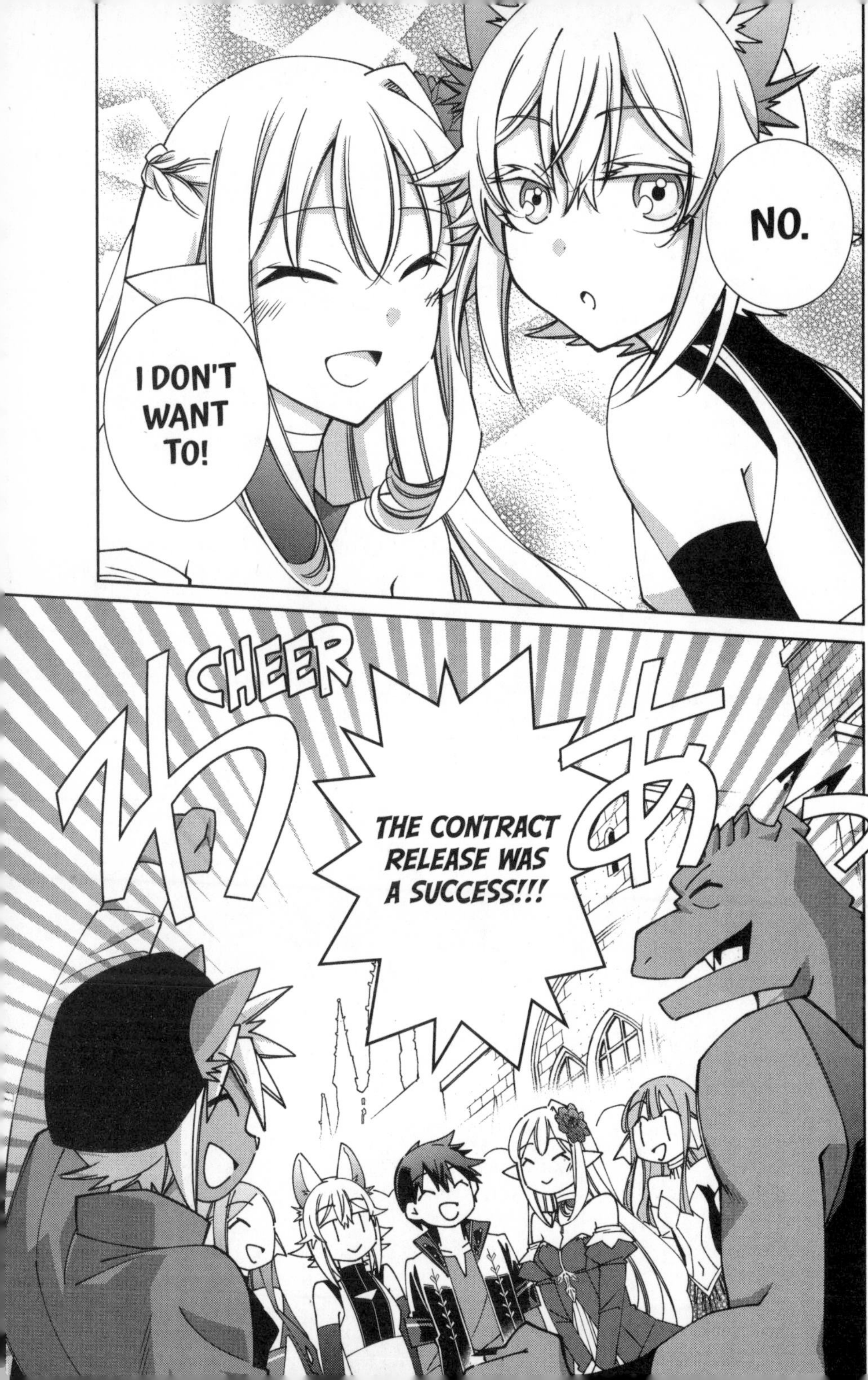
NO.
I DON'T WANT TO!
CHEER
わあっ
THE CONTRACT RELEASE WAS A SUCCESS!!!

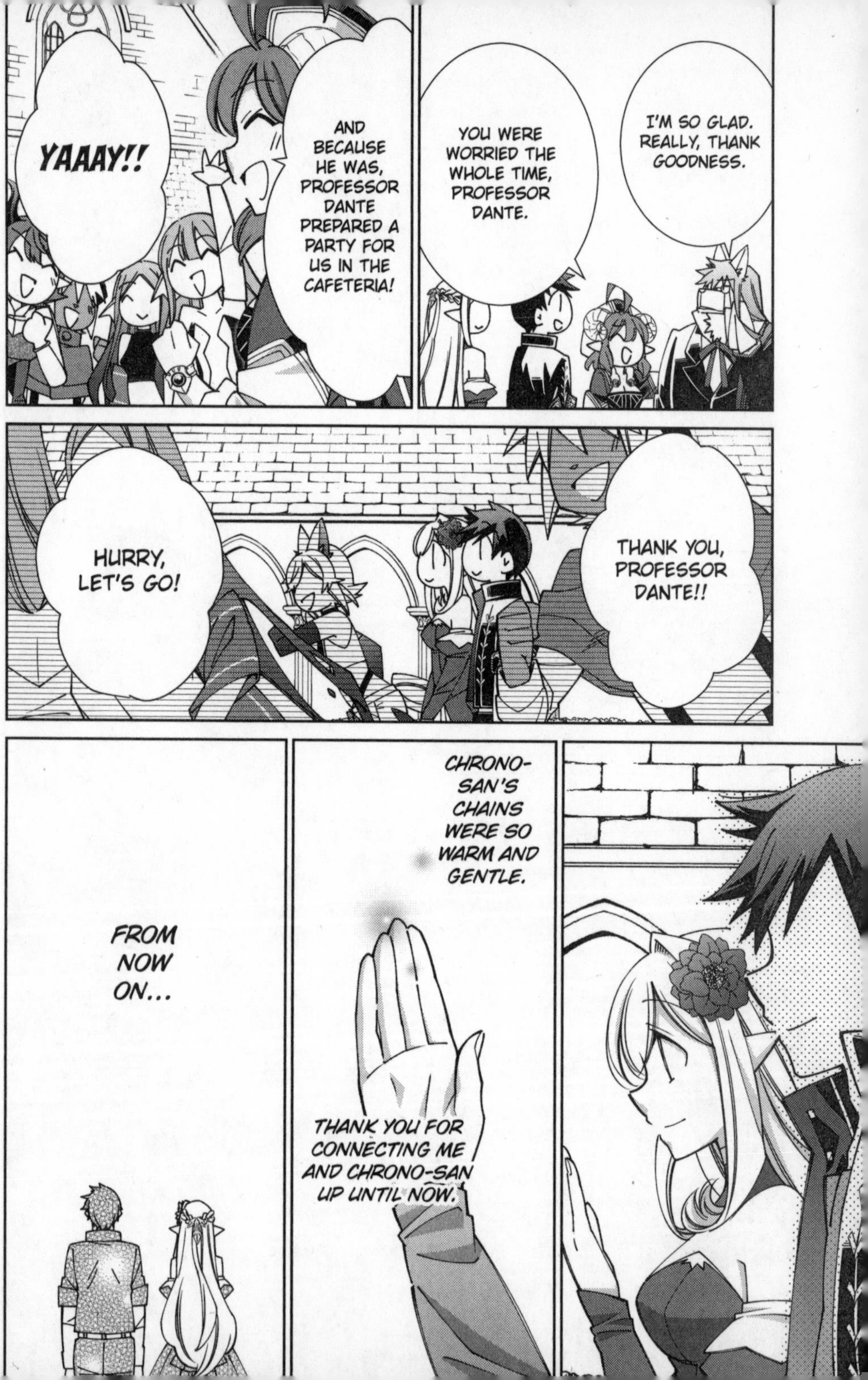
I'M SO GLAD. REALLY, THANK GOODNESS.
YOU WERE WORRIED THE WHOLE TIME, PROFESSOR DANTE.
AND BECAUSE HE WAS, PROFESSOR DANTE PREPARED A PARTY FOR US IN THE CAFETERIA!
YAAAY!!
THANK YOU, PROFESSOR DANTE!!
HURRY, LET'S GO!
CHRONO-SAN'S CHAINS WERE SO WARM AND GENTLE.
THANK YOU FOR CONNECTING ME AND CHRONO-SAN UP UNTIL NOW.
FROM NOW ON...

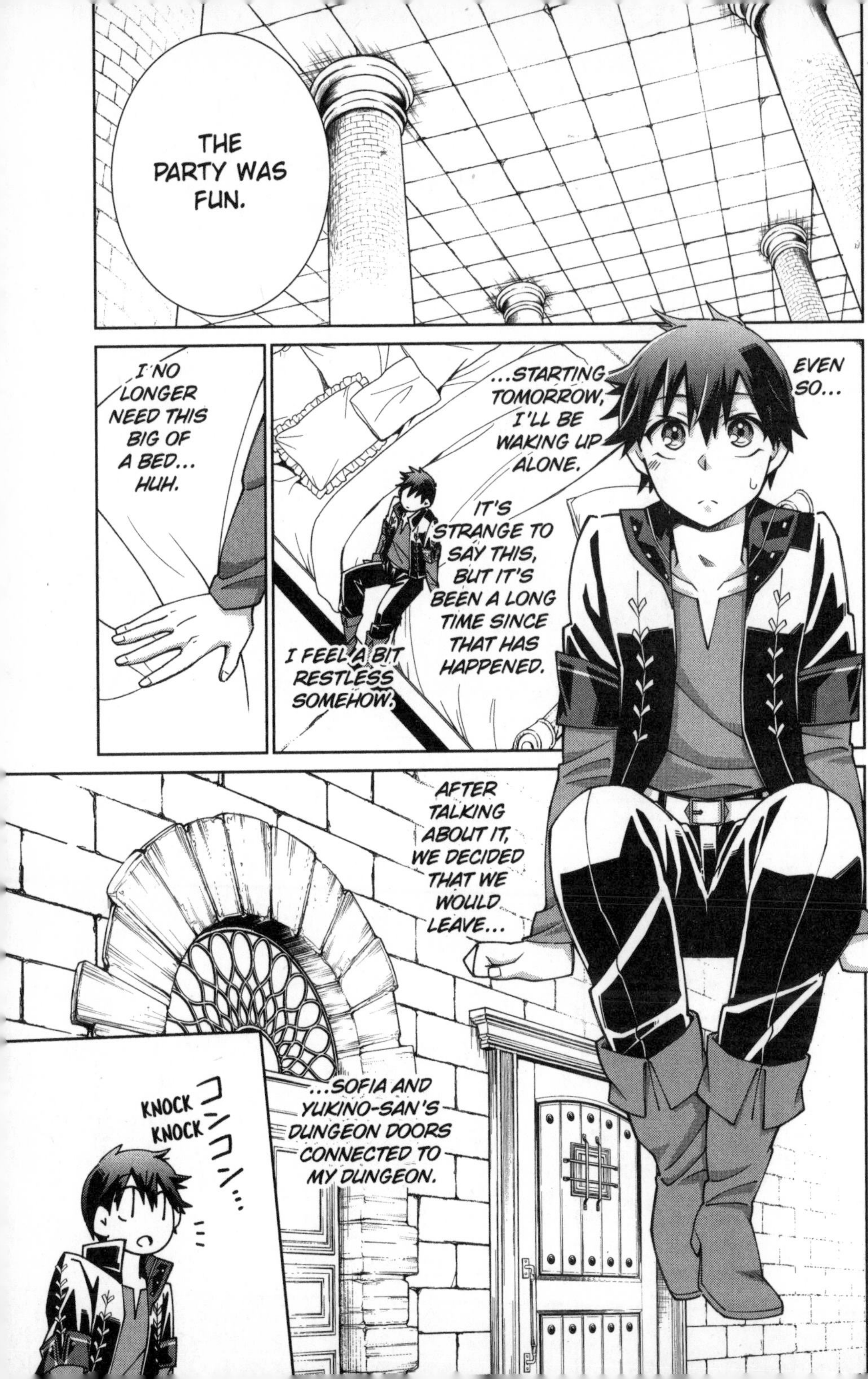
THE PARTY WAS FUN.
EVEN SO...
...STARTING TOMORROW, I'LL BE WAKING UP ALONE.
IT'S STRANGE TO SAY THIS, BUT IT'S BEEN A LONG TIME SINCE THAT HAS HAPPENED.
I FEEL A BIT RESTLESS SOMEHOW.
I NO LONGER NEED THIS BIG OF A BED... HUH.
AFTER TALKING ABOUT IT, WE DECIDED THAT WE WOULD LEAVE...
...SOFIA AND YUKINO-SAN'S DUNGEON DOORS CONNECTED TO MY DUNGEON.
KNOCK KNOCK

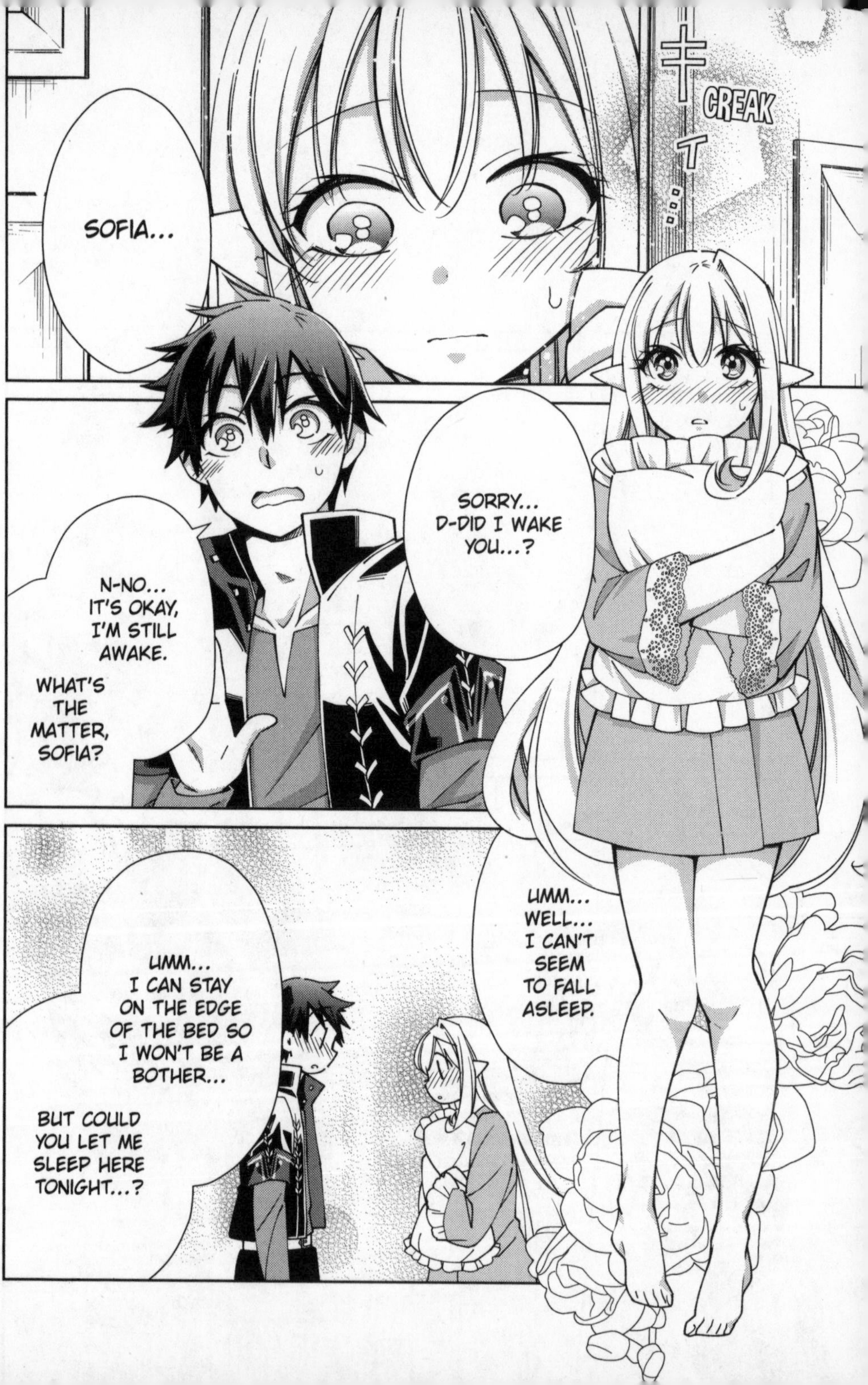
CREAK
SOFIA...
SORRY... D-DID I WAKE YOU...?
N-NO... IT'S OKAY, I'M STILL AWAKE.
WHAT'S THE MATTER, SOFIA?
UMM... WELL... I CAN'T SEEM TO FALL ASLEEP.
UMM... I CAN STAY ON THE EDGE OF THE BED SO I WON'T BE A BOTHER...
BUT COULD YOU LET ME SLEEP HERE TONIGHT...?

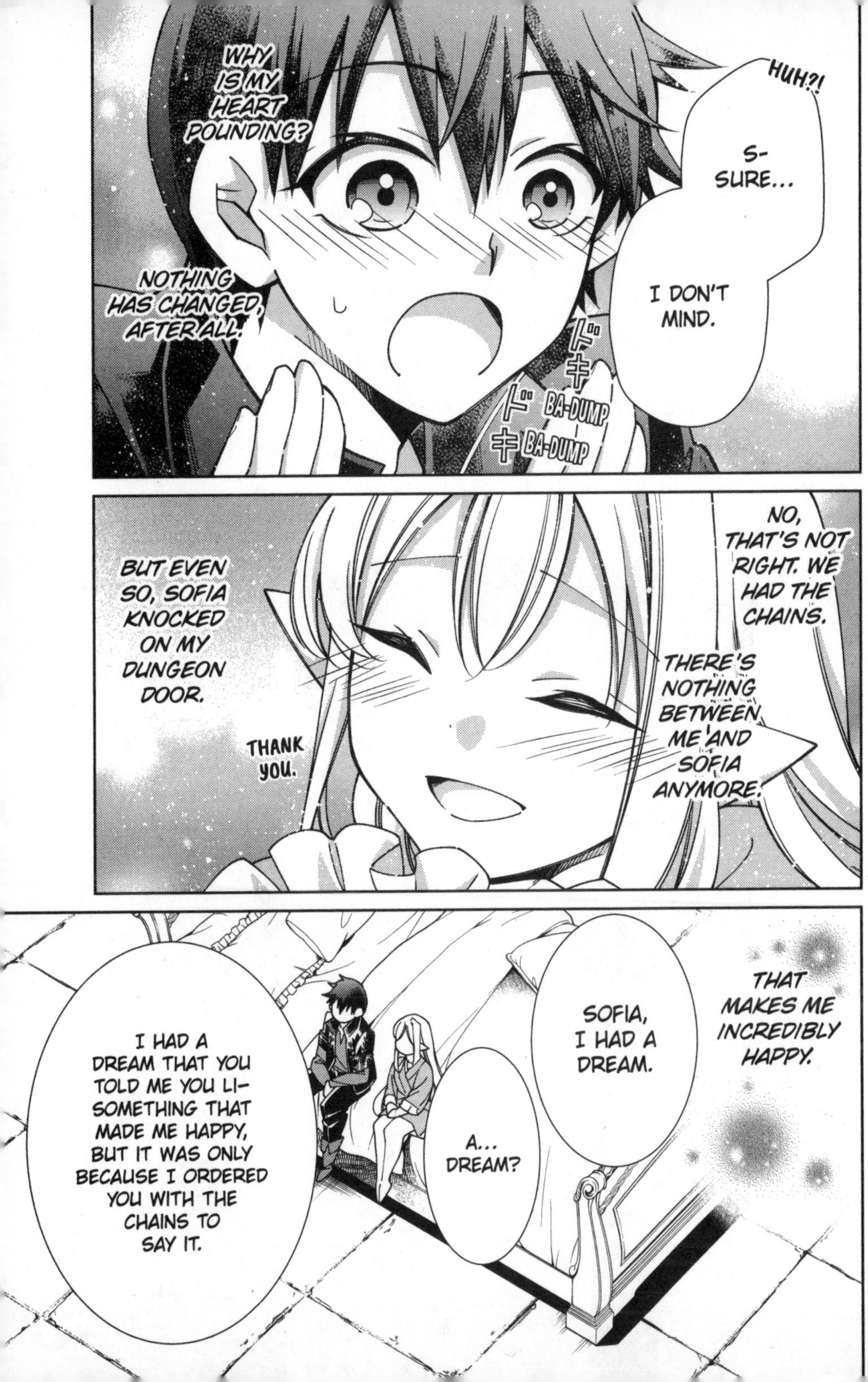
HUH?!
S-SURE...
I DON'T MIND.
WHY IS MY HEART POUNDING?
ドキ BA-DUMP
ドキ BA-DUMP
NOTHING HAS CHANGED, AFTER ALL.
NO, THAT'S NOT RIGHT. WE HAD THE CHAINS.
THERE'S NOTHING BETWEEN ME AND SOFIA ANYMORE.
BUT EVEN SO, SOFIA KNOCKED ON MY DUNGEON DOOR.
THANK YOU.
THAT MAKES ME INCREDIBLY HAPPY.
SOFIA, I HAD A DREAM.
A... DREAM?
I HAD A DREAM THAT YOU TOLD ME YOU LI- SOMETHING THAT MADE ME HAPPY, BUT IT WAS ONLY BECAUSE I ORDERED YOU WITH THE CHAINS TO SAY IT.

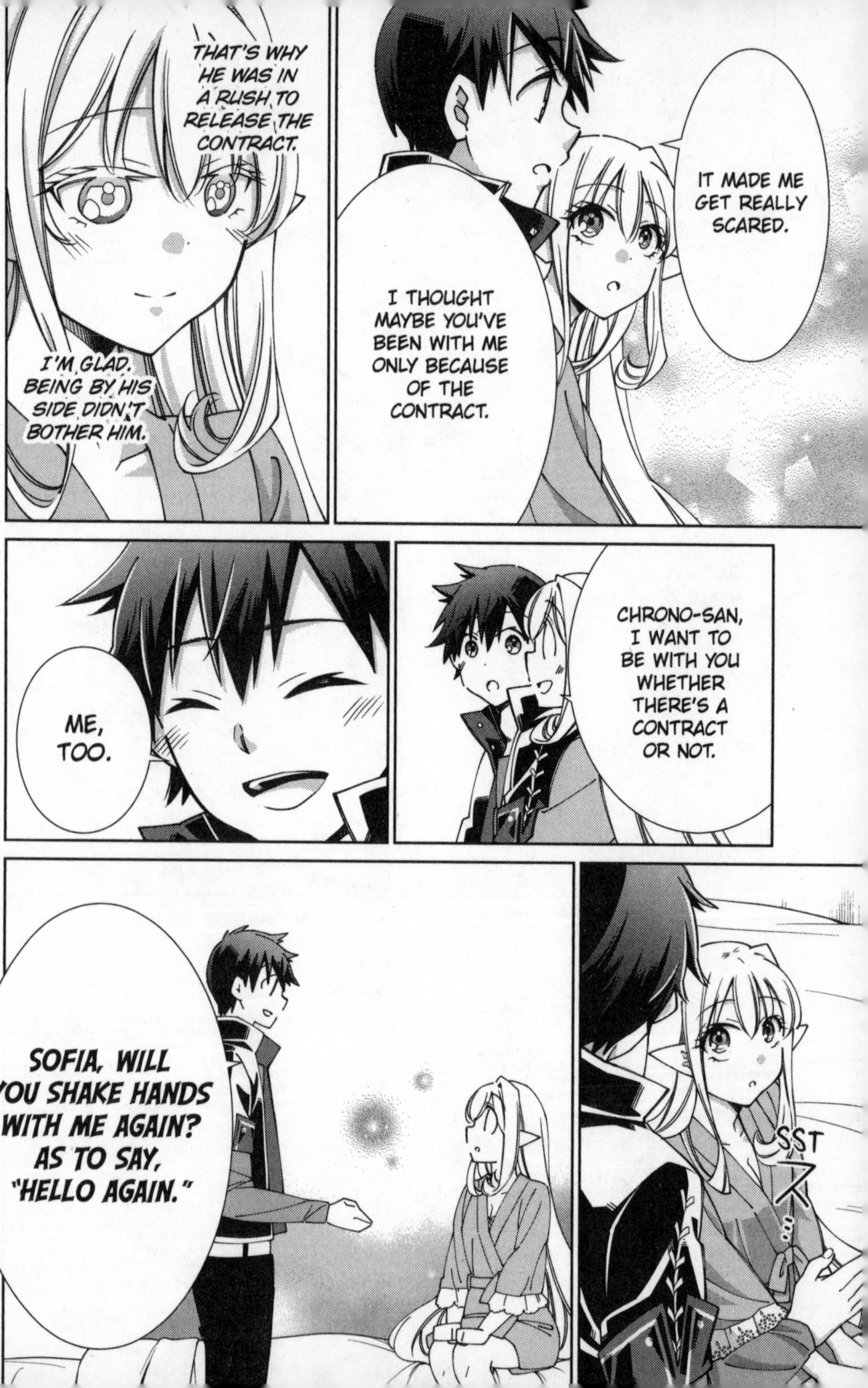
IT MADE ME GET REALLY SCARED.
I THOUGHT MAYBE YOU'VE BEEN WITH ME ONLY BECAUSE OF THE CONTRACT.
THAT'S WHY HE WAS IN A RUSH TO RELEASE THE CONTRACT.
I'M GLAD. BEING BY HIS SIDE DIDN'T BOTHER HIM.
CHRONO-SAN, I WANT TO BE WITH YOU WHETHER THERE'S A CONTRACT OR NOT.
ME, TOO.
SST
SOFIA, WILL YOU SHAKE HANDS WITH ME AGAIN? AS TO SAY, "HELLO AGAIN."

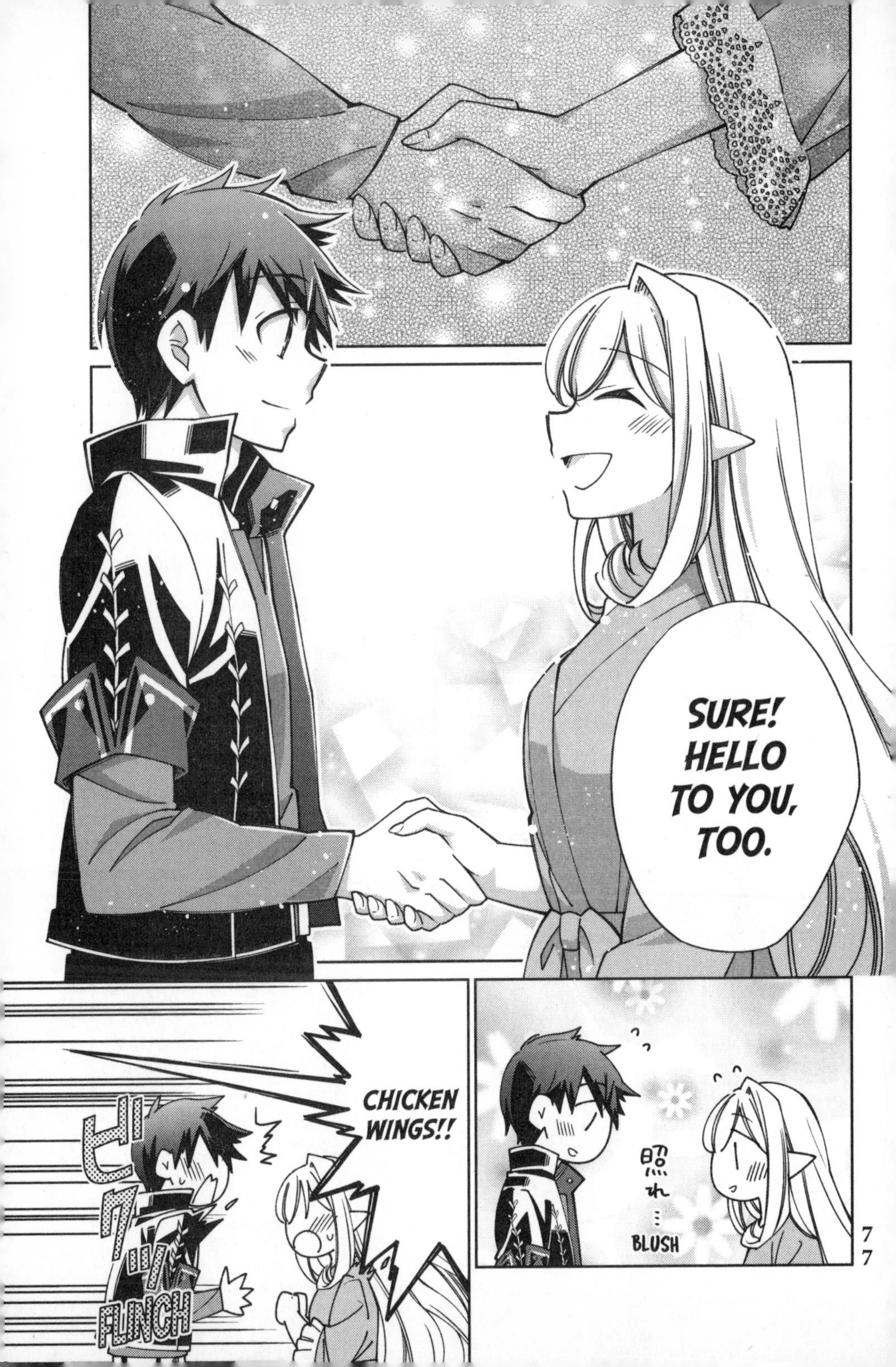
SURE! HELLO TO YOU, TOO.
照れ…
BLUSH
CHICKEN WINGS!!
ビクッ
FLINCH

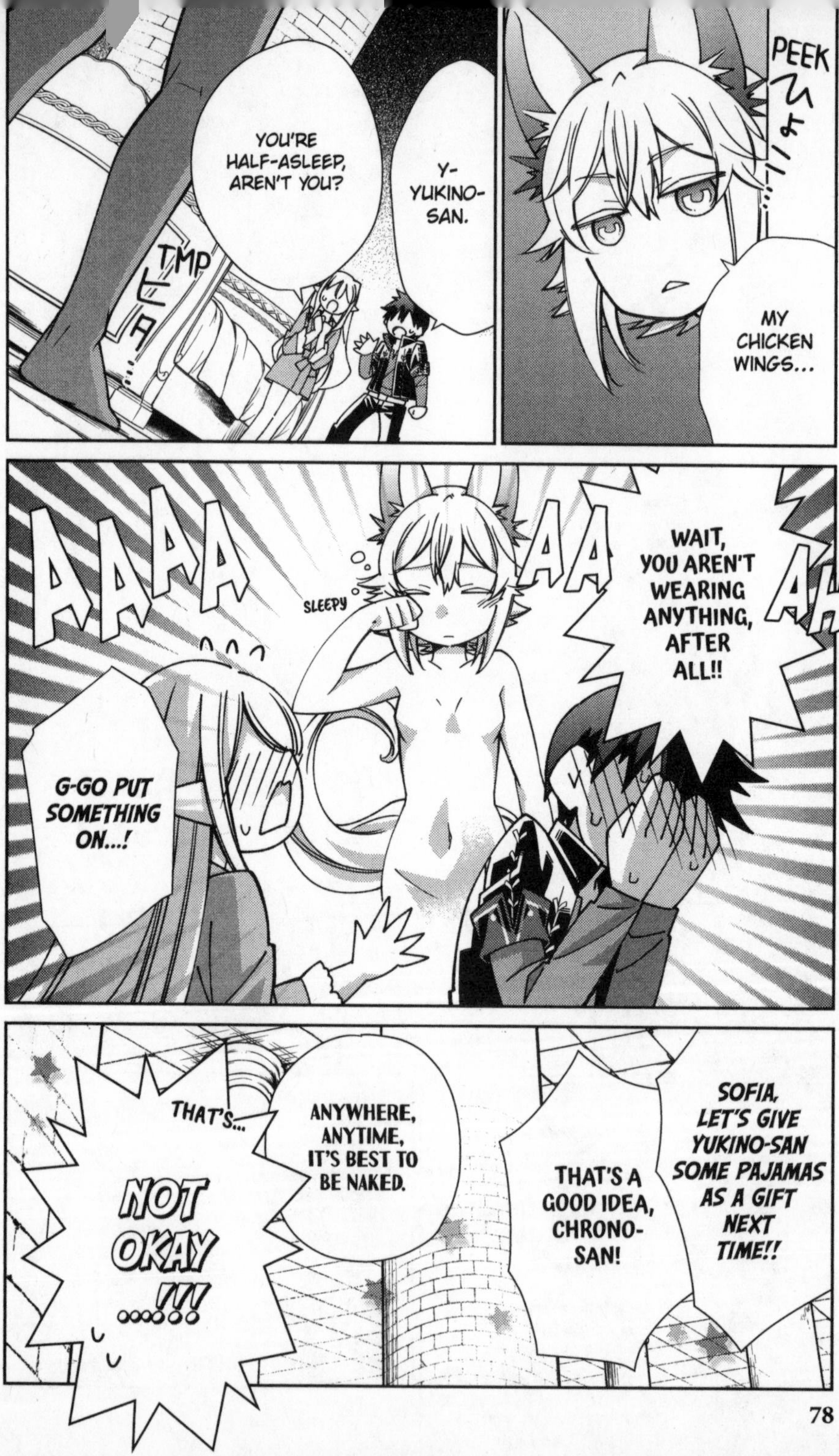
PEEK
MY CHICKEN WINGS...
Y-YUKINO-SAN.
YOU'RE HALF-ASLEEP, AREN'T YOU?
TMP
WAIT, YOU AREN'T WEARING ANYTHING, AFTER ALL!!
AAAAAAH
SLEEPY
G-GO PUT SOMETHING ON...!
SOFIA, LET'S GIVE YUKINO-SAN SOME PAJAMAS AS A GIFT NEXT TIME!!
THAT'S A GOOD IDEA, CHRONO-SAN!
ANYWHERE, ANYTIME, IT'S BEST TO BE NAKED.
THAT'S...
NOT OKAY.....!!!

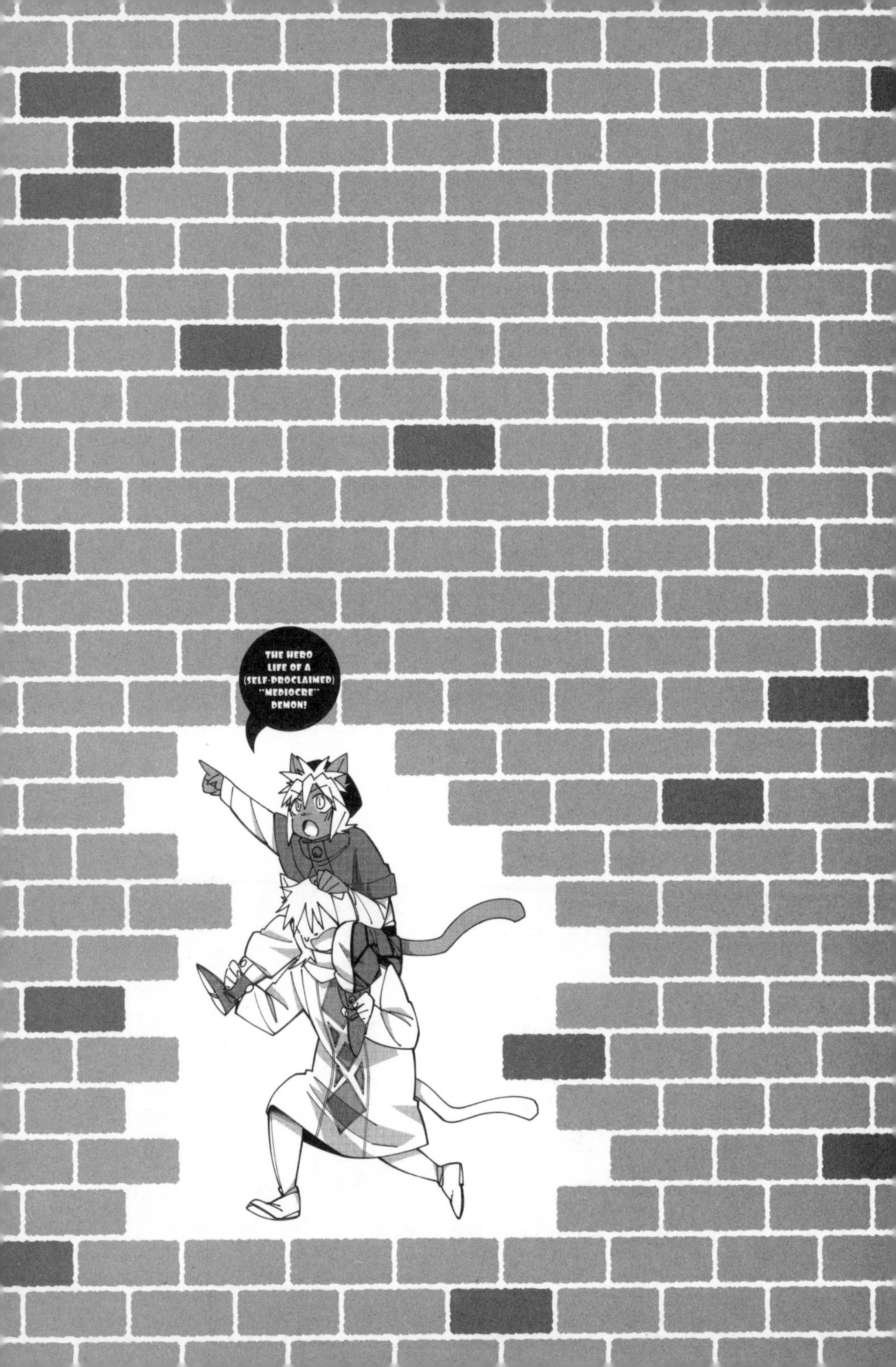
THE HERO LIFE OF A (SELF-PROCLAIMED) "MEDIOCRE" DEMON!

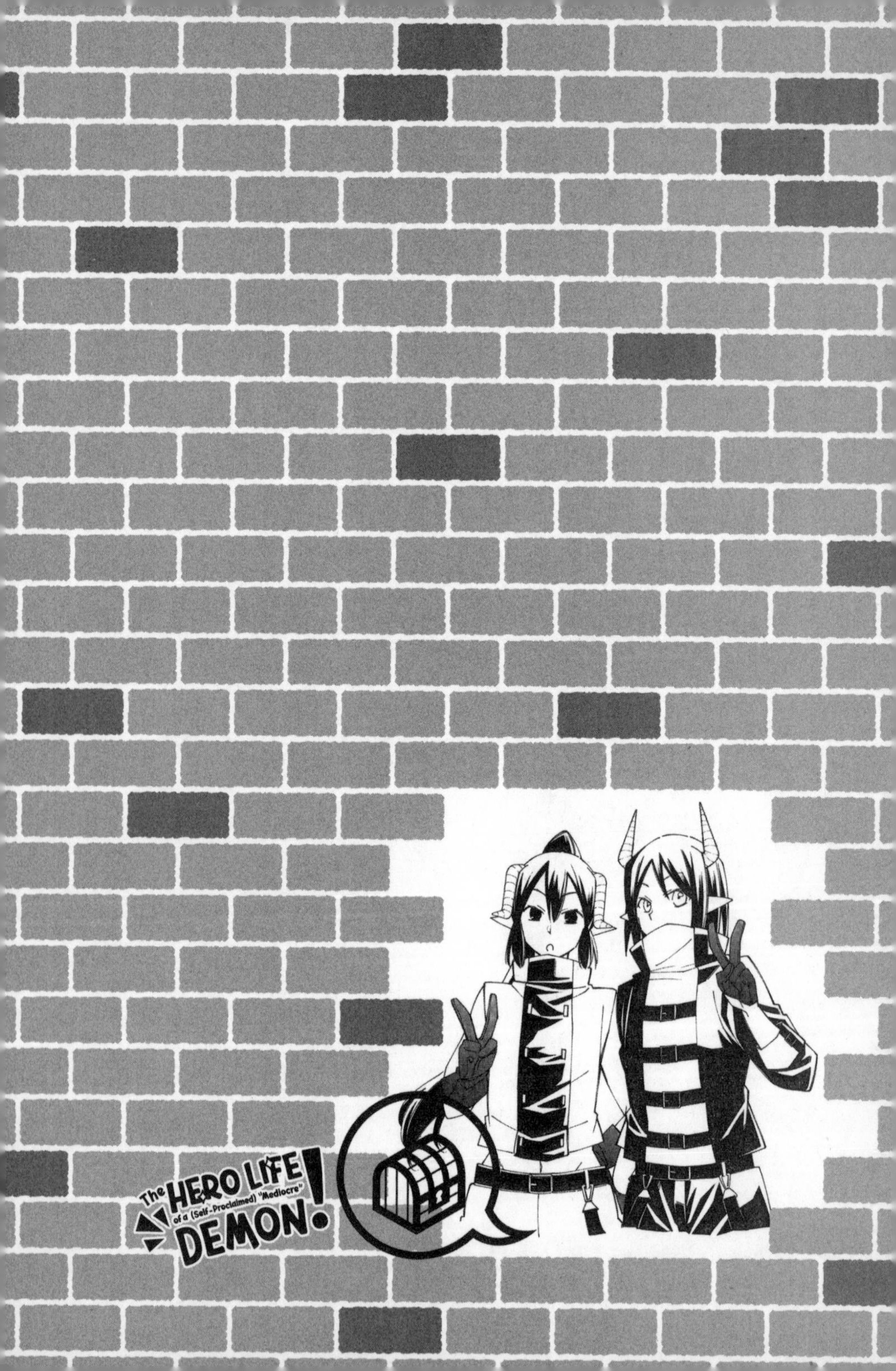
The HERO LIFE of a (Self-Proclaimed) "Mediocre" DEMON!

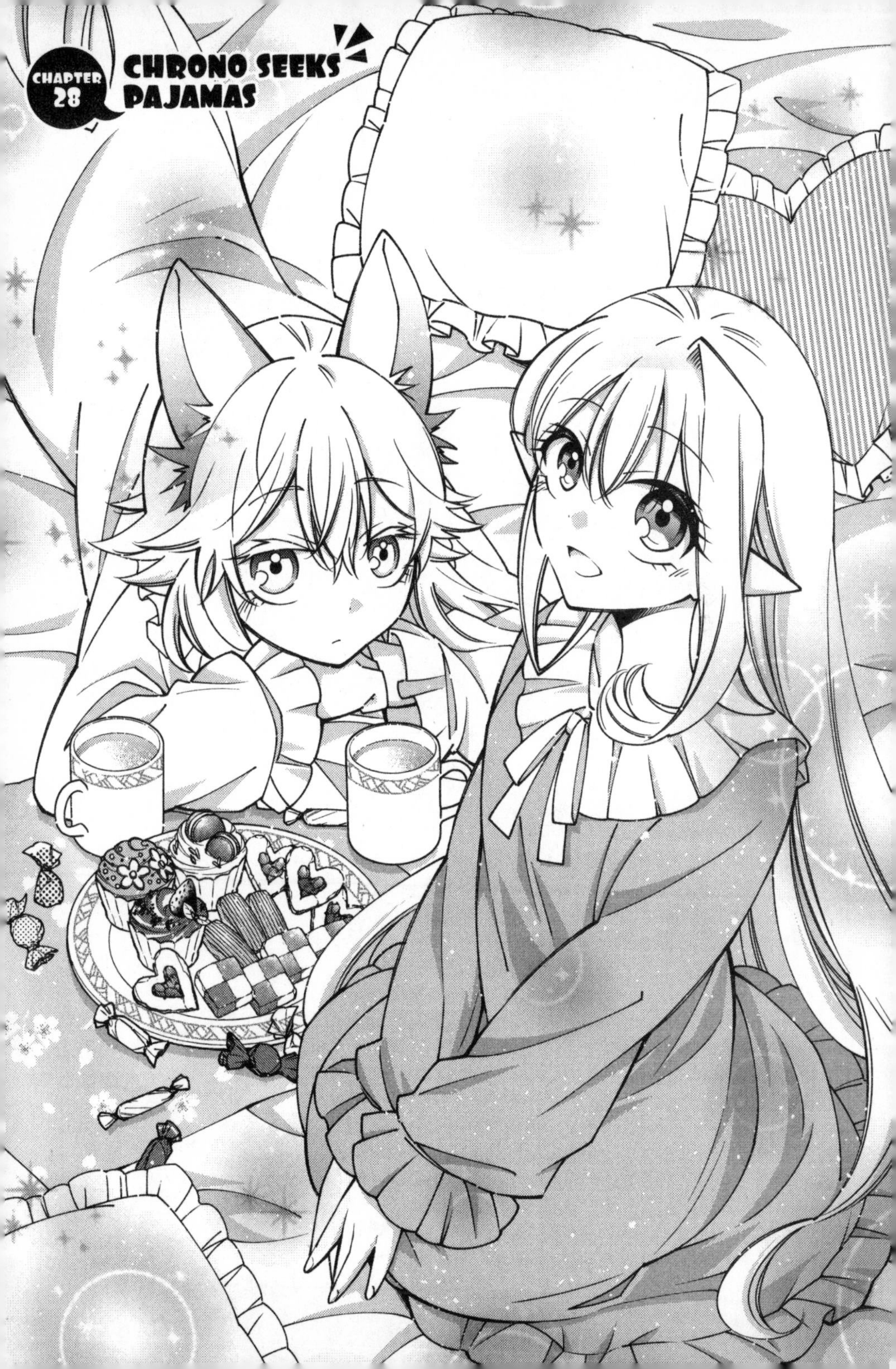
CHAPTER 28
CHRONO SEEKS PAJAMAS

I SEE...
SO YOU
FINALLY...

RELEASED
THE THRALL
CONTRACT.

**VLAD GRAVE
VAMPIRE KING
SOFIA'S DAD**

NICE
WORK...

SOFIA,
YUKINO-KUN,
PHILANIKOS...

SORRY FOR
WORRYING YOU,
OLD MAN.

...AND
YOUNG
CHRONO.

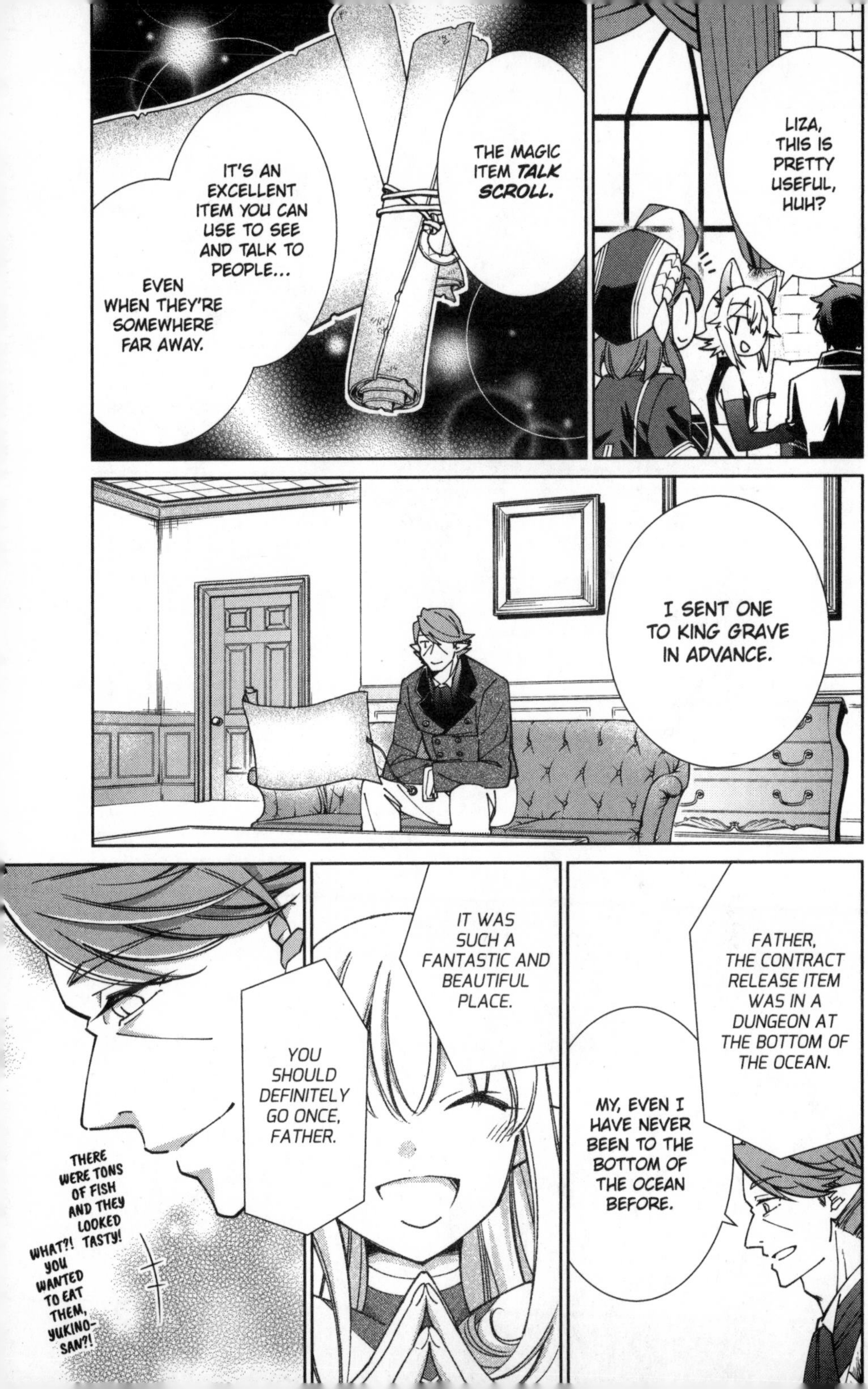

LIZA, THIS IS PRETTY USEFUL, HUH?
THE MAGIC ITEM *TALK SCROLL.*
IT'S AN EXCELLENT ITEM YOU CAN USE TO SEE AND TALK TO PEOPLE...
EVEN WHEN THEY'RE SOMEWHERE FAR AWAY.
I SENT ONE TO KING GRAVE IN ADVANCE.
FATHER, THE CONTRACT RELEASE ITEM WAS IN A DUNGEON AT THE BOTTOM OF THE OCEAN.
MY, EVEN I HAVE NEVER BEEN TO THE BOTTOM OF THE OCEAN BEFORE.
IT WAS SUCH A FANTASTIC AND BEAUTIFUL PLACE.
YOU SHOULD DEFINITELY GO ONCE, FATHER.
THERE WERE TONS OF FISH AND THEY LOOKED TASTY!
WHAT?! YOU WANTED TO EAT THEM, YUKINO-SAN?!

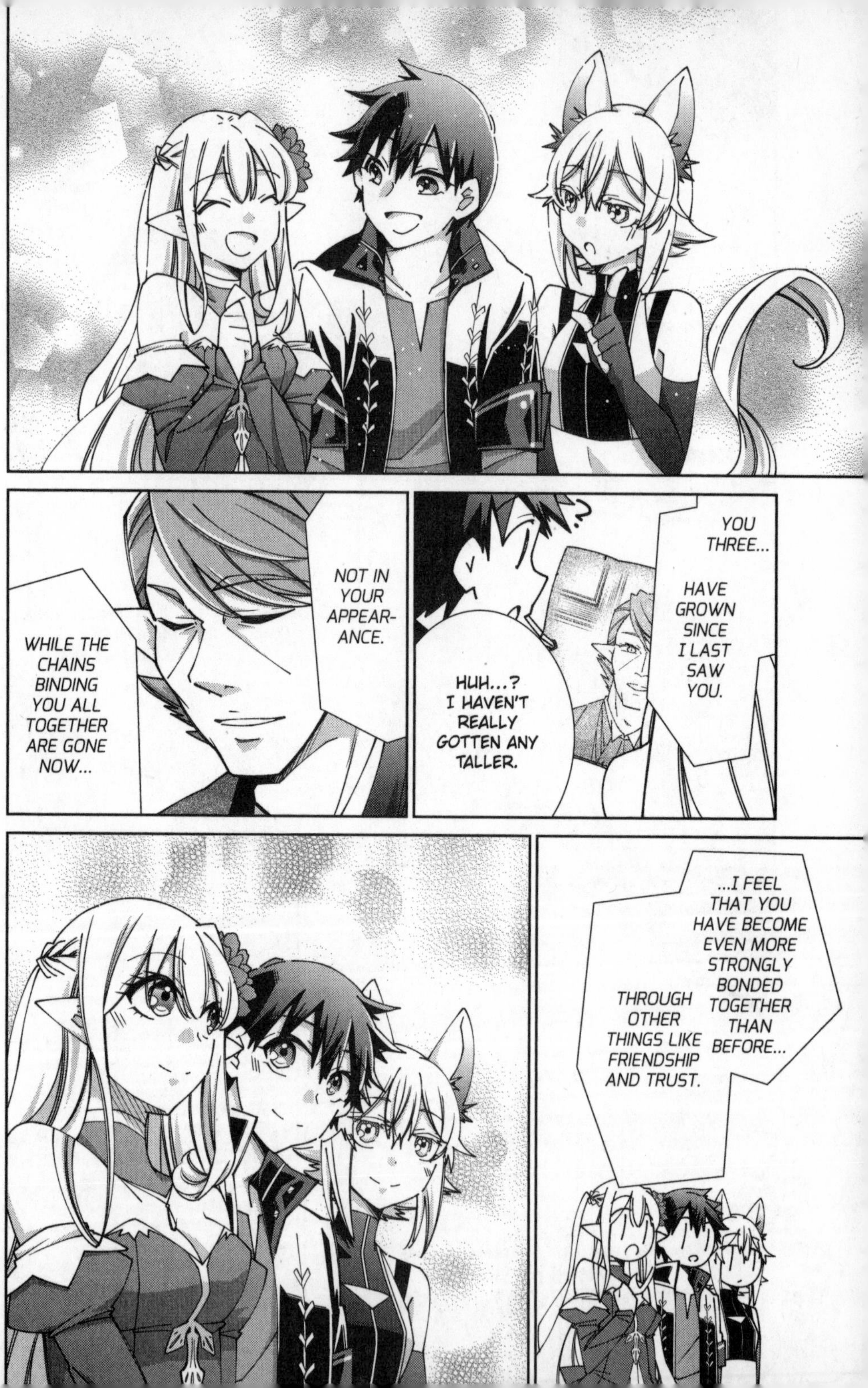
YOU THREE...
HAVE GROWN SINCE I LAST SAW YOU.
HUH...? I HAVEN'T REALLY GOTTEN ANY TALLER.
NOT IN YOUR APPEARANCE.
WHILE THE CHAINS BINDING YOU ALL TOGETHER ARE GONE NOW...
...I FEEL THAT YOU HAVE BECOME EVEN MORE STRONGLY BONDED TOGETHER THAN BEFORE...
THROUGH OTHER THINGS LIKE FRIENDSHIP AND TRUST.

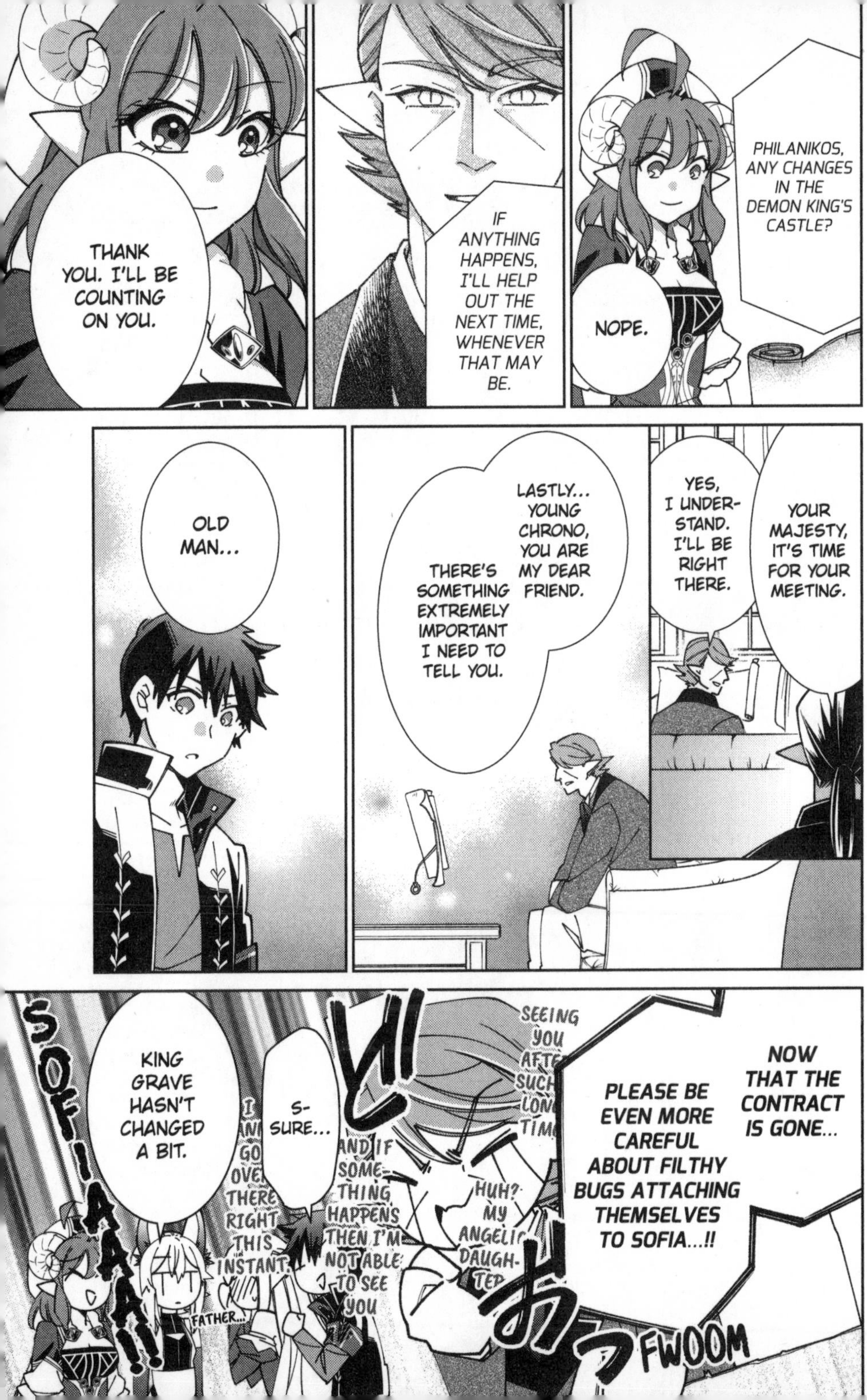
PHILANIKOS, ANY CHANGES IN THE DEMON KING'S CASTLE?
NOPE.
IF ANYTHING HAPPENS, I'LL HELP OUT THE NEXT TIME, WHENEVER THAT MAY BE.
THANK YOU. I'LL BE COUNTING ON YOU.
YOUR MAJESTY, IT'S TIME FOR YOUR MEETING.
YES, I UNDERSTAND. I'LL BE RIGHT THERE.
LASTLY... YOUNG CHRONO, YOU ARE MY DEAR FRIEND.
THERE'S SOMETHING EXTREMELY IMPORTANT I NEED TO TELL YOU.
OLD MAN...
NOW THAT THE CONTRACT IS GONE...
PLEASE BE EVEN MORE CAREFUL ABOUT FILTHY BUGS ATTACHING THEMSELVES TO SOFIA...!!
SEEING YOU
HUH? MY ANGELIC DAUGH-
AND IF SOMETHING HAPPENS THEN I'M NOT ABLE TO SEE YOU
FWOOM
S-SURE...
THERE RIGHT THIS INSTANT.
KING GRAVE HASN'T CHANGED A BIT.
SOFIAAA!!
FATHER...

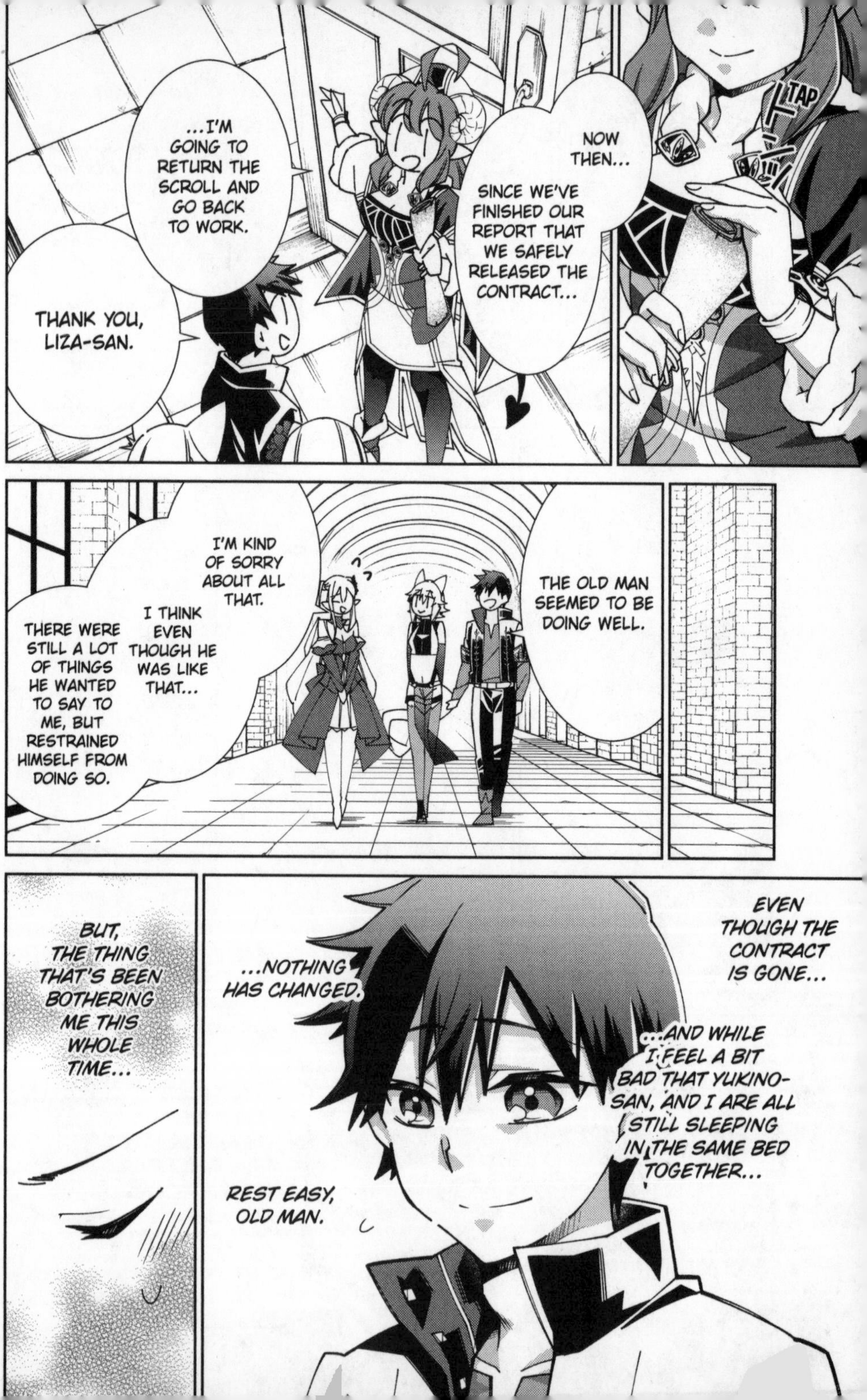
TAP
NOW THEN... SINCE WE'VE FINISHED OUR REPORT THAT WE SAFELY RELEASED THE CONTRACT...
...I'M GOING TO RETURN THE SCROLL AND GO BACK TO WORK.
THANK YOU, LIZA-SAN.
THE OLD MAN SEEMED TO BE DOING WELL.
I'M KIND OF SORRY ABOUT ALL THAT.
I THINK EVEN THOUGH HE WAS LIKE THAT...
THERE WERE STILL A LOT OF THINGS HE WANTED TO SAY TO ME, BUT RESTRAINED HIMSELF FROM DOING SO.
EVEN THOUGH THE CONTRACT IS GONE...
...AND WHILE I FEEL A BIT BAD THAT YUKINO-SAN, AND I ARE ALL STILL SLEEPING IN THE SAME BED TOGETHER...
...NOTHING HAS CHANGED.
REST EASY, OLD MAN.
BUT, THE THING THAT'S BEEN BOTHERING ME THIS WHOLE TIME...

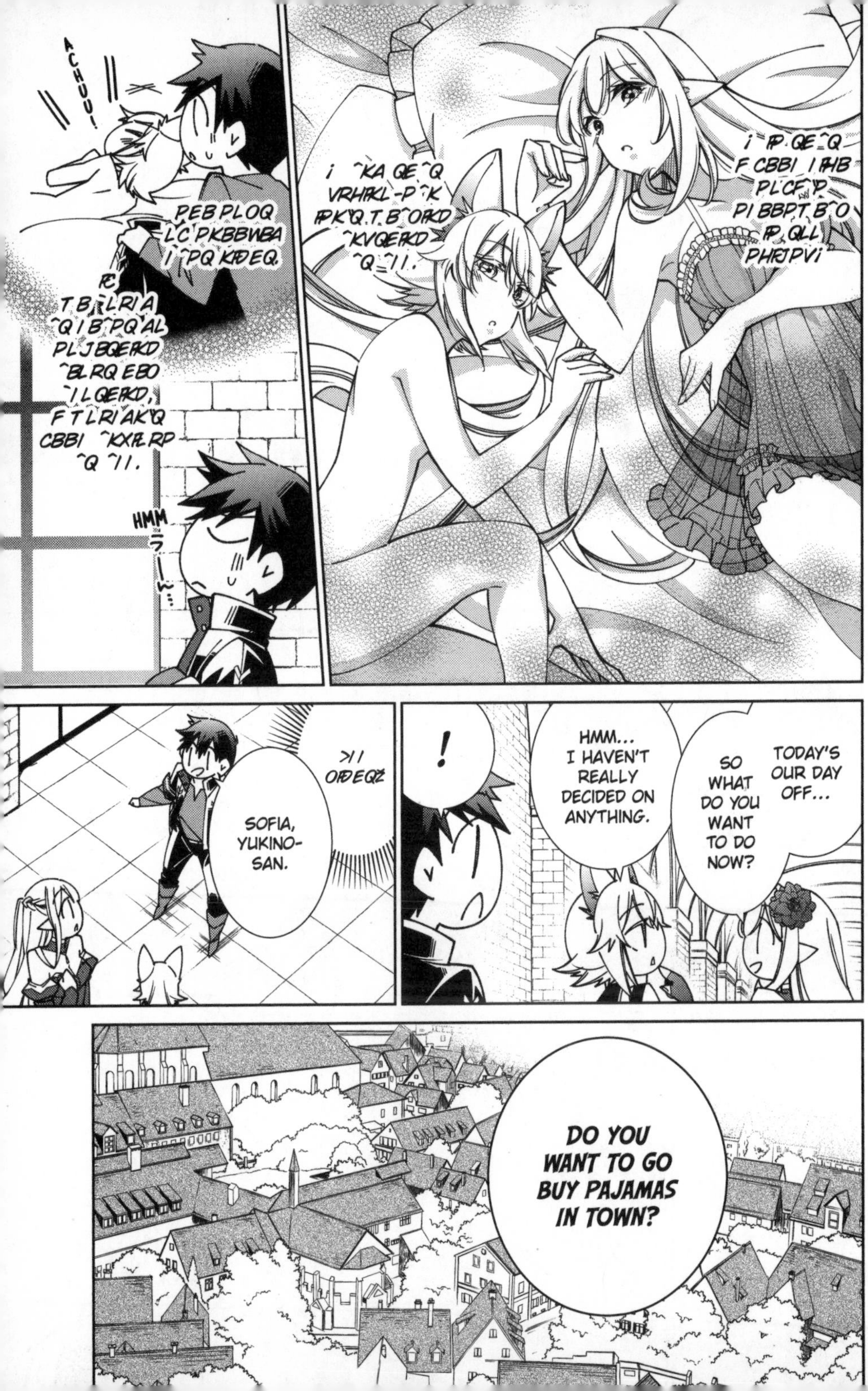
ACHUU!
HMM
TODAY'S OUR DAY OFF...
SO WHAT DO YOU WANT TO DO NOW?
HMM... I HAVEN'T REALLY DECIDED ON ANYTHING.
!
SOFIA, YUKINO-SAN.
DO YOU WANT TO GO BUY PAJAMAS IN TOWN?

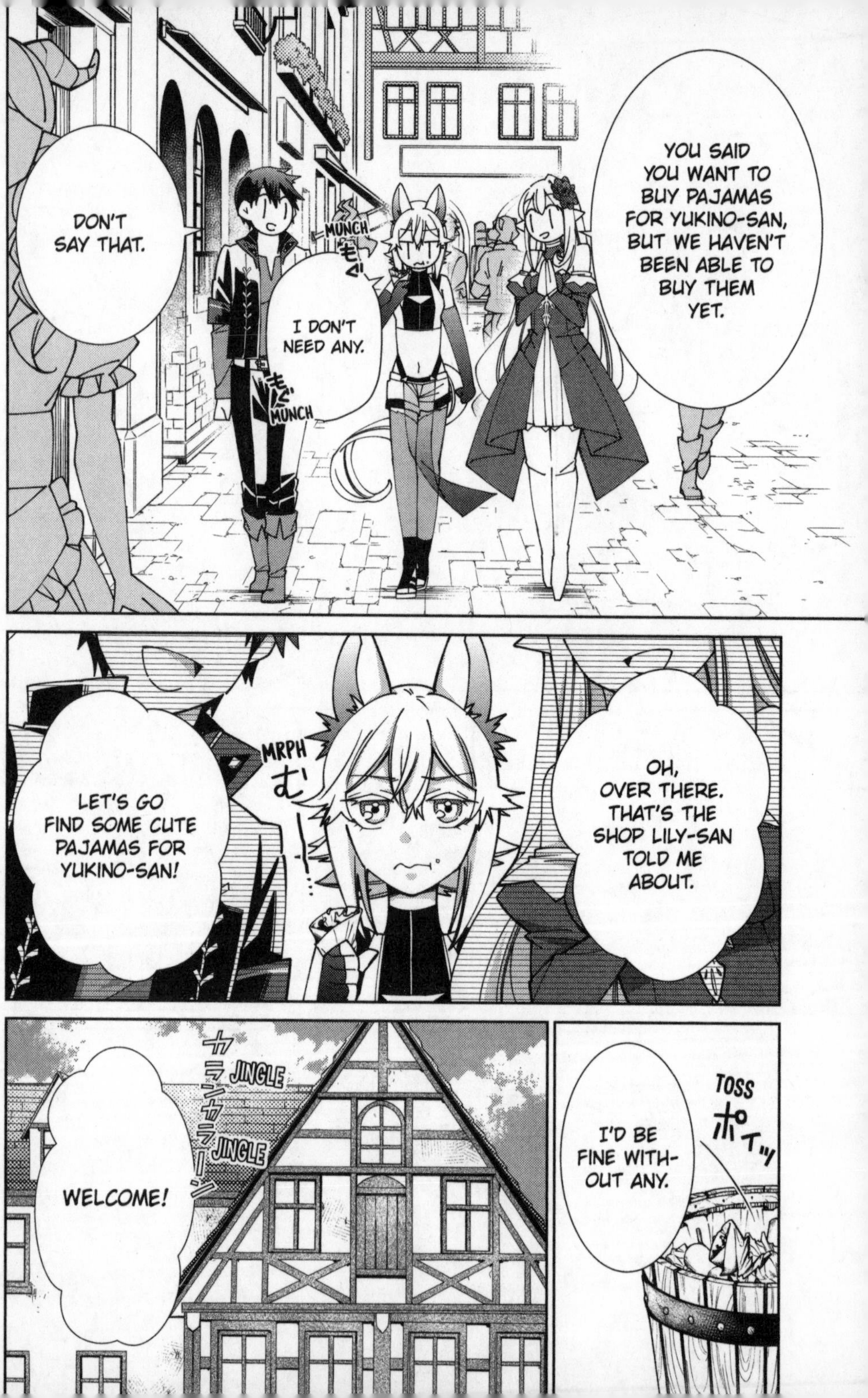

YOU SAID YOU WANT TO BUY PAJAMAS FOR YUKINO-SAN, BUT WE HAVEN'T BEEN ABLE TO BUY THEM YET.
MUNCH もぐ
I DON'T NEED ANY.
もぐ MUNCH
DON'T SAY THAT.
OH, OVER THERE. THAT'S THE SHOP LILY-SAN TOLD ME ABOUT.
MRPH む
LET'S GO FIND SOME CUTE PAJAMAS FOR YUKINO-SAN!
TOSS ポイッ
I'D BE FINE WITH-OUT ANY.
カランカラーン JINGLE JINGLE
WELCOME!

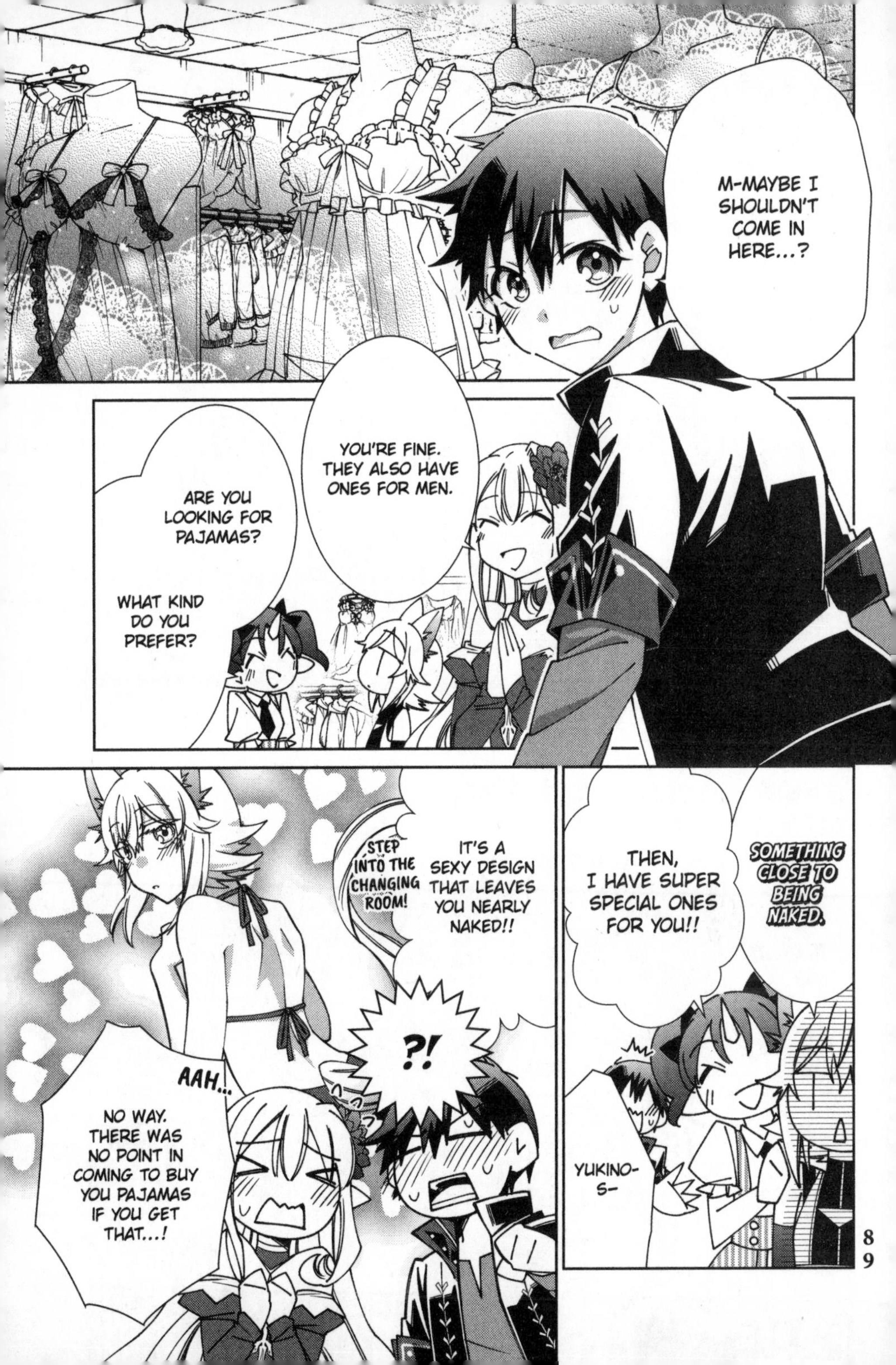
M-MAYBE I SHOULDN'T COME IN HERE...?
YOU'RE FINE. THEY ALSO HAVE ONES FOR MEN.
ARE YOU LOOKING FOR PAJAMAS?
WHAT KIND DO YOU PREFER?
SOMETHING CLOSE TO BEING NAKED.
THEN, I HAVE SUPER SPECIAL ONES FOR YOU!!
YUKINO-S-
IT'S A SEXY DESIGN THAT LEAVES YOU NEARLY NAKED!!
STEP INTO THE CHANGING ROOM!
?!
AAH...
NO WAY. THERE WAS NO POINT IN COMING TO BUY YOU PAJAMAS IF YOU GET THAT...!

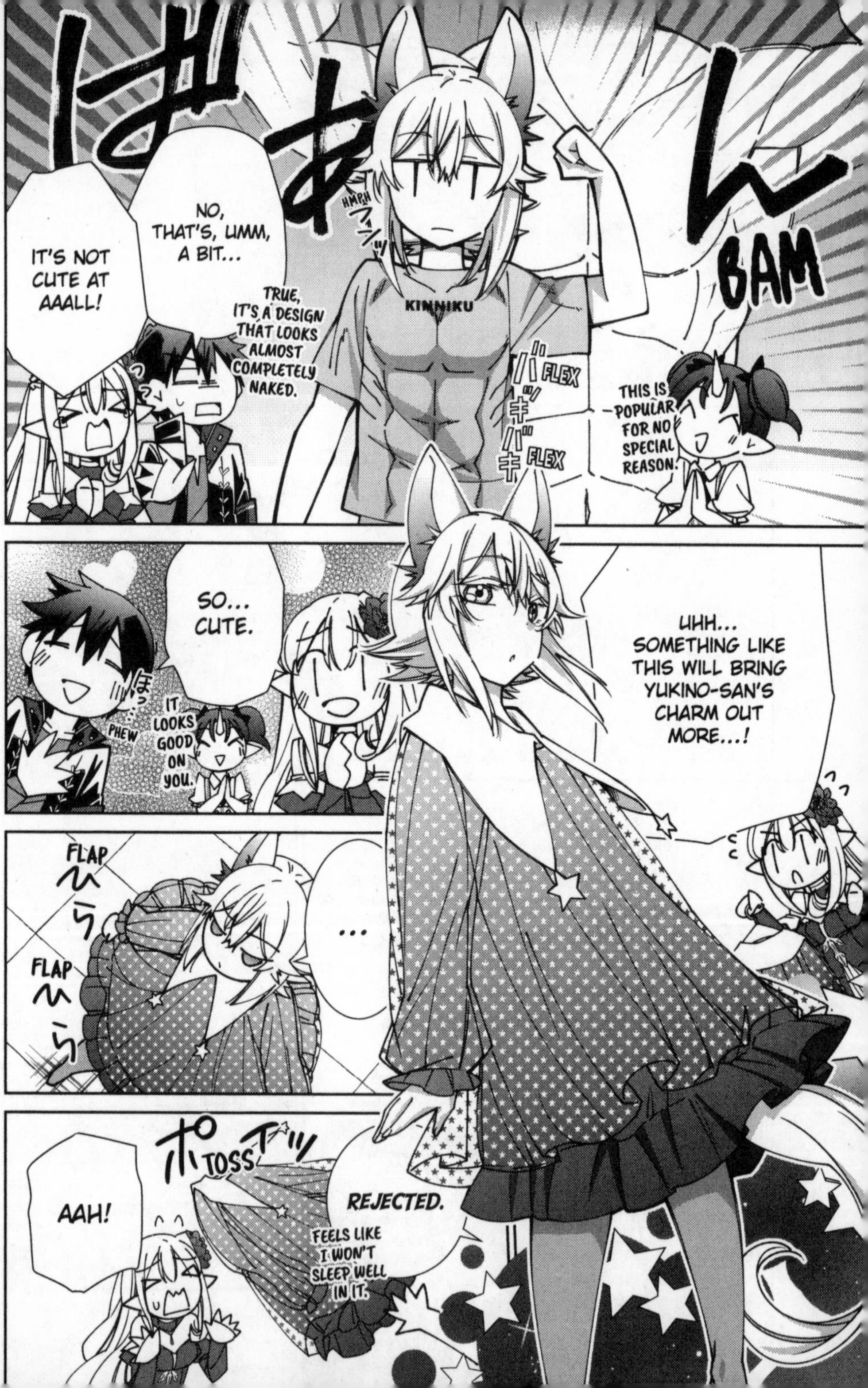
BAM
HMPH
KINNIKU
FLEX
FLEX
THIS IS POPULAR FOR NO SPECIAL REASON.
TRUE, IT'S A DESIGN THAT LOOKS ALMOST COMPLETELY NAKED.
NO, THAT'S, UMM, A BIT...
IT'S NOT CUTE AT AAALL!
UHH... SOMETHING LIKE THIS WILL BRING YUKINO-SAN'S CHARM OUT MORE...!
SO... CUTE.
PHEW
IT LOOKS GOOD ON YOU.
FLAP
FLAP
...
TOSS
REJECTED.
FEELS LIKE I WON'T SLEEP WELL IN IT.
AAH!

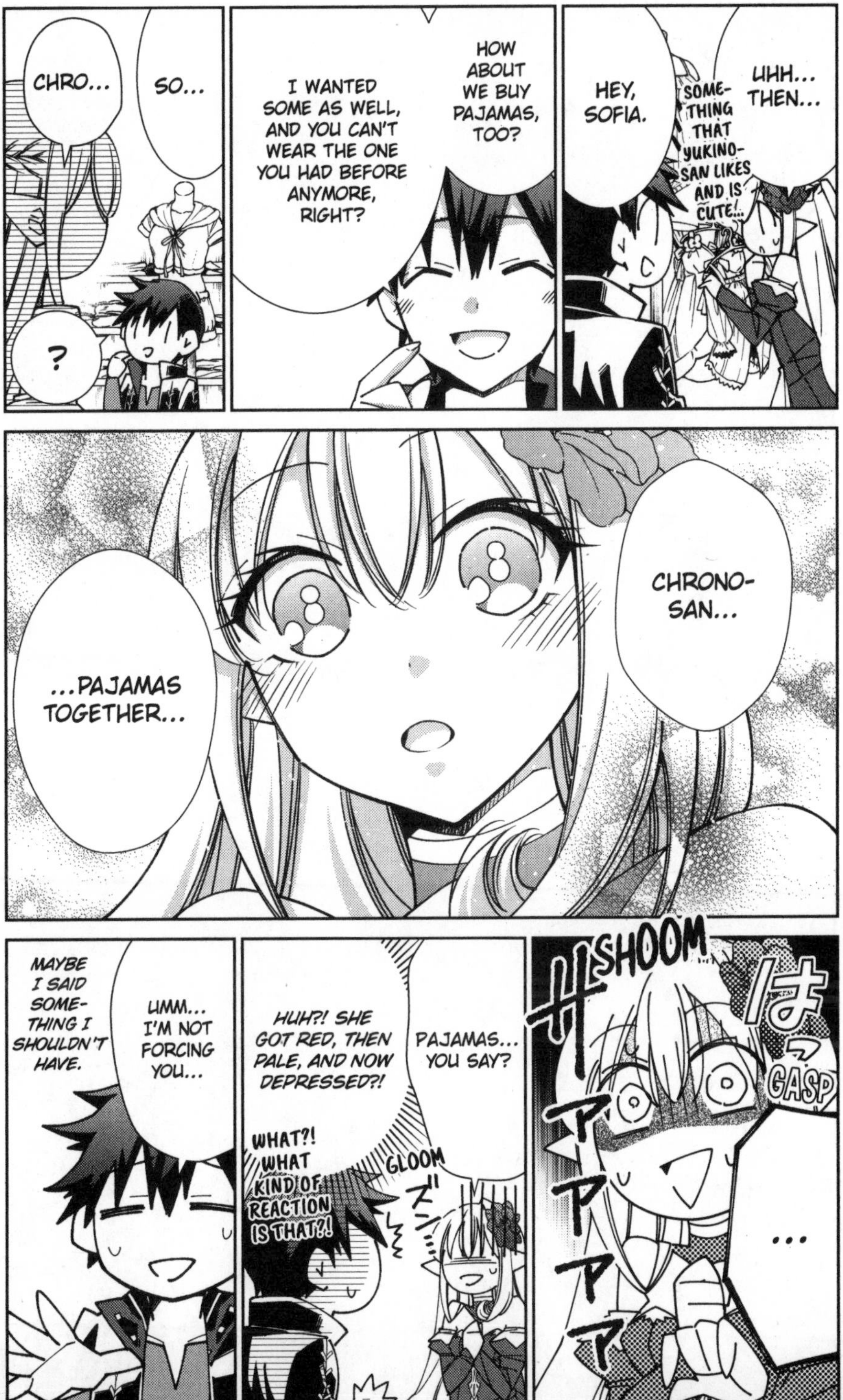
UHH... THEN...
SOME-THING THAT YUKINO-SAN LIKES AND IS CUTE...
HEY, SOFIA.
HOW ABOUT WE BUY PAJAMAS, TOO?
I WANTED SOME AS WELL, AND YOU CAN'T WEAR THE ONE YOU HAD BEFORE ANYMORE, RIGHT?
SO...
CHRO...
?
CHRONO-SAN...
...PAJAMAS TOGETHER...
SHOOM
GASP
...
PAJAMAS... YOU SAY?
HUH?! SHE GOT RED, THEN PALE, AND NOW DEPRESSED?!
GLOOM
WHAT?! WHAT KIND OF REACTION IS THAT?!
UMM... I'M NOT FORCING YOU...
MAYBE I SAID SOMETHING I SHOULDN'T HAVE.

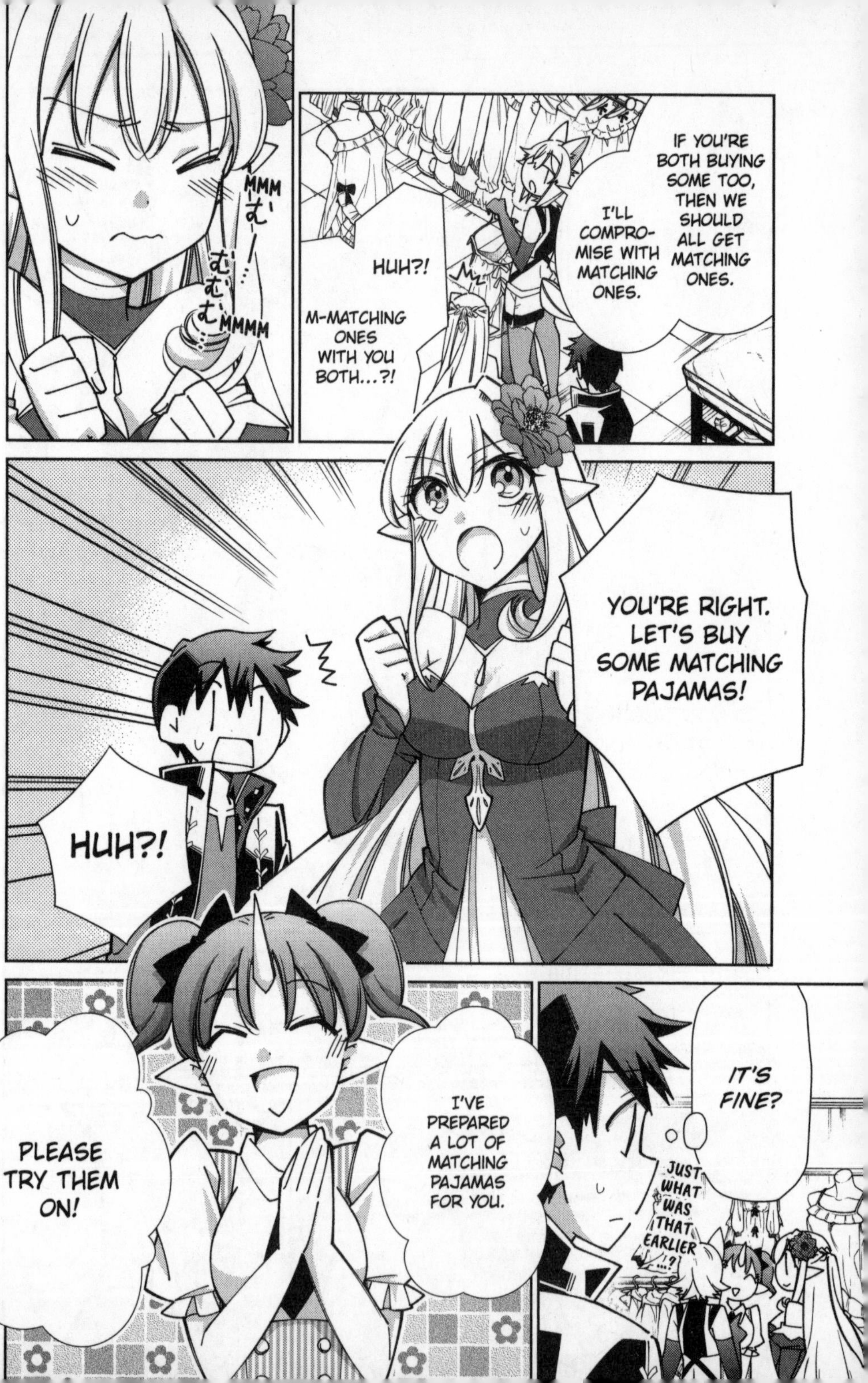
IF YOU'RE BOTH BUYING SOME TOO, THEN WE SHOULD ALL GET MATCHING ONES.
I'LL COMPRO-MISE WITH MATCHING ONES.
HUH?!
M-MATCHING ONES WITH YOU BOTH...?!
MMM むー…
むむむ MMMM
YOU'RE RIGHT. LET'S BUY SOME MATCHING PAJAMAS!
HUH?!
IT'S FINE?
JUST WHAT WAS THAT EARLIER...?
I'VE PREPARED A LOT OF MATCHING PAJAMAS FOR YOU.
PLEASE TRY THEM ON!

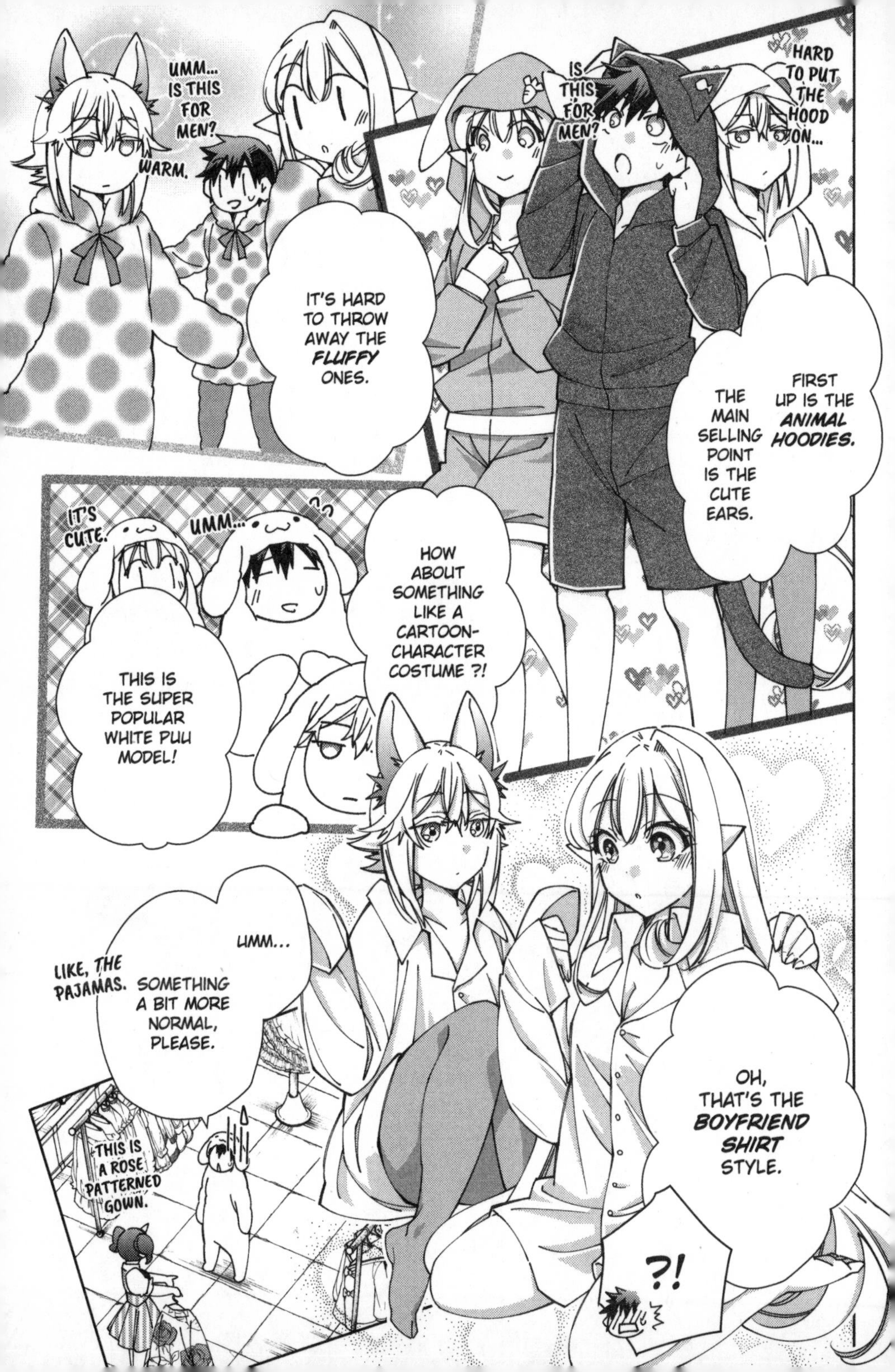
HARD TO PUT THE HOOD ON...
IS THIS FOR MEN?
FIRST UP IS THE ANIMAL HOODIES.
THE MAIN SELLING POINT IS THE CUTE EARS.
UMM... IS THIS FOR MEN?
IT'S HARD TO THROW AWAY THE FLUFFY ONES.
WARM.
HOW ABOUT SOMETHING LIKE A CARTOON-CHARACTER COSTUME ?!
UMM...
IT'S CUTE.
THIS IS THE SUPER POPULAR WHITE PUU MODEL!
OH, THAT'S THE BOYFRIEND SHIRT STYLE.
?!
UMM...
SOMETHING A BIT MORE NORMAL, PLEASE.
LIKE, THE PAJAMAS.
THIS IS A ROSE PATTERNED GOWN.

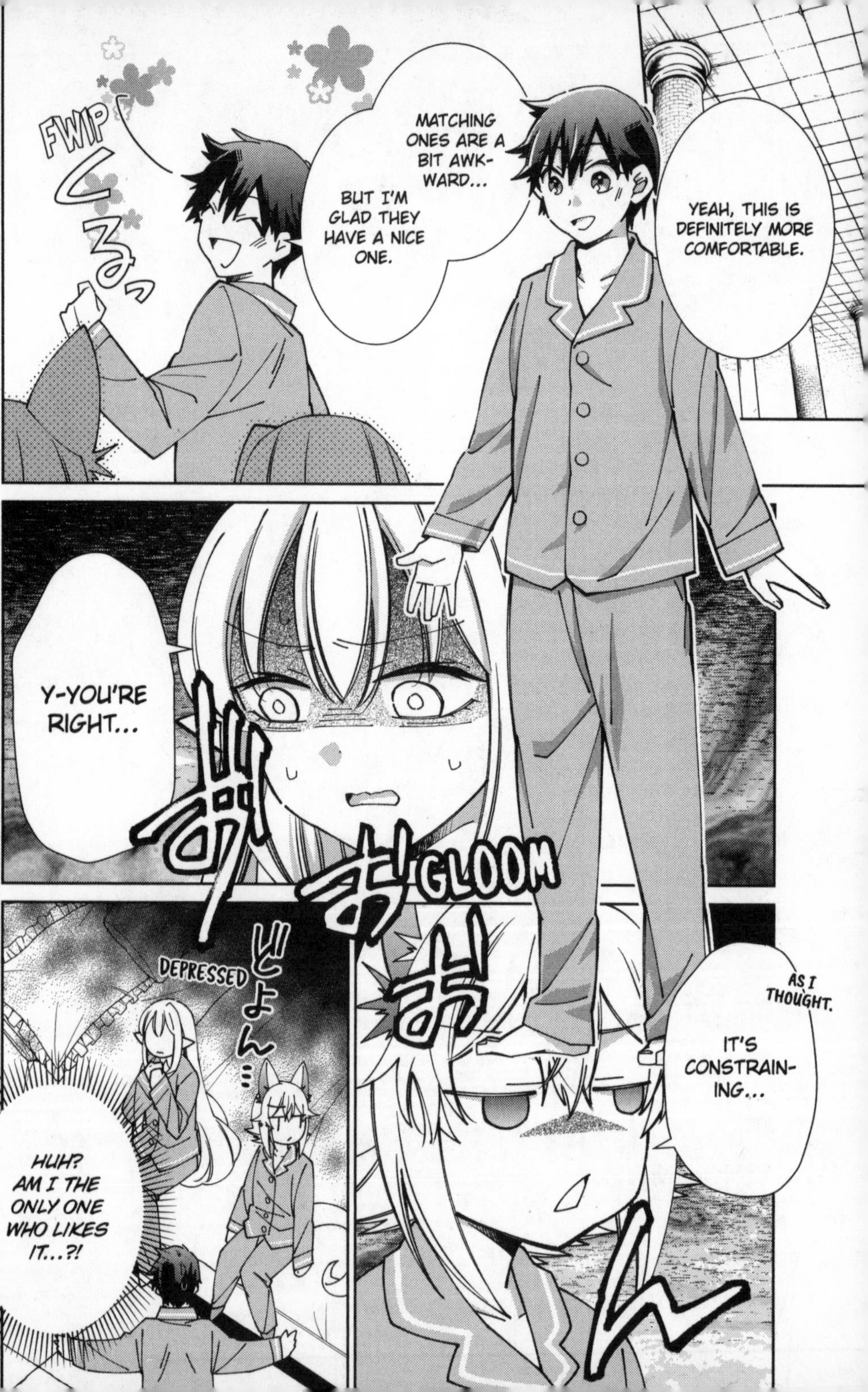
YEAH, THIS IS DEFINITELY MORE COMFORTABLE.
MATCHING ONES ARE A BIT AWK-WARD...
BUT I'M GLAD THEY HAVE A NICE ONE.
FWIP
くるっ
Y-YOU'RE RIGHT...
おおお
GLOOM
AS I THOUGHT.
IT'S CONSTRAIN-ING...
DEPRESSED
どよん…
HUH? AM I THE ONLY ONE WHO LIKES IT...?!

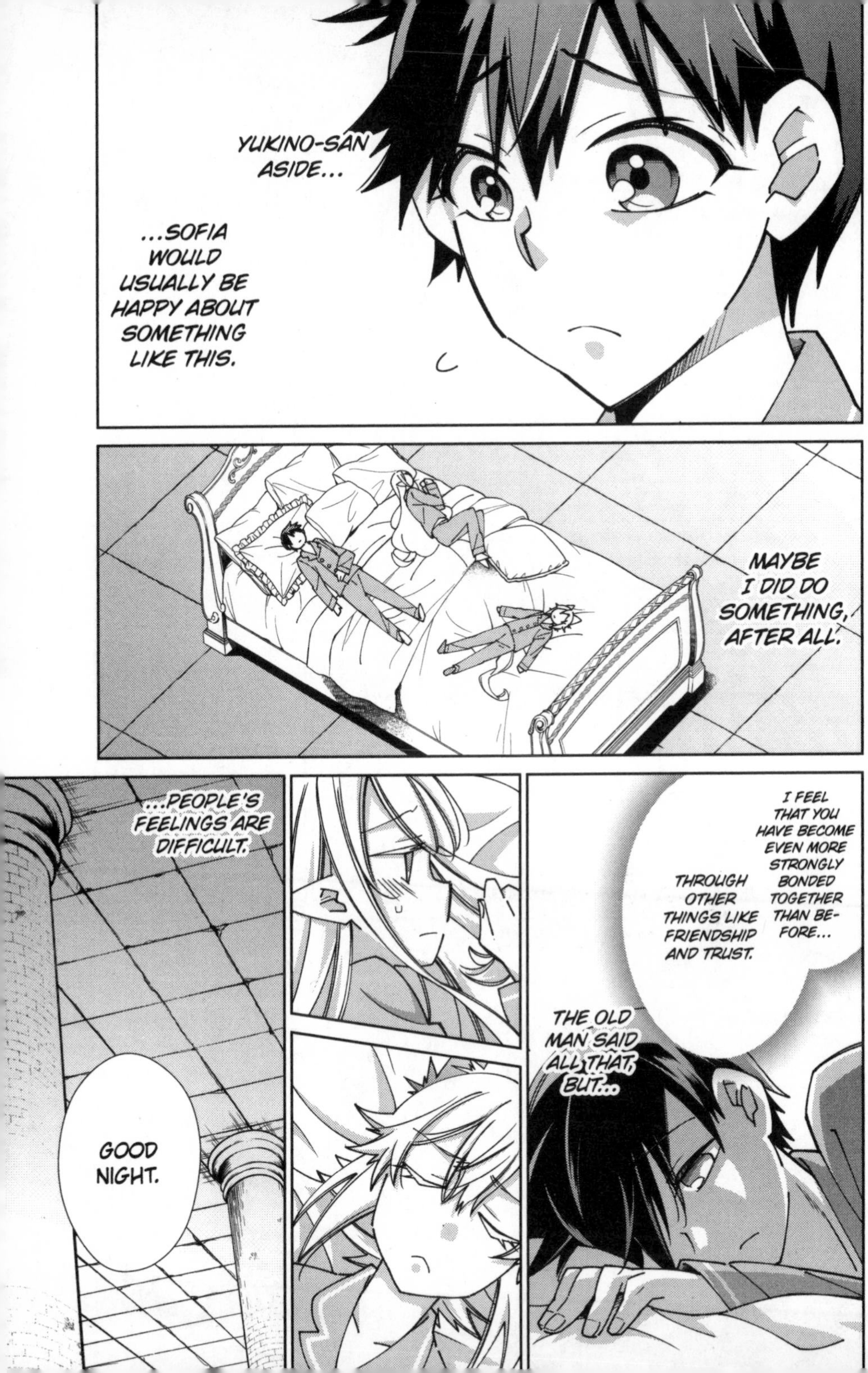
YUKINO-SAN ASIDE...
...SOFIA WOULD USUALLY BE HAPPY ABOUT SOMETHING LIKE THIS.
MAYBE I DID DO SOMETHING, AFTER ALL.
I FEEL THAT YOU HAVE BECOME EVEN MORE STRONGLY BONDED TOGETHER THAN BE-FORE...
THROUGH OTHER THINGS LIKE FRIENDSHIP AND TRUST.
THE OLD MAN SAID ALL THAT, BUT...
...PEOPLE'S FEELINGS ARE DIFFICULT.
GOOD NIGHT.

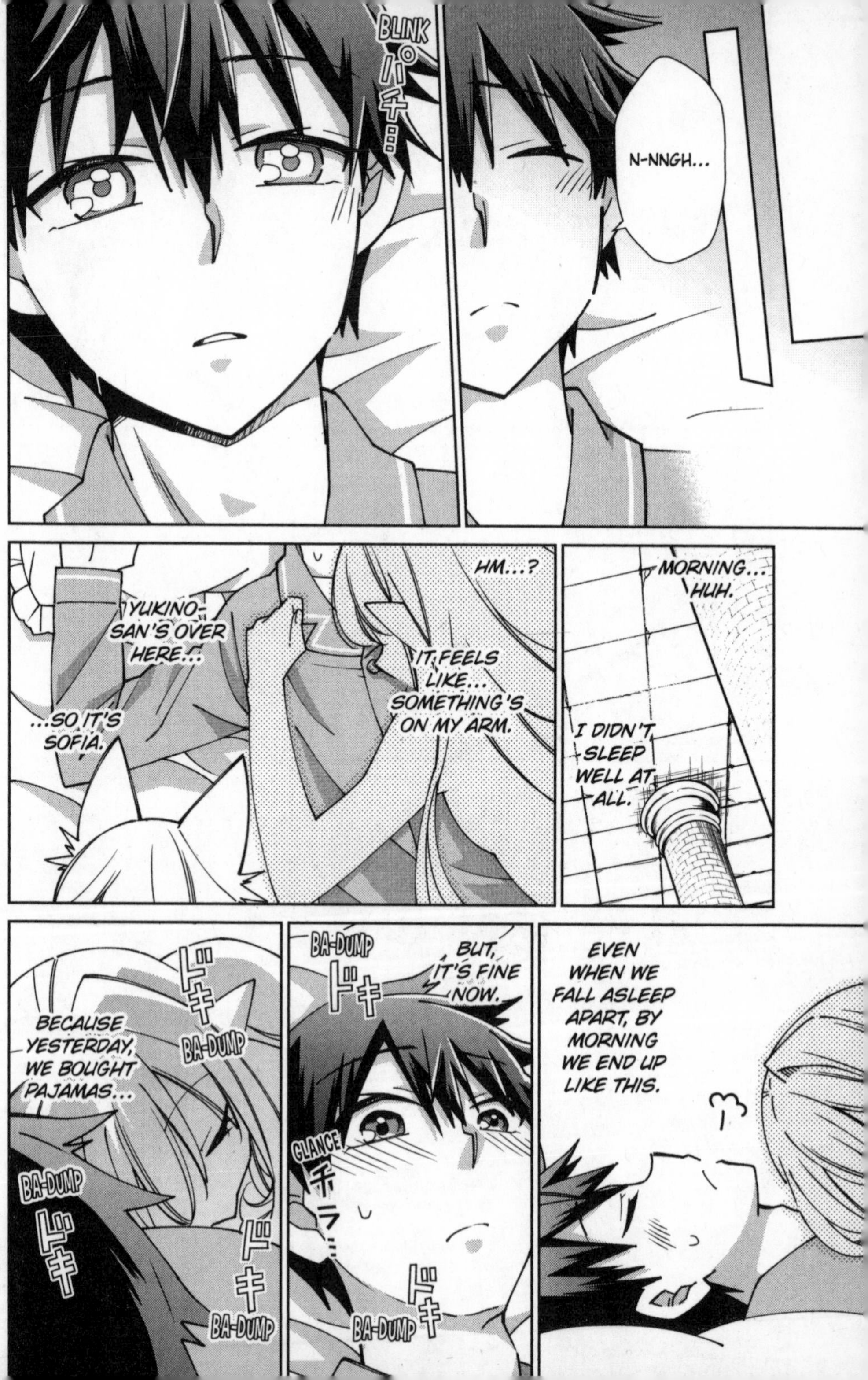
N-NNGH...
BLINK
パチ...
MORNING... HUH.
I DIDN'T SLEEP WELL AT ALL.
HM...?
IT FEELS LIKE... SOMETHING'S ON MY ARM.
YUKINO-SAN'S OVER HERE...
...SO IT'S SOFIA.
EVEN WHEN WE FALL ASLEEP APART, BY MORNING WE END UP LIKE THIS.
BA-DUMP
ドキ
BUT, IT'S FINE NOW.
GLANCE
チラ...
BA-DUMP
ドキ
ドキ
BA-DUMP
BA-DUMP
ドキ
BECAUSE YESTERDAY, WE BOUGHT PAJAMAS...
BA-DUMP
ドッキ
ドキ
BA-DUMP

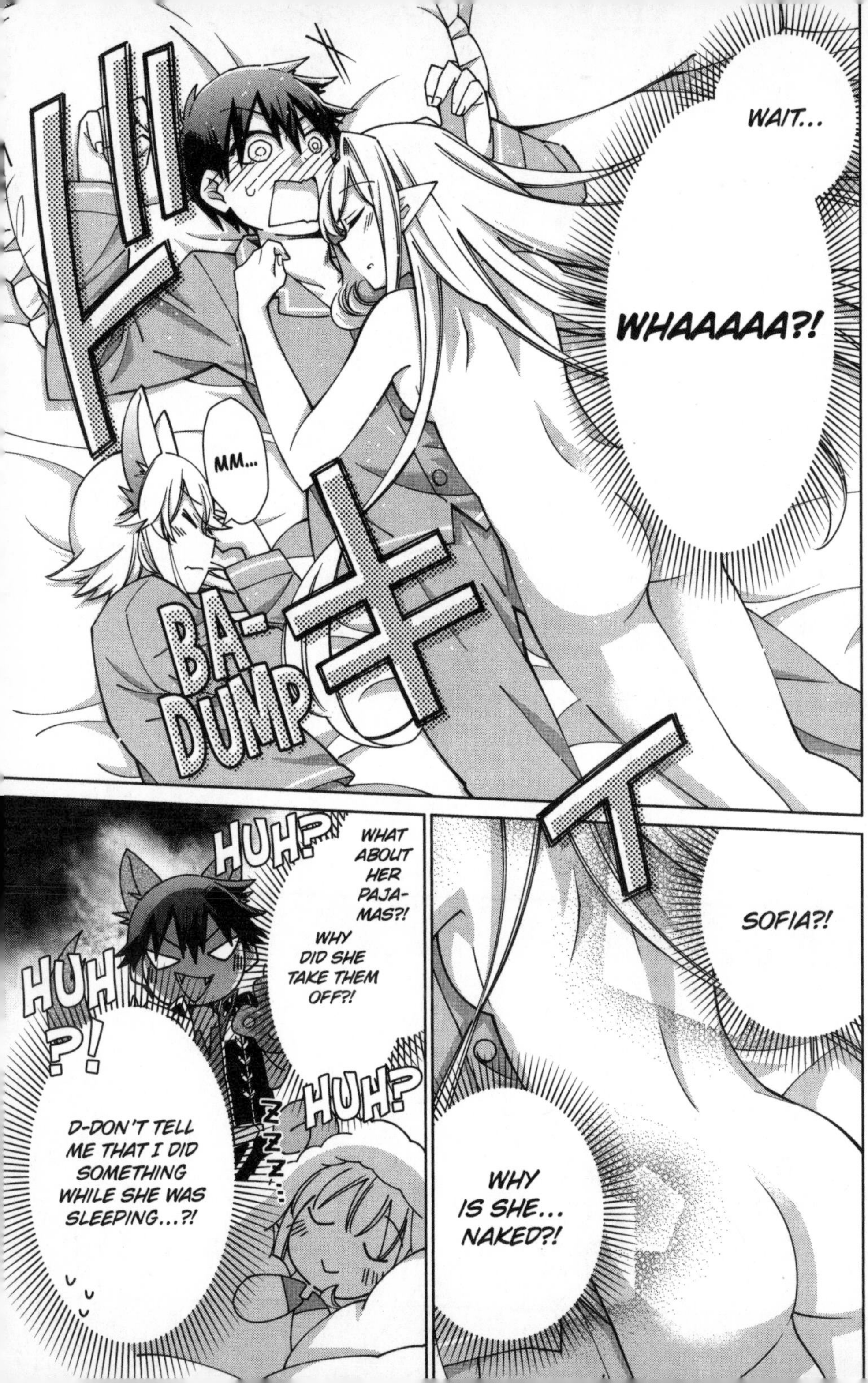
WAIT…
WHAAAAA?!
MM…
BA-DUMP
SOFIA?!
WHY IS SHE… NAKED?!
HUH?
WHAT ABOUT HER PAJAMAS?!
WHY DID SHE TAKE THEM OFF?!
HUH?!
D-DON'T TELL ME THAT I DID SOMETHING WHILE SHE WAS SLEEPING…?!
HUH?

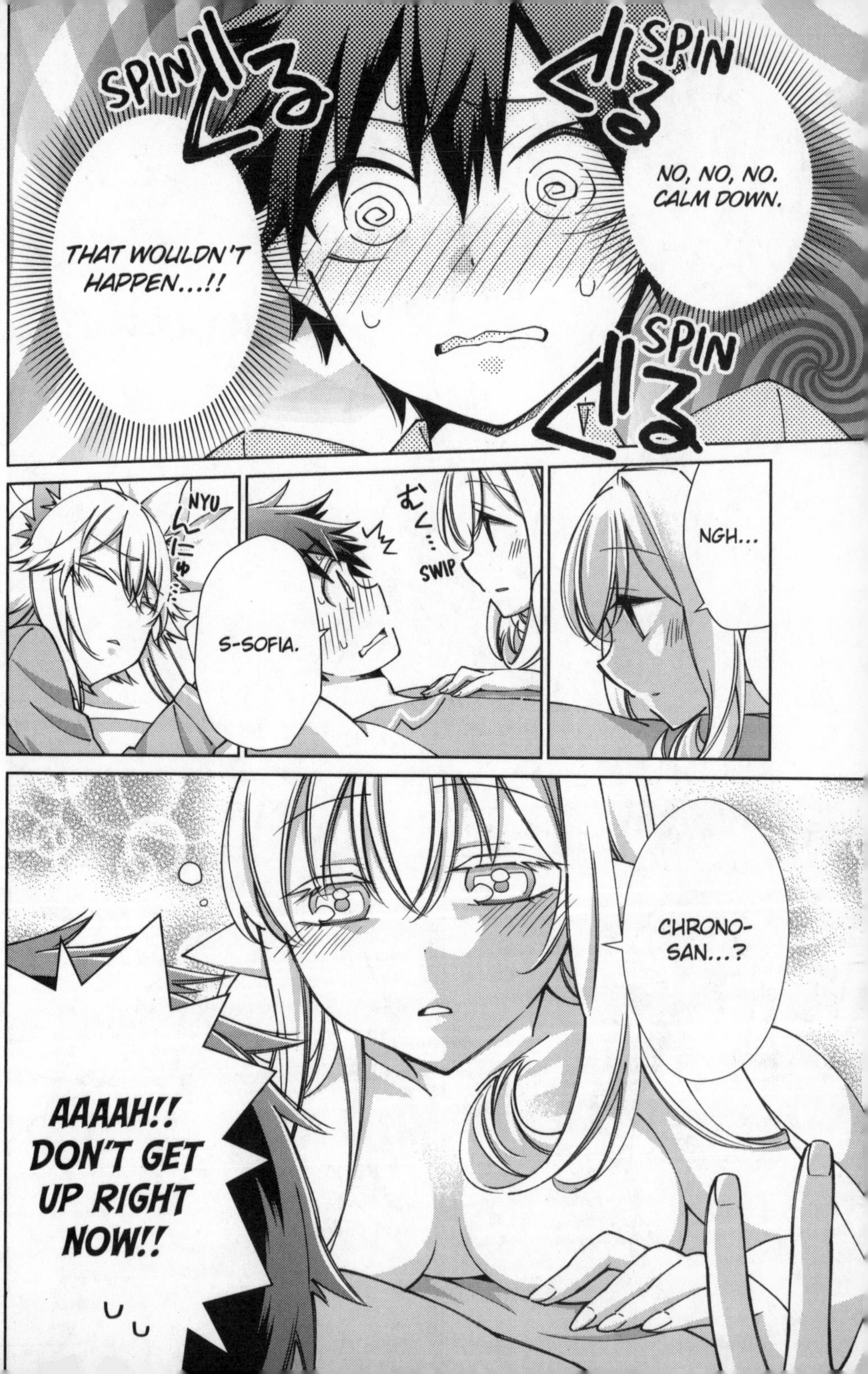
SPIN くる
NO, NO, NO. CALM DOWN.
SPIN くる
SPIN くる
THAT WOULDN'T HAPPEN...!!
NGH...
むく… SWIP
S-SOFIA.
NYU んにゅ
CHRONO-SAN...?
AAAAH!! DON'T GET UP RIGHT NOW!!

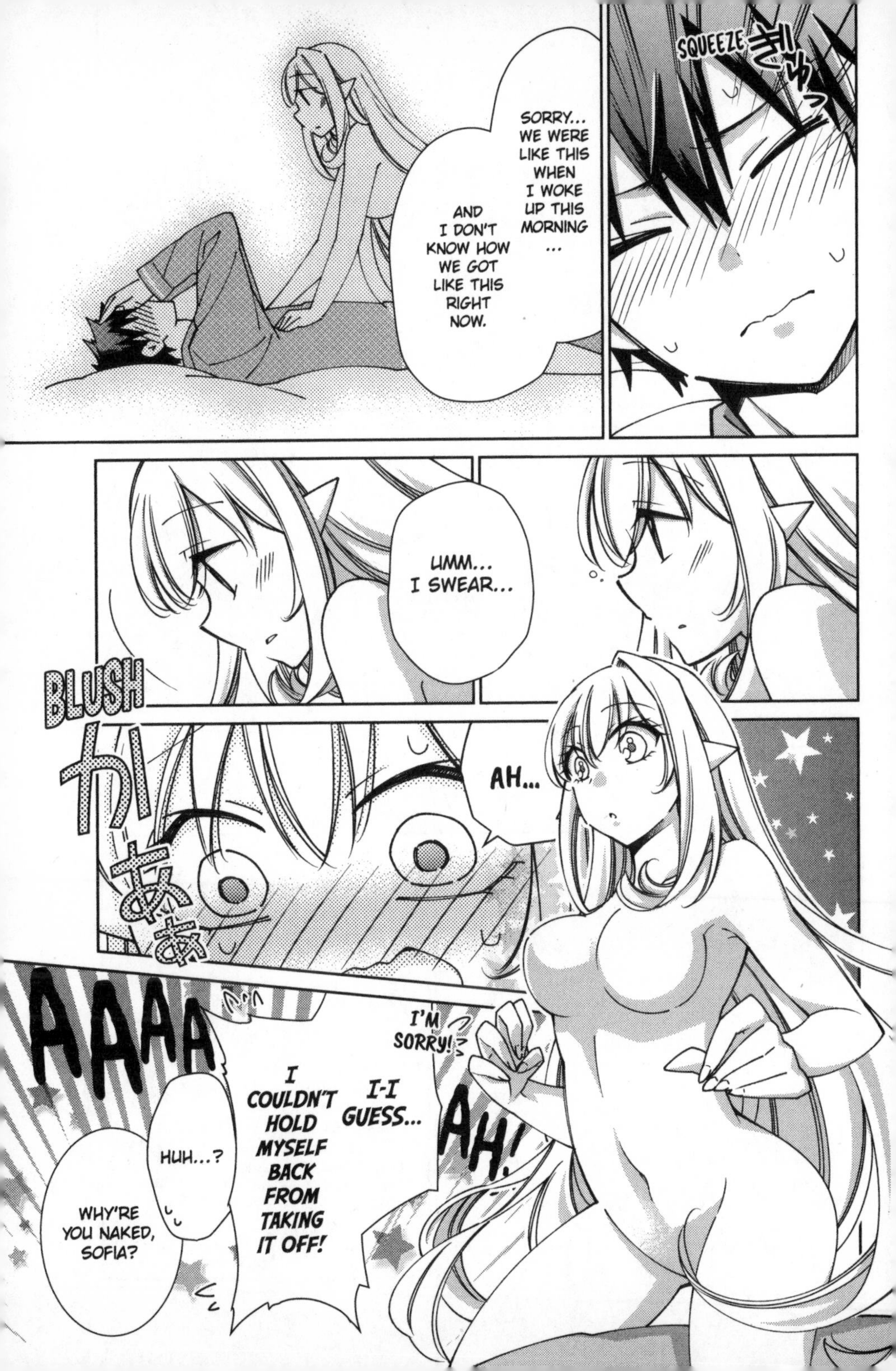
SQUEEZE ぎゅっ
SORRY... WE WERE LIKE THIS WHEN I WOKE UP THIS MORNING ...
AND I DON'T KNOW HOW WE GOT LIKE THIS RIGHT NOW.
UMM... I SWEAR...
BLUSH
AH...
わぁあ
AAAA AH!
I'M SORRY!
I-I GUESS...
I COULDN'T HOLD MYSELF BACK FROM TAKING IT OFF!
HUH...?
WHY'RE YOU NAKED, SOFIA?

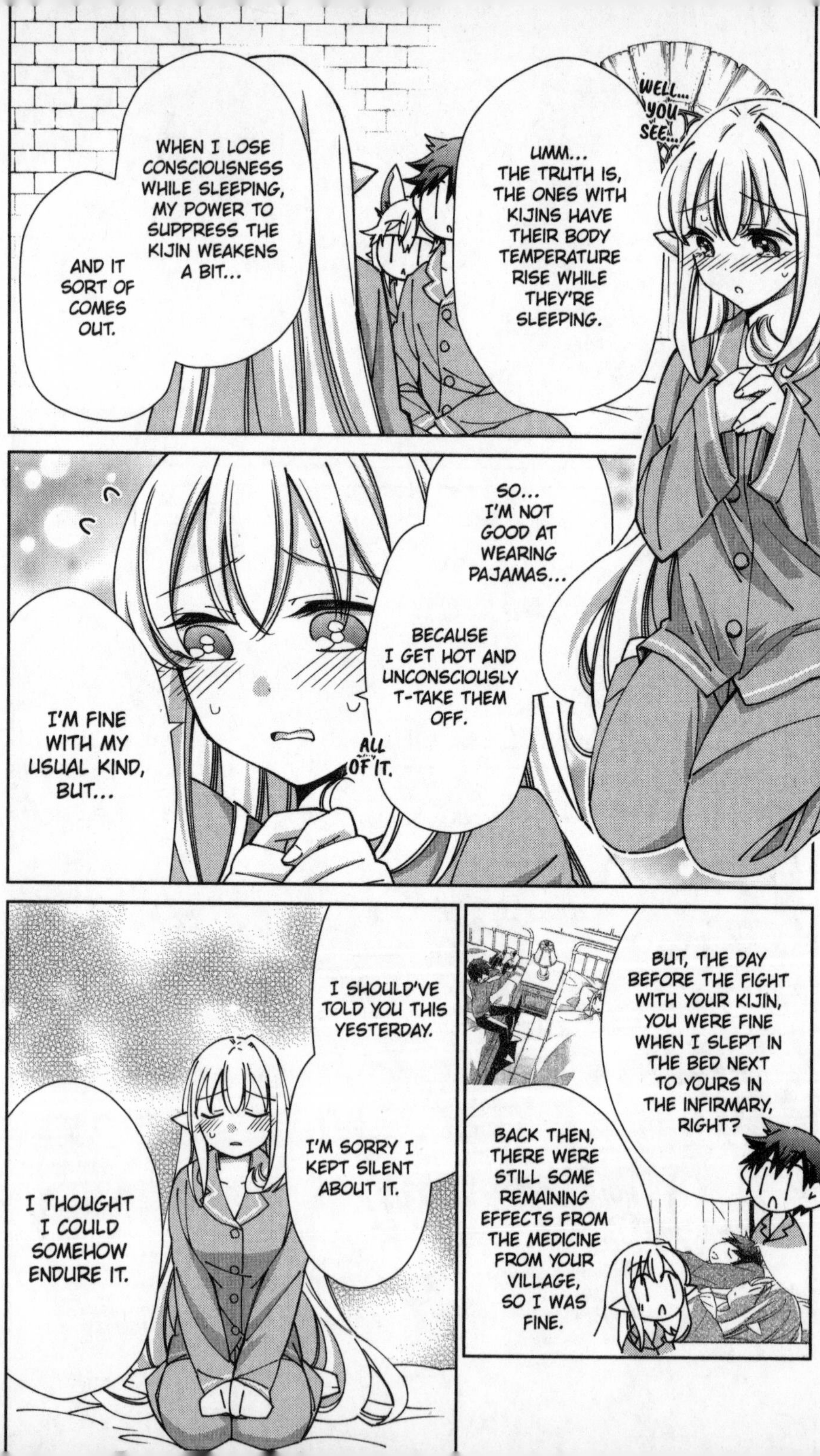
WELL... YOU SEE...
UMM... THE TRUTH IS, THE ONES WITH KIJINS HAVE THEIR BODY TEMPERATURE RISE WHILE THEY'RE SLEEPING.
WHEN I LOSE CONSCIOUSNESS WHILE SLEEPING, MY POWER TO SUPPRESS THE KIJIN WEAKENS A BIT...
AND IT SORT OF COMES OUT.
SO... I'M NOT GOOD AT WEARING PAJAMAS...
BECAUSE I GET HOT AND UNCONSCIOUSLY T-TAKE THEM OFF.
ALL OF IT.
I'M FINE WITH MY USUAL KIND, BUT...
BUT, THE DAY BEFORE THE FIGHT WITH YOUR KIJIN, YOU WERE FINE WHEN I SLEPT IN THE BED NEXT TO YOURS IN THE INFIRMARY, RIGHT?
BACK THEN, THERE WERE STILL SOME REMAINING EFFECTS FROM THE MEDICINE FROM YOUR VILLAGE, SO I WAS FINE.
I SHOULD'VE TOLD YOU THIS YESTERDAY.
I'M SORRY I KEPT SILENT ABOUT IT.
I THOUGHT I COULD SOMEHOW ENDURE IT.

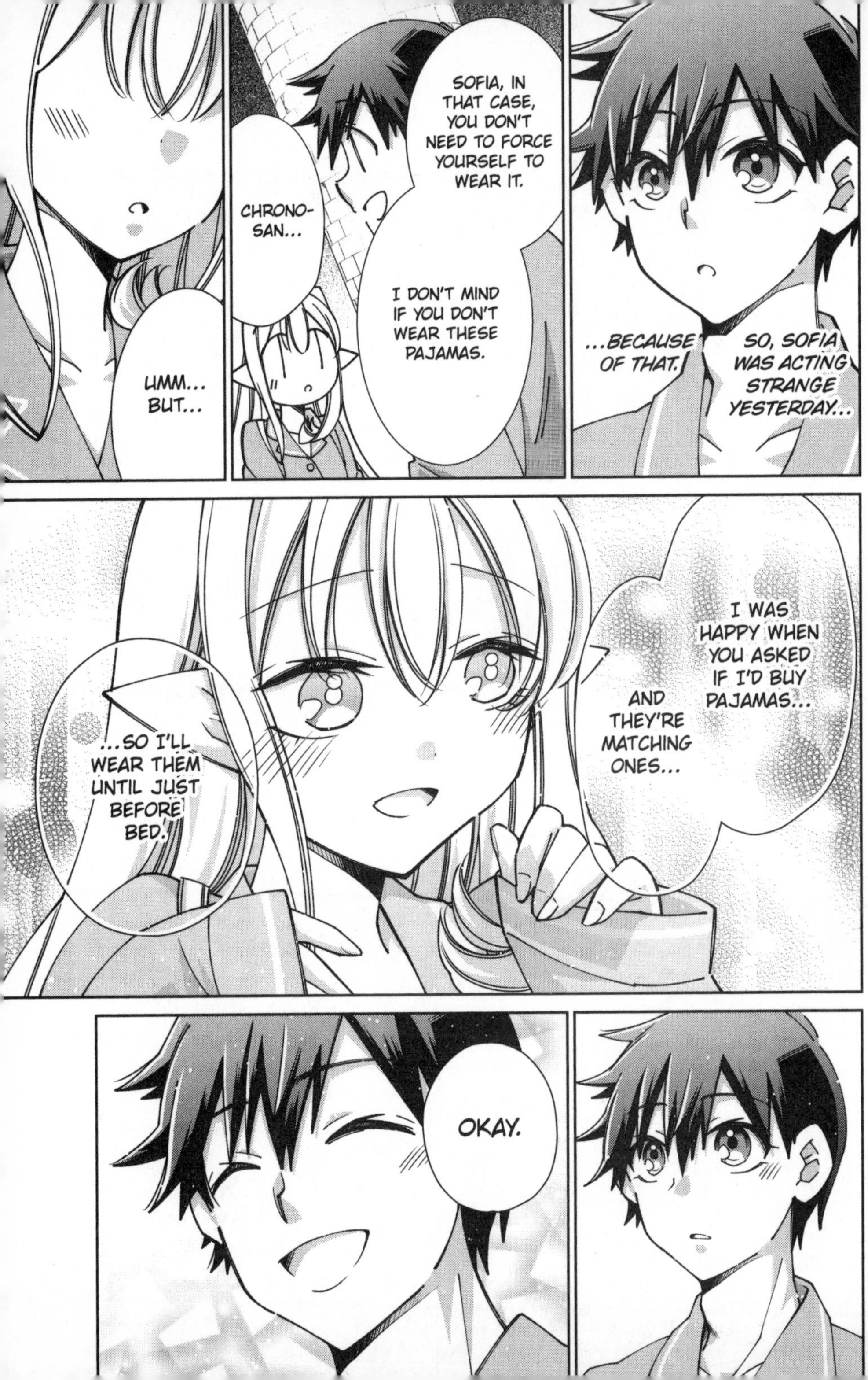
SO, SOFIA WAS ACTING STRANGE YESTERDAY...
...BECAUSE OF THAT.
SOFIA, IN THAT CASE, YOU DON'T NEED TO FORCE YOURSELF TO WEAR IT.
I DON'T MIND IF YOU DON'T WEAR THESE PAJAMAS.
CHRONO-SAN...
UMM... BUT...
I WAS HAPPY WHEN YOU ASKED IF I'D BUY PAJAMAS...
AND THEY'RE MATCHING ONES...
...SO I'LL WEAR THEM UNTIL JUST BEFORE BED.
OKAY.

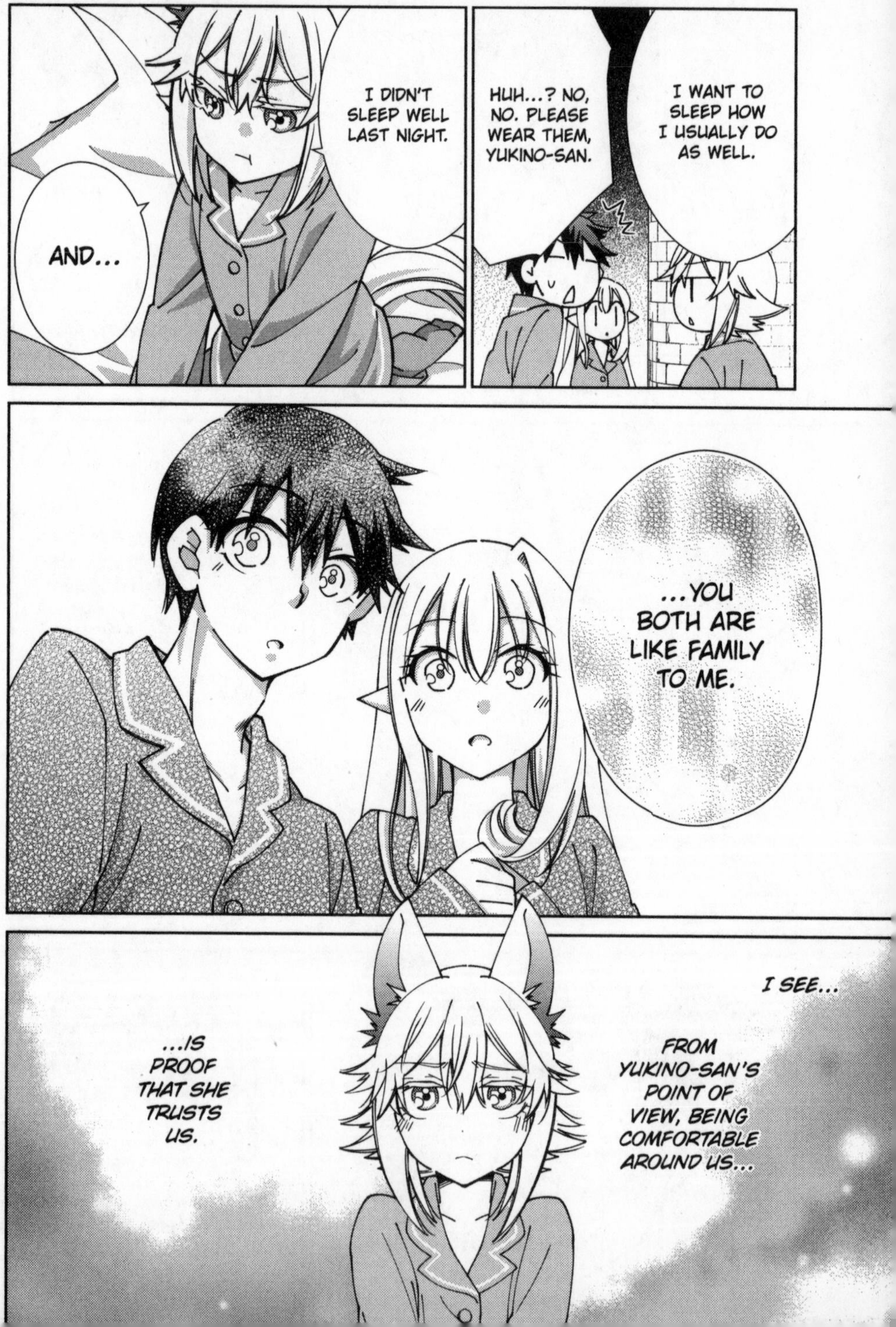
I WANT TO SLEEP HOW I USUALLY DO AS WELL.
HUH...? NO, NO. PLEASE WEAR THEM, YUKINO-SAN.
I DIDN'T SLEEP WELL LAST NIGHT.
AND...
...YOU BOTH ARE LIKE FAMILY TO ME.
I SEE...
FROM YUKINO-SAN'S POINT OF VIEW, BEING COMFORTABLE AROUND US...
...IS PROOF THAT SHE TRUSTS US.

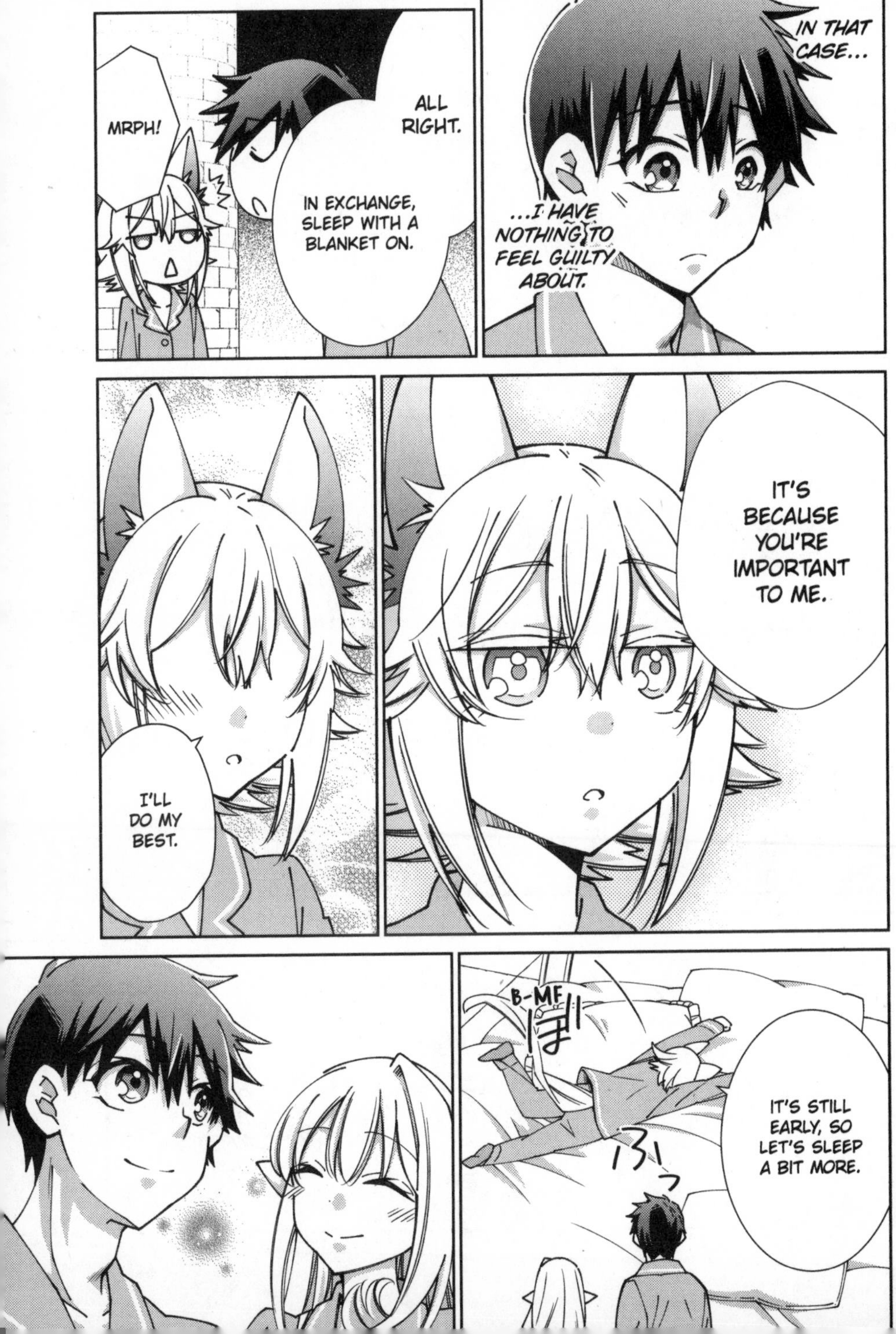
IN THAT CASE...
...I HAVE NOTHING TO FEEL GUILTY ABOUT.
ALL RIGHT.
IN EXCHANGE, SLEEP WITH A BLANKET ON.
MRPH!
IT'S BECAUSE YOU'RE IMPORTANT TO ME.
I'LL DO MY BEST.
B-MF
IT'S STILL EARLY, SO LET'S SLEEP A BIT MORE.

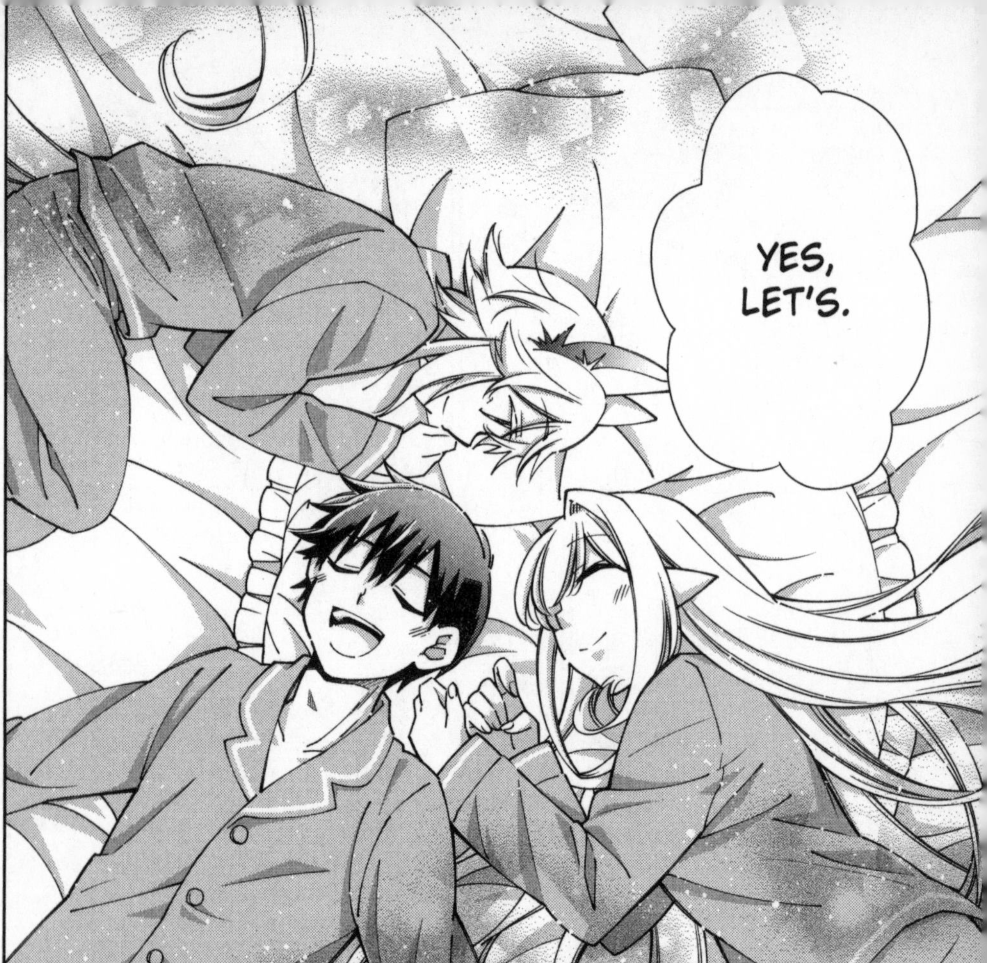
YES, LET'S.

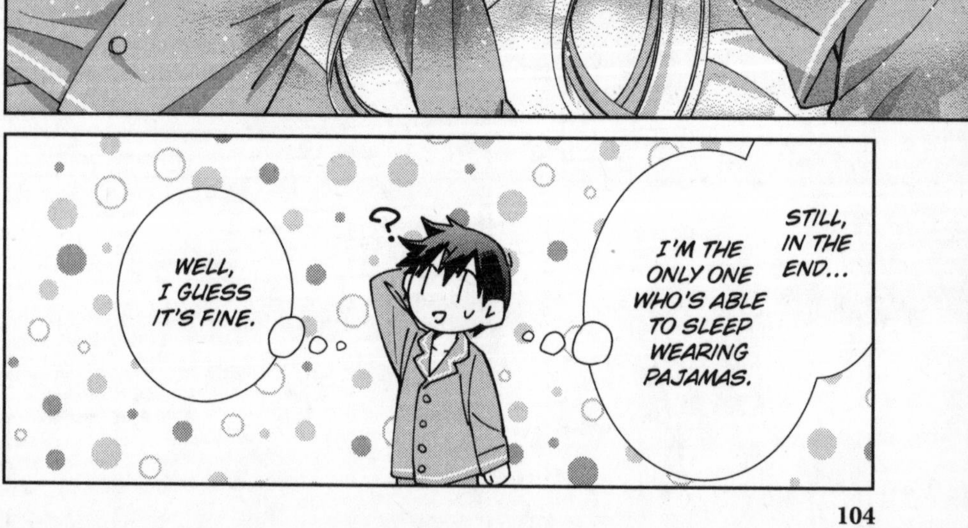
STILL, IN THE END...
I'M THE ONLY ONE WHO'S ABLE TO SLEEP WEARING PAJAMAS.
WELL, I GUESS IT'S FINE.

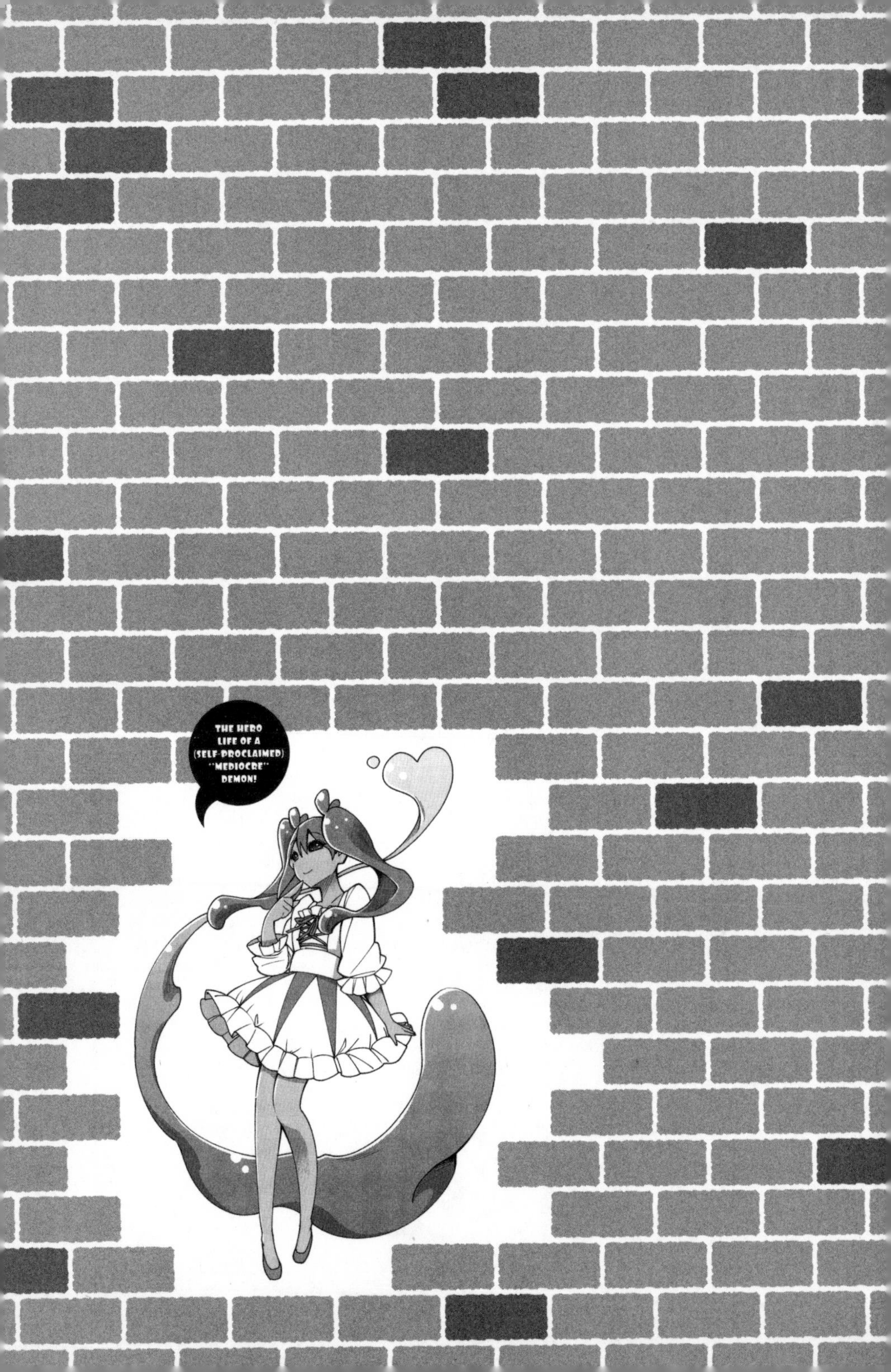
THE HERO LIFE OF A (SELF-PROCLAIMED) "MEDIOCRE" DEMON!

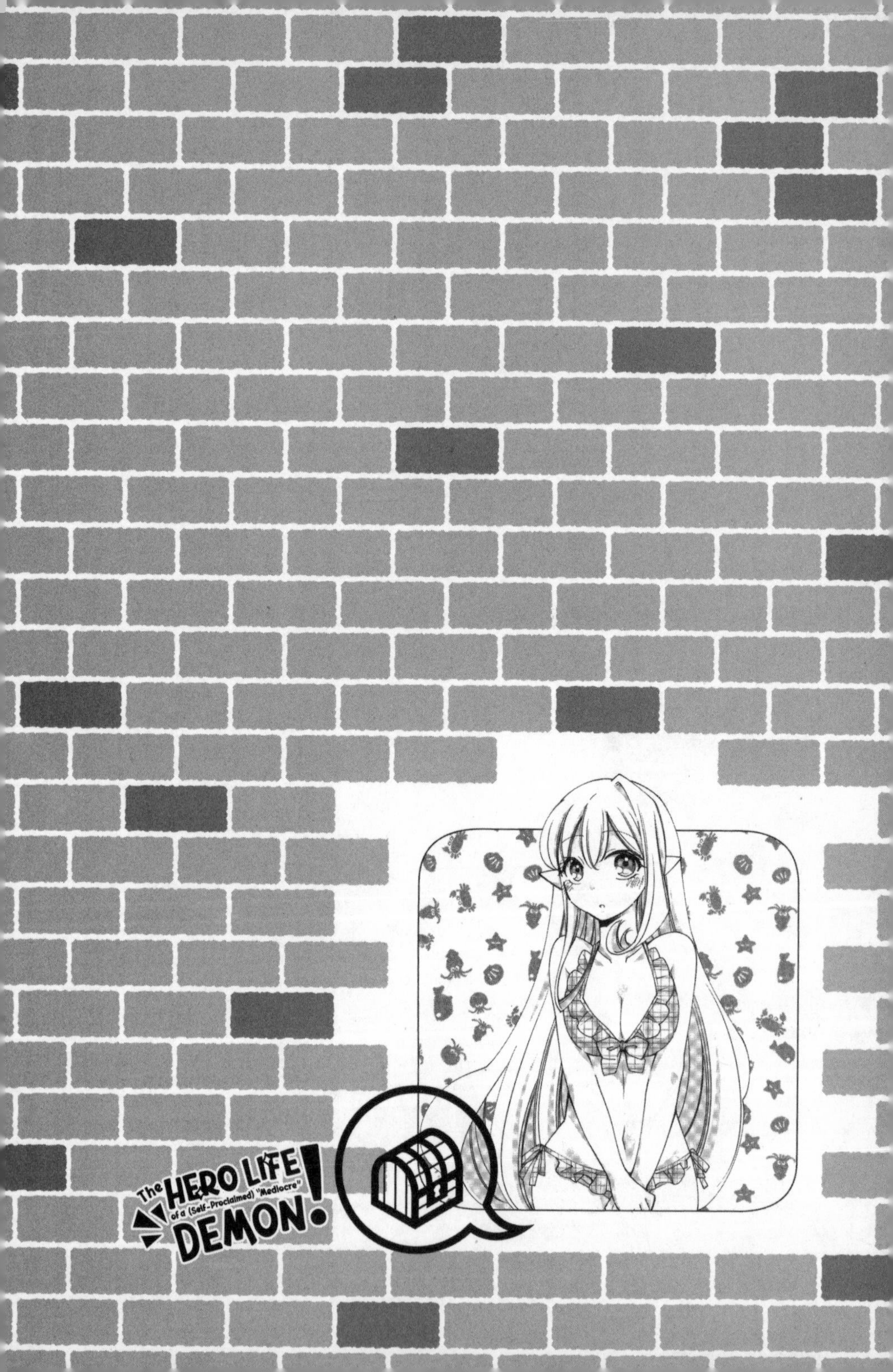
The HERO LIFE of a (Self-Proclaimed) "Mediocre" DEMON!

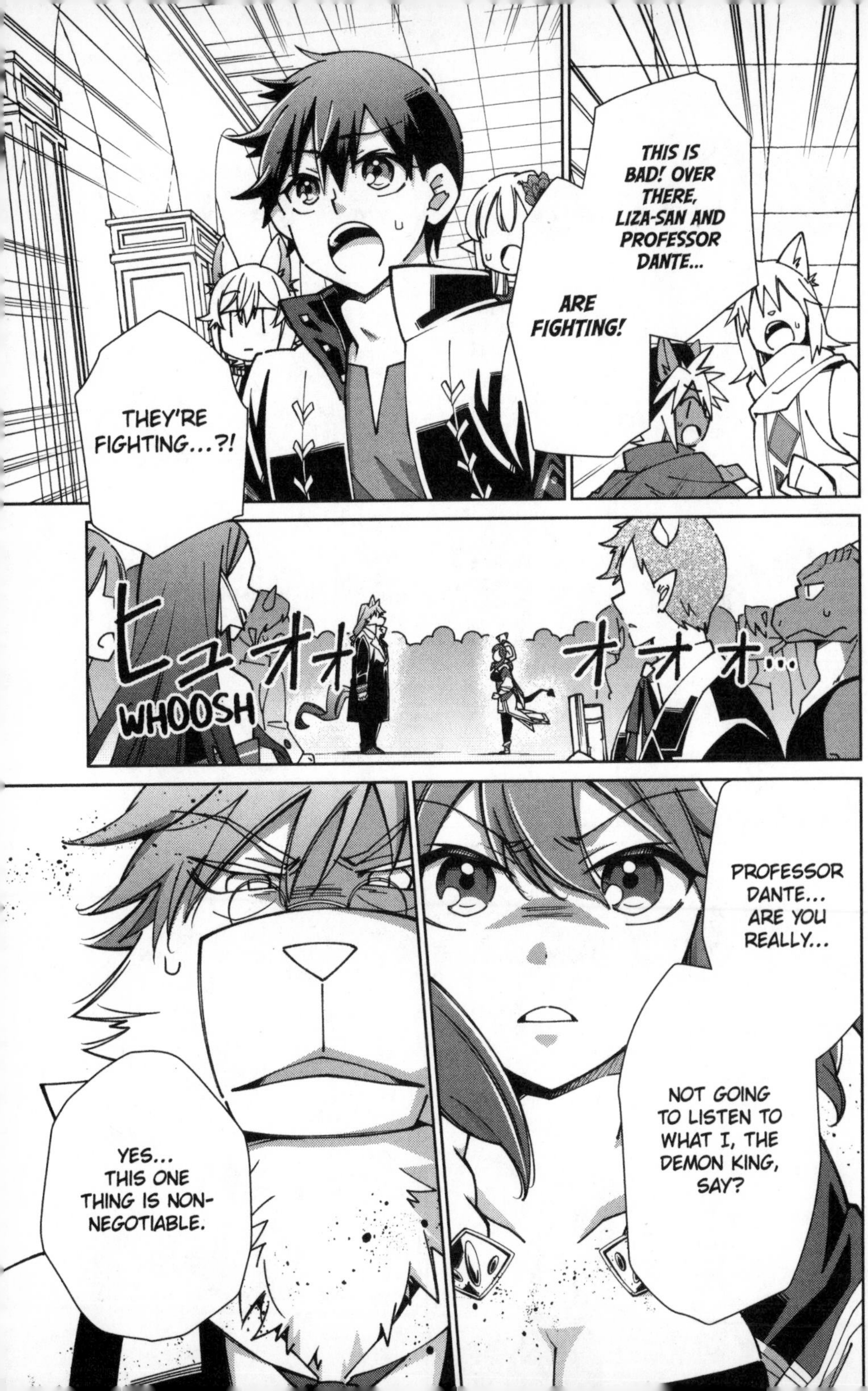
THIS IS BAD! OVER THERE, LIZA-SAN AND PROFESSOR DANTE...
ARE FIGHTING!
THEY'RE FIGHTING...?!
ヒュオオ オオオ…
WHOOSH
PROFESSOR DANTE... ARE YOU REALLY...
NOT GOING TO LISTEN TO WHAT I, THE DEMON KING, SAY?
YES... THIS ONE THING IS NON-NEGOTIABLE.

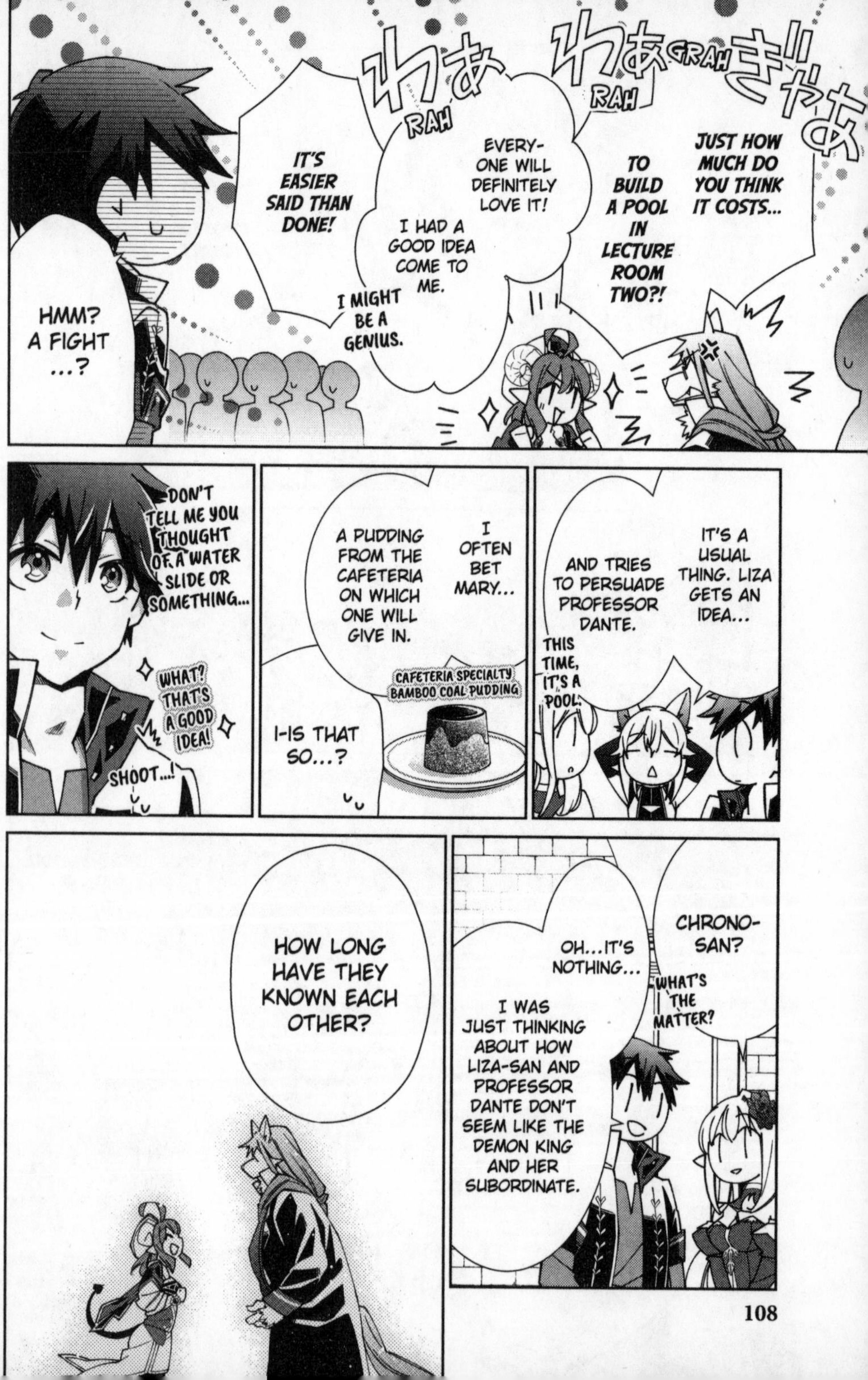
わあ わあ きゃあ
RAH
RAH
GRAH
JUST HOW MUCH DO YOU THINK IT COSTS...
TO BUILD A POOL IN LECTURE ROOM TWO?!
EVERY-ONE WILL DEFINITELY LOVE IT!
I HAD A GOOD IDEA COME TO ME.
I MIGHT BE A GENIUS.
IT'S EASIER SAID THAN DONE!
HMM? A FIGHT ...?
IT'S A USUAL THING. LIZA GETS AN IDEA...
AND TRIES TO PERSUADE PROFESSOR DANTE.
THIS TIME, IT'S A POOL.
I OFTEN BET MARY...
A PUDDING FROM THE CAFETERIA ON WHICH ONE WILL GIVE IN.
CAFETERIA SPECIALTY BAMBOO COAL PUDDING
I-IS THAT SO...?
DON'T TELL ME YOU THOUGHT OF A WATER SLIDE OR SOMETHING...
WHAT? THAT'S A GOOD IDEA!
SHOOT...!
CHRONO-SAN?
WHAT'S THE MATTER?
OH...IT'S NOTHING...
I WAS JUST THINKING ABOUT HOW LIZA-SAN AND PROFESSOR DANTE DON'T SEEM LIKE THE DEMON KING AND HER SUBORDINATE.
HOW LONG HAVE THEY KNOWN EACH OTHER?

# CHAPTER 29 LIZA SPEAKS WITH DANTE

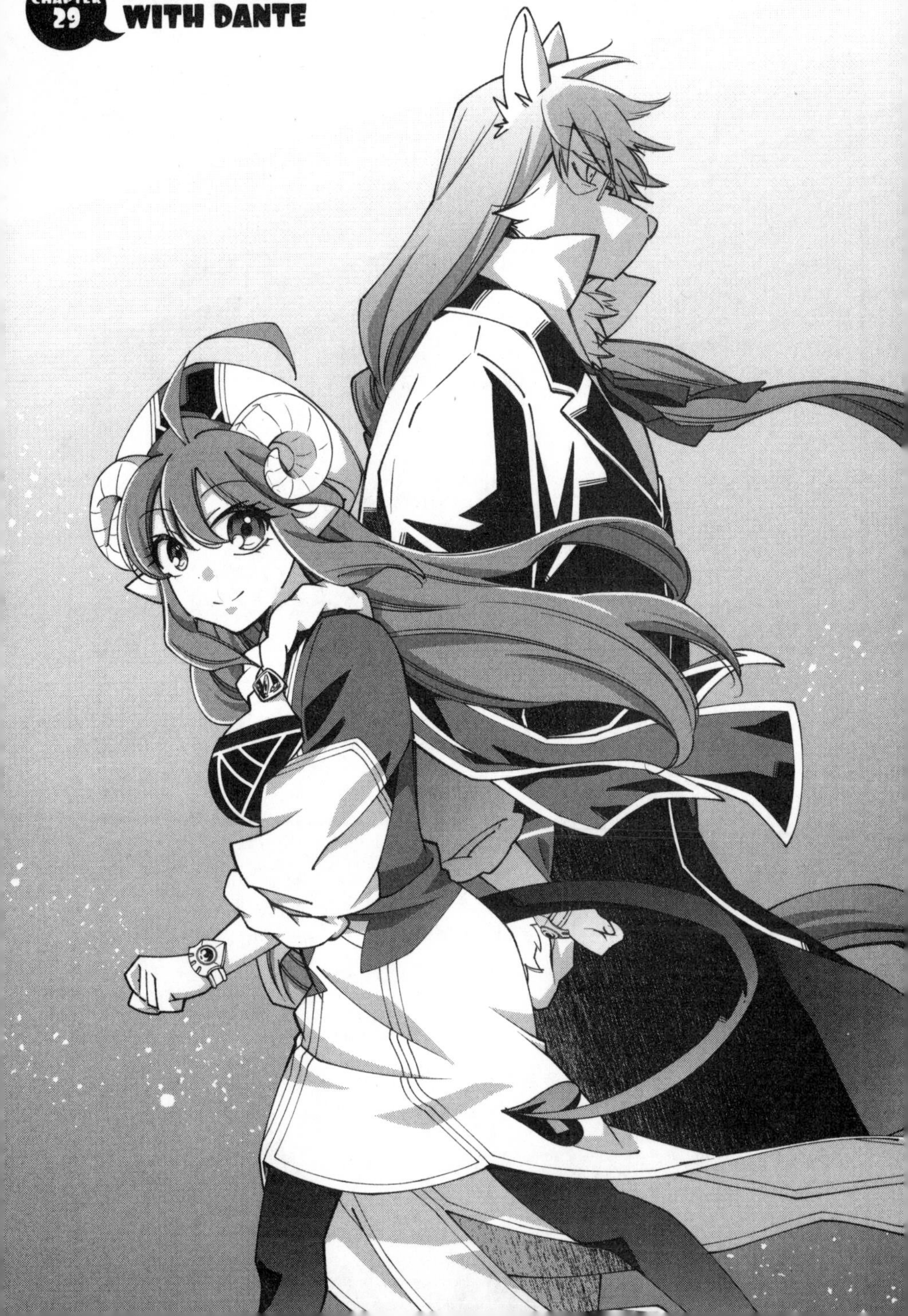

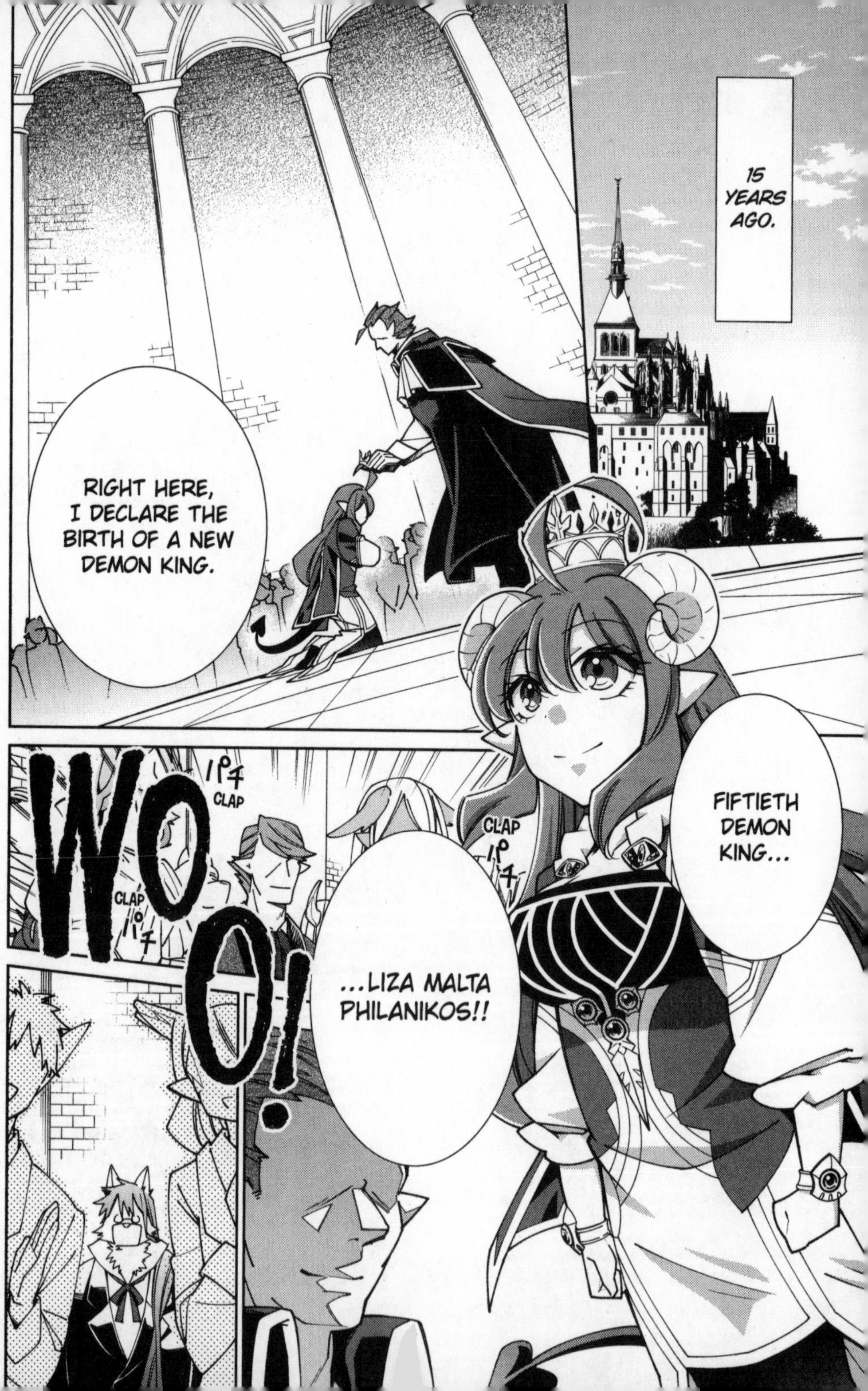
15 YEARS AGO.
RIGHT HERE, I DECLARE THE BIRTH OF A NEW DEMON KING.
FIFTIETH DEMON KING...
CLAP パチ
...LIZA MALTA PHILANIKOS!!
パチ CLAP
WOO!
CLAP パチ

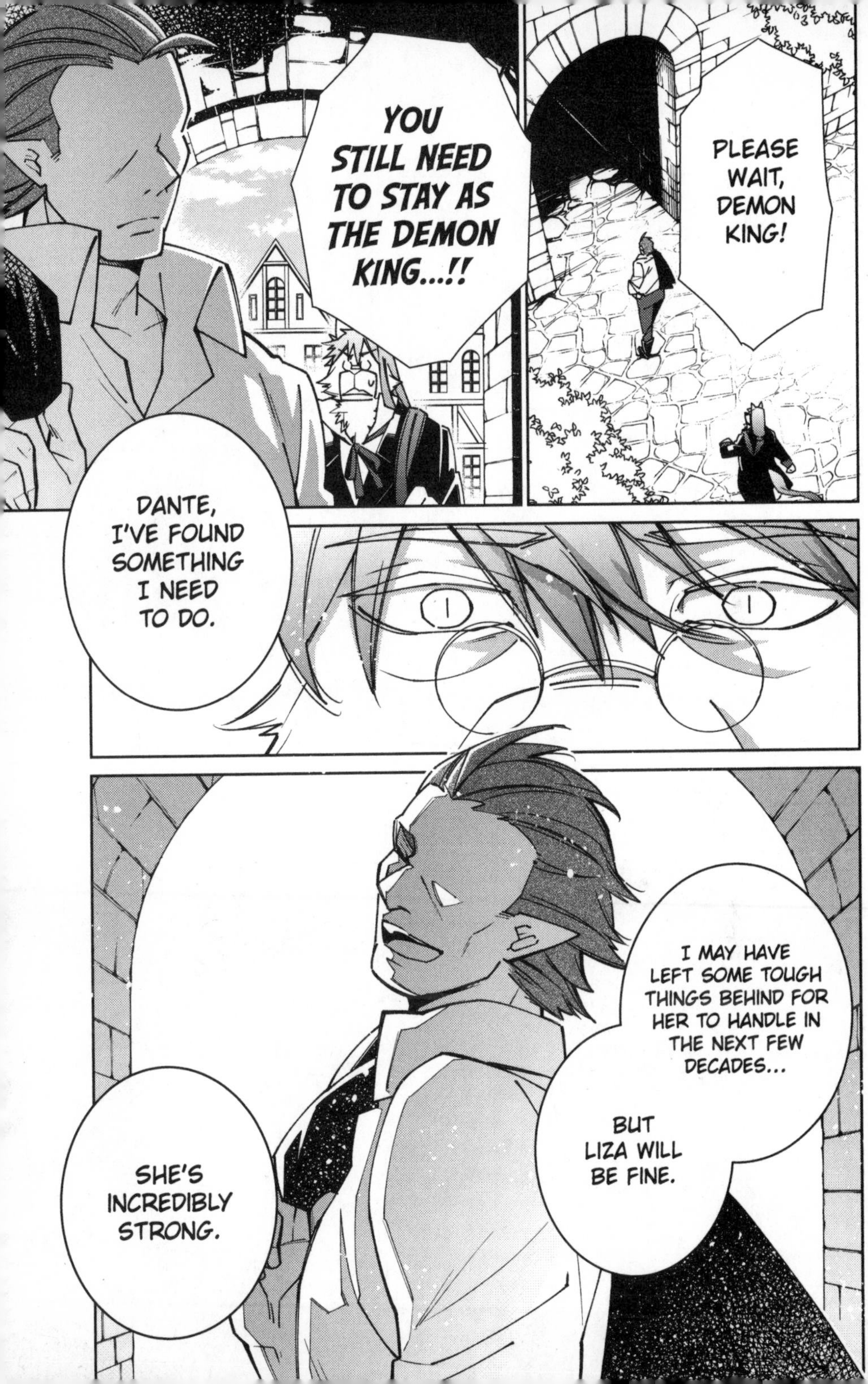
PLEASE WAIT, DEMON KING!
YOU STILL NEED TO STAY AS THE DEMON KING...!!
DANTE, I'VE FOUND SOMETHING I NEED TO DO.
I MAY HAVE LEFT SOME TOUGH THINGS BEHIND FOR HER TO HANDLE IN THE NEXT FEW DECADES...
BUT LIZA WILL BE FINE.
SHE'S INCREDIBLY STRONG.

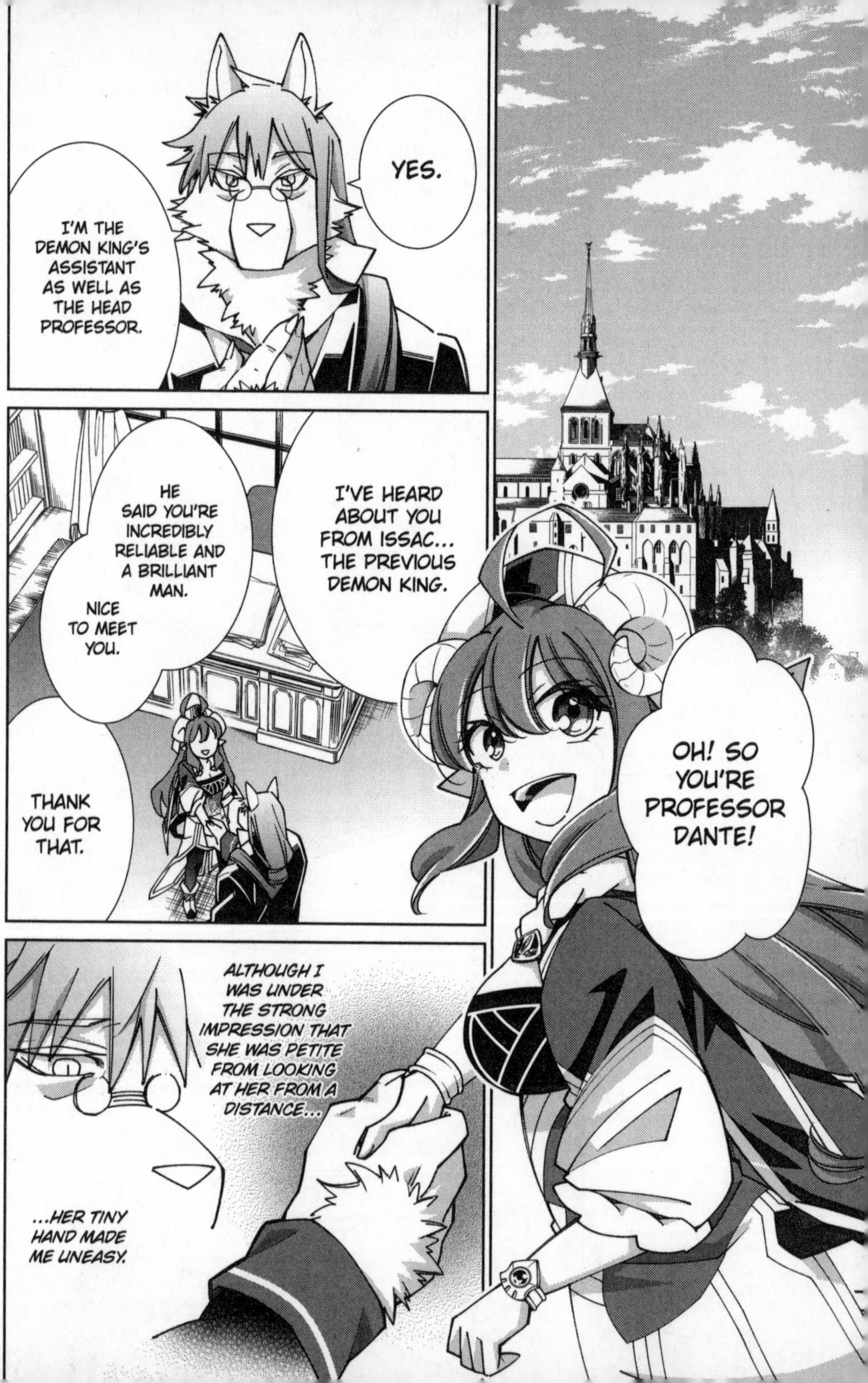

OH! SO YOU'RE PROFESSOR DANTE!
YES.
I'M THE DEMON KING'S ASSISTANT AS WELL AS THE HEAD PROFESSOR.
I'VE HEARD ABOUT YOU FROM ISSAC... THE PREVIOUS DEMON KING.
HE SAID YOU'RE INCREDIBLY RELIABLE AND A BRILLIANT MAN.
NICE TO MEET YOU.
THANK YOU FOR THAT.
ALTHOUGH I WAS UNDER THE STRONG IMPRESSION THAT SHE WAS PETITE FROM LOOKING AT HER FROM A DISTANCE...
...HER TINY HAND MADE ME UNEASY.

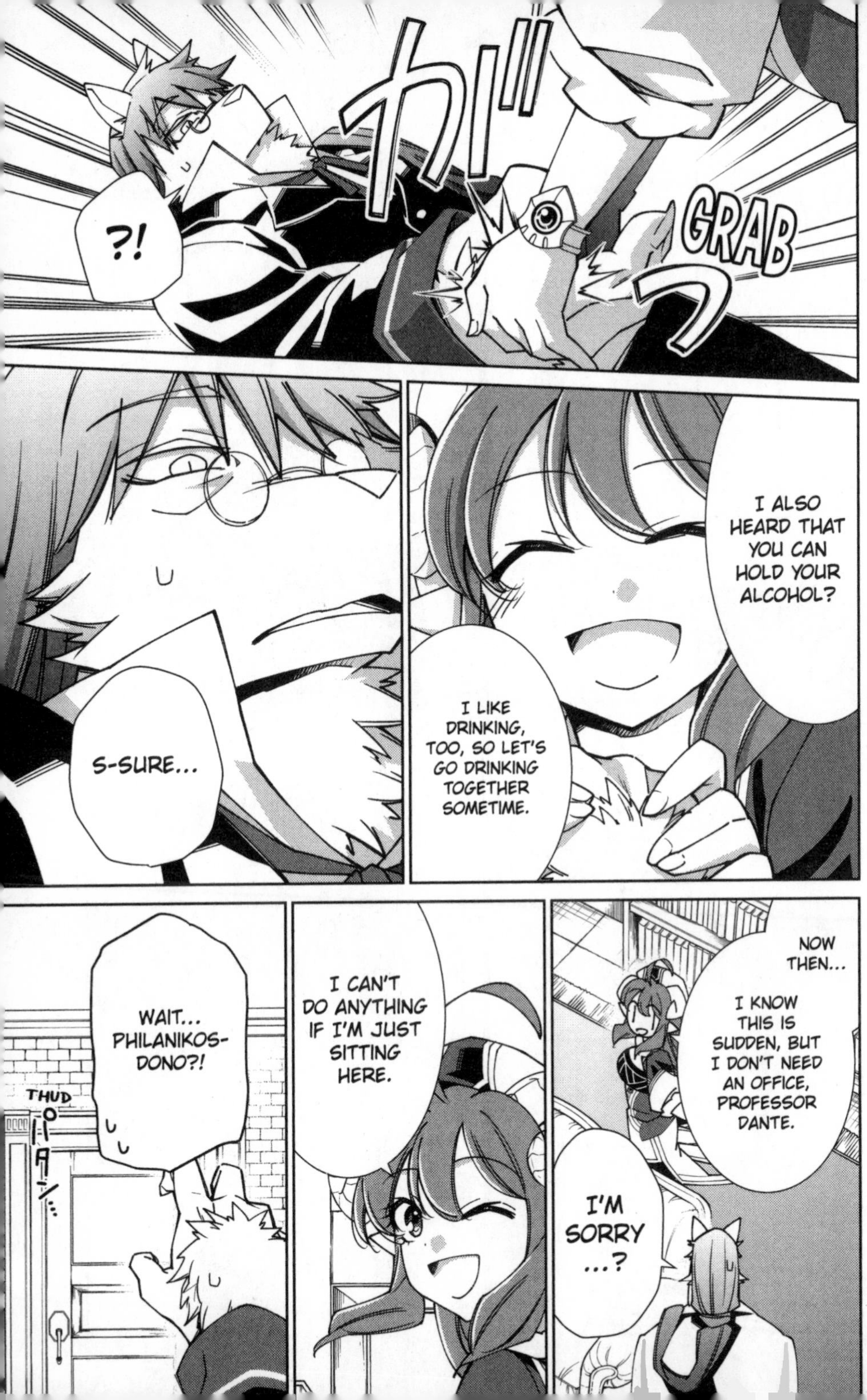
GRAB
?!
I ALSO HEARD THAT YOU CAN HOLD YOUR ALCOHOL?
I LIKE DRINKING, TOO, SO LET'S GO DRINKING TOGETHER SOMETIME.
S-SURE...
NOW THEN...
I KNOW THIS IS SUDDEN, BUT I DON'T NEED AN OFFICE, PROFESSOR DANTE.
I'M SORRY ...?
I CAN'T DO ANYTHING IF I'M JUST SITTING HERE.
WAIT... PHILANIKOS-DONO?!
THUD

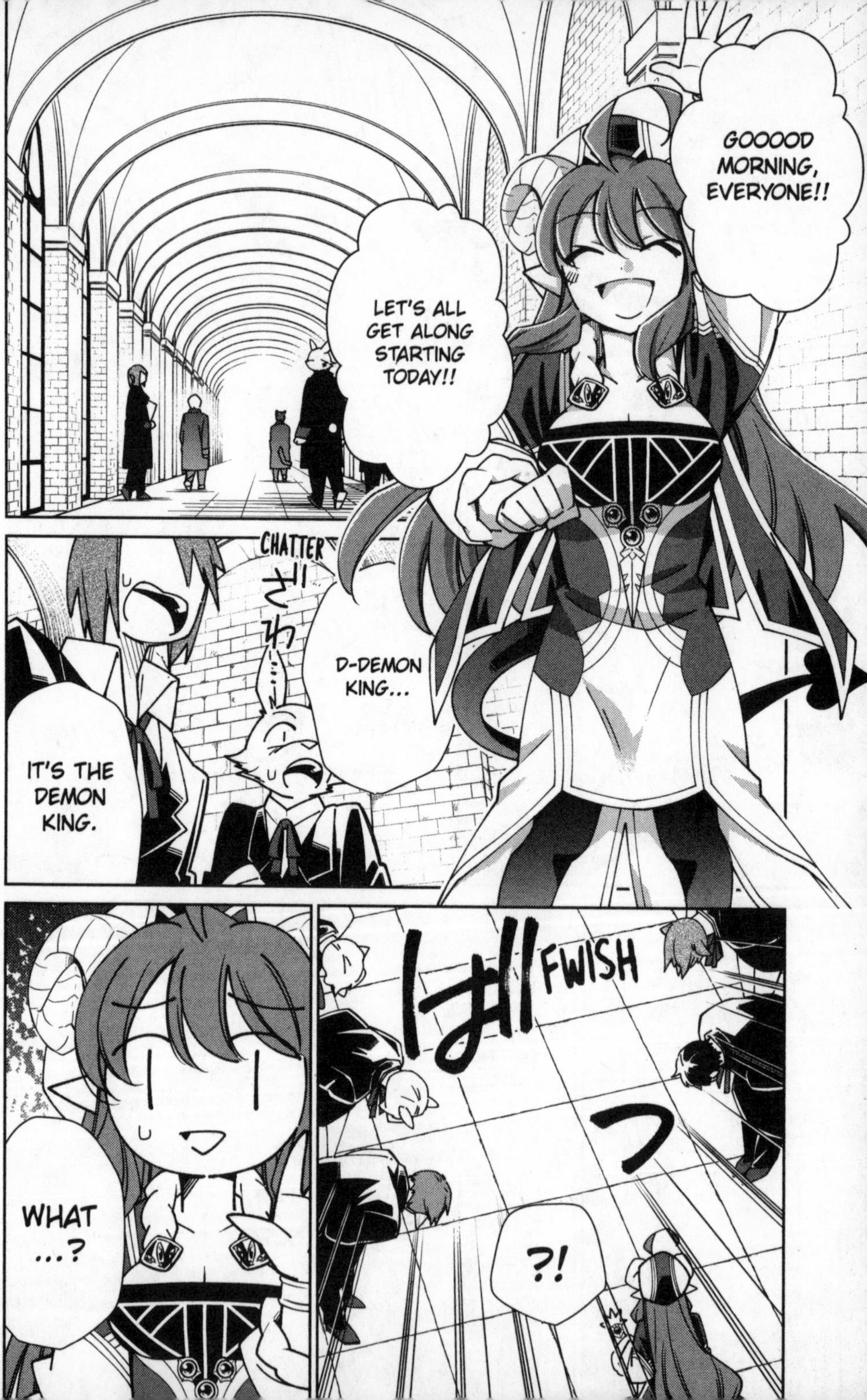
GOOOOD MORNING, EVERYONE!!
LET'S ALL GET ALONG STARTING TODAY!!
CHATTER
ざわ…
D-DEMON KING...
IT'S THE DEMON KING.
はっ
FWISH
?!
WHAT ...?

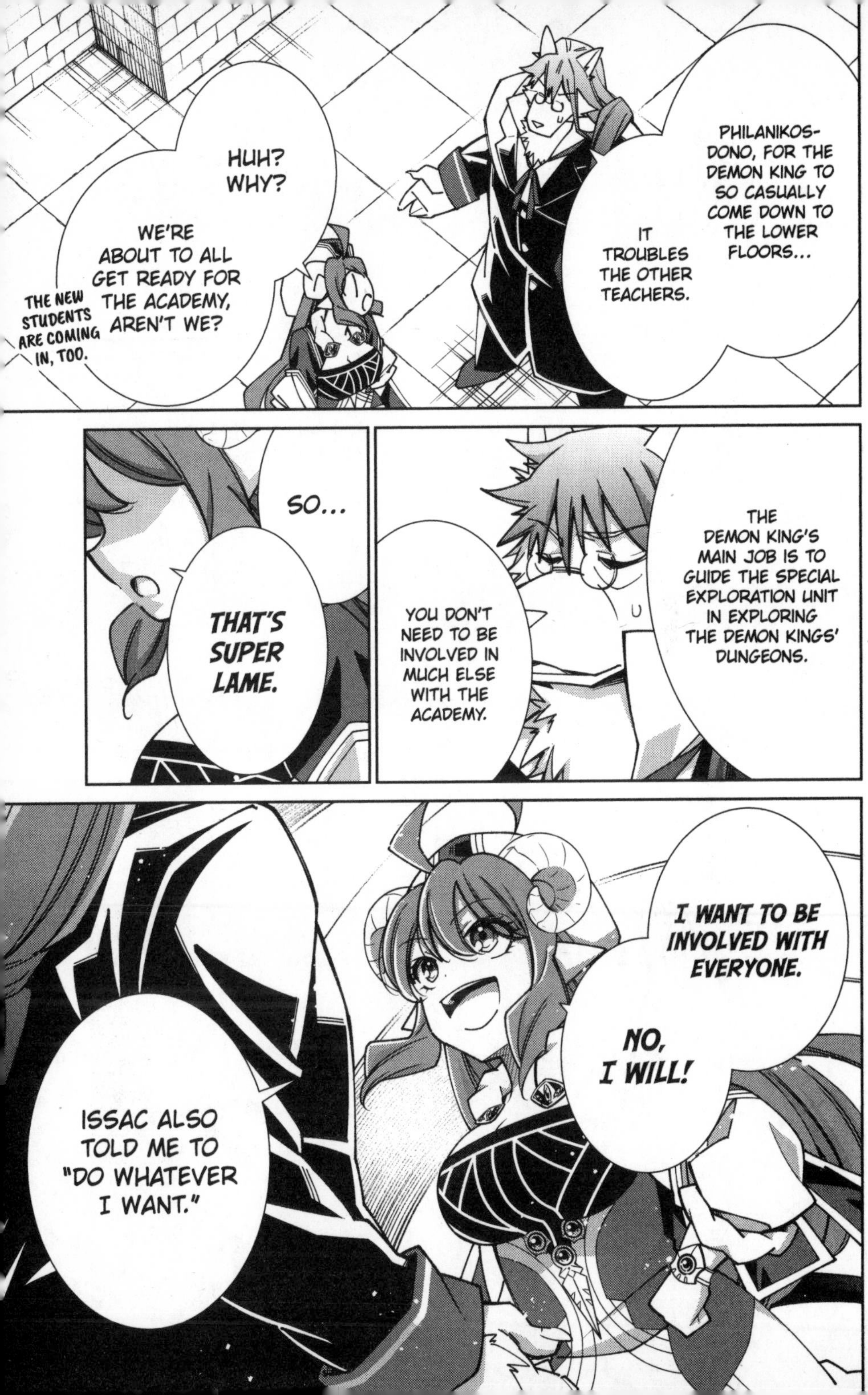
PHILANIKOS-DONO, FOR THE DEMON KING TO SO CASUALLY COME DOWN TO THE LOWER FLOORS...
IT TROUBLES THE OTHER TEACHERS.
HUH? WHY?
WE'RE ABOUT TO ALL GET READY FOR THE ACADEMY, AREN'T WE?
THE NEW STUDENTS ARE COMING IN, TOO.
THE DEMON KING'S MAIN JOB IS TO GUIDE THE SPECIAL EXPLORATION UNIT IN EXPLORING THE DEMON KINGS' DUNGEONS.
YOU DON'T NEED TO BE INVOLVED IN MUCH ELSE WITH THE ACADEMY.
SO...
THAT'S SUPER LAME.
I WANT TO BE INVOLVED WITH EVERYONE.
NO, I WILL!
ISSAC ALSO TOLD ME TO "DO WHATEVER I WANT."

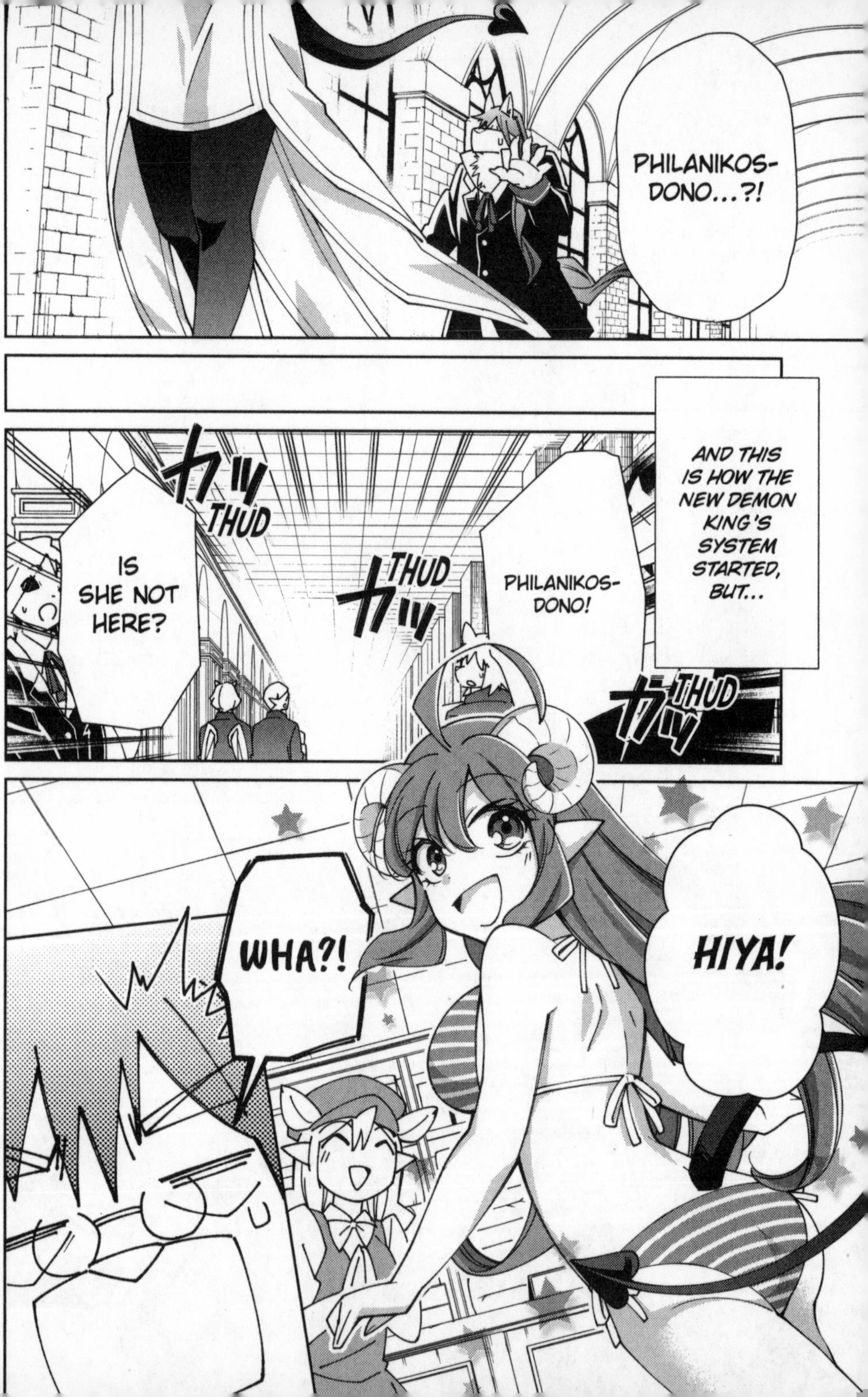
PHILANIKOS-DONO...?!
AND THIS IS HOW THE NEW DEMON KING'S SYSTEM STARTED, BUT...
PHILANIKOS-DONO!
カッ THUD
カッ THUD
カッ THUD
IS SHE NOT HERE?
HIYA!
WHA?!

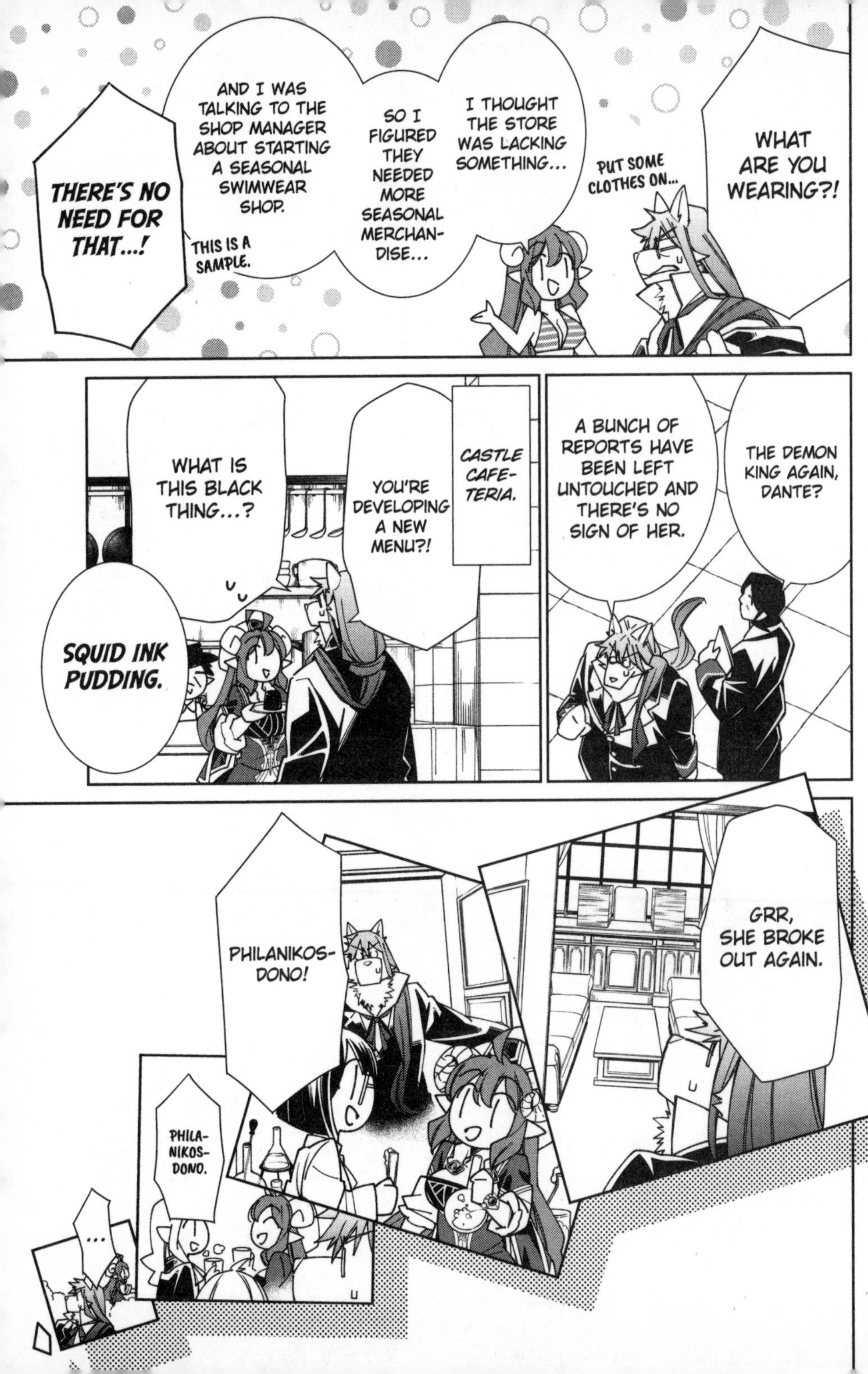
WHAT ARE YOU WEARING?!
PUT SOME CLOTHES ON...
I THOUGHT THE STORE WAS LACKING SOMETHING...
SO I FIGURED THEY NEEDED MORE SEASONAL MERCHANDISE...
AND I WAS TALKING TO THE SHOP MANAGER ABOUT STARTING A SEASONAL SWIMWEAR SHOP.
THIS IS A SAMPLE.
THERE'S NO NEED FOR THAT...!
THE DEMON KING AGAIN, DANTE?
A BUNCH OF REPORTS HAVE BEEN LEFT UNTOUCHED AND THERE'S NO SIGN OF HER.
CASTLE CAFETERIA.
YOU'RE DEVELOPING A NEW MENU?!
WHAT IS THIS BLACK THING...?
SQUID INK PUDDING.
GRR, SHE BROKE OUT AGAIN.
PHILANIKOS-DONO!
PHILANIKOS-DONO.
...

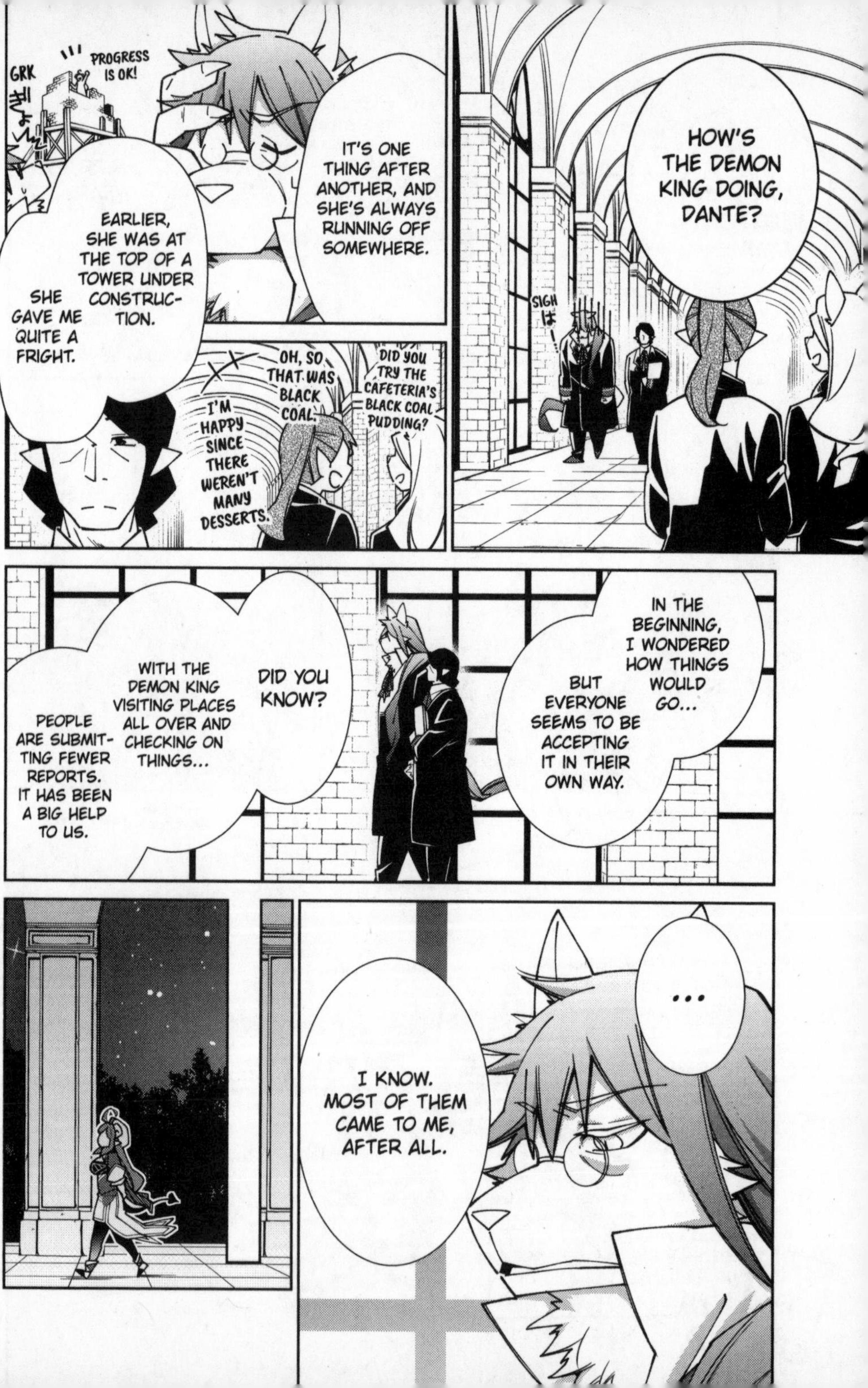
HOW'S THE DEMON KING DOING, DANTE?
SIGH
IT'S ONE THING AFTER ANOTHER, AND SHE'S ALWAYS RUNNING OFF SOMEWHERE.
PROGRESS IS OK!
GRK
EARLIER, SHE WAS AT THE TOP OF A TOWER UNDER CONSTRUCTION.
SHE GAVE ME QUITE A FRIGHT.
DID YOU TRY THE CAFETERIA'S BLACK COAL PUDDING?
OH, SO THAT WAS BLACK COAL.
I'M HAPPY SINCE THERE WEREN'T MANY DESSERTS.
IN THE BEGINNING, I WONDERED HOW THINGS WOULD GO...
BUT EVERYONE SEEMS TO BE ACCEPTING IT IN THEIR OWN WAY.
DID YOU KNOW?
WITH THE DEMON KING VISITING PLACES ALL OVER AND CHECKING ON THINGS...
PEOPLE ARE SUBMITTING FEWER REPORTS. IT HAS BEEN A BIG HELP TO US.
...
I KNOW. MOST OF THEM CAME TO ME, AFTER ALL.

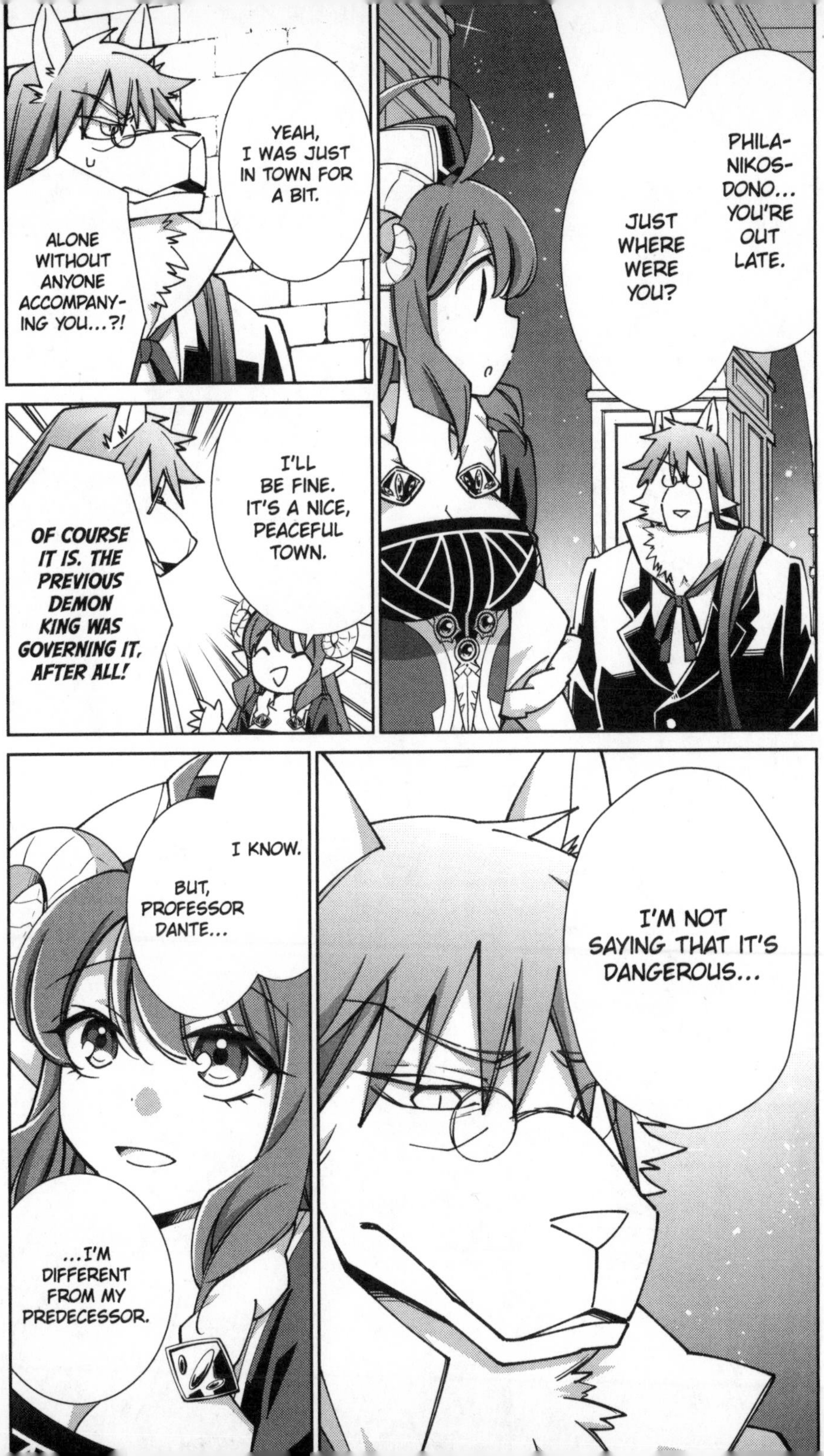
PHILA-NIKOS-DONO... YOU'RE OUT LATE.
JUST WHERE WERE YOU?
YEAH, I WAS JUST IN TOWN FOR A BIT.
ALONE WITHOUT ANYONE ACCOMPANY-ING YOU...?!
I'LL BE FINE. IT'S A NICE, PEACEFUL TOWN.
OF COURSE IT IS. THE PREVIOUS DEMON KING WAS GOVERNING IT, AFTER ALL!
I'M NOT SAYING THAT IT'S DANGEROUS...
I KNOW.
BUT, PROFESSOR DANTE...
...I'M DIFFERENT FROM MY PREDECESSOR.

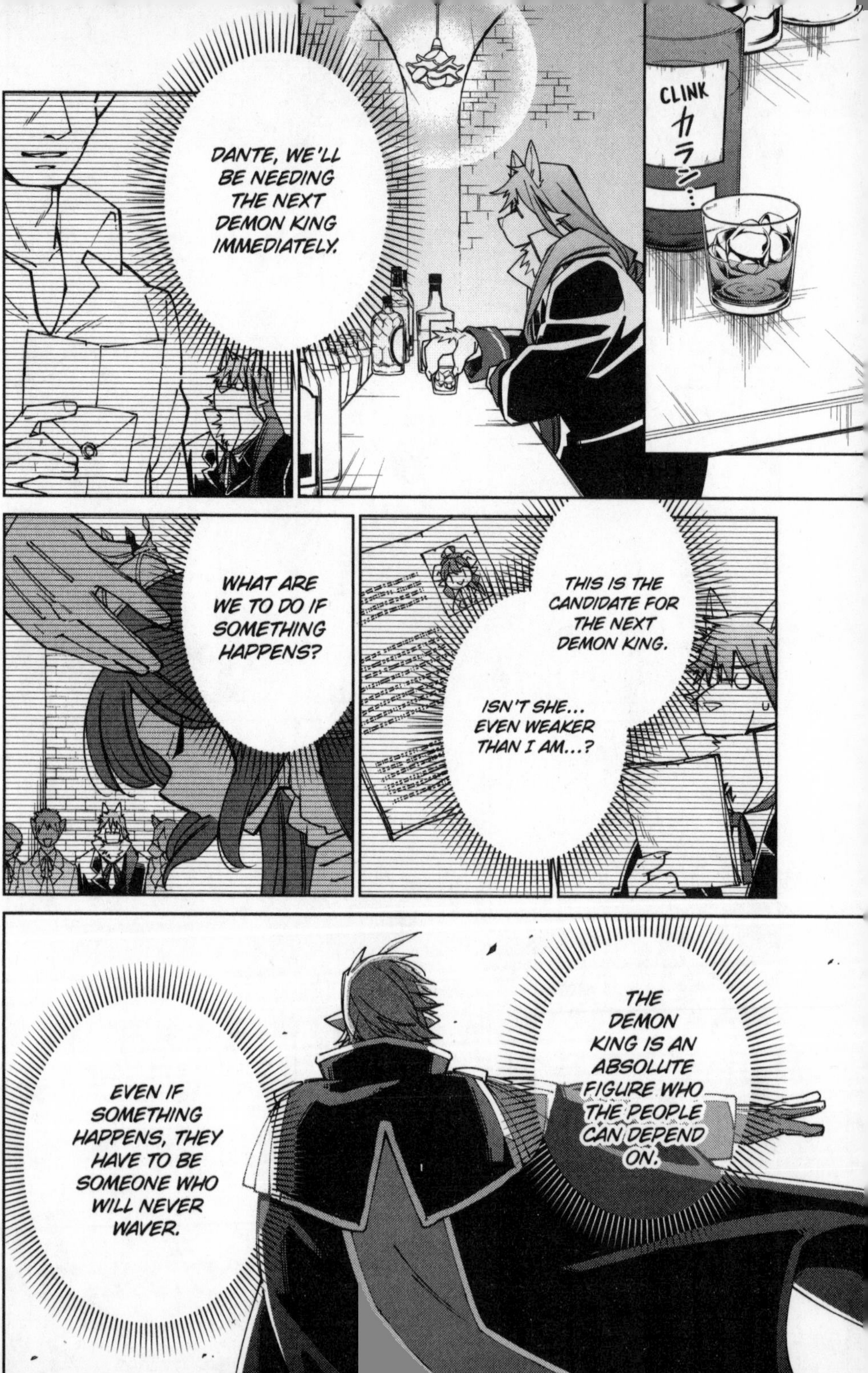

CLINK
カラン…
DANTE, WE'LL BE NEEDING THE NEXT DEMON KING IMMEDIATELY.
THIS IS THE CANDIDATE FOR THE NEXT DEMON KING.
ISN'T SHE... EVEN WEAKER THAN I AM...?
WHAT ARE WE TO DO IF SOMETHING HAPPENS?
THE DEMON KING IS AN ABSOLUTE FIGURE WHO THE PEOPLE CAN DEPEND ON.
EVEN IF SOMETHING HAPPENS, THEY HAVE TO BE SOMEONE WHO WILL NEVER WAVER.

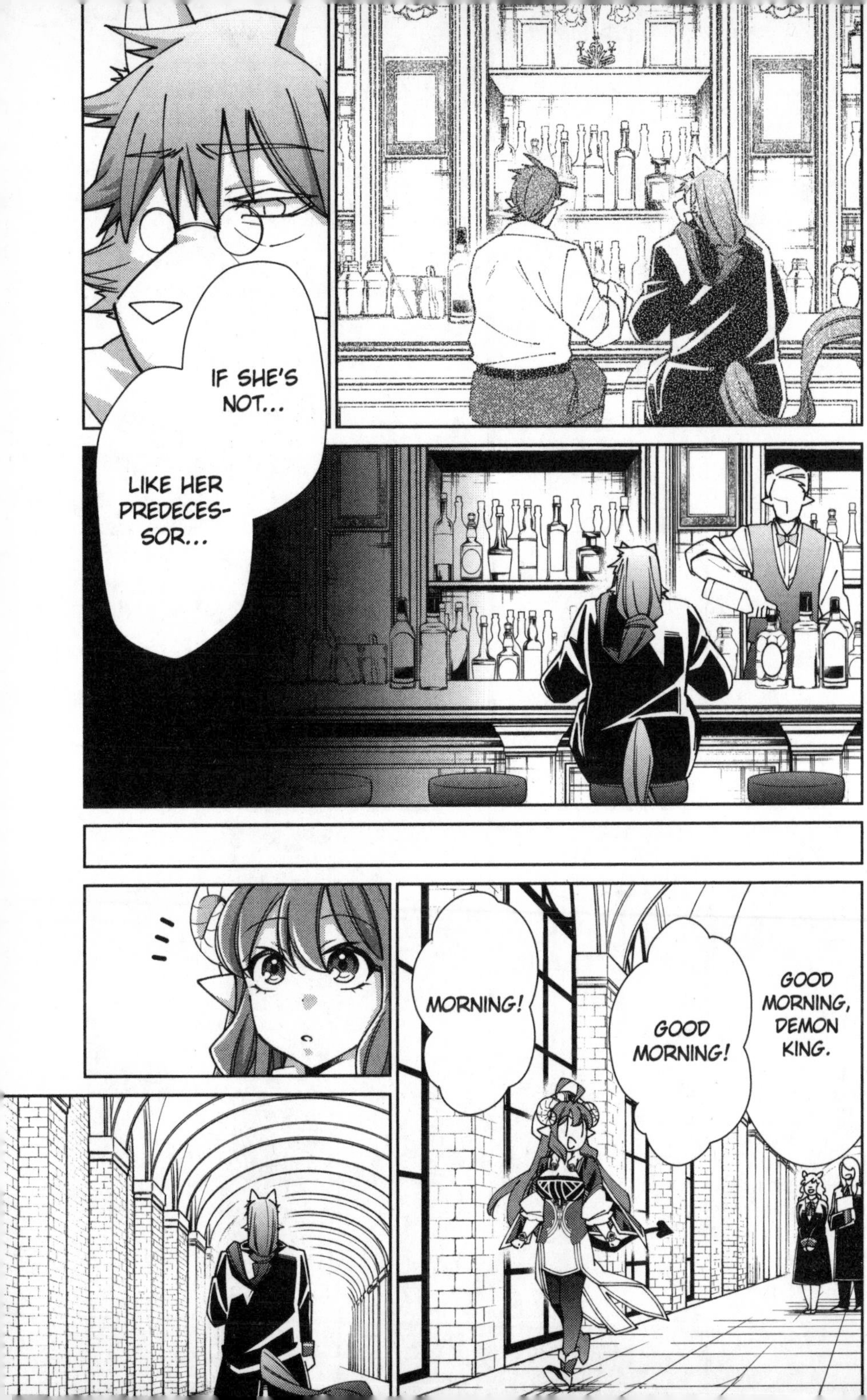
IF SHE'S NOT...
LIKE HER PREDECES-SOR...
GOOD MORNING, DEMON KING.
GOOD MORNING!
MORNING!

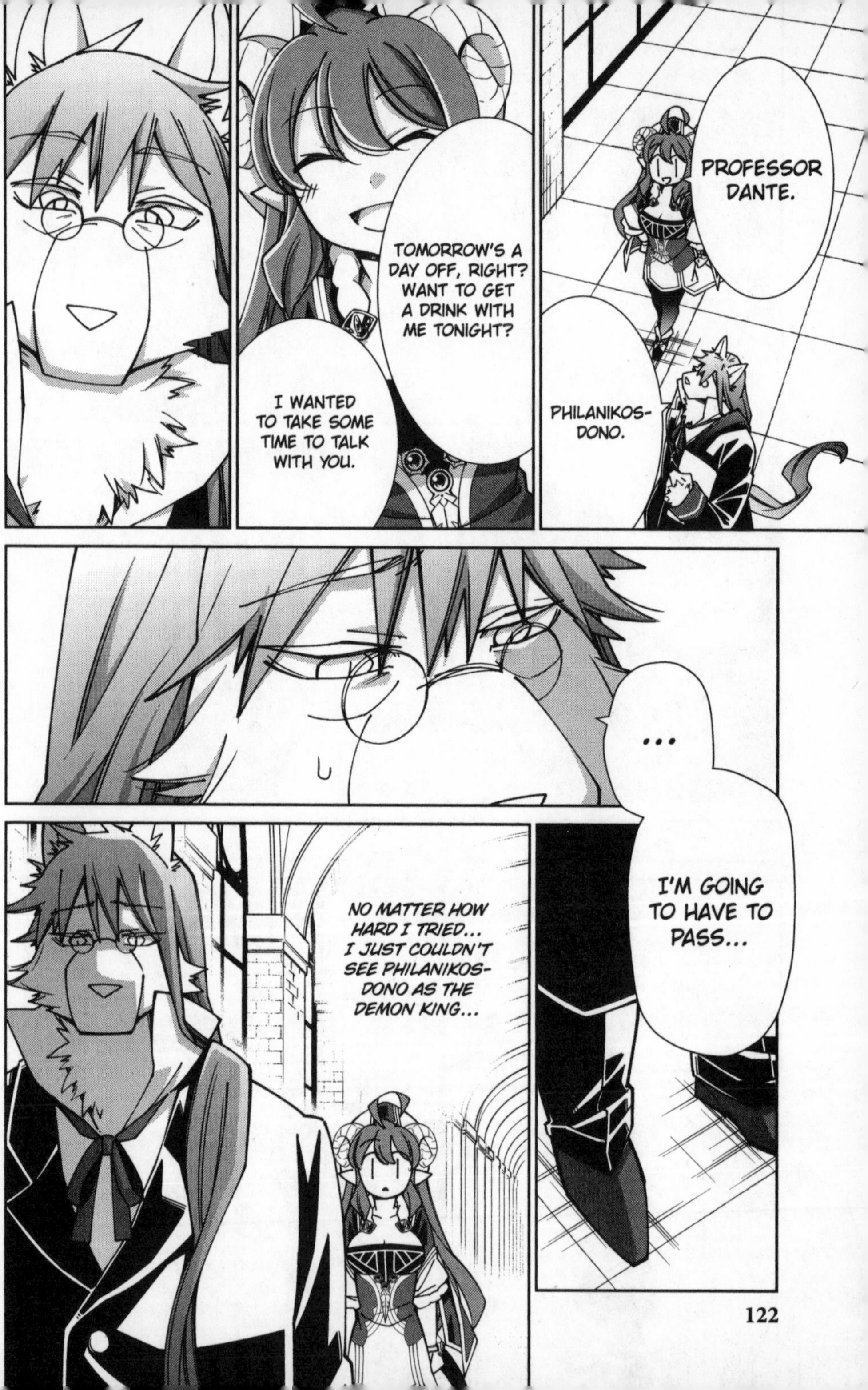
PROFESSOR DANTE.
PHILANIKOS-DONO.
TOMORROW'S A DAY OFF, RIGHT? WANT TO GET A DRINK WITH ME TONIGHT?
I WANTED TO TAKE SOME TIME TO TALK WITH YOU.
...
I'M GOING TO HAVE TO PASS...
NO MATTER HOW HARD I TRIED... I JUST COULDN'T SEE PHILANIKOS-DONO AS THE DEMON KING...

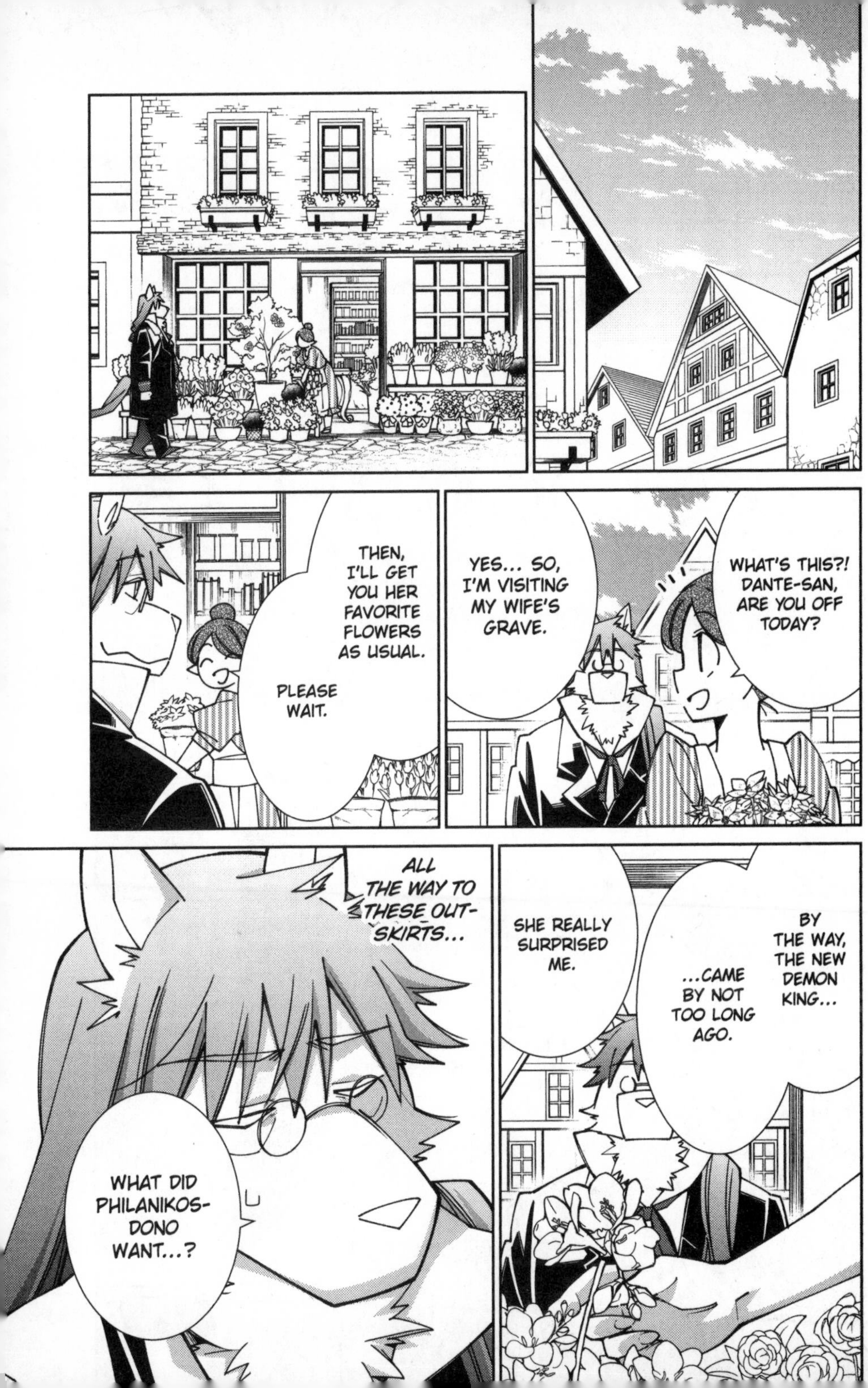
WHAT'S THIS?! DANTE-SAN, ARE YOU OFF TODAY?
YES... SO, I'M VISITING MY WIFE'S GRAVE.
THEN, I'LL GET YOU HER FAVORITE FLOWERS AS USUAL.
PLEASE WAIT.
BY THE WAY, THE NEW DEMON KING...
...CAME BY NOT TOO LONG AGO.
SHE REALLY SURPRISED ME.
ALL THE WAY TO THESE OUT-SKIRTS...
WHAT DID PHILANIKOS-DONO WANT...?

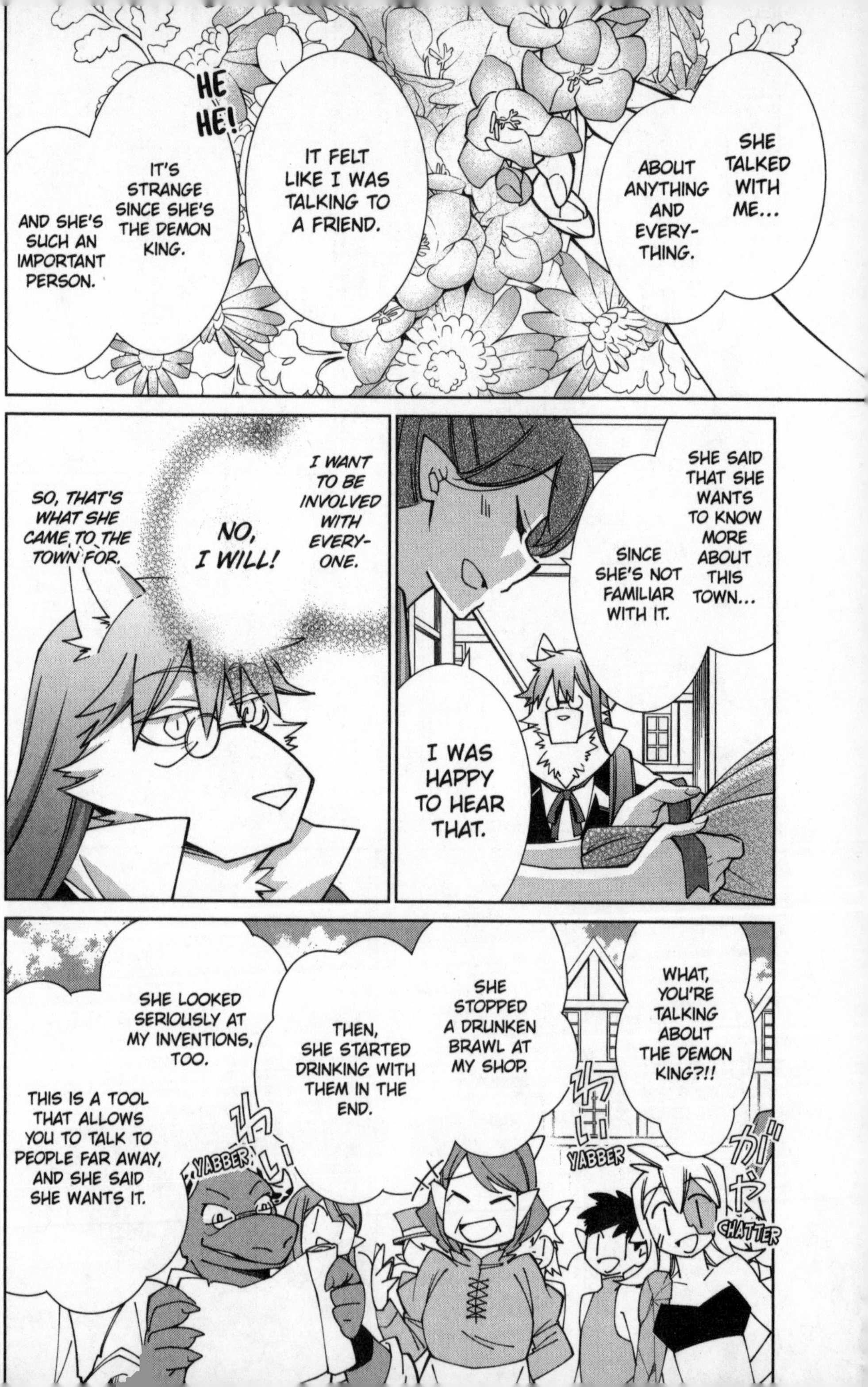
SHE TALKED WITH ME...
ABOUT ANYTHING AND EVERYTHING.
IT FELT LIKE I WAS TALKING TO A FRIEND.
HE HE!
IT'S STRANGE SINCE SHE'S THE DEMON KING.
AND SHE'S SUCH AN IMPORTANT PERSON.
SHE SAID THAT SHE WANTS TO KNOW MORE ABOUT THIS TOWN...
SINCE SHE'S NOT FAMILIAR WITH IT.
I WAS HAPPY TO HEAR THAT.
I WANT TO BE INVOLVED WITH EVERYONE.
NO, I WILL!
SO, THAT'S WHAT SHE CAME TO THE TOWN FOR.
WHAT, YOU'RE TALKING ABOUT THE DEMON KING?!!
CHATTER
YABBER
SHE STOPPED A DRUNKEN BRAWL AT MY SHOP.
THEN, SHE STARTED DRINKING WITH THEM IN THE END.
SHE LOOKED SERIOUSLY AT MY INVENTIONS, TOO.
YABBER
THIS IS A TOOL THAT ALLOWS YOU TO TALK TO PEOPLE FAR AWAY, AND SHE SAID SHE WANTS IT.

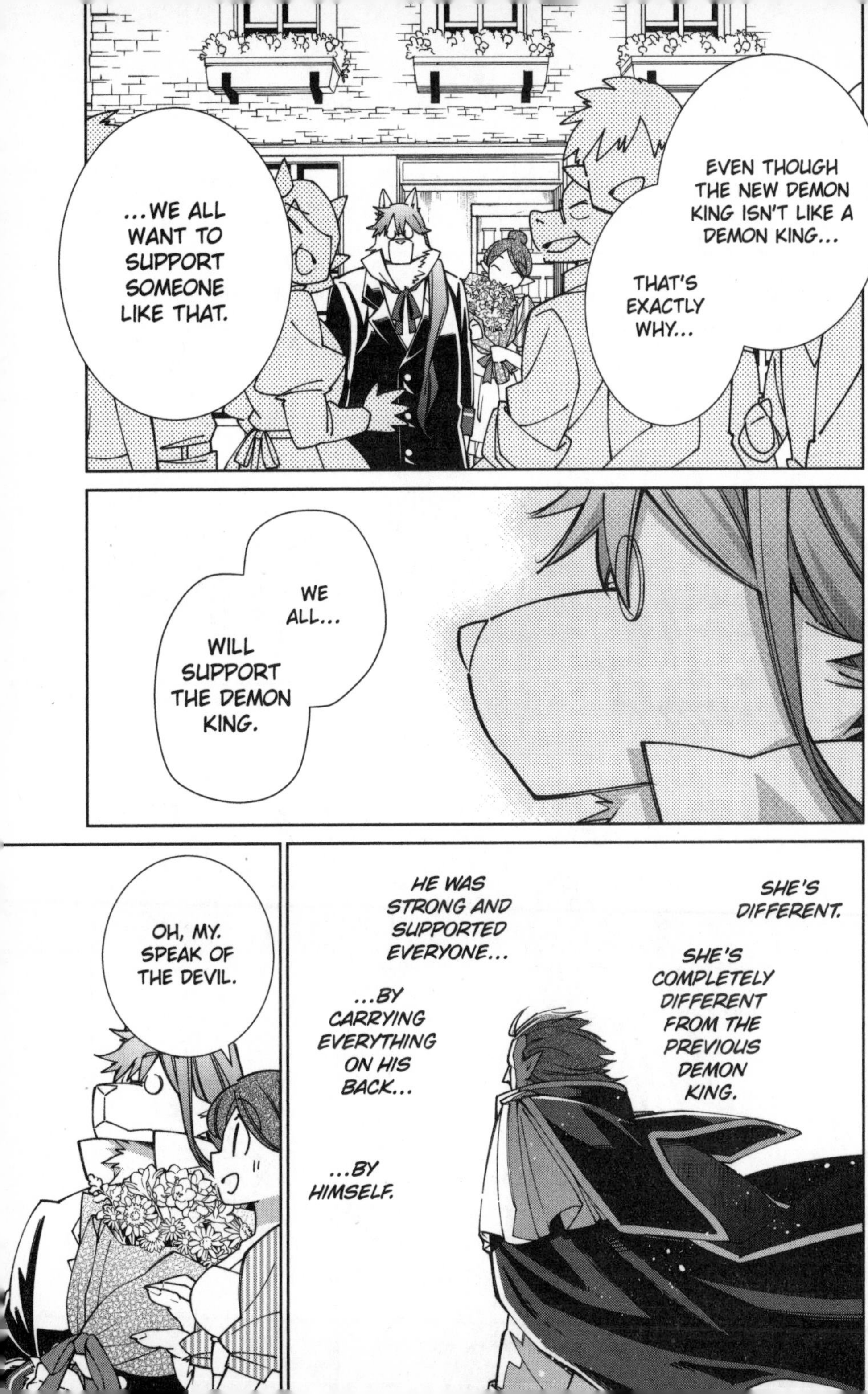
EVEN THOUGH THE NEW DEMON KING ISN'T LIKE A DEMON KING...
THAT'S EXACTLY WHY...
...WE ALL WANT TO SUPPORT SOMEONE LIKE THAT.
WE ALL...
WILL SUPPORT THE DEMON KING.
SHE'S DIFFERENT.
SHE'S COMPLETELY DIFFERENT FROM THE PREVIOUS DEMON KING.
HE WAS STRONG AND SUPPORTED EVERYONE...
...BY CARRYING EVERYTHING ON HIS BACK...
...BY HIMSELF.
OH, MY. SPEAK OF THE DEVIL.

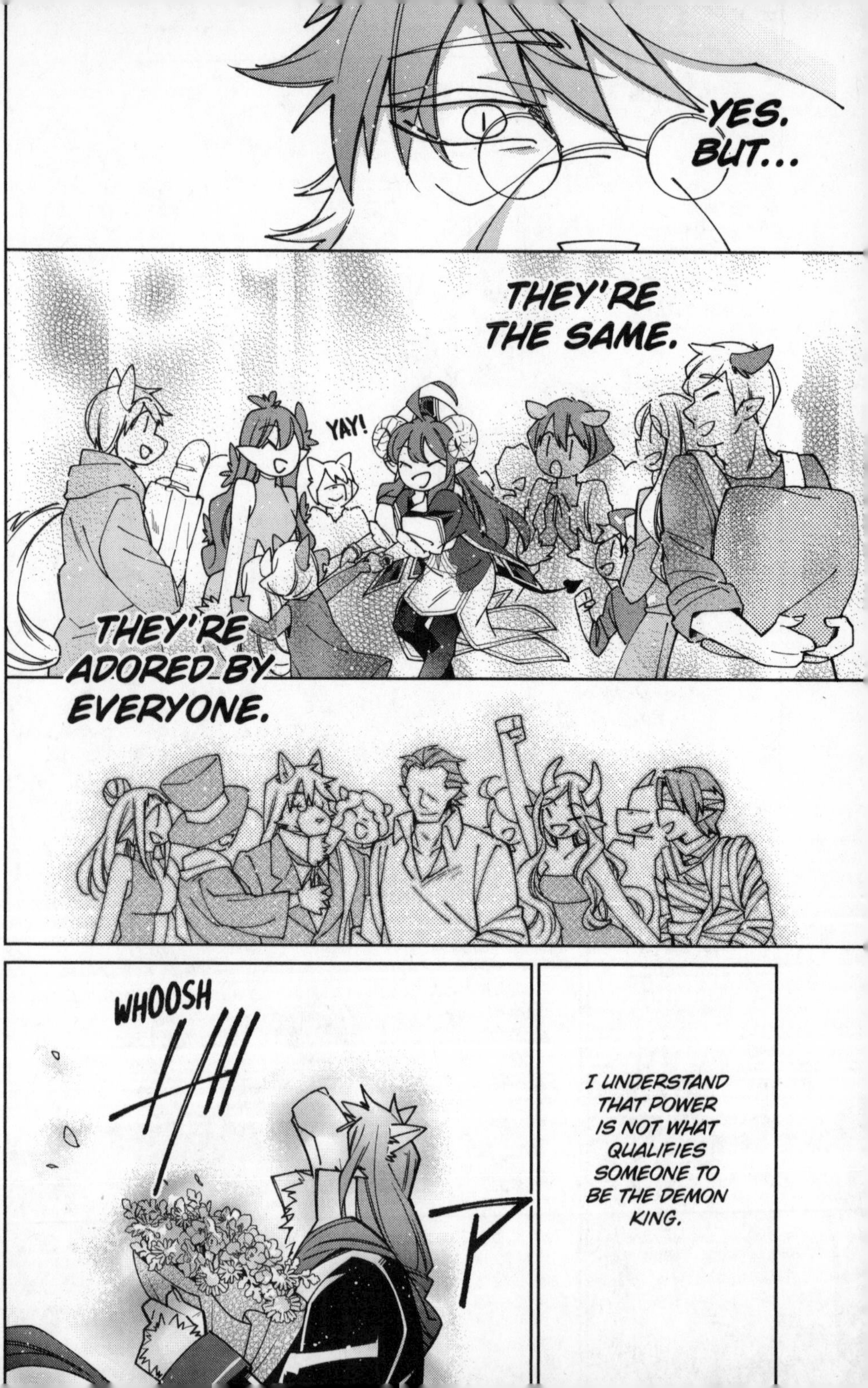
YES. BUT...
THEY'RE THE SAME.
YAY!
THEY'RE ADORED BY EVERYONE.
I UNDERSTAND THAT POWER IS NOT WHAT QUALIFIES SOMEONE TO BE THE DEMON KING.
WHOOSH

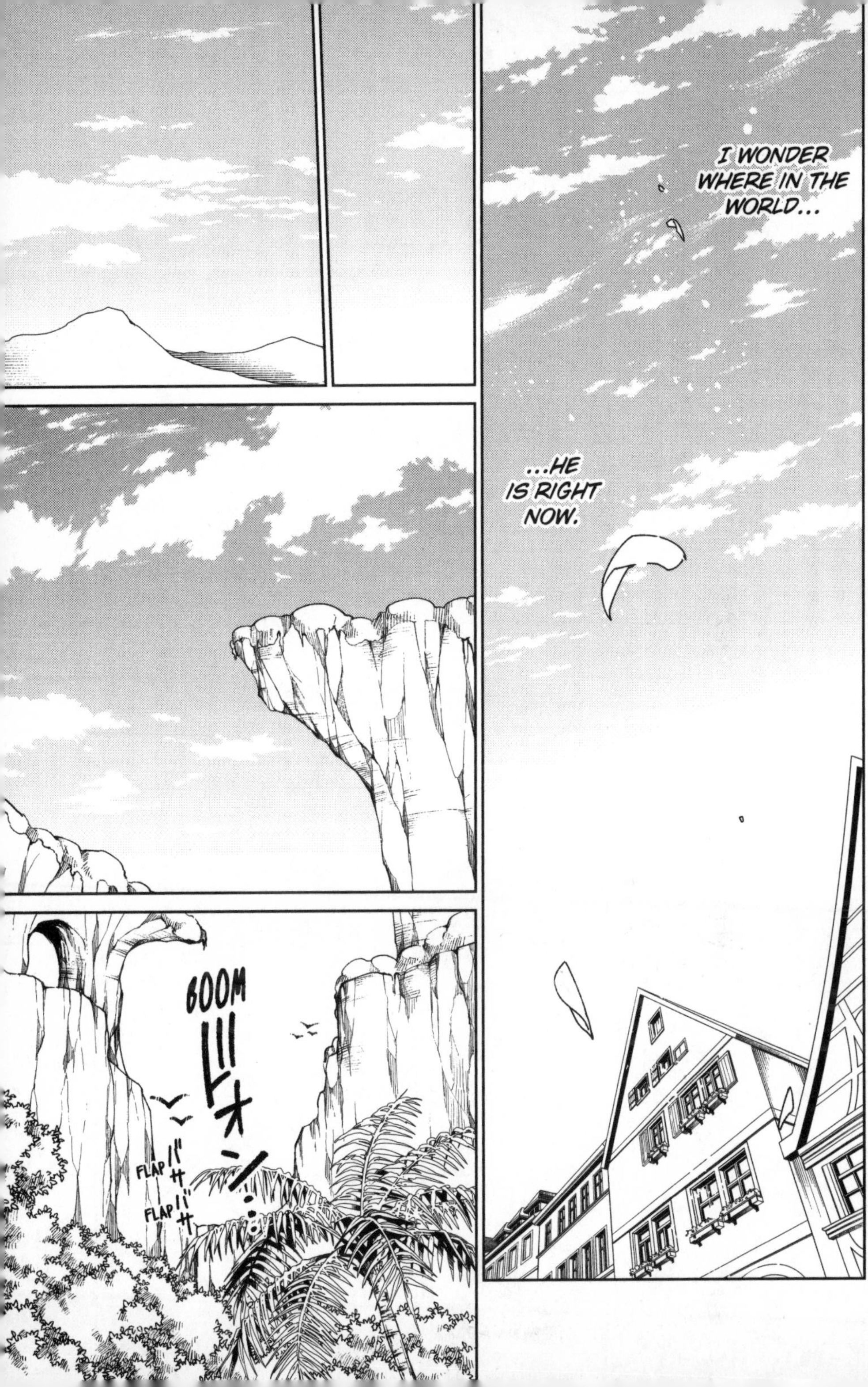
I WONDER WHERE IN THE WORLD...
...HE IS RIGHT NOW.
GOOM
ドォン
FLAP バサ
FLAP バサ

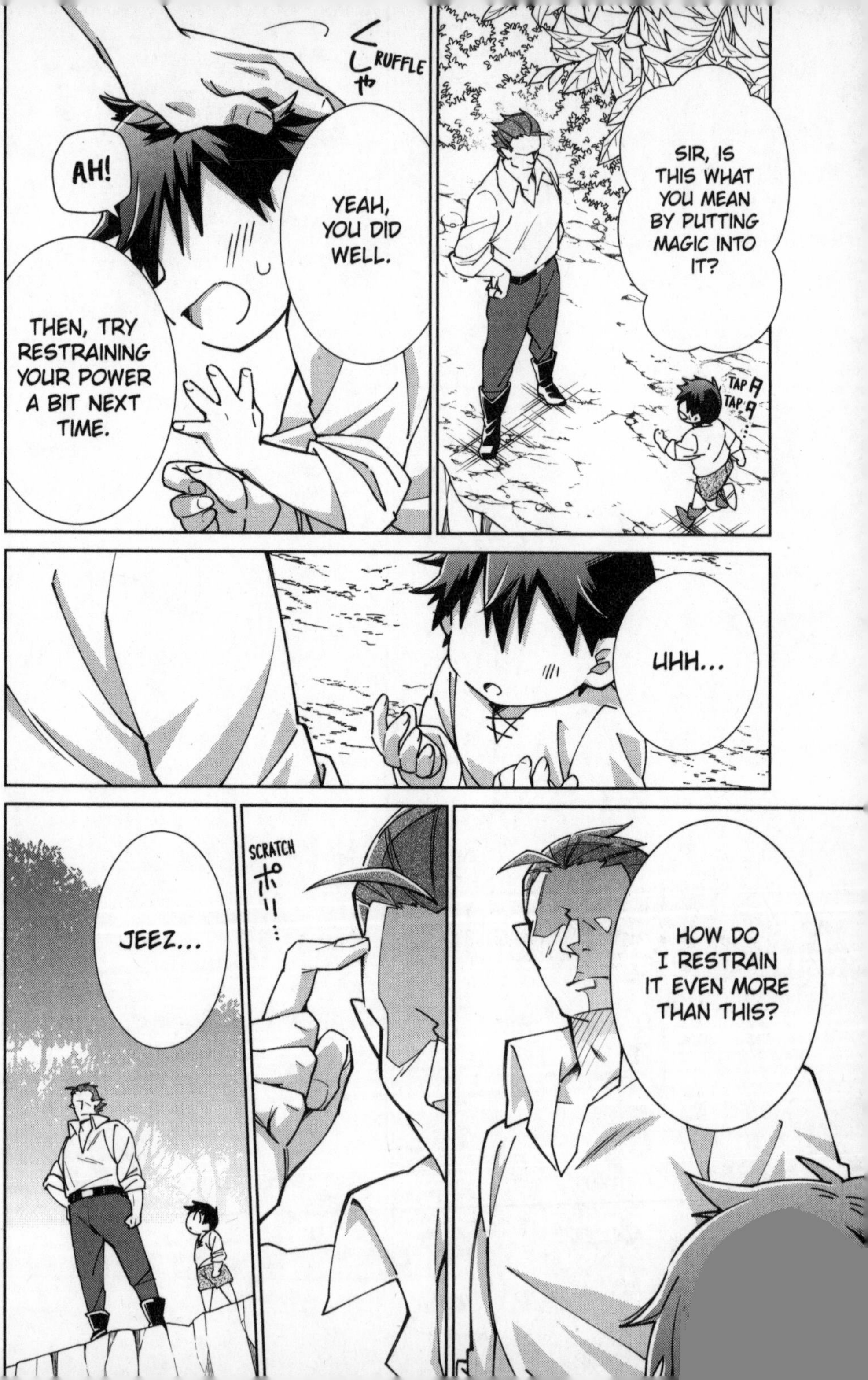
SIR, IS THIS WHAT YOU MEAN BY PUTTING MAGIC INTO IT?
TAP TAP
くしゃ RUFFLE
YEAH, YOU DID WELL.
AH!
THEN, TRY RESTRAINING YOUR POWER A BIT NEXT TIME.
UHH...
HOW DO I RESTRAIN IT EVEN MORE THAN THIS?
SCRATCH ポリ…
JEEZ...

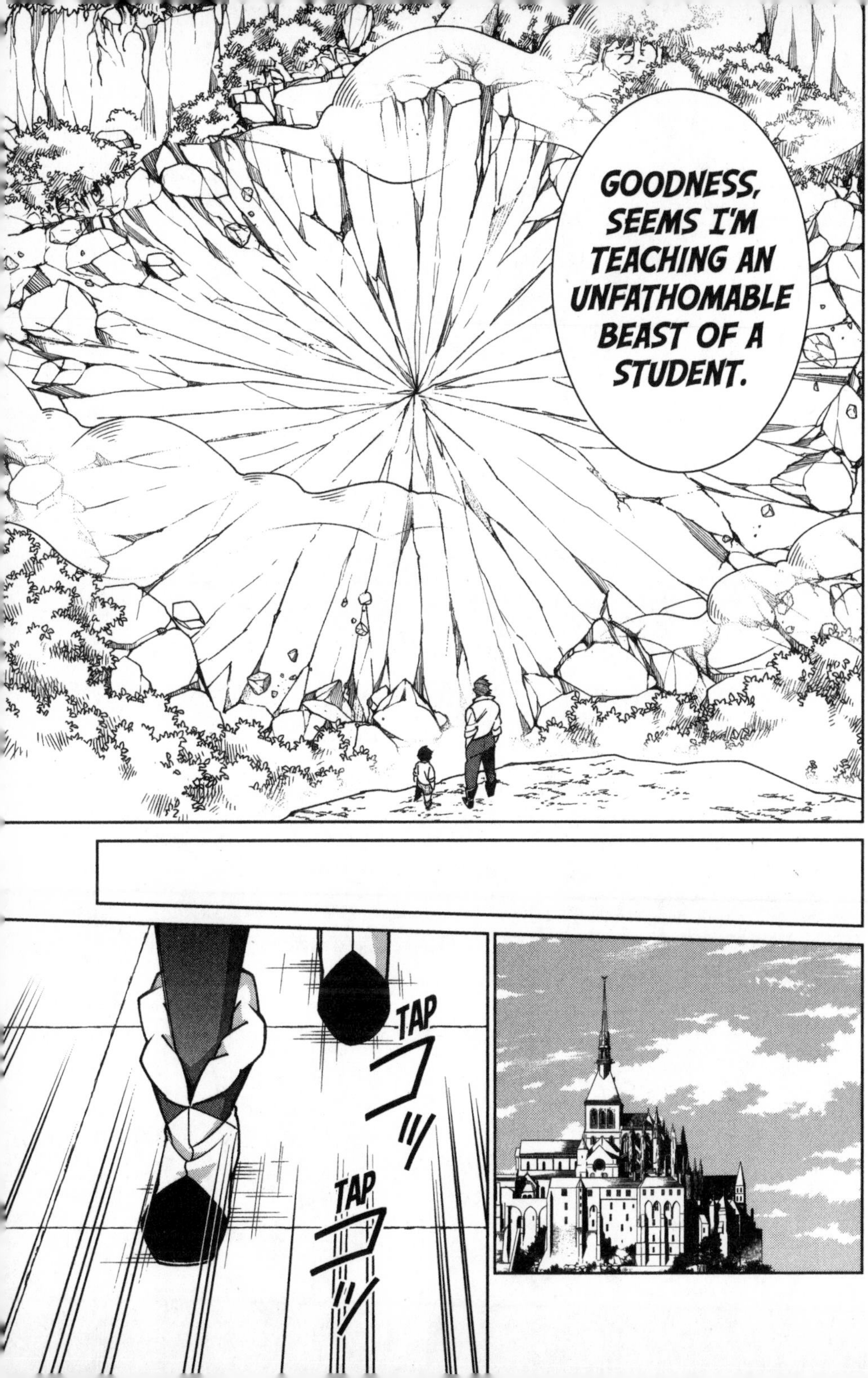
GOODNESS, SEEMS I'M TEACHING AN UNFATHOMABLE BEAST OF A STUDENT.
TAP
TAP

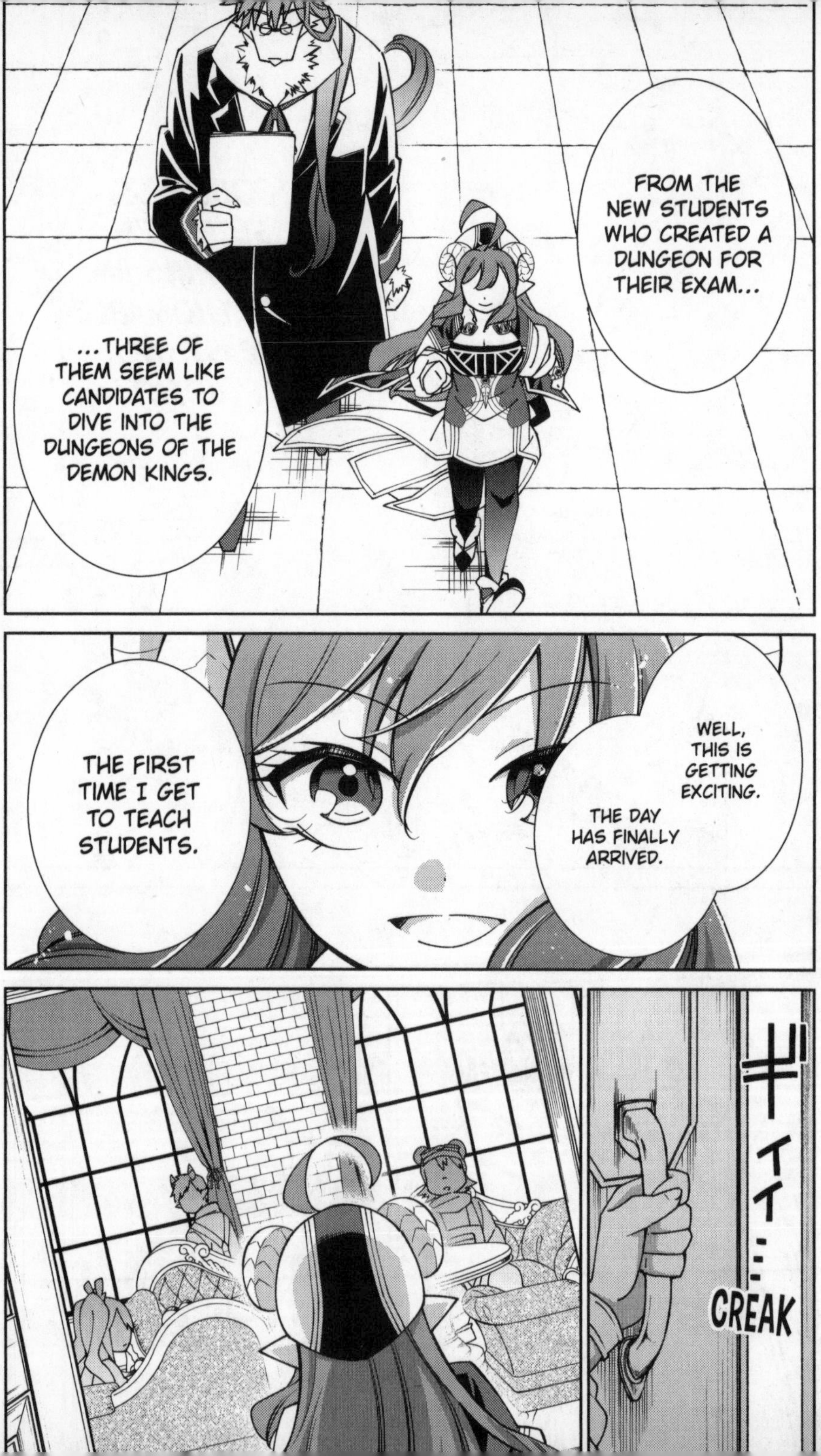
FROM THE NEW STUDENTS WHO CREATED A DUNGEON FOR THEIR EXAM...
...THREE OF THEM SEEM LIKE CANDIDATES TO DIVE INTO THE DUNGEONS OF THE DEMON KINGS.
WELL, THIS IS GETTING EXCITING.
THE DAY HAS FINALLY ARRIVED.
THE FIRST TIME I GET TO TEACH STUDENTS.
CREAK

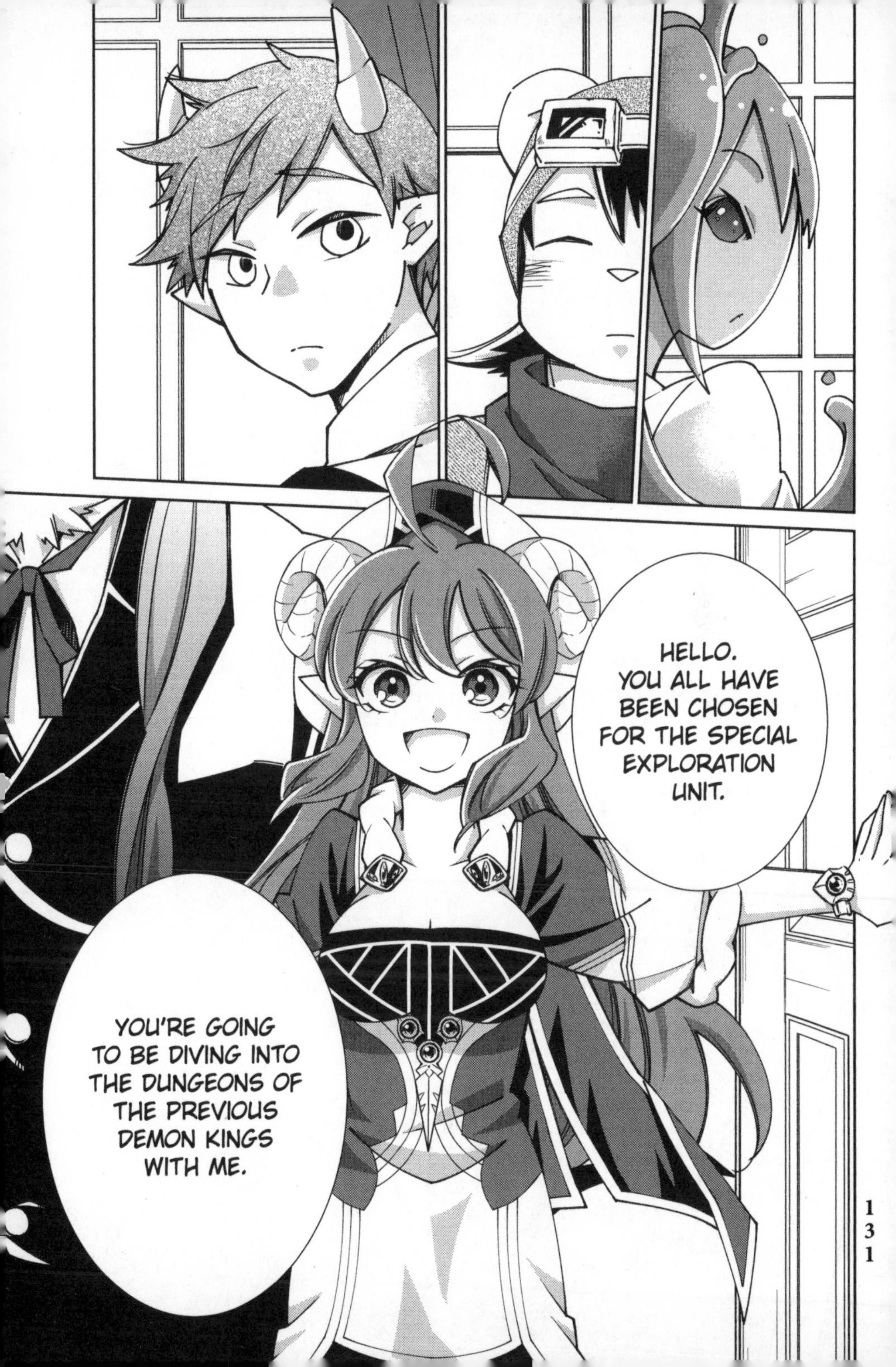
HELLO. YOU ALL HAVE BEEN CHOSEN FOR THE SPECIAL EXPLORATION UNIT.
YOU'RE GOING TO BE DIVING INTO THE DUNGEONS OF THE PREVIOUS DEMON KINGS WITH ME.

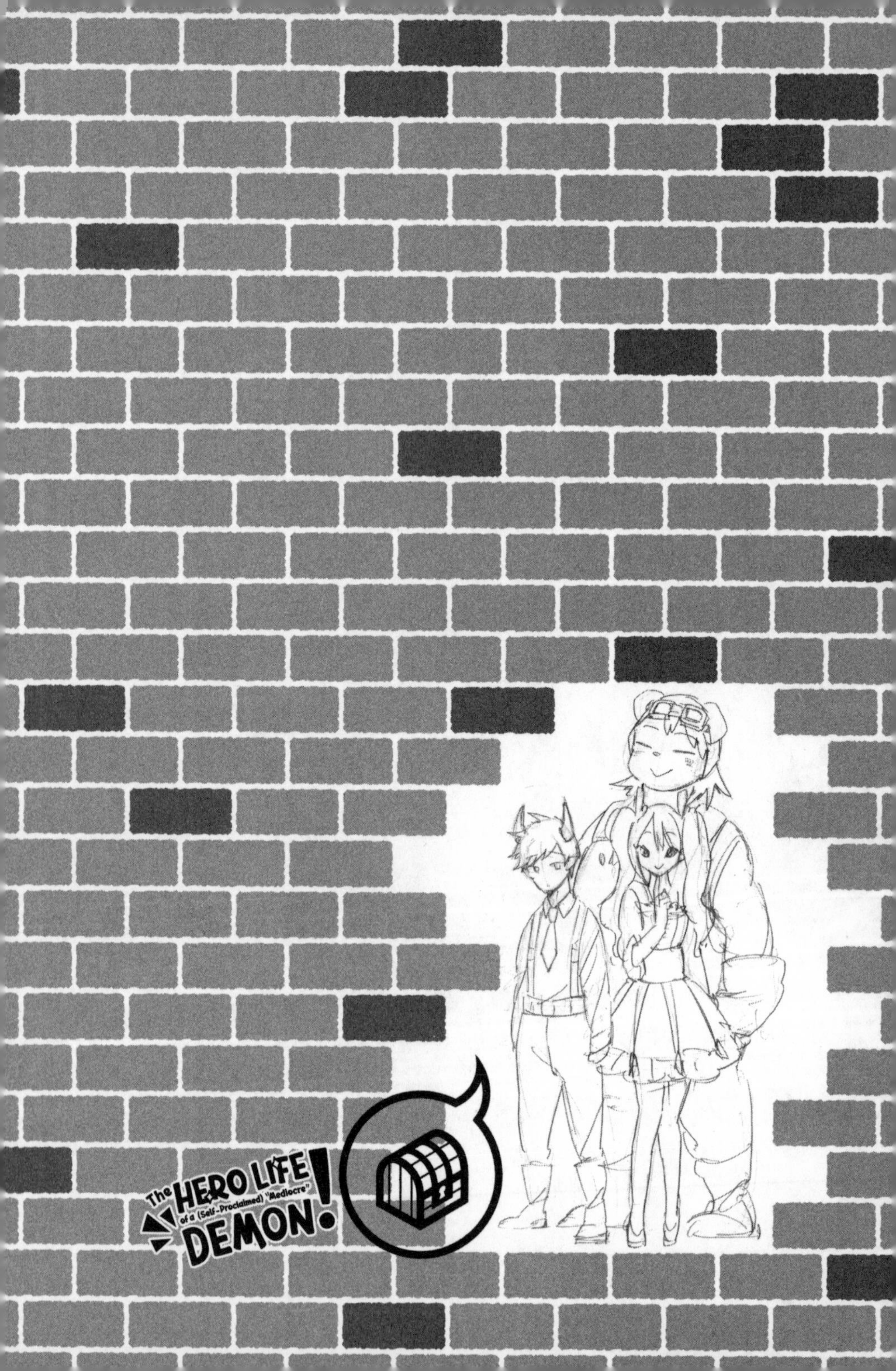
The HERO LIFE of a (Self-Proclaimed) "Mediocre" DEMON!

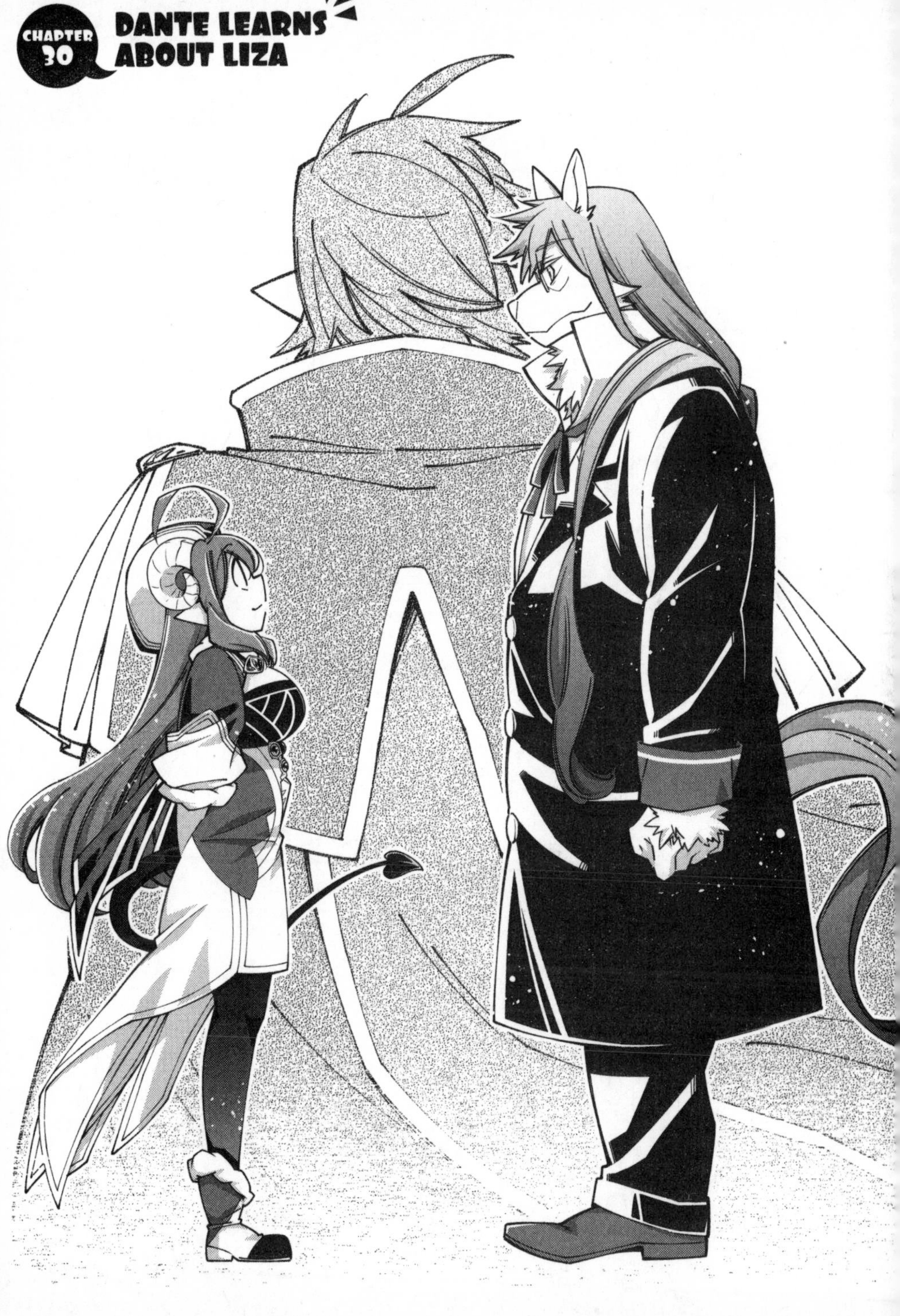
CHAPTER 30
DANTE LEARNS ABOUT LIZA

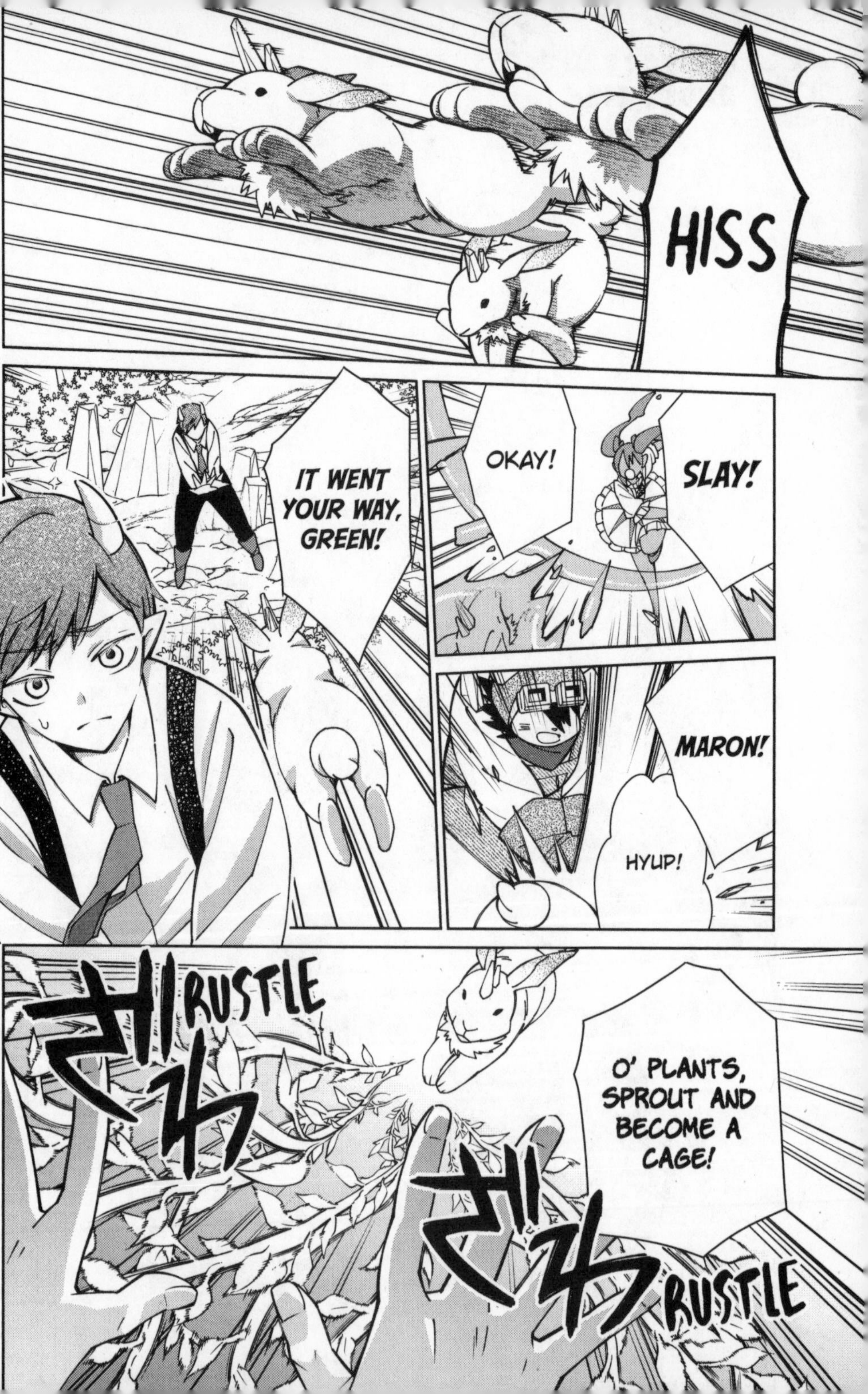
HISS
SLAY!
OKAY!
MARON!
HYUP!
IT WENT YOUR WAY, GREEN!
O' PLANTS, SPROUT AND BECOME A CAGE!
RUSTLE
RUSTLE

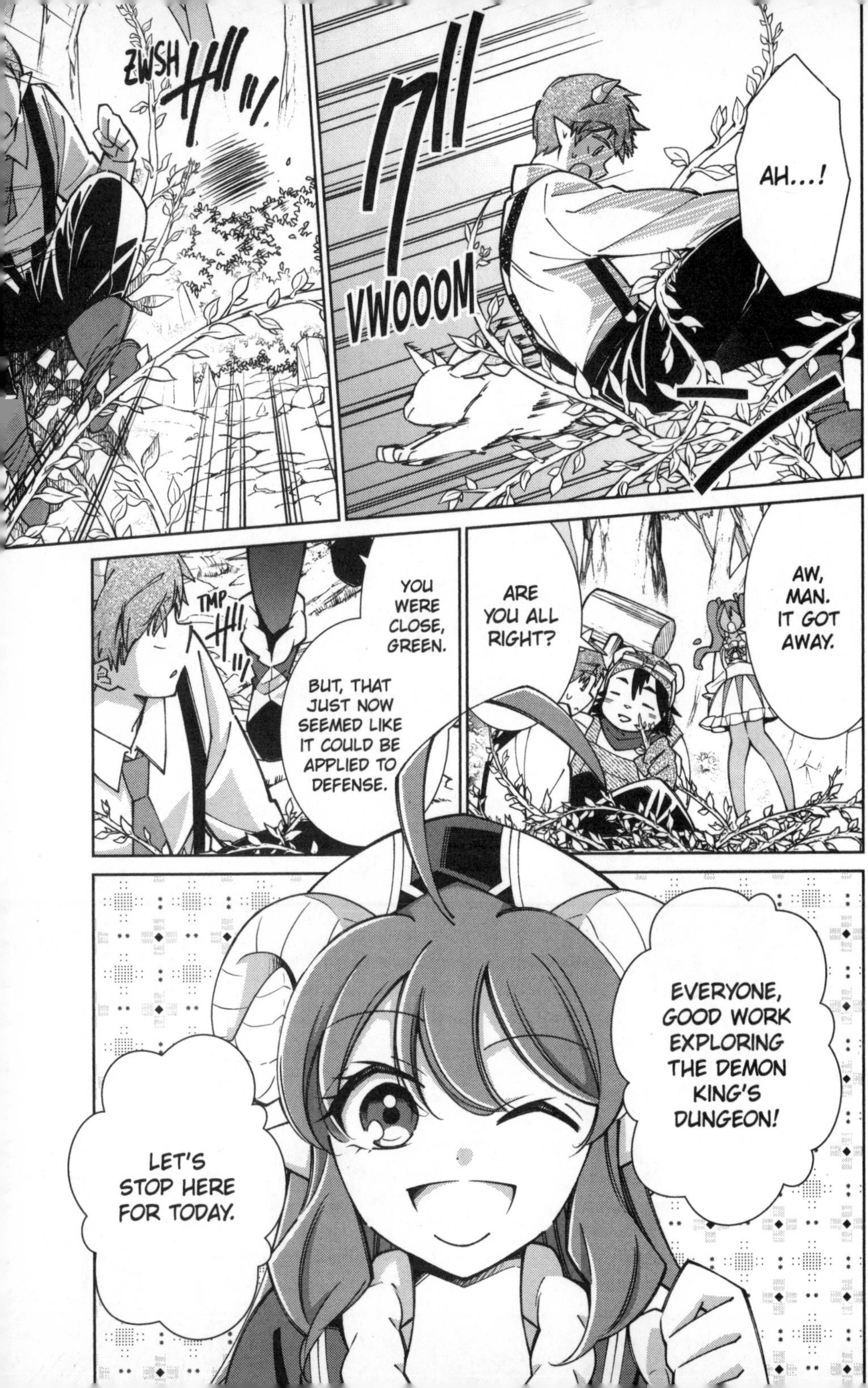
AH...!
VWOOOM
ZWSH
AW, MAN. IT GOT AWAY.
ARE YOU ALL RIGHT?
YOU WERE CLOSE, GREEN.
BUT, THAT JUST NOW SEEMED LIKE IT COULD BE APPLIED TO DEFENSE.
TMP
EVERYONE, GOOD WORK EXPLORING THE DEMON KING'S DUNGEON!
LET'S STOP HERE FOR TODAY.

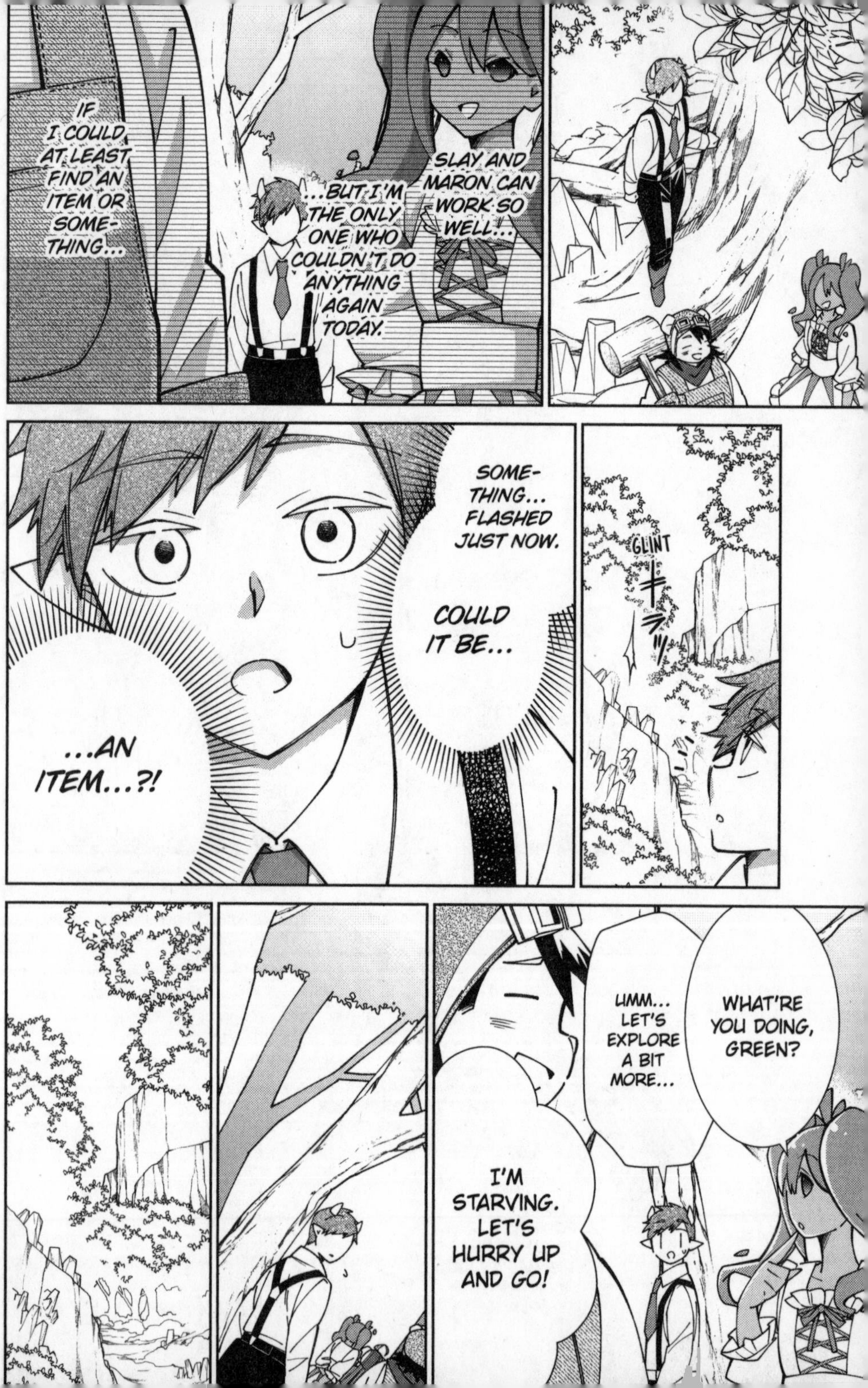
SLAY AND MARON CAN WORK SO WELL...
...BUT I'M THE ONLY ONE WHO COULDN'T DO ANYTHING AGAIN TODAY.
IF I COULD AT LEAST FIND AN ITEM OR SOME-THING...
GLINT
SOME-THING... FLASHED JUST NOW.
COULD IT BE...
...AN ITEM...?!
WHAT'RE YOU DOING, GREEN?
UMM... LET'S EXPLORE A BIT MORE...
I'M STARVING. LET'S HURRY UP AND GO!

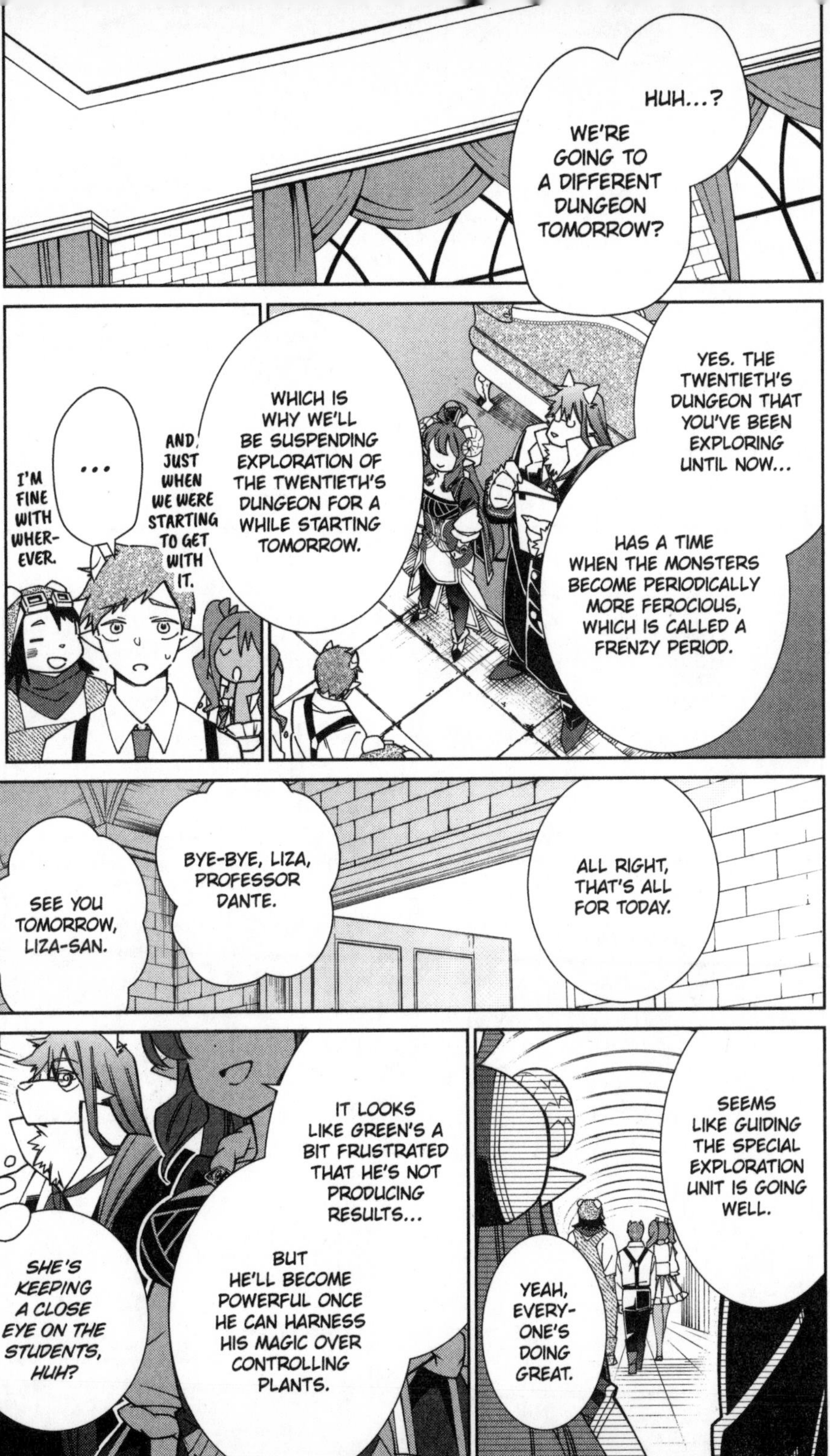
HUH...?
WE'RE GOING TO A DIFFERENT DUNGEON TOMORROW?
YES. THE TWENTIETH'S DUNGEON THAT YOU'VE BEEN EXPLORING UNTIL NOW...
HAS A TIME WHEN THE MONSTERS BECOME PERIODICALLY MORE FEROCIOUS, WHICH IS CALLED A FRENZY PERIOD.
WHICH IS WHY WE'LL BE SUSPENDING EXPLORATION OF THE TWENTIETH'S DUNGEON FOR A WHILE STARTING TOMORROW.
AND, JUST WHEN WE WERE STARTING TO GET WITH IT.
...
I'M FINE WITH WHER-EVER.
ALL RIGHT, THAT'S ALL FOR TODAY.
BYE-BYE, LIZA, PROFESSOR DANTE.
SEE YOU TOMORROW, LIZA-SAN.
SEEMS LIKE GUIDING THE SPECIAL EXPLORATION UNIT IS GOING WELL.
YEAH, EVERY-ONE'S DOING GREAT.
IT LOOKS LIKE GREEN'S A BIT FRUSTRATED THAT HE'S NOT PRODUCING RESULTS...
BUT HE'LL BECOME POWERFUL ONCE HE CAN HARNESS HIS MAGIC OVER CONTROLLING PLANTS.
SHE'S KEEPING A CLOSE EYE ON THE STUDENTS, HUH?

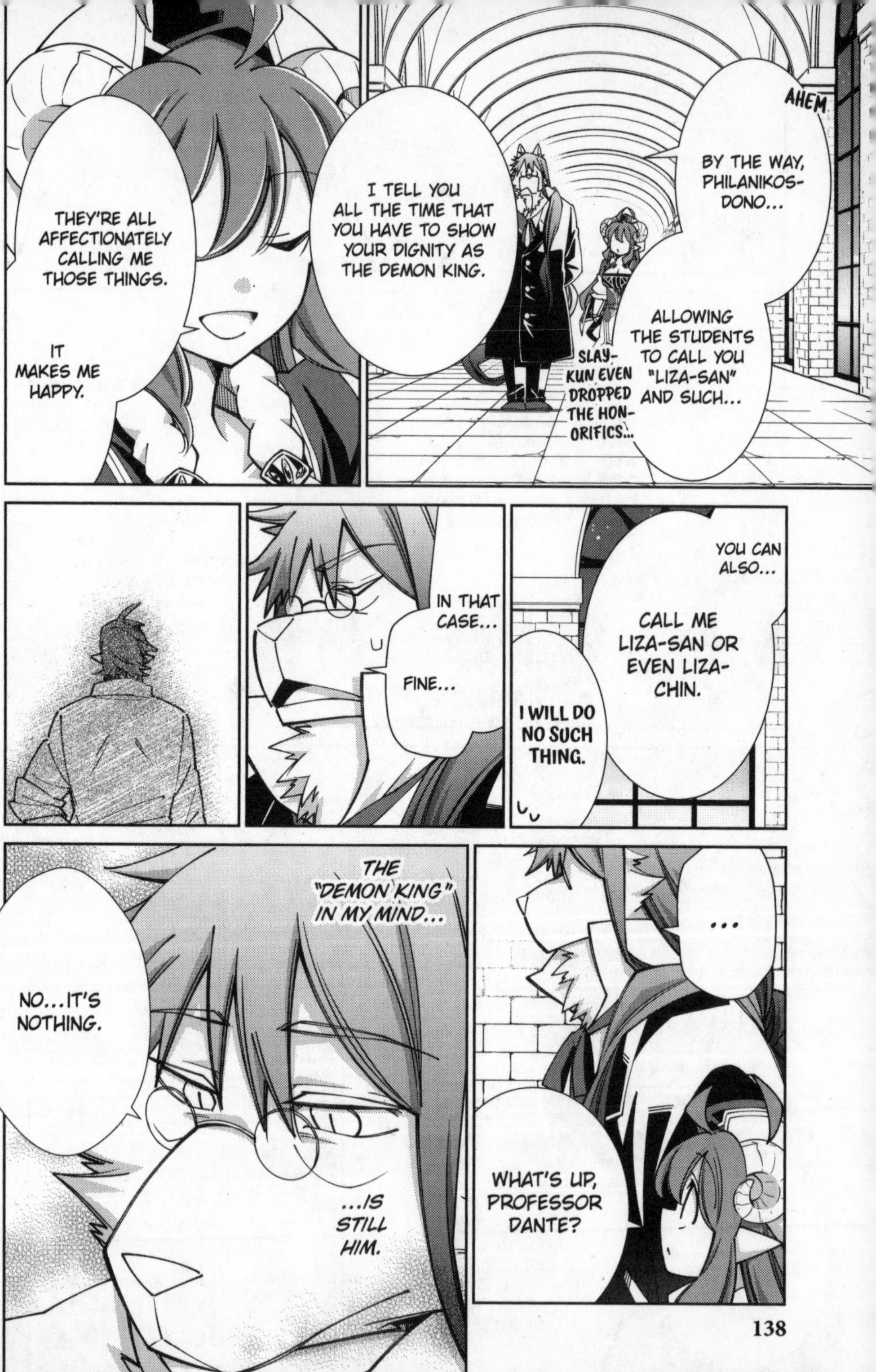
AHEM
BY THE WAY, PHILANIKOS-DONO...
ALLOWING THE STUDENTS TO CALL YOU "LIZA-SAN" AND SUCH...
SLAY-KUN EVEN DROPPED THE HONORIFICS...
I TELL YOU ALL THE TIME THAT YOU HAVE TO SHOW YOUR DIGNITY AS THE DEMON KING.
THEY'RE ALL AFFECTIONATELY CALLING ME THOSE THINGS.
IT MAKES ME HAPPY.
YOU CAN ALSO...
CALL ME LIZA-SAN OR EVEN LIZA-CHIN.
I WILL DO NO SUCH THING.
IN THAT CASE...
FINE...
...
WHAT'S UP, PROFESSOR DANTE?
THE "DEMON KING" IN MY MIND...
...IS STILL HIM.
NO...IT'S NOTHING.

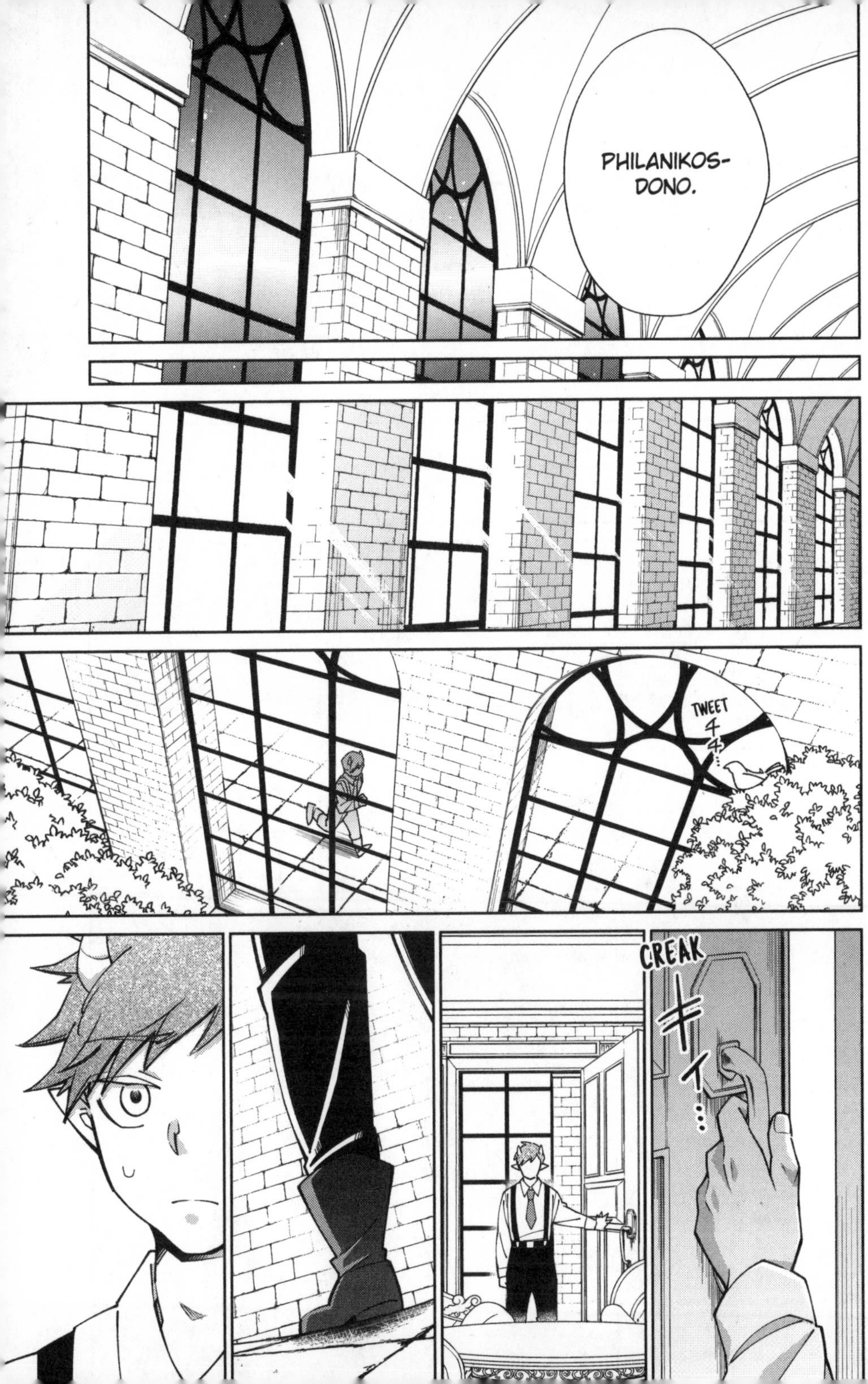
PHILANIKOS-
DONO.
TWEET
チチ…
CREAK
キイ…

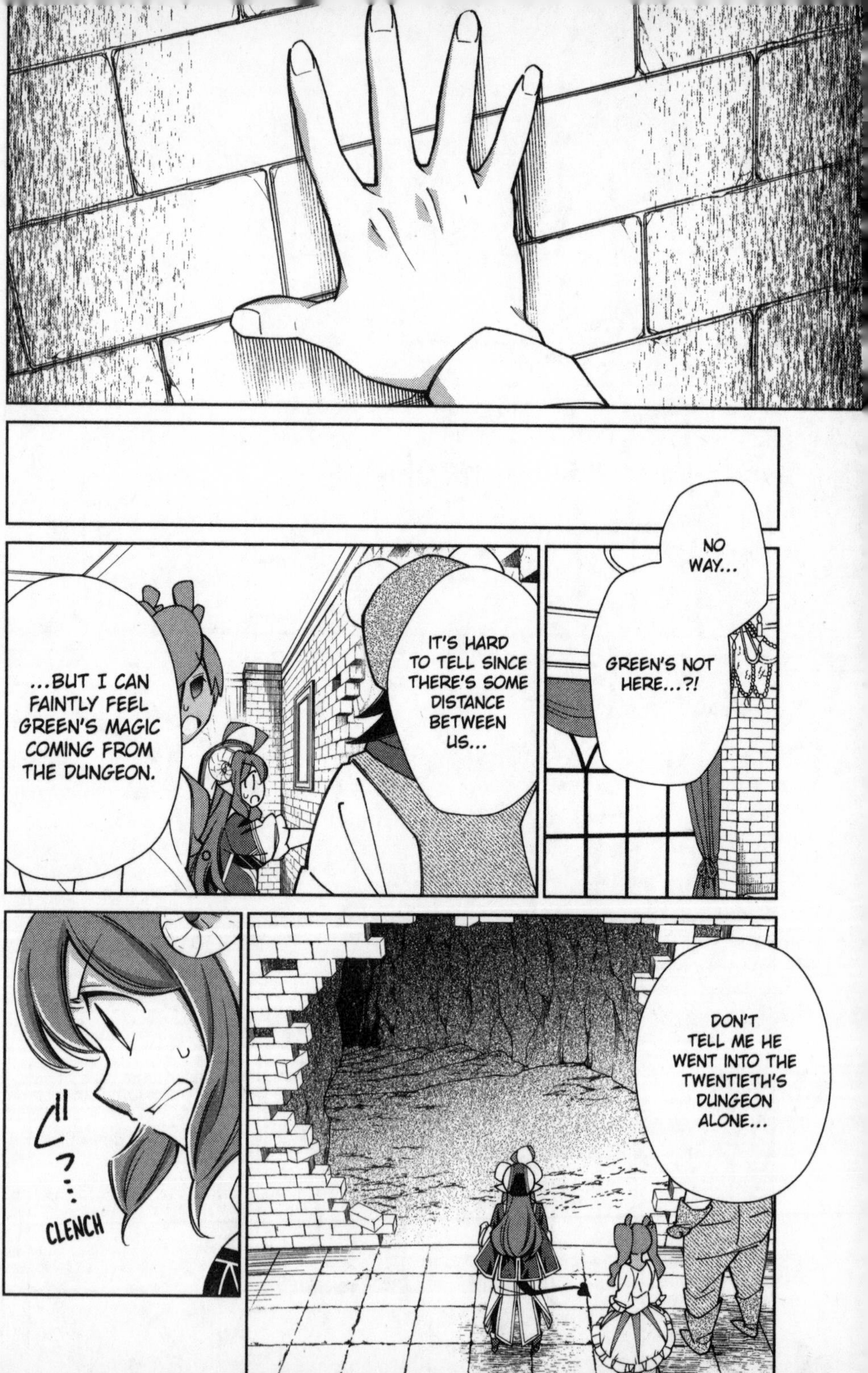
NO WAY...
GREEN'S NOT HERE...?!
IT'S HARD TO TELL SINCE THERE'S SOME DISTANCE BETWEEN US...
...BUT I CAN FAINTLY FEEL GREEN'S MAGIC COMING FROM THE DUNGEON.
DON'T TELL ME HE WENT INTO THE TWENTIETH'S DUNGEON ALONE...
CLENCH

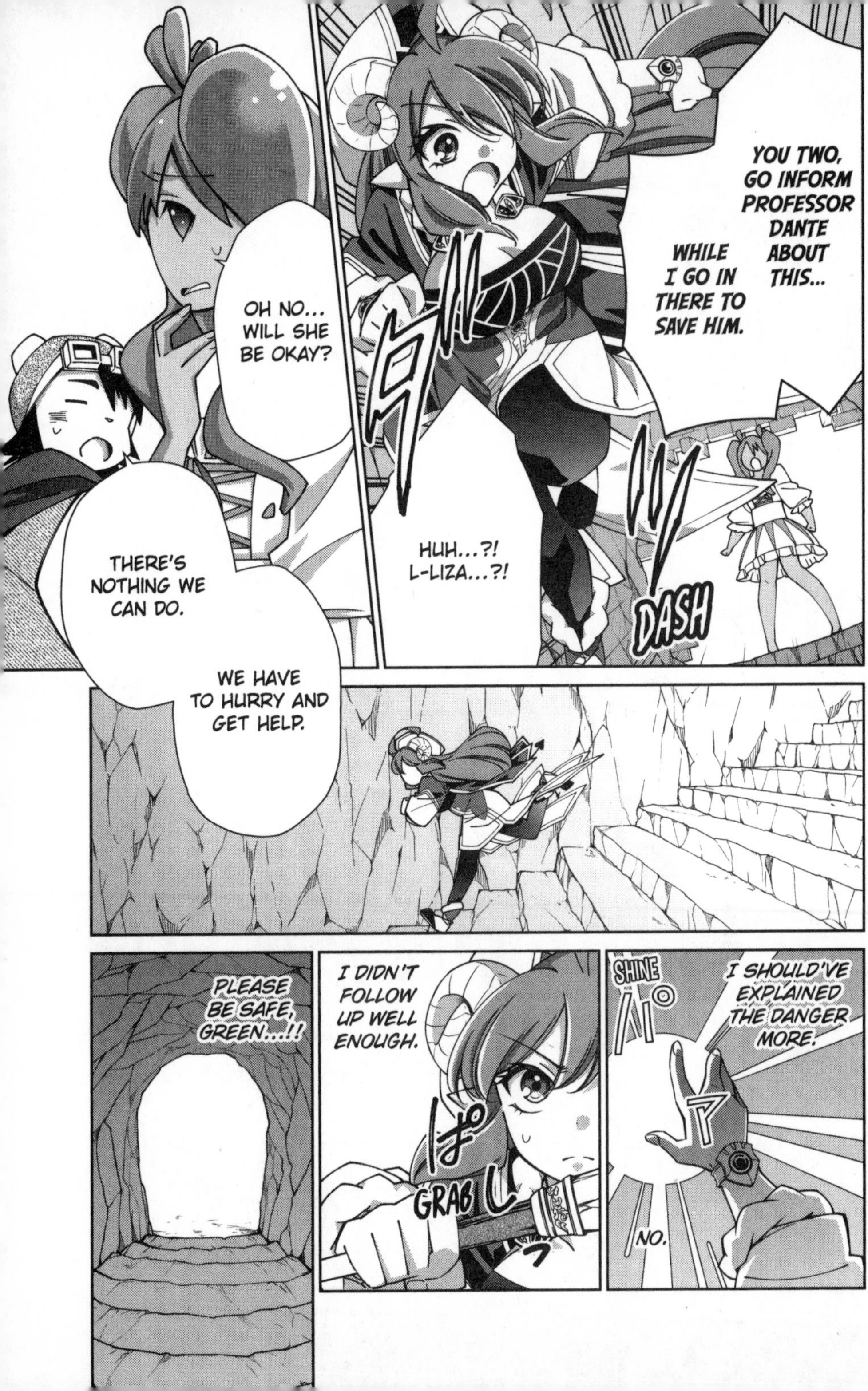
YOU TWO, GO INFORM PROFESSOR DANTE ABOUT THIS...
WHILE I GO IN THERE TO SAVE HIM.
HUH...?! L-LIZA...?!
DASH
OH NO... WILL SHE BE OKAY?
THERE'S NOTHING WE CAN DO.
WE HAVE TO HURRY AND GET HELP.
SHINE
I SHOULD'VE EXPLAINED THE DANGER MORE.
NO.
I DIDN'T FOLLOW UP WELL ENOUGH.
GRAB
PLEASE BE SAFE, GREEN...!!

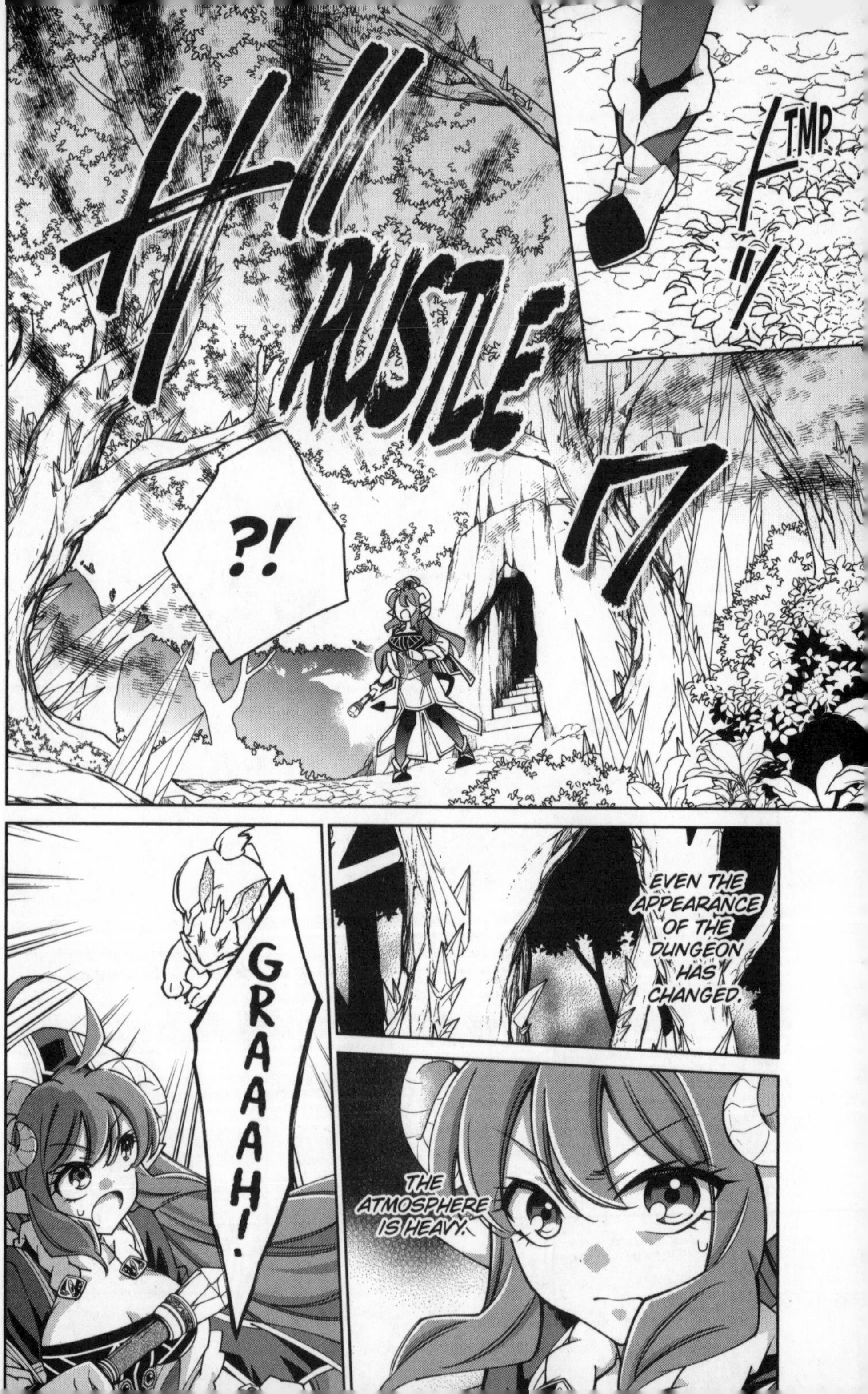
TMP
RUSTLE
?!
EVEN THE APPEARANCE OF THE DUNGEON HAS CHANGED.
THE ATMOSPHERE IS HEAVY.
GRAAAAH!

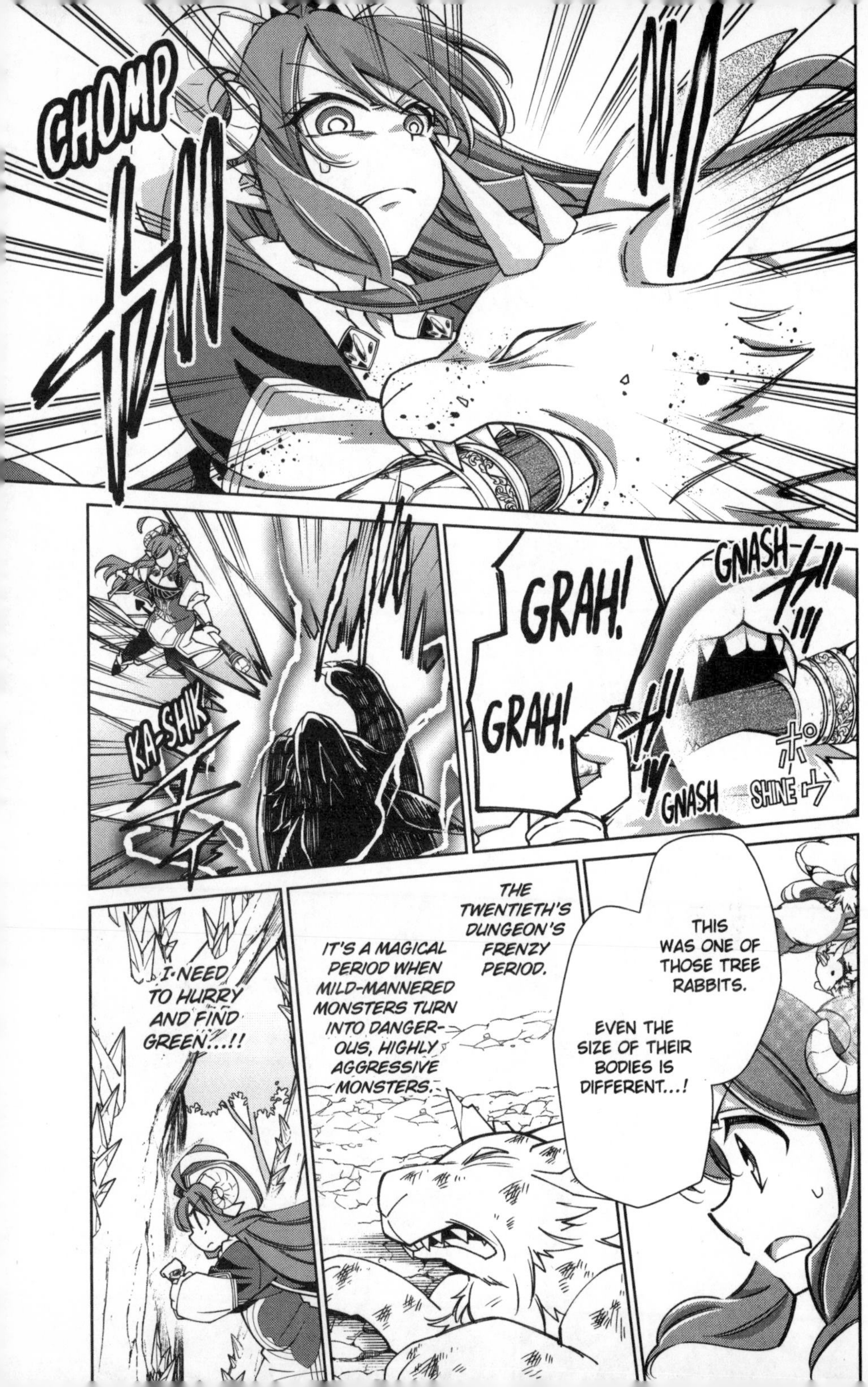

CHOMP
GNASH
GRAH!
GRAH!
GNASH
SHINE
KA-SHIK
THIS WAS ONE OF THOSE TREE RABBITS.
EVEN THE SIZE OF THEIR BODIES IS DIFFERENT...!
THE TWENTIETH'S DUNGEON'S FRENZY PERIOD.
IT'S A MAGICAL PERIOD WHEN MILD-MANNERED MONSTERS TURN INTO DANGEROUS, HIGHLY AGGRESSIVE MONSTERS.
I NEED TO HURRY AND FIND GREEN...!!

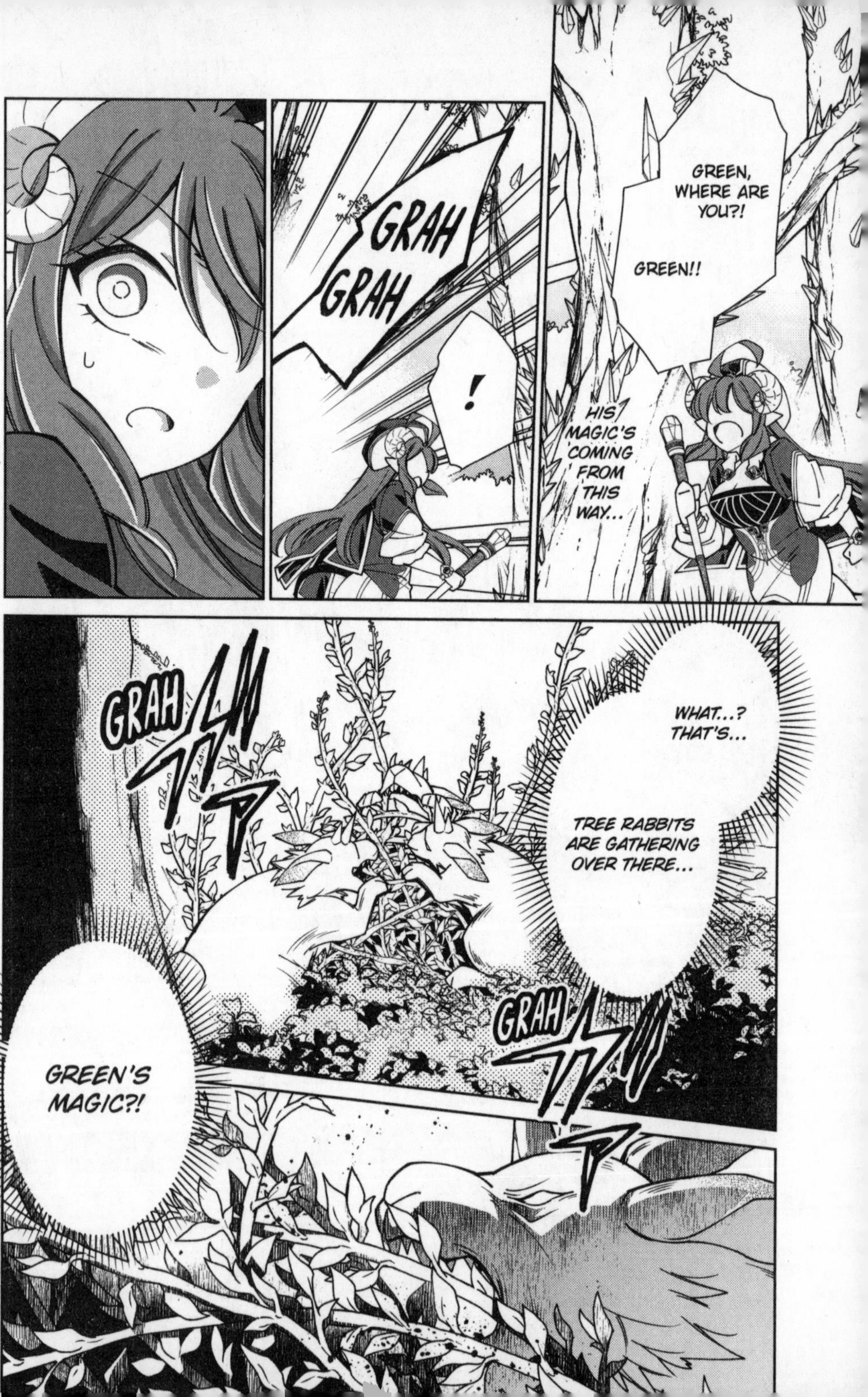
GREEN, WHERE ARE YOU?!
GREEN!!
HIS MAGIC'S COMING FROM THIS WAY...
GRAH GRAH
!
WHAT...? THAT'S...
TREE RABBITS ARE GATHERING OVER THERE...
GRAH
GRAH
GREEN'S MAGIC?!

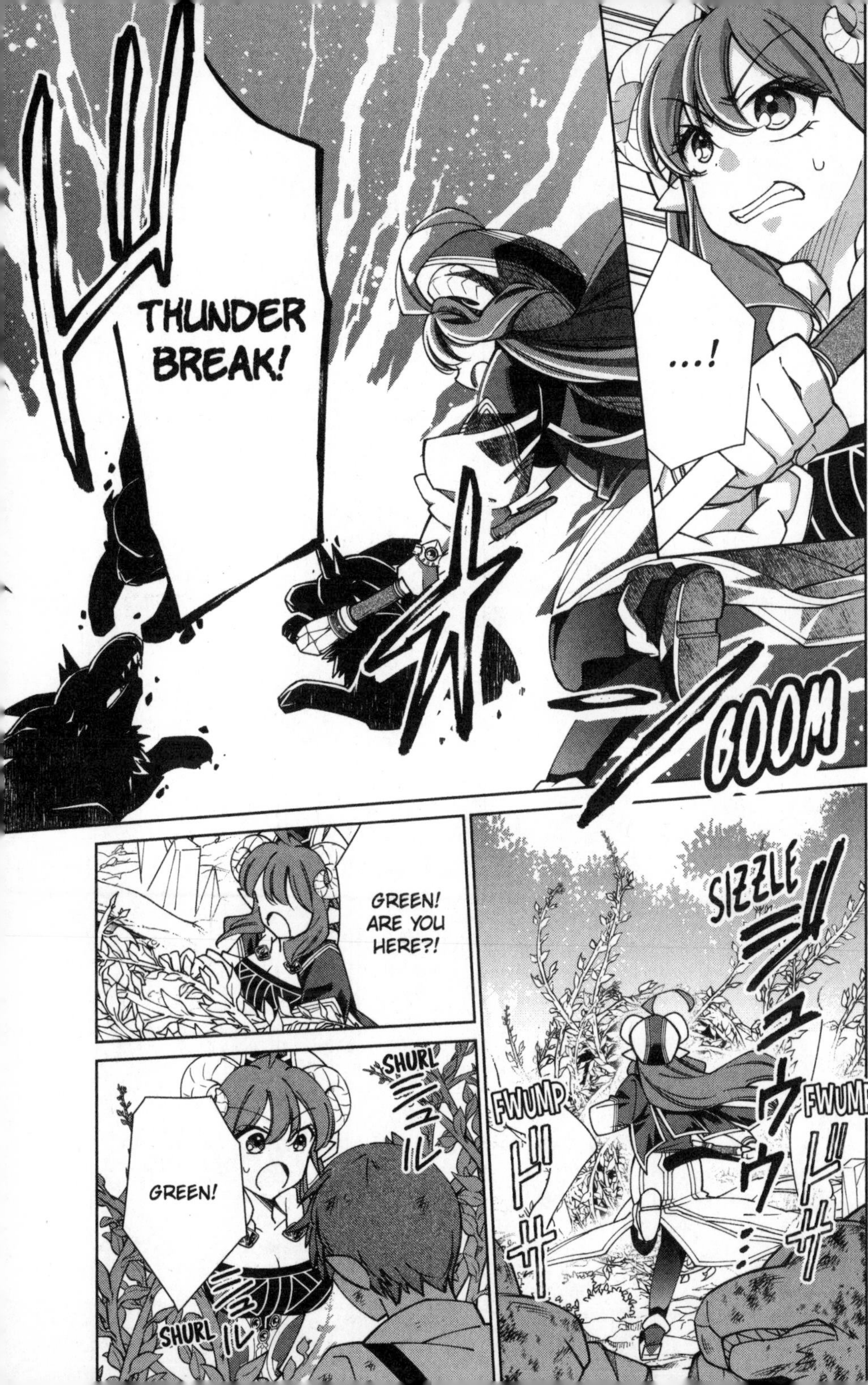
...!
THUNDER BREAK!
BOOM
SIZZLE
FWUMP
FWUMP
GREEN! ARE YOU HERE?!
SHURL
GREEN!
SHURL

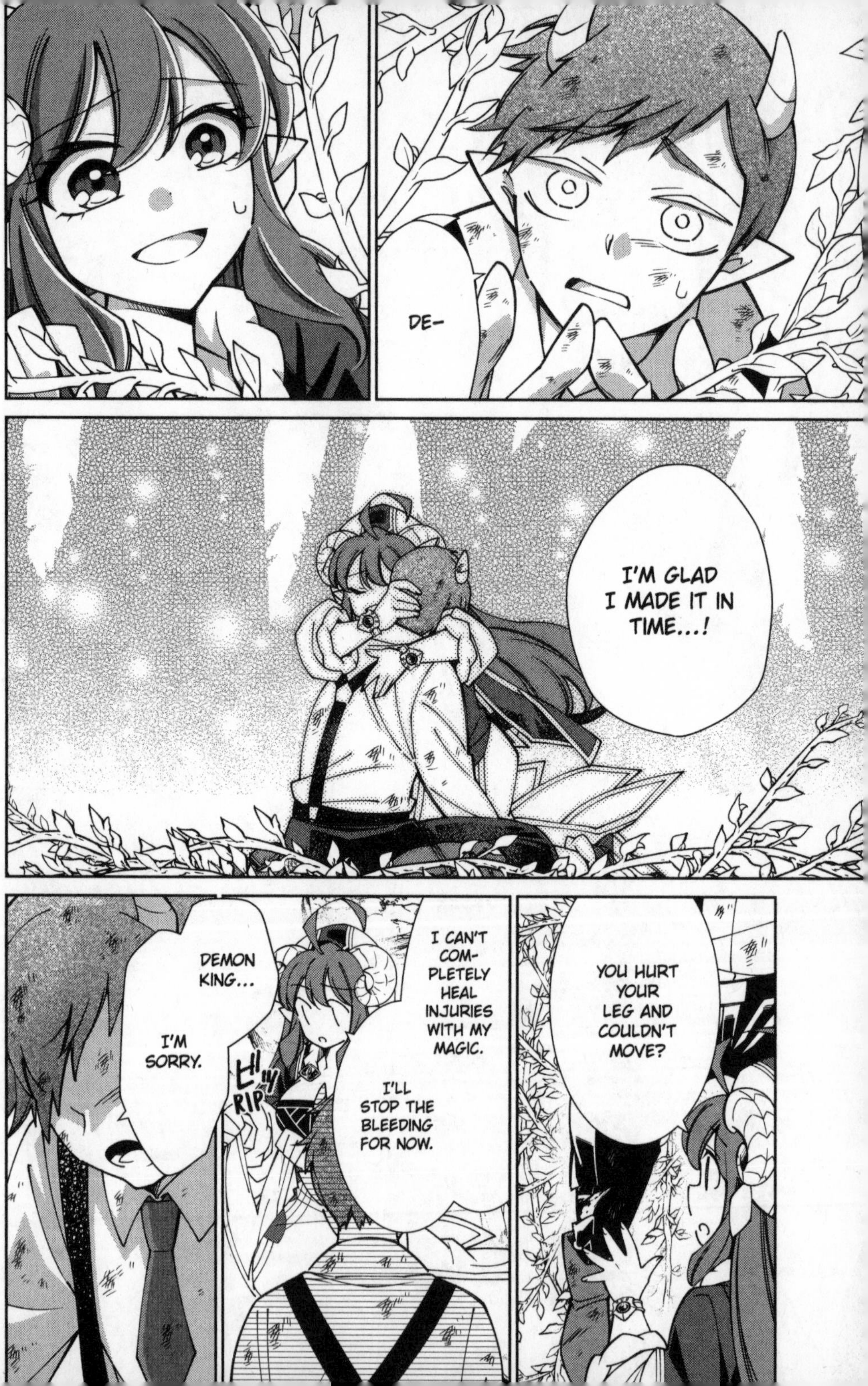
DE-
I'M GLAD I MADE IT IN TIME...!
YOU HURT YOUR LEG AND COULDN'T MOVE?
I CAN'T COM-PLETELY HEAL INJURIES WITH MY MAGIC.
I'LL STOP THE BLEEDING FOR NOW.
ビリッ RIP
DEMON KING...
I'M SORRY.

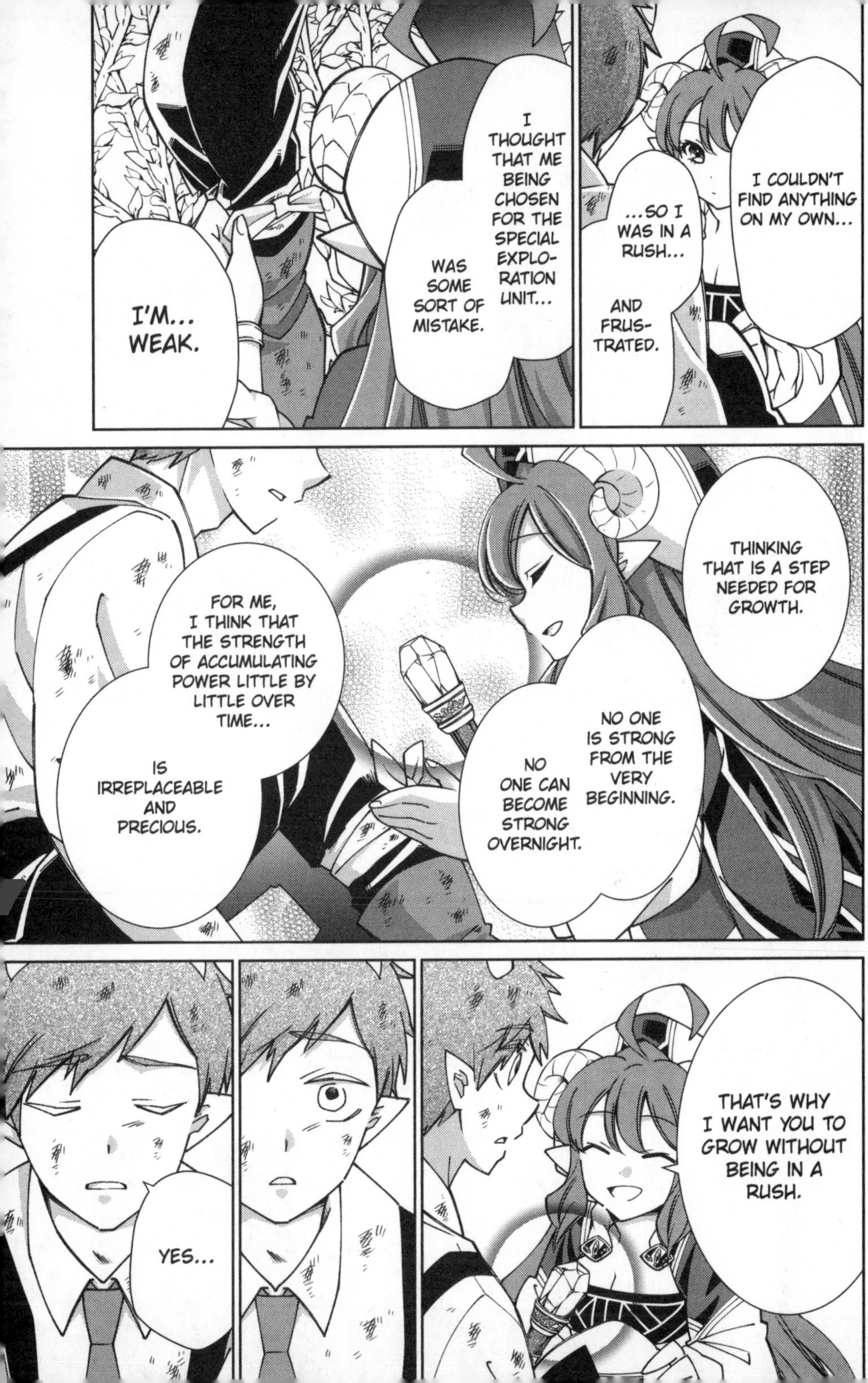
I COULDN'T FIND ANYTHING ON MY OWN...
...SO I WAS IN A RUSH...
AND FRUS-TRATED.
I THOUGHT THAT ME BEING CHOSEN FOR THE SPECIAL EXPLO-RATION UNIT...
WAS SOME SORT OF MISTAKE.
I'M... WEAK.
THINKING THAT IS A STEP NEEDED FOR GROWTH.
NO ONE IS STRONG FROM THE VERY BEGINNING.
NO ONE CAN BECOME STRONG OVERNIGHT.
FOR ME, I THINK THAT THE STRENGTH OF ACCUMULATING POWER LITTLE BY LITTLE OVER TIME...
IS IRREPLACEABLE AND PRECIOUS.
THAT'S WHY I WANT YOU TO GROW WITHOUT BEING IN A RUSH.
YES...

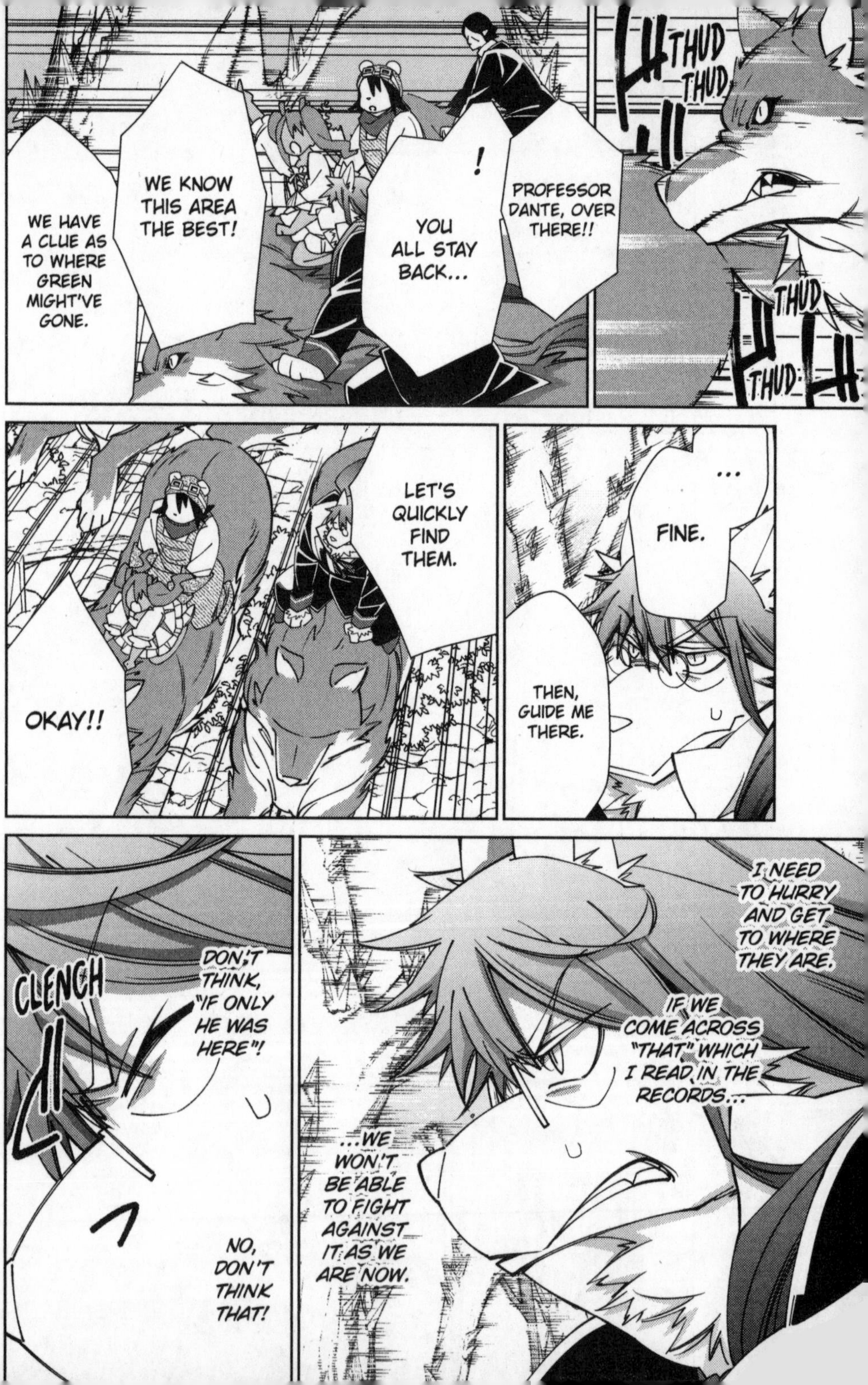
THUD
THUD
THUD
THUD
PROFESSOR DANTE, OVER THERE!!
!
YOU ALL STAY BACK...
WE KNOW THIS AREA THE BEST!
WE HAVE A CLUE AS TO WHERE GREEN MIGHT'VE GONE.
...
FINE.
THEN, GUIDE ME THERE.
LET'S QUICKLY FIND THEM.
OKAY!!
I NEED TO HURRY AND GET TO WHERE THEY ARE.
IF WE COME ACROSS "THAT" WHICH I READ IN THE RECORDS...
...WE WON'T BE ABLE TO FIGHT AGAINST IT AS WE ARE NOW.
DON'T THINK, "IF ONLY HE WAS HERE"!
CLENCH
NO, DON'T THINK THAT!

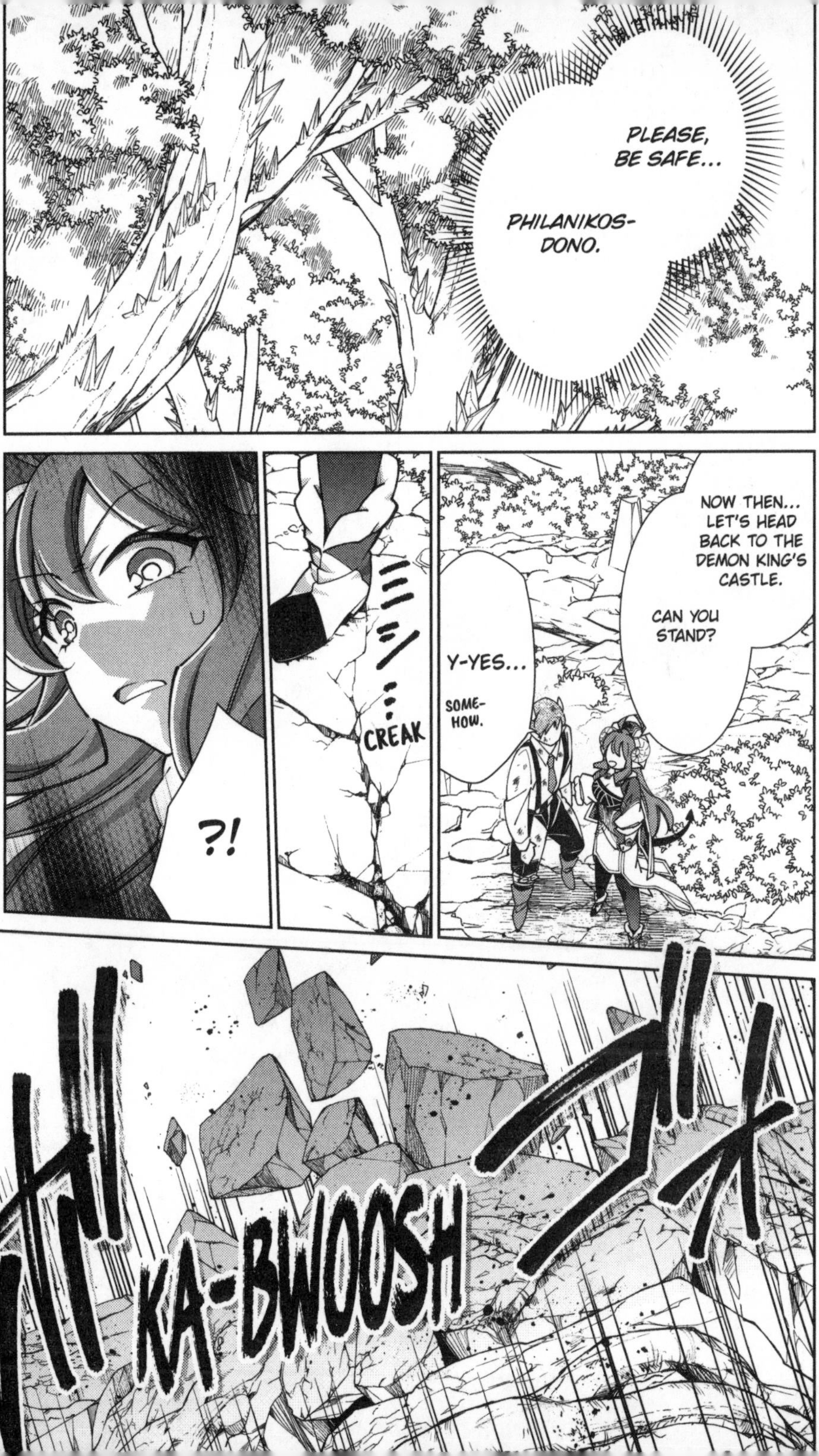
PLEASE, BE SAFE...
PHILANIKOS-DONO.
NOW THEN... LET'S HEAD BACK TO THE DEMON KING'S CASTLE.
CAN YOU STAND?
Y-YES...
SOME-HOW.
CREAK
?!
KA-BWOOSH

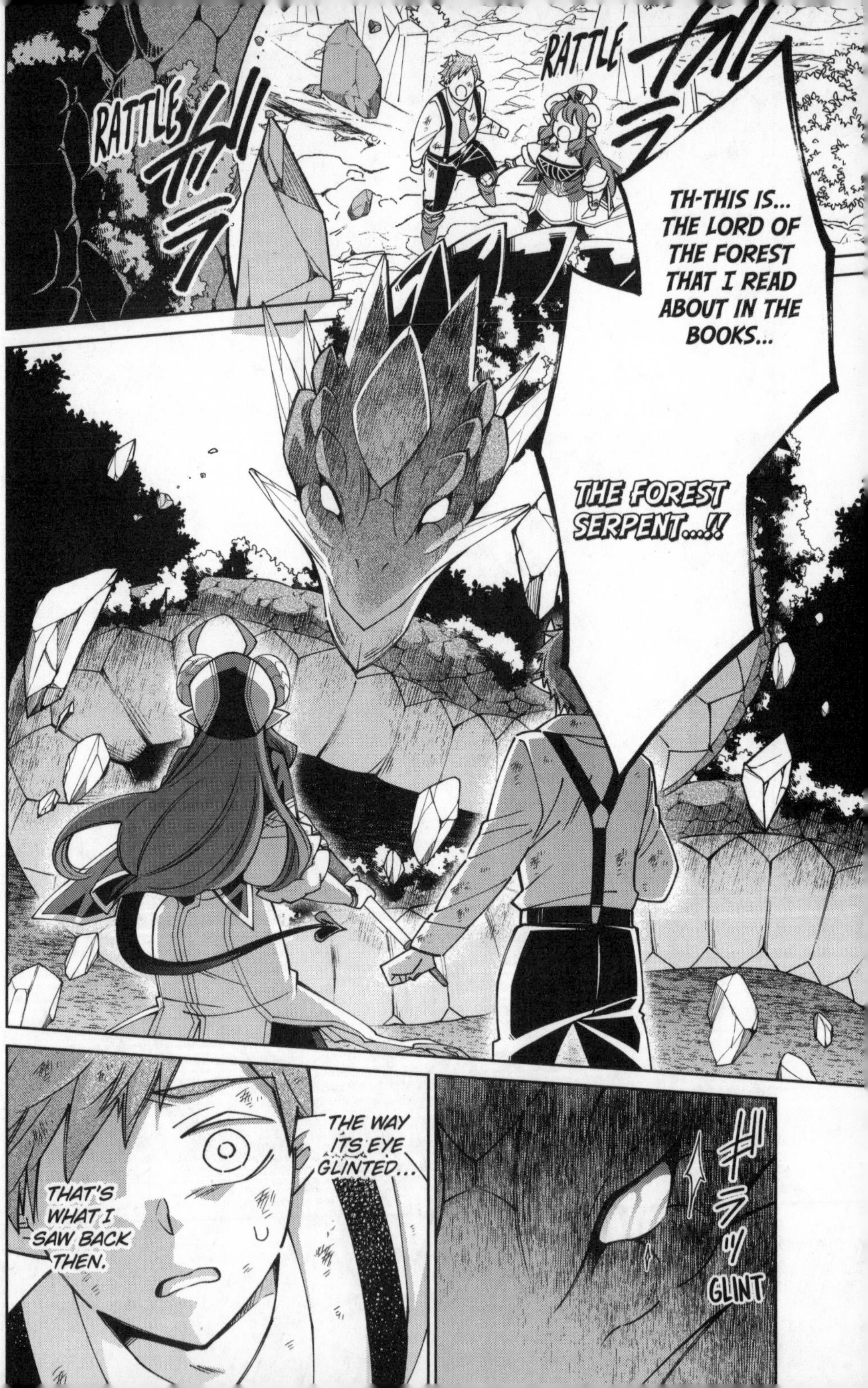
RATTLE
RATTLE
TH-THIS IS... THE LORD OF THE FOREST THAT I READ ABOUT IN THE BOOKS...
THE FOREST SERPENT...!!
GLINT
THE WAY ITS EYE GLINTED...
THAT'S WHAT I SAW BACK THEN.

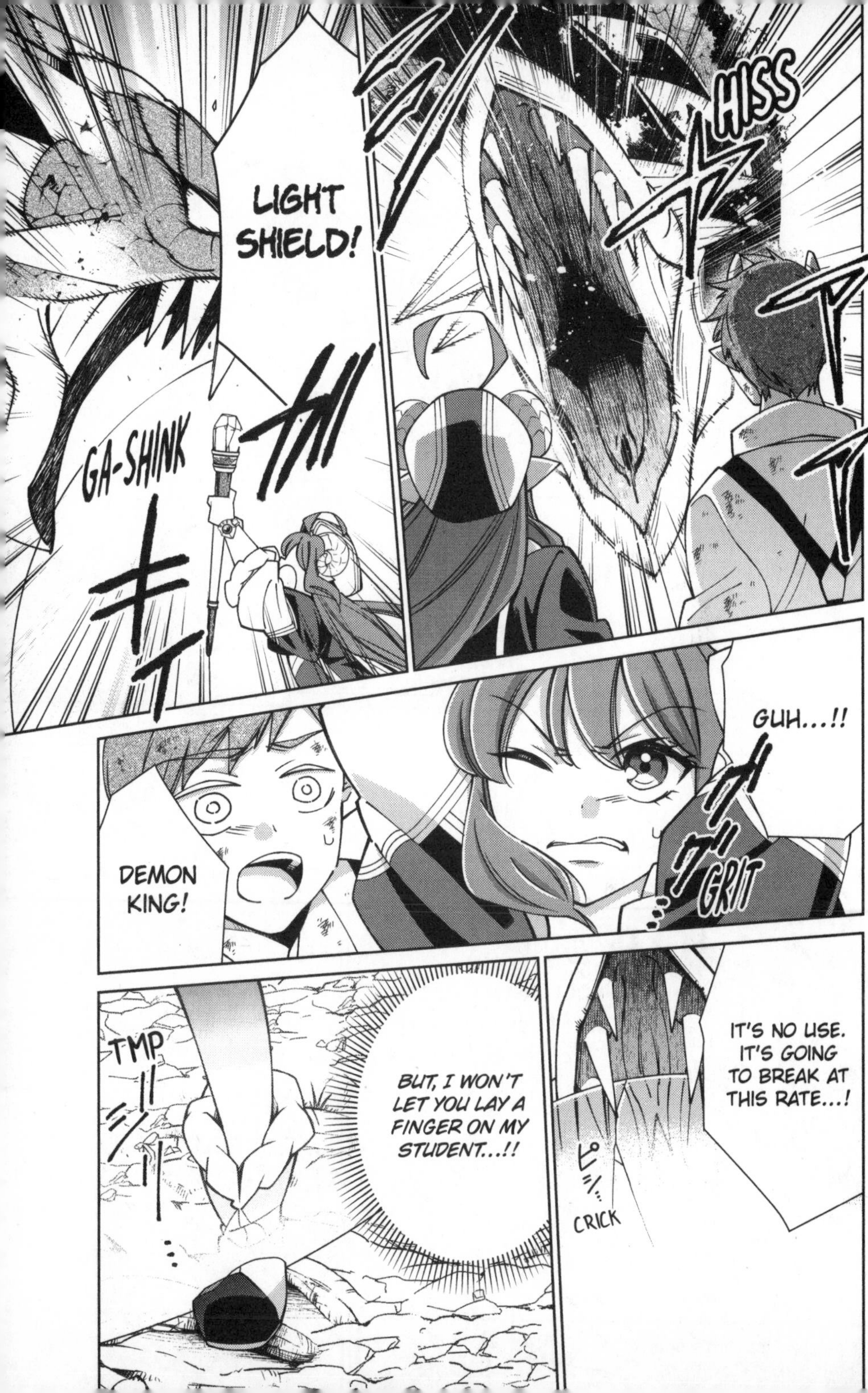
HISS
LIGHT SHIELD!
GA-SHINK
GUH...!!
GRIT
DEMON KING!
IT'S NO USE. IT'S GOING TO BREAK AT THIS RATE...!
CRICK
BUT, I WON'T LET YOU LAY A FINGER ON MY STUDENT...!!
TMP

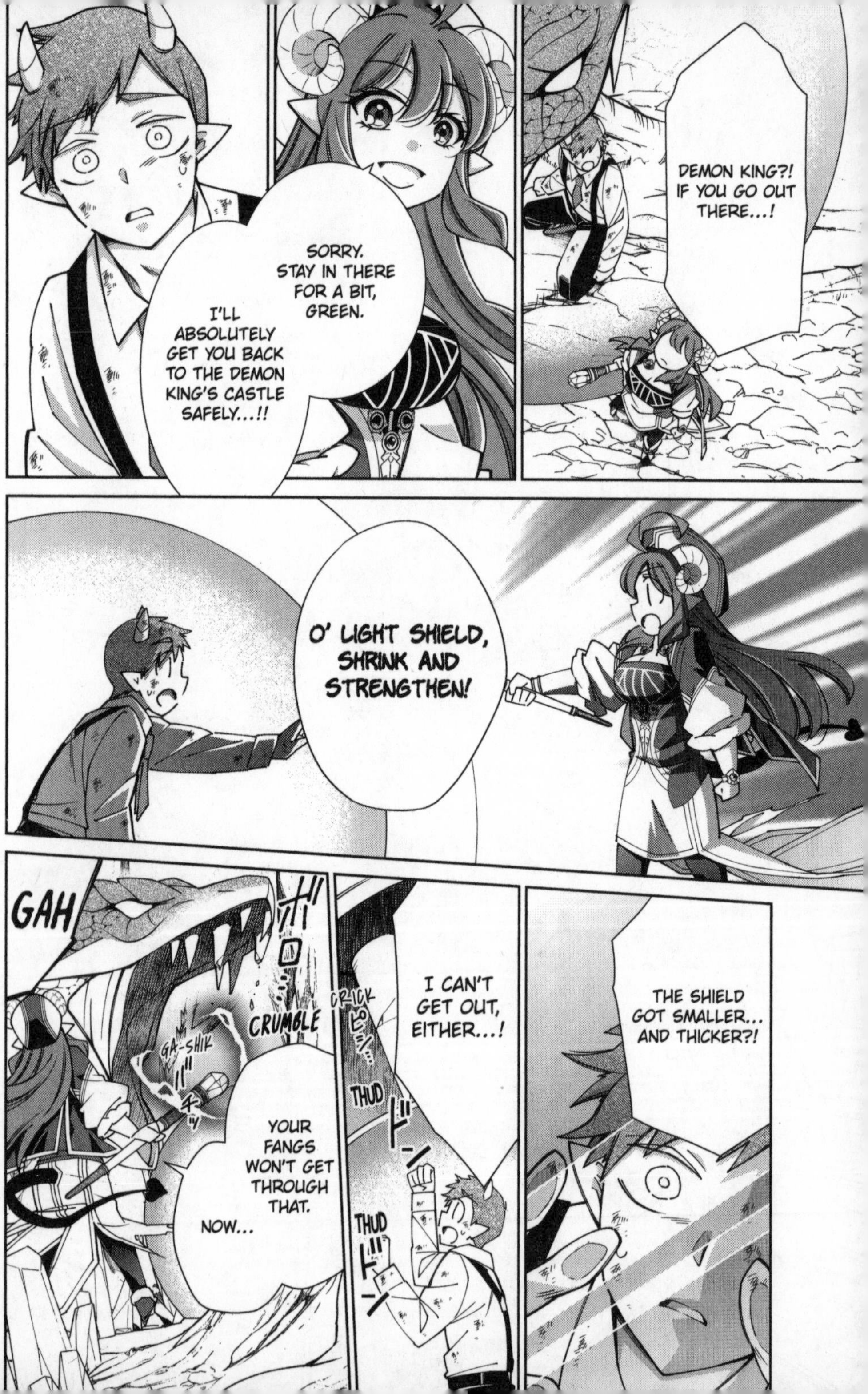
DEMON KING?! IF YOU GO OUT THERE...!
SORRY. STAY IN THERE FOR A BIT, GREEN.
I'LL ABSOLUTELY GET YOU BACK TO THE DEMON KING'S CASTLE SAFELY...!!
O' LIGHT SHIELD, SHRINK AND STRENGTHEN!
THE SHIELD GOT SMALLER... AND THICKER?!
I CAN'T GET OUT, EITHER...!
THUD
THUD
GAH
CRUMBLE
CRICK
GA-SHIK
YOUR FANGS WON'T GET THROUGH THAT.
NOW...

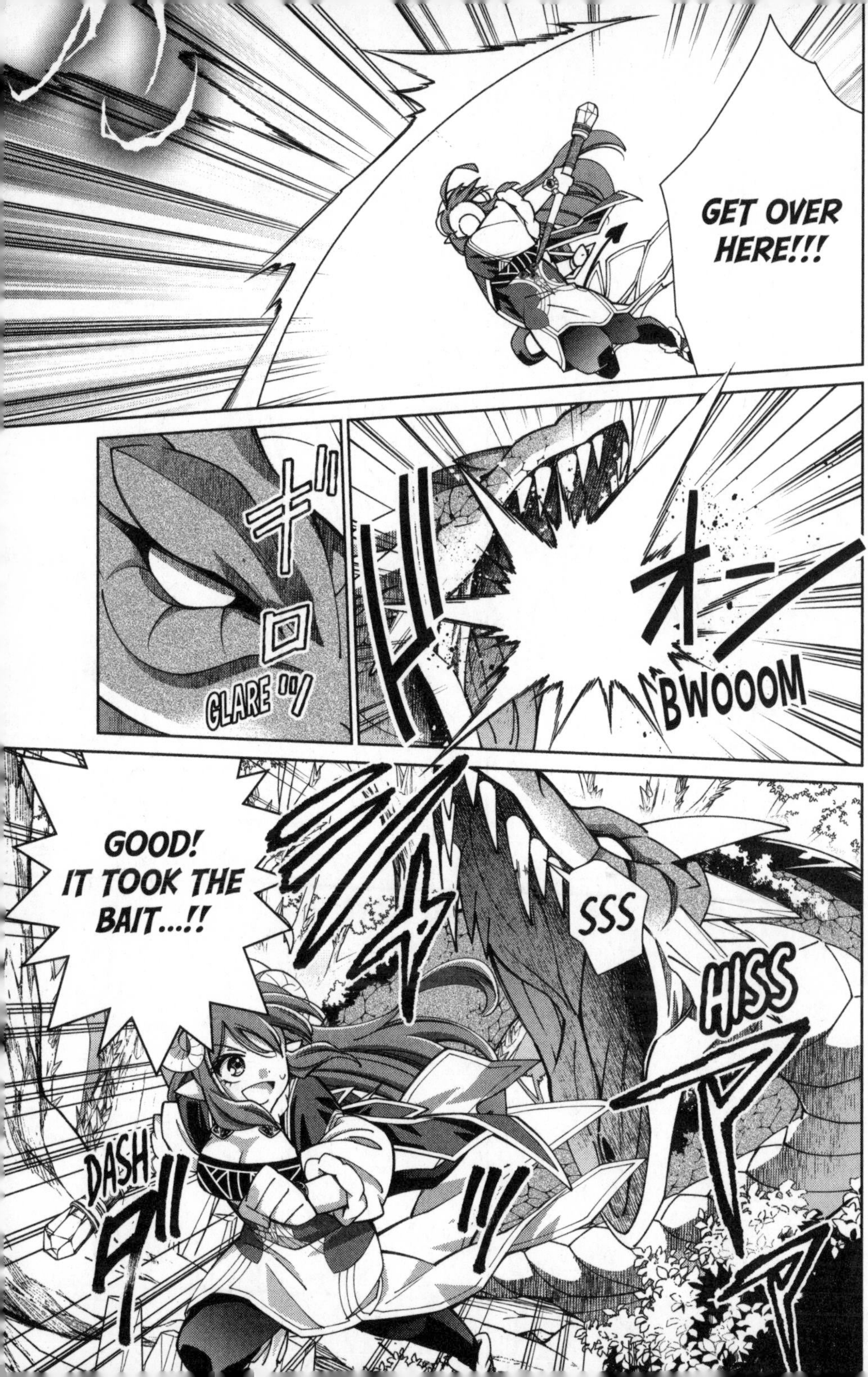
GET OVER HERE!!!
BWOOOM
GLARE
GOOD! IT TOOK THE BAIT...!!
SSS
HISS
DASH

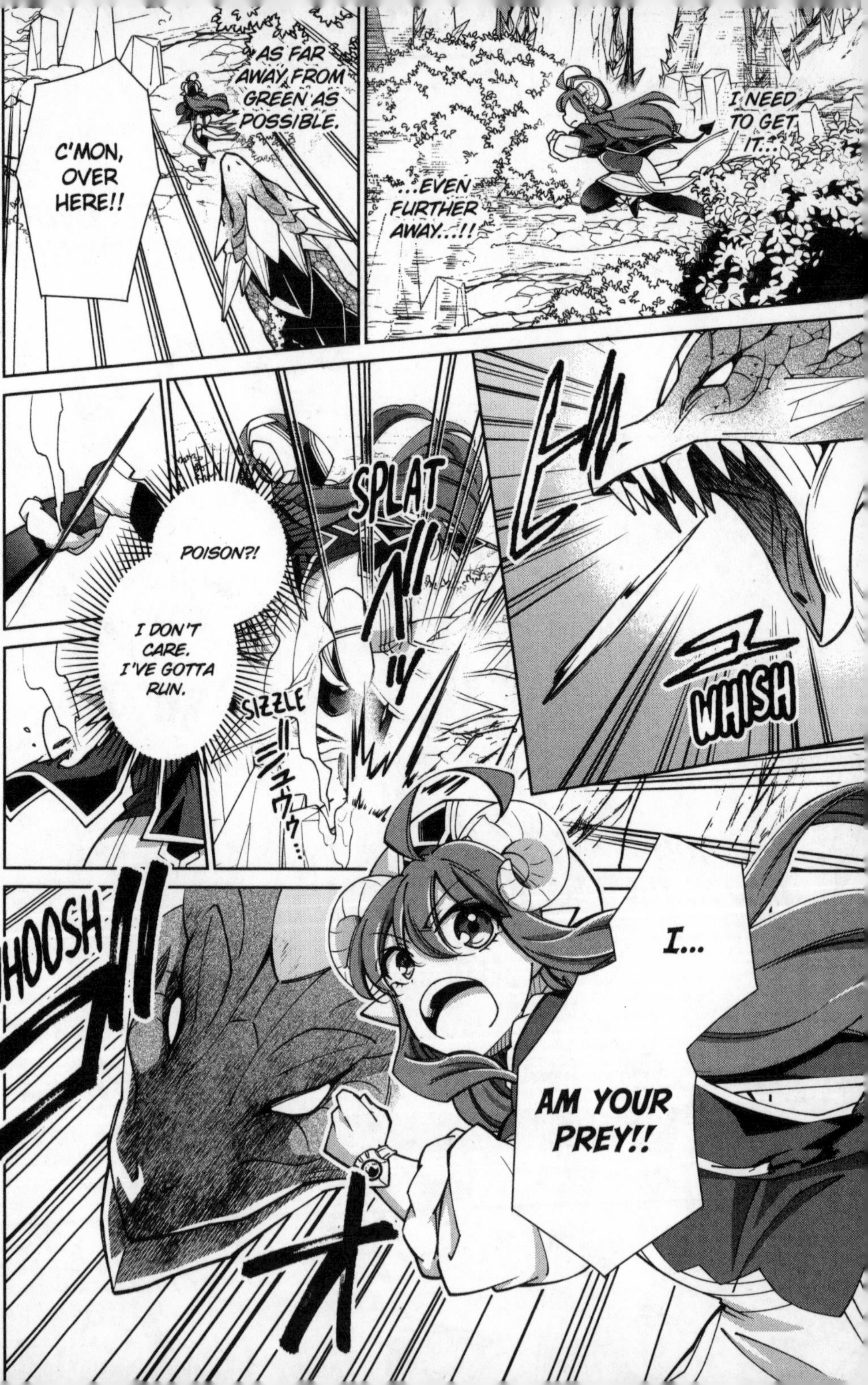

I NEED TO GET IT...
...EVEN FURTHER AWAY...!!
AS FAR AWAY FROM GREEN AS POSSIBLE.
C'MON, OVER HERE!!
WHISH
SPLAT
POISON?!
I DON'T CARE. I'VE GOTTA RUN.
SIZZLE
ジュウウ…
I...
AM YOUR PREY!!
WHOOSH

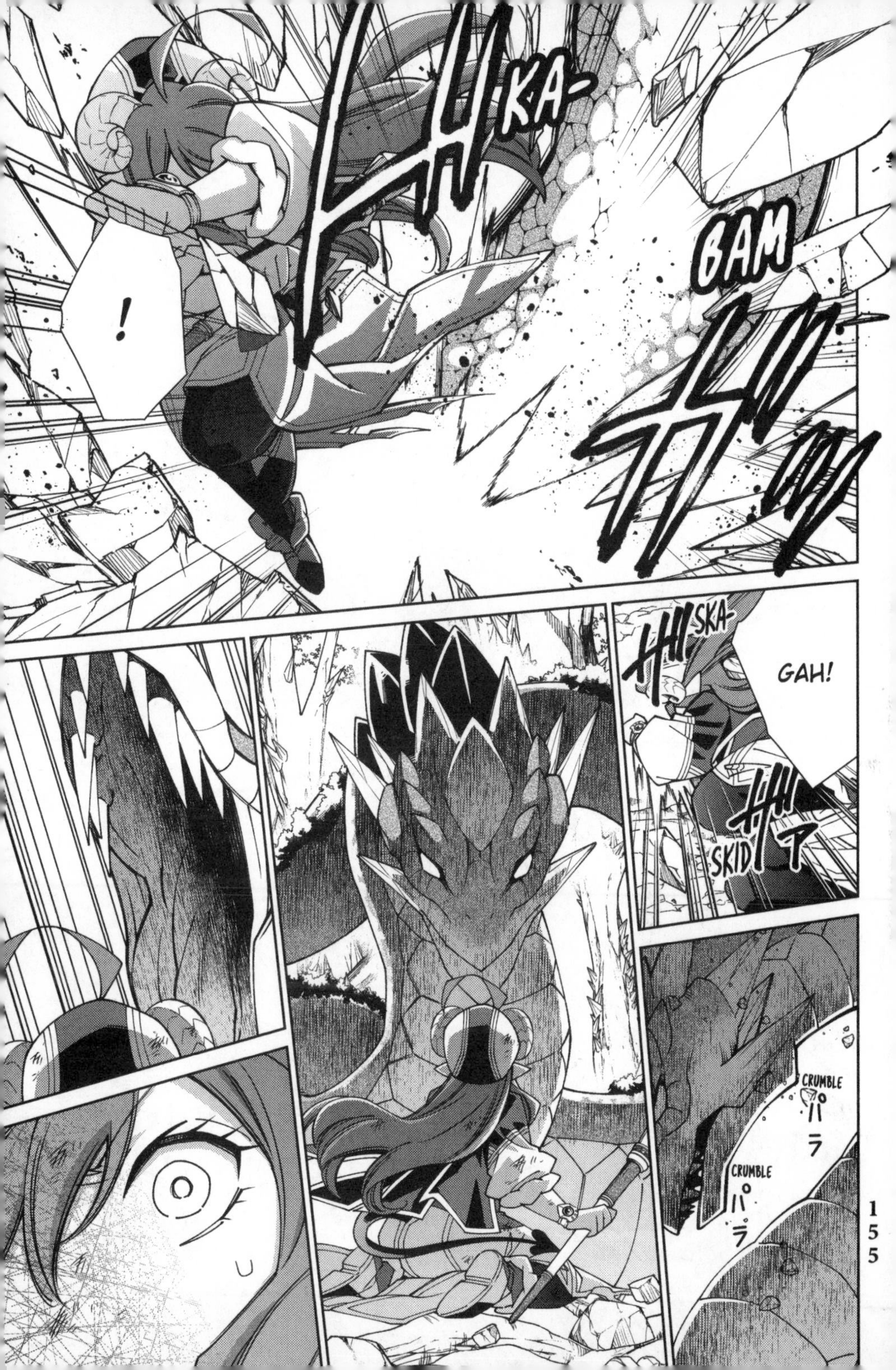
KA-
BAM
!
SKA
GAH!
SKID
CRUMBLE
パラ
CRUMBLE
パラ

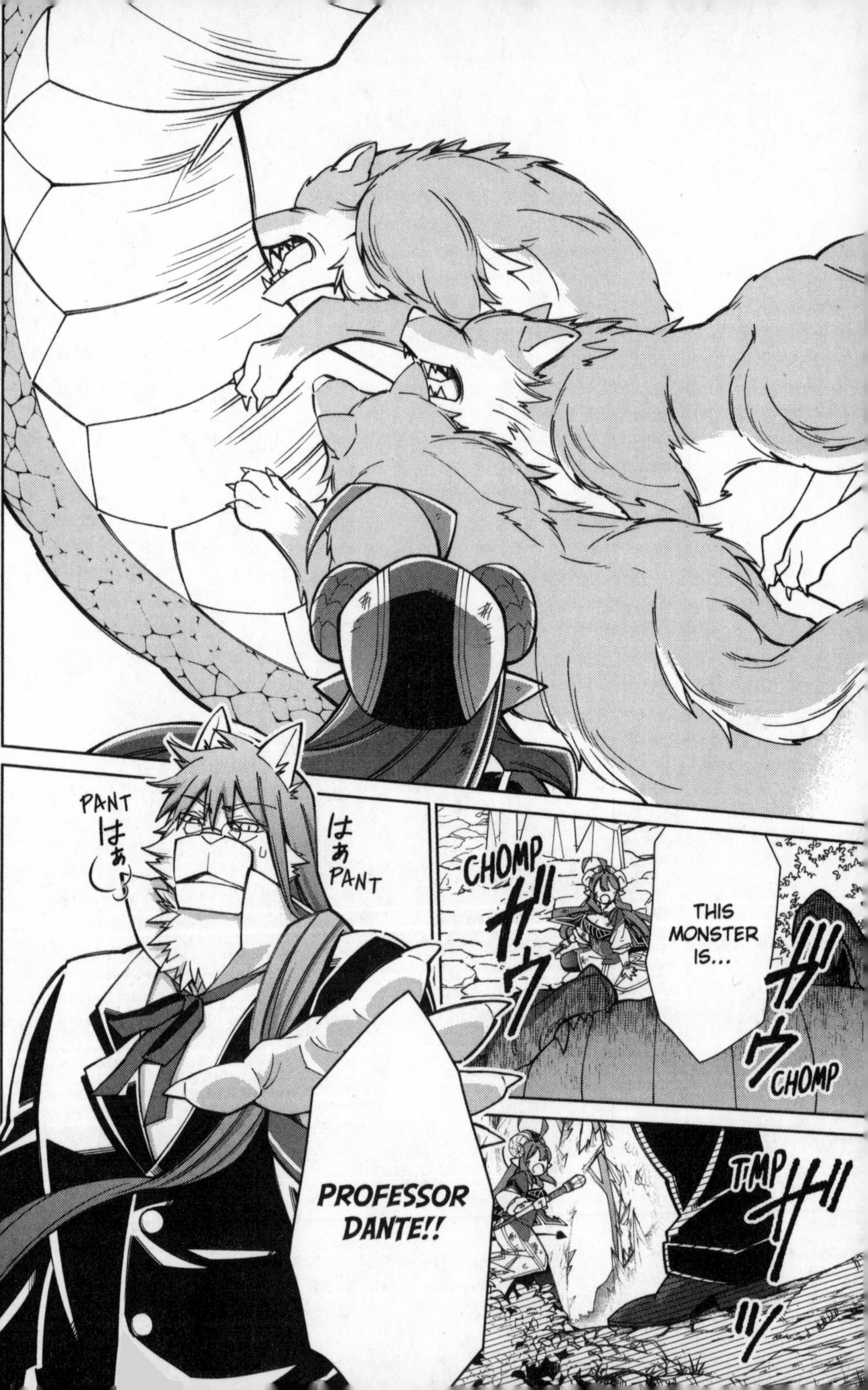
ガウ
CHOMP
THIS MONSTER IS...
ガウ
CHOMP
PANT
はぁ
はぁ
PANT
PROFESSOR DANTE!!
TMP
ザッ

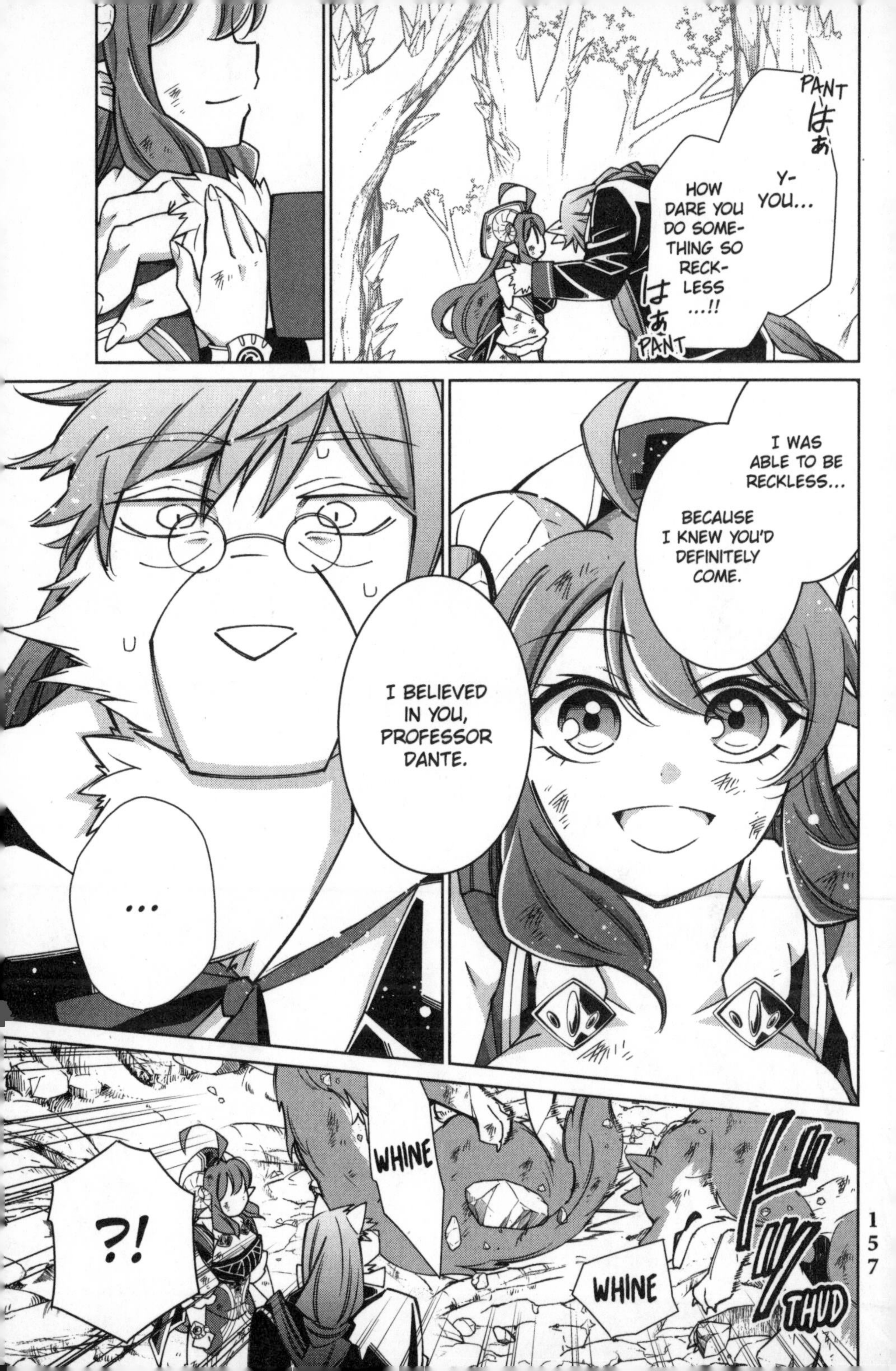
PANT はぁ
Y-YOU...
HOW DARE YOU DO SOMETHING SO RECKLESS...!!
はぁ PANT
I WAS ABLE TO BE RECKLESS...
BECAUSE I KNEW YOU'D DEFINITELY COME.
I BELIEVED IN YOU, PROFESSOR DANTE.
...
THUD
WHINE
WHINE
?!

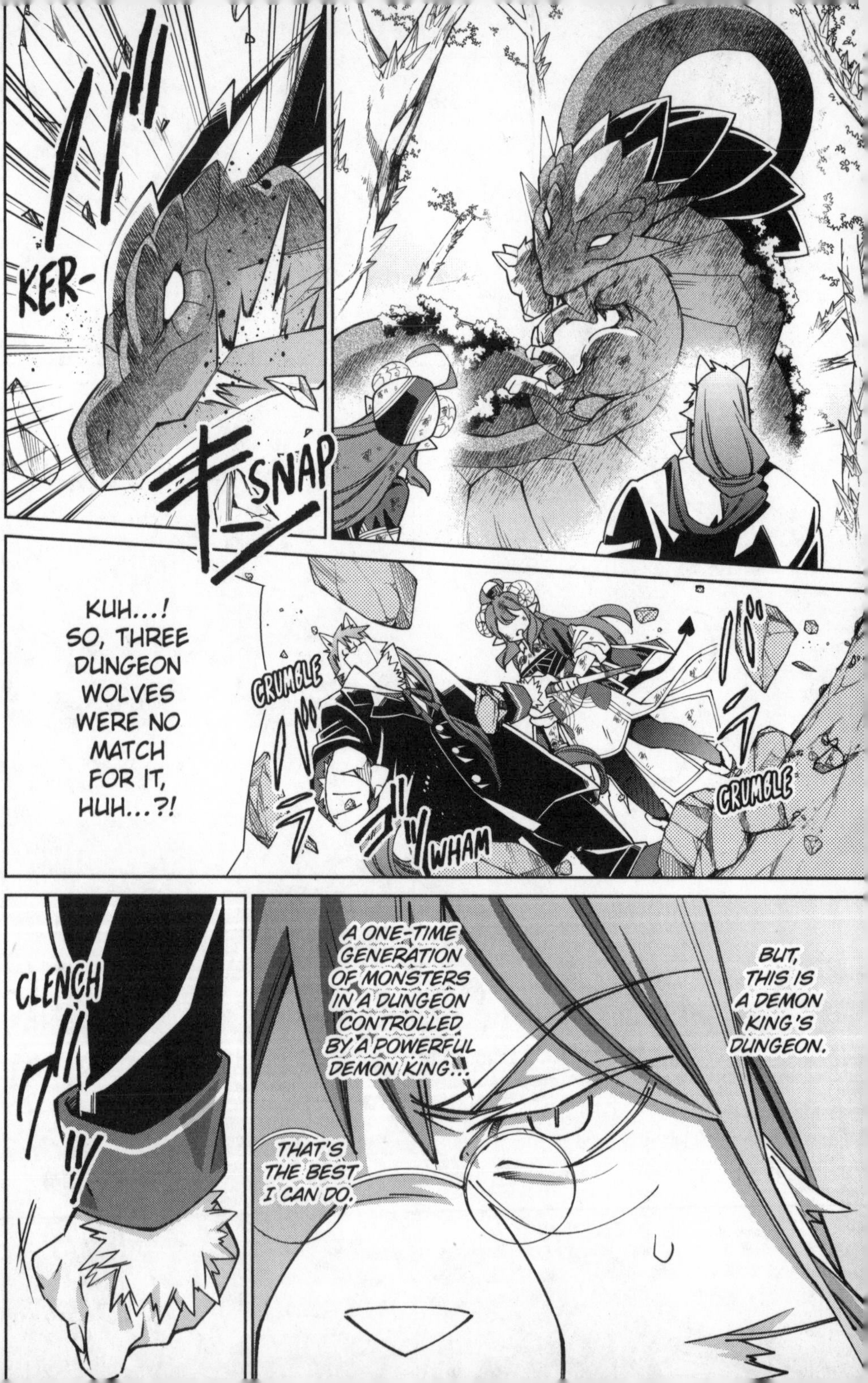
KER-
SNAP
KUH...! SO, THREE DUNGEON WOLVES WERE NO MATCH FOR IT, HUH...?!
CRUMBLE
CRUMBLE
WHAM
BUT, THIS IS A DEMON KING'S DUNGEON.
A ONE-TIME GENERATION OF MONSTERS IN A DUNGEON CONTROLLED BY A POWERFUL DEMON KING...
THAT'S THE BEST I CAN DO.
CLENCH

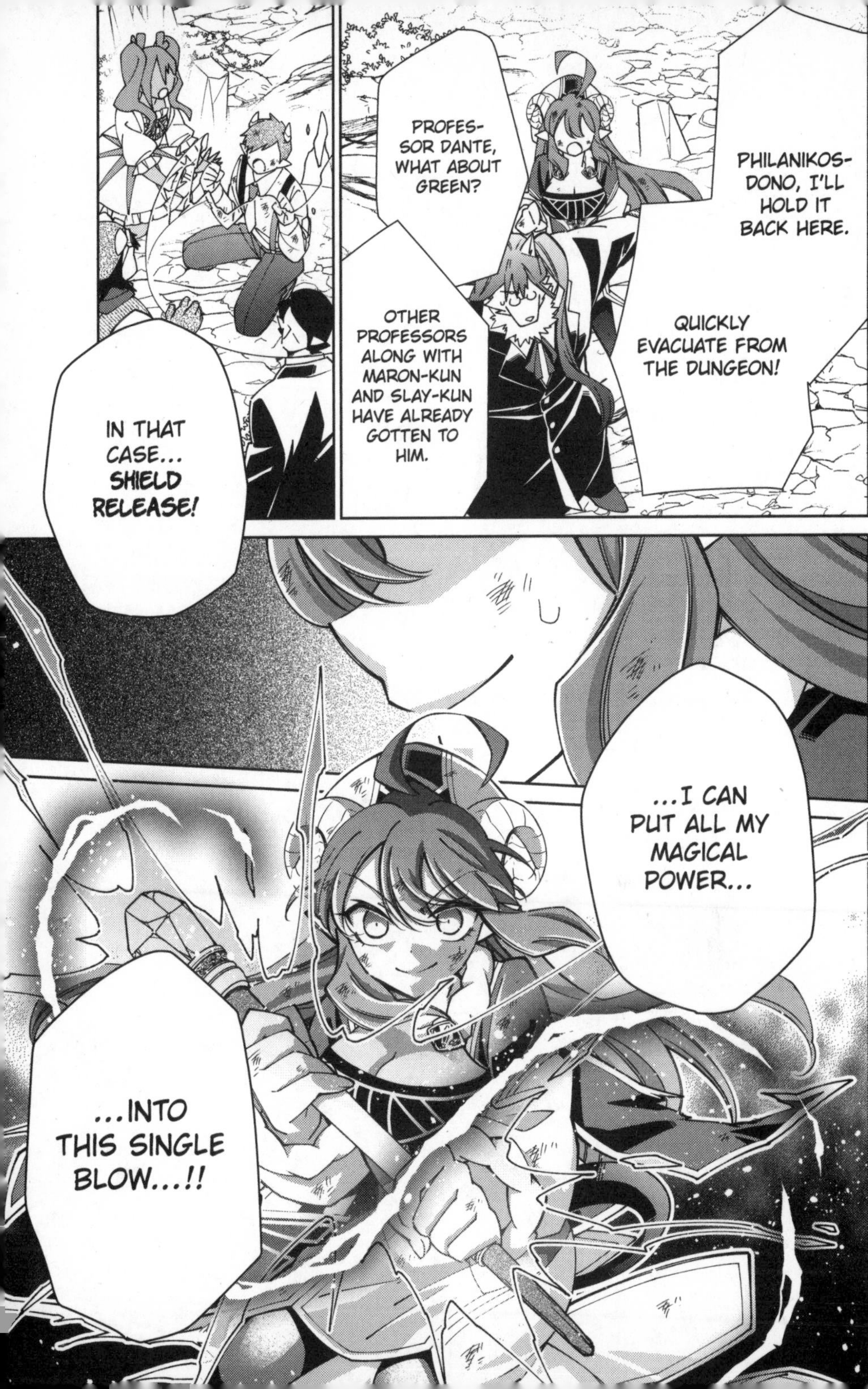
PHILANIKOS-DONO, I'LL HOLD IT BACK HERE.
QUICKLY EVACUATE FROM THE DUNGEON!
PROFES-SOR DANTE, WHAT ABOUT GREEN?
OTHER PROFESSORS ALONG WITH MARON-KUN AND SLAY-KUN HAVE ALREADY GOTTEN TO HIM.
IN THAT CASE... **SHIELD RELEASE!**
...I CAN PUT ALL MY MAGICAL POWER...
...INTO THIS SINGLE BLOW...!!

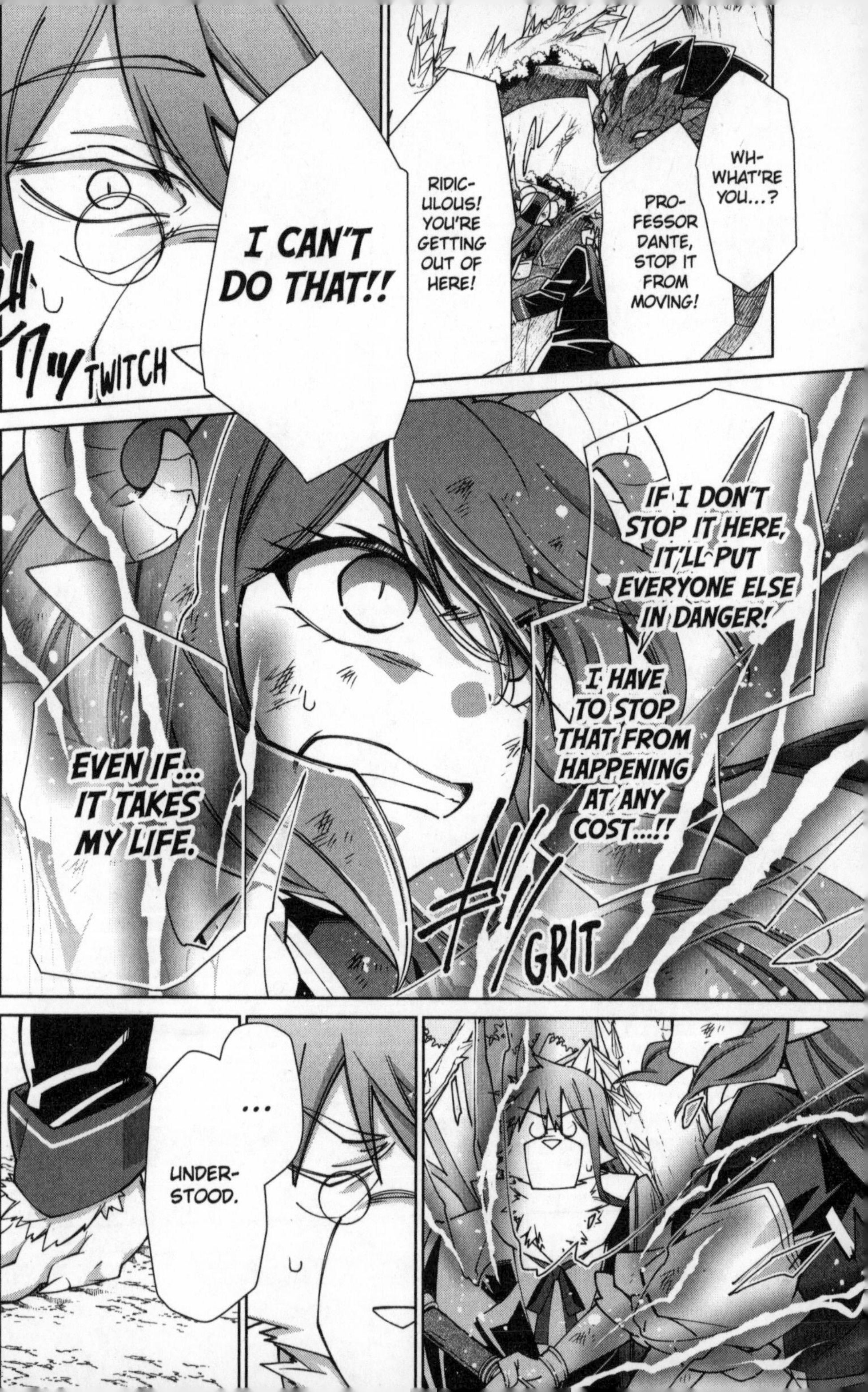
WH- WHAT'RE YOU...?
PRO- FESSOR DANTE, STOP IT FROM MOVING!
RIDIC- ULOUS! YOU'RE GETTING OUT OF HERE!
I CAN'T DO THAT!!
TWITCH
IF I DON'T STOP IT HERE, IT'LL PUT EVERYONE ELSE IN DANGER!
I HAVE TO STOP THAT FROM HAPPENING AT ANY COST...!!
EVEN IF... IT TAKES MY LIFE.
GRIT
...
UNDER- STOOD.

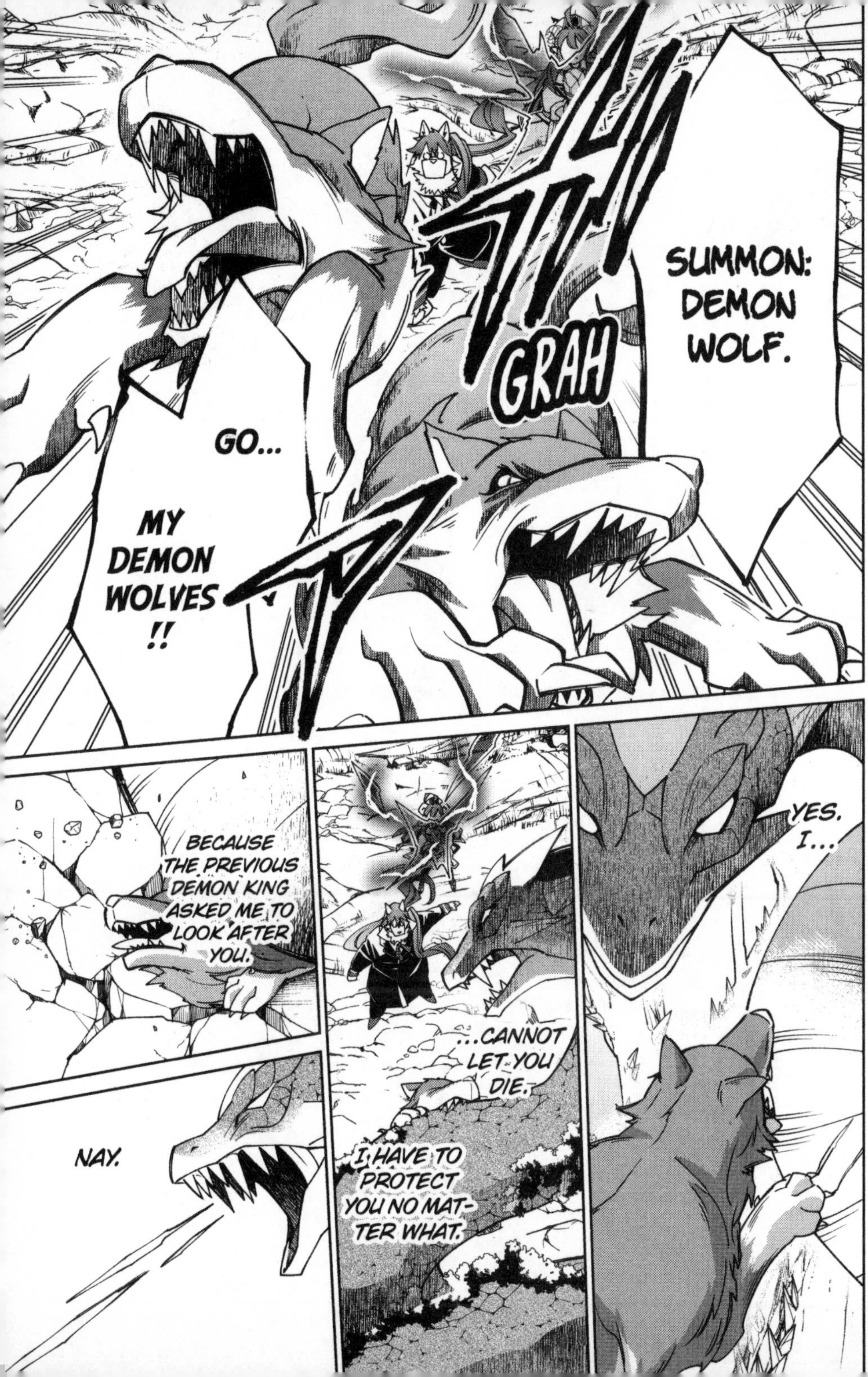
SUMMON: DEMON WOLF.
GRAH
GO...
MY DEMON WOLVES !!
YES. I...
...CANNOT LET YOU DIE.
I HAVE TO PROTECT YOU NO MATTER WHAT.
BECAUSE THE PREVIOUS DEMON KING ASKED ME TO LOOK AFTER YOU.
NAY.

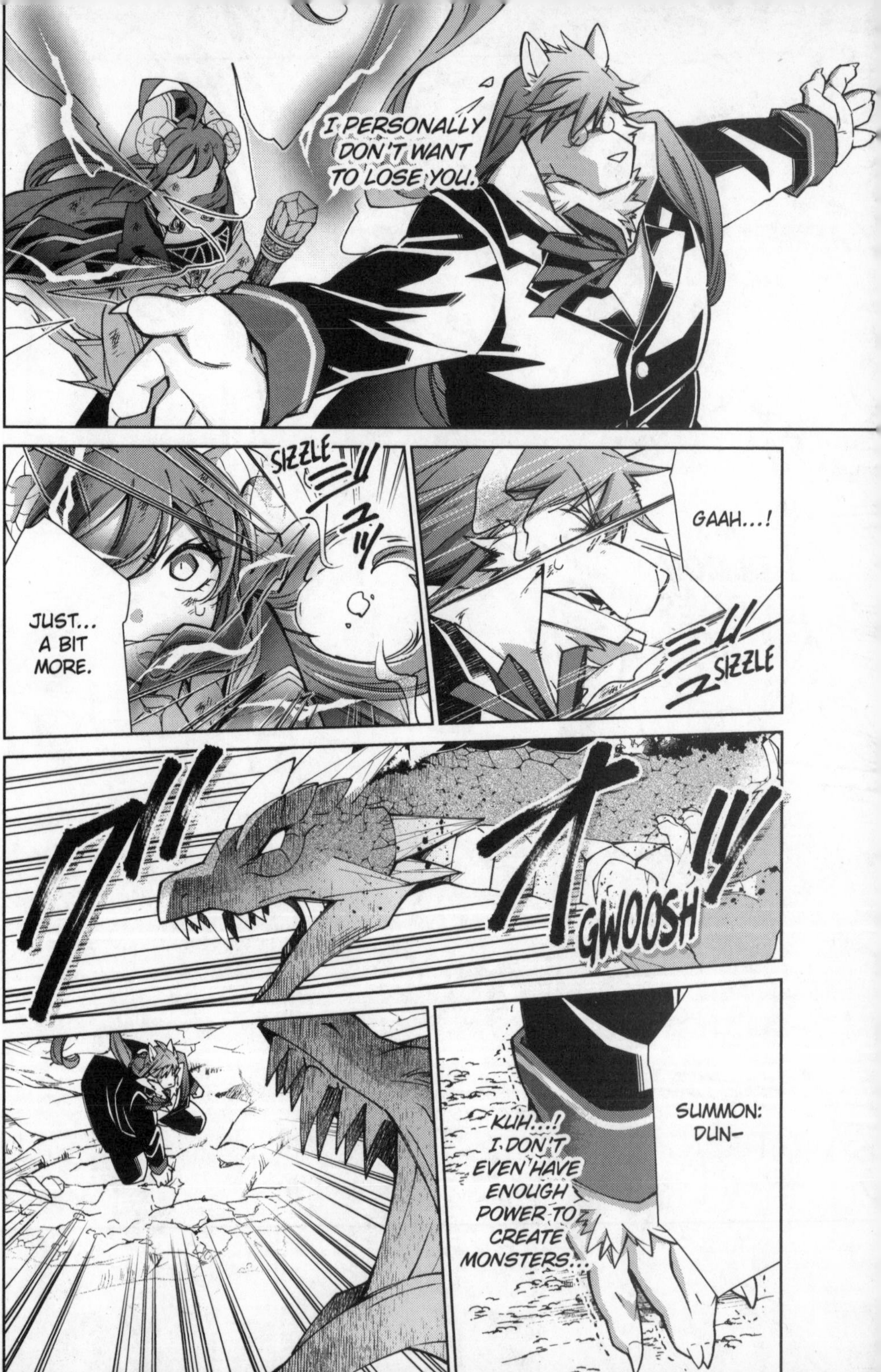
I PERSONALLY DON'T WANT TO LOSE YOU.
GAAH...!
SIZZLE
SIZZLE
JUST... A BIT MORE.
GWOOSH
SUMMON: DUN-
KUH...! I DON'T EVEN HAVE ENOUGH POWER TO CREATE MONSTERS...

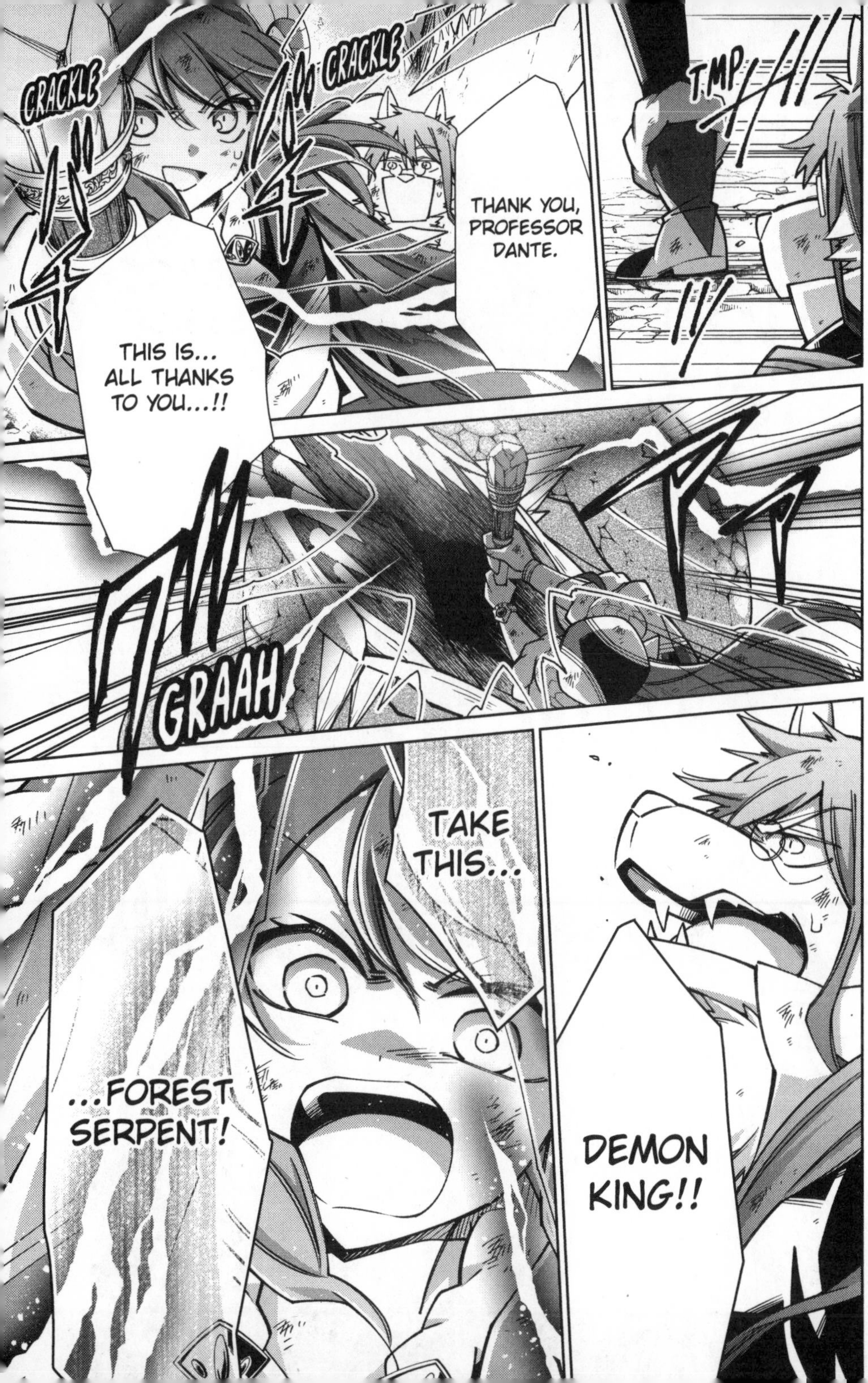
TMP
CRACKLE
CRACKLE
THANK YOU, PROFESSOR DANTE.
THIS IS... ALL THANKS TO YOU...!!
GRAAH
DEMON KING!!
TAKE THIS...
...FOREST SERPENT!

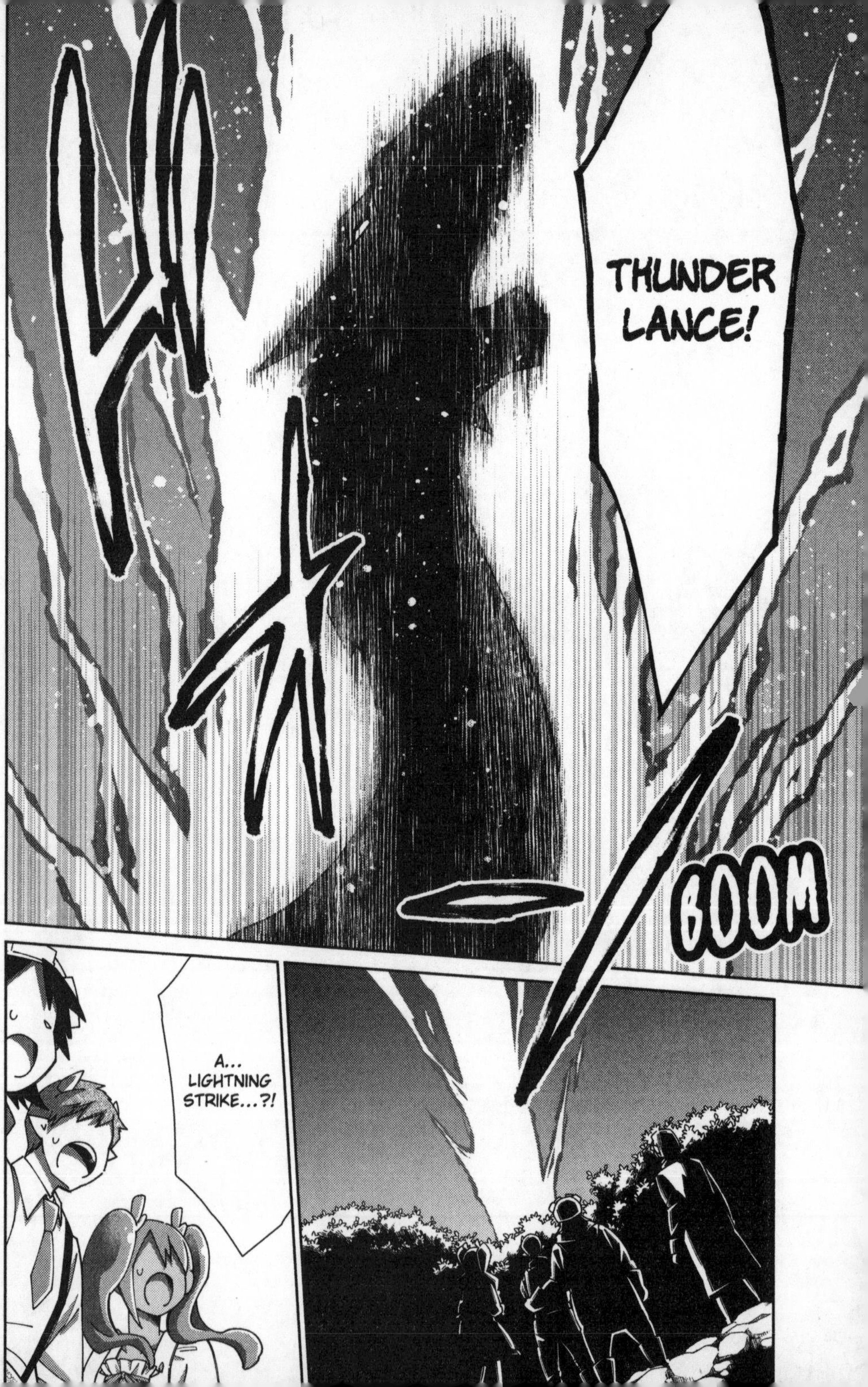
THUNDER LANCE!
BOOM
A... LIGHTNING STRIKE...?!

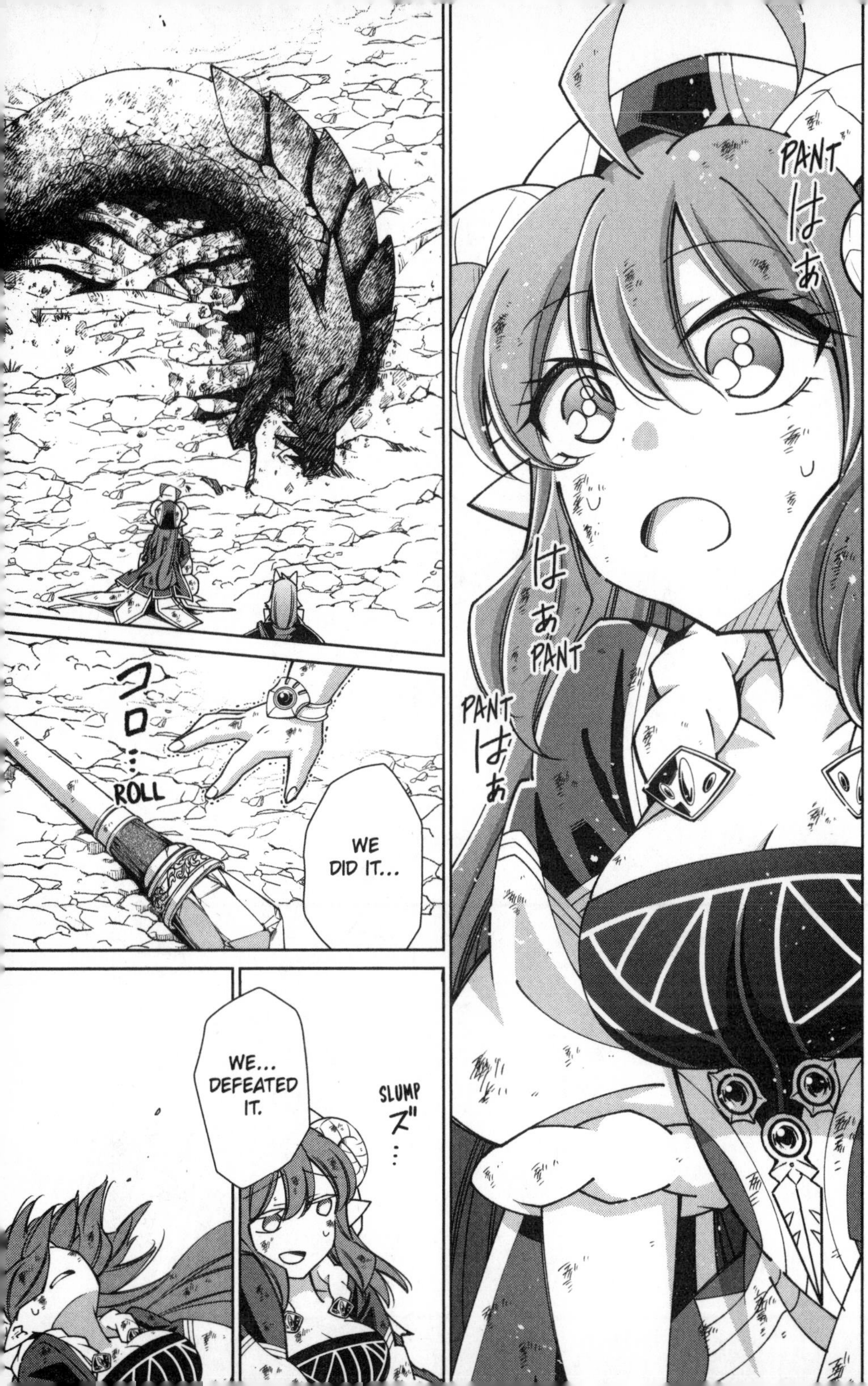
PANT
はぁ
はぁ
PANT
PANT
ぱぁ
コロ…
ROLL
WE DID IT…
WE… DEFEATED IT.
SLUMP
ズ…

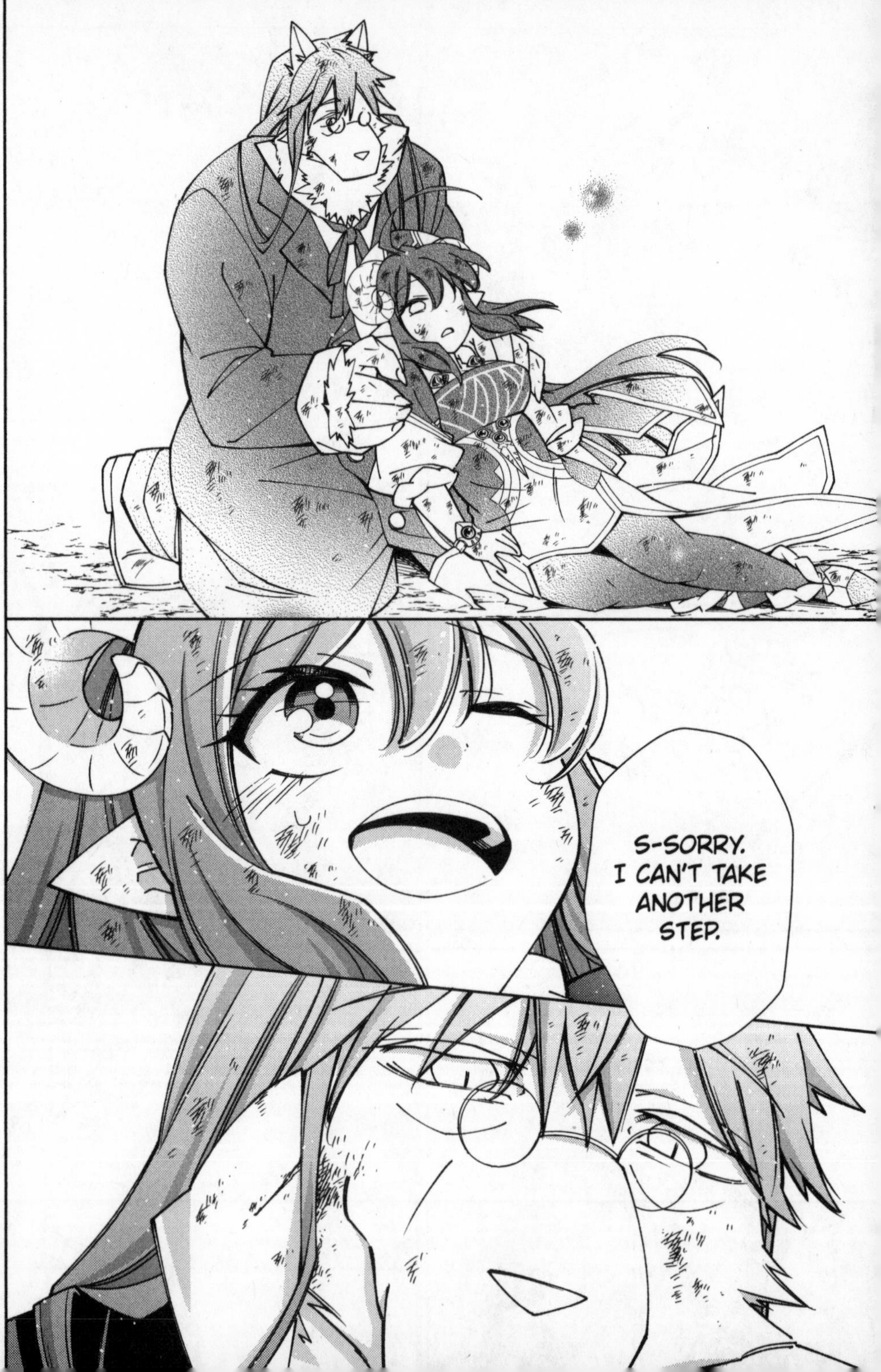
S-SORRY. I CAN'T TAKE ANOTHER STEP.

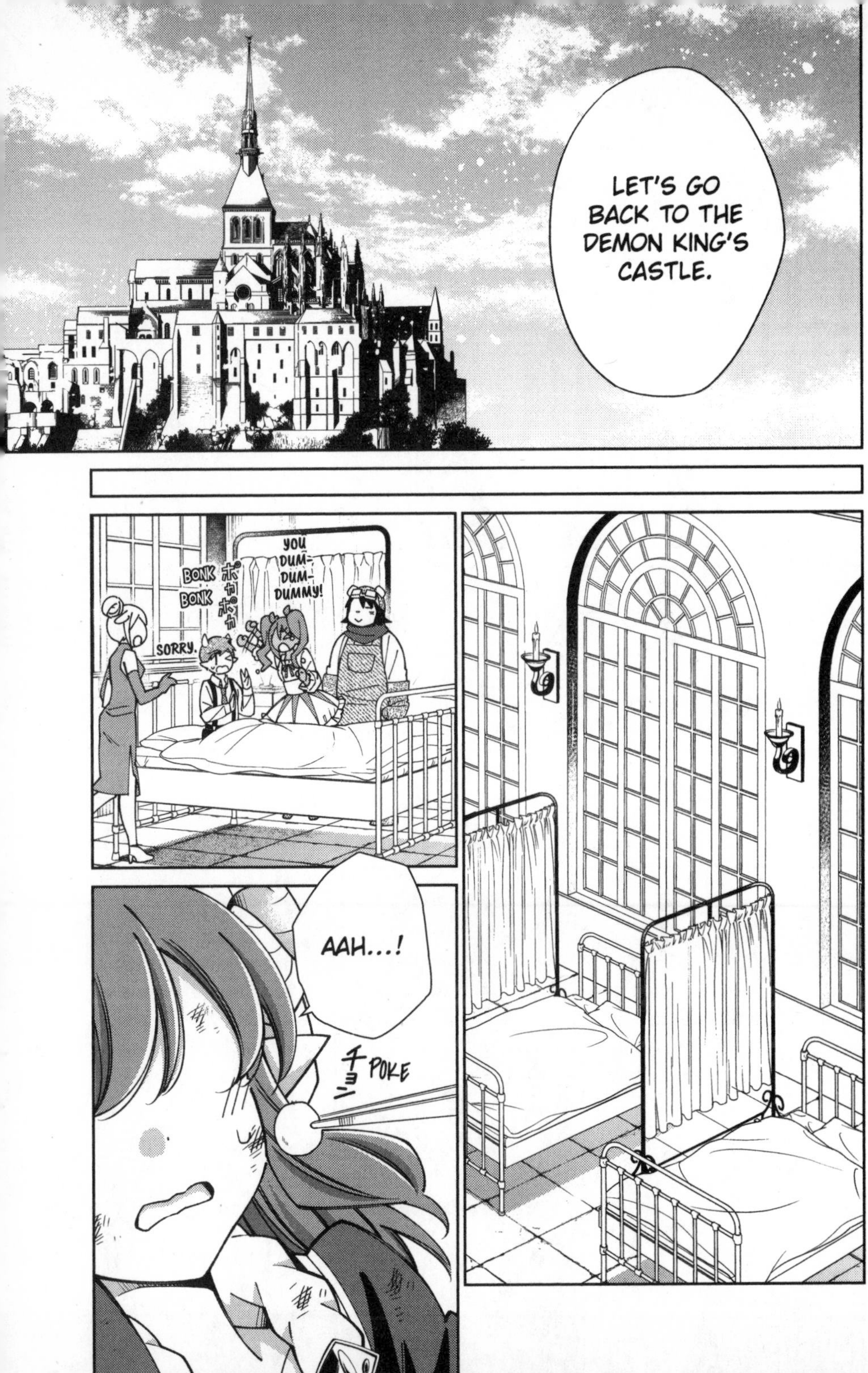
LET'S GO BACK TO THE DEMON KING'S CASTLE.
YOU DUM-DUM-DUMMY!
BONK BONK
ポカポカ
SORRY.
AAH...!
チョン
POKE

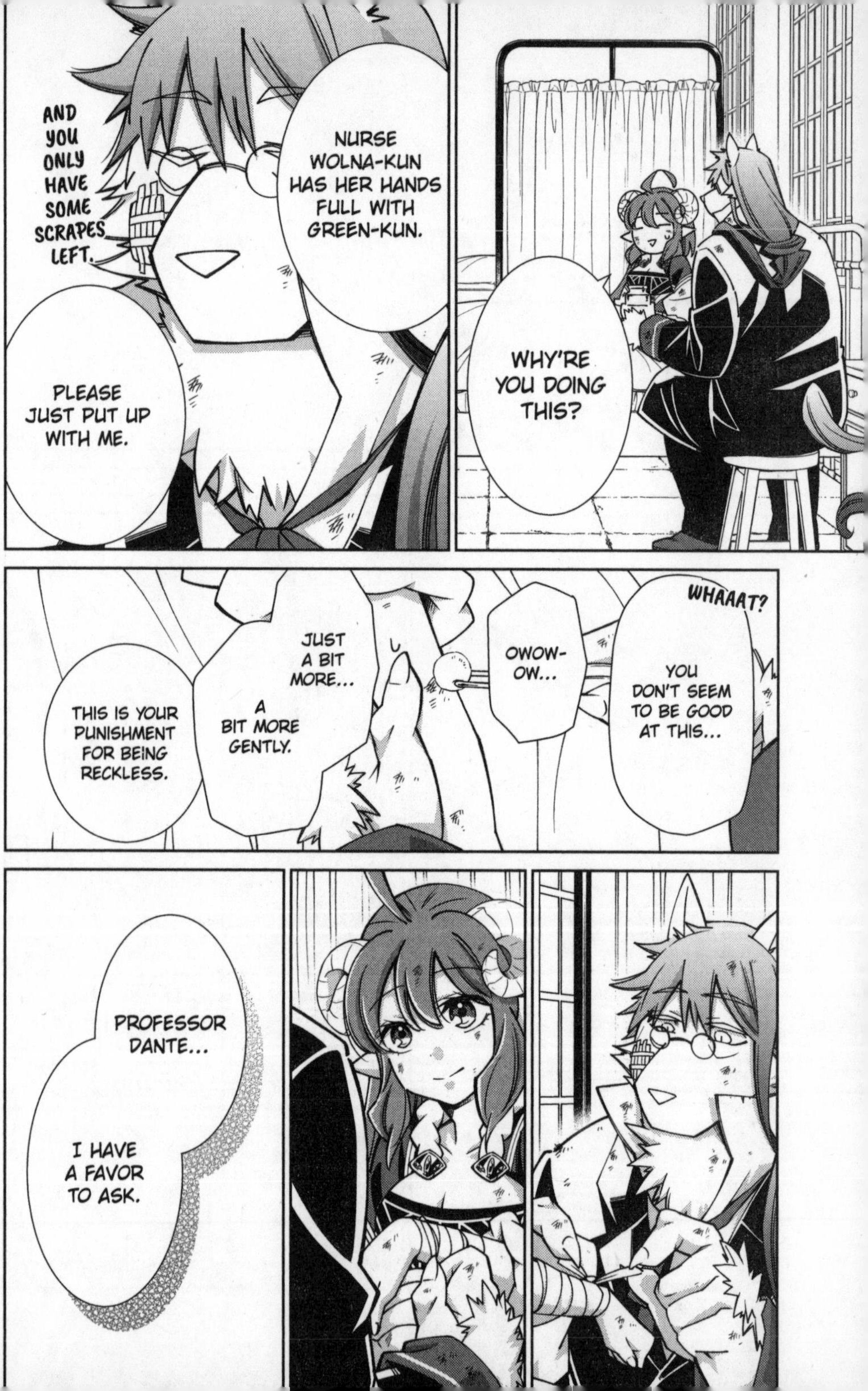
WHY'RE YOU DOING THIS?
NURSE WOLNA-KUN HAS HER HANDS FULL WITH GREEN-KUN.
AND YOU ONLY HAVE SOME SCRAPES LEFT.
PLEASE JUST PUT UP WITH ME.
WHAAAT?
YOU DON'T SEEM TO BE GOOD AT THIS...
OWOW-OW...
JUST A BIT MORE...
A BIT MORE GENTLY.
THIS IS YOUR PUNISHMENT FOR BEING RECKLESS.
PROFESSOR DANTE...
I HAVE A FAVOR TO ASK.

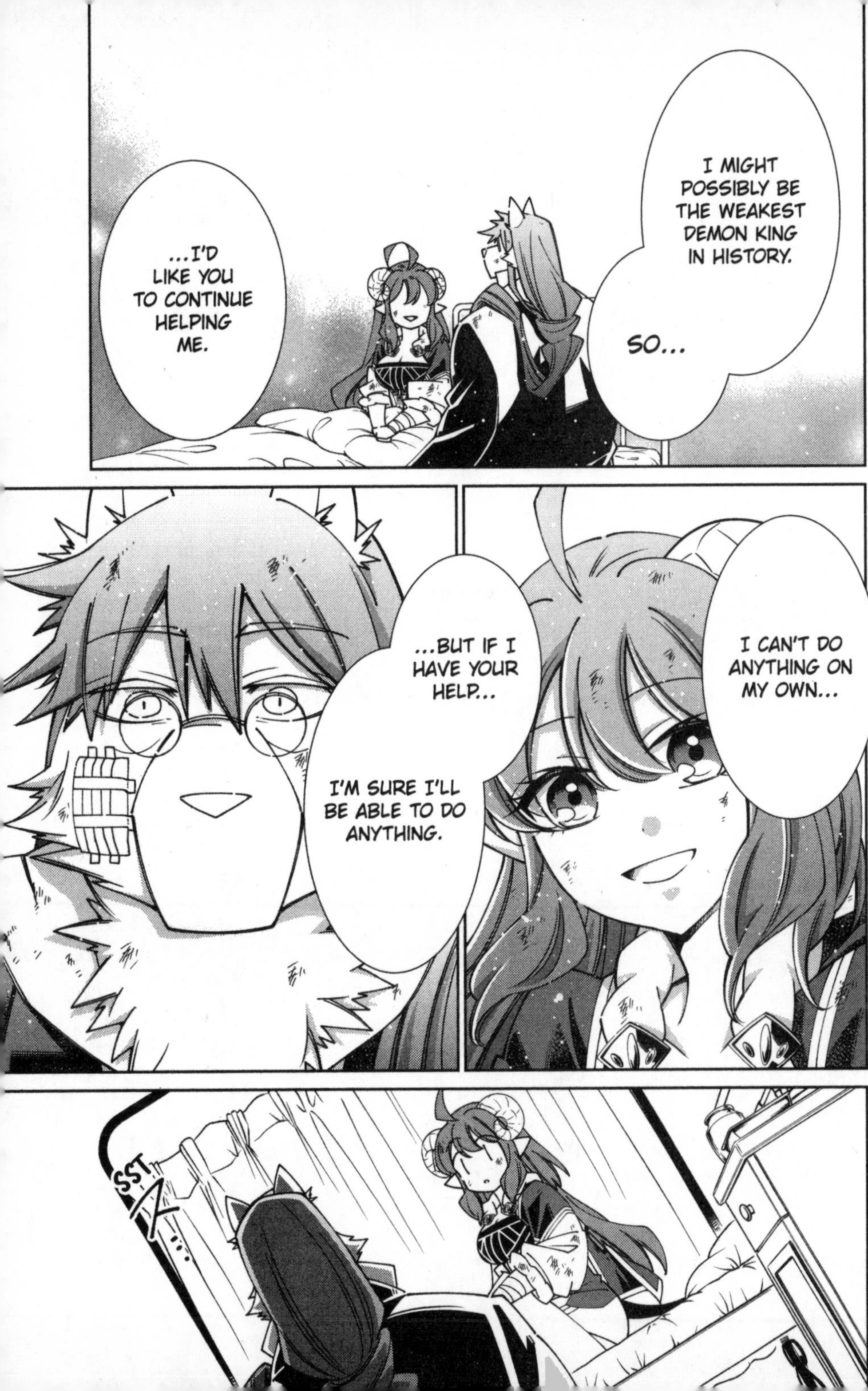
I MIGHT POSSIBLY BE THE WEAKEST DEMON KING IN HISTORY.
SO...
...I'D LIKE YOU TO CONTINUE HELPING ME.
I CAN'T DO ANYTHING ON MY OWN...
...BUT IF I HAVE YOUR HELP...
I'M SURE I'LL BE ABLE TO DO ANYTHING.
SST
...

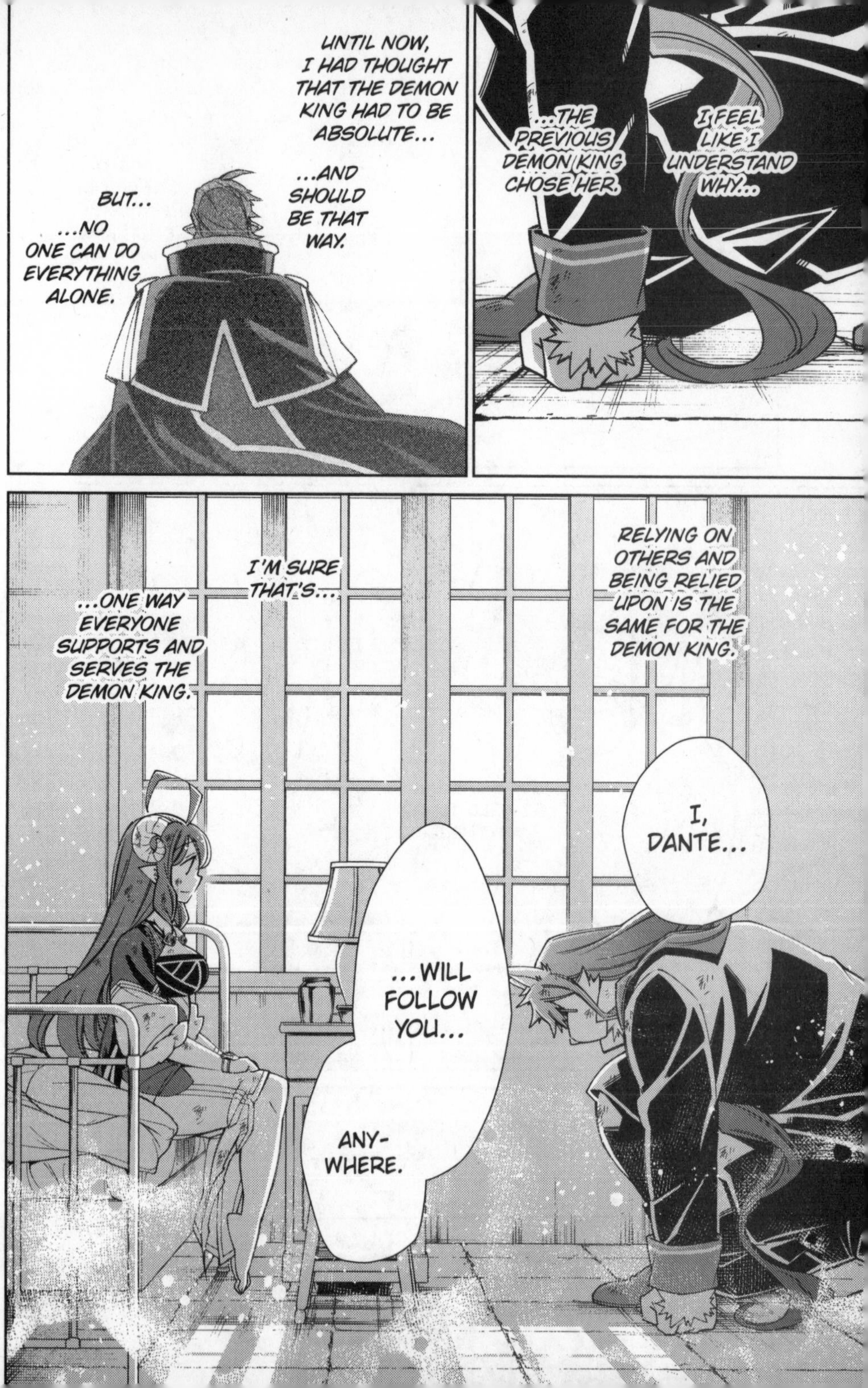
I FEEL LIKE I UNDERSTAND WHY...
...THE PREVIOUS DEMON KING CHOSE HER.
UNTIL NOW, I HAD THOUGHT THAT THE DEMON KING HAD TO BE ABSOLUTE...
...AND SHOULD BE THAT WAY.
BUT...
...NO ONE CAN DO EVERYTHING ALONE.
RELYING ON OTHERS AND BEING RELIED UPON IS THE SAME FOR THE DEMON KING.
I'M SURE THAT'S...
...ONE WAY EVERYONE SUPPORTS AND SERVES THE DEMON KING.
I, DANTE...
...WILL FOLLOW YOU...
ANY-WHERE.

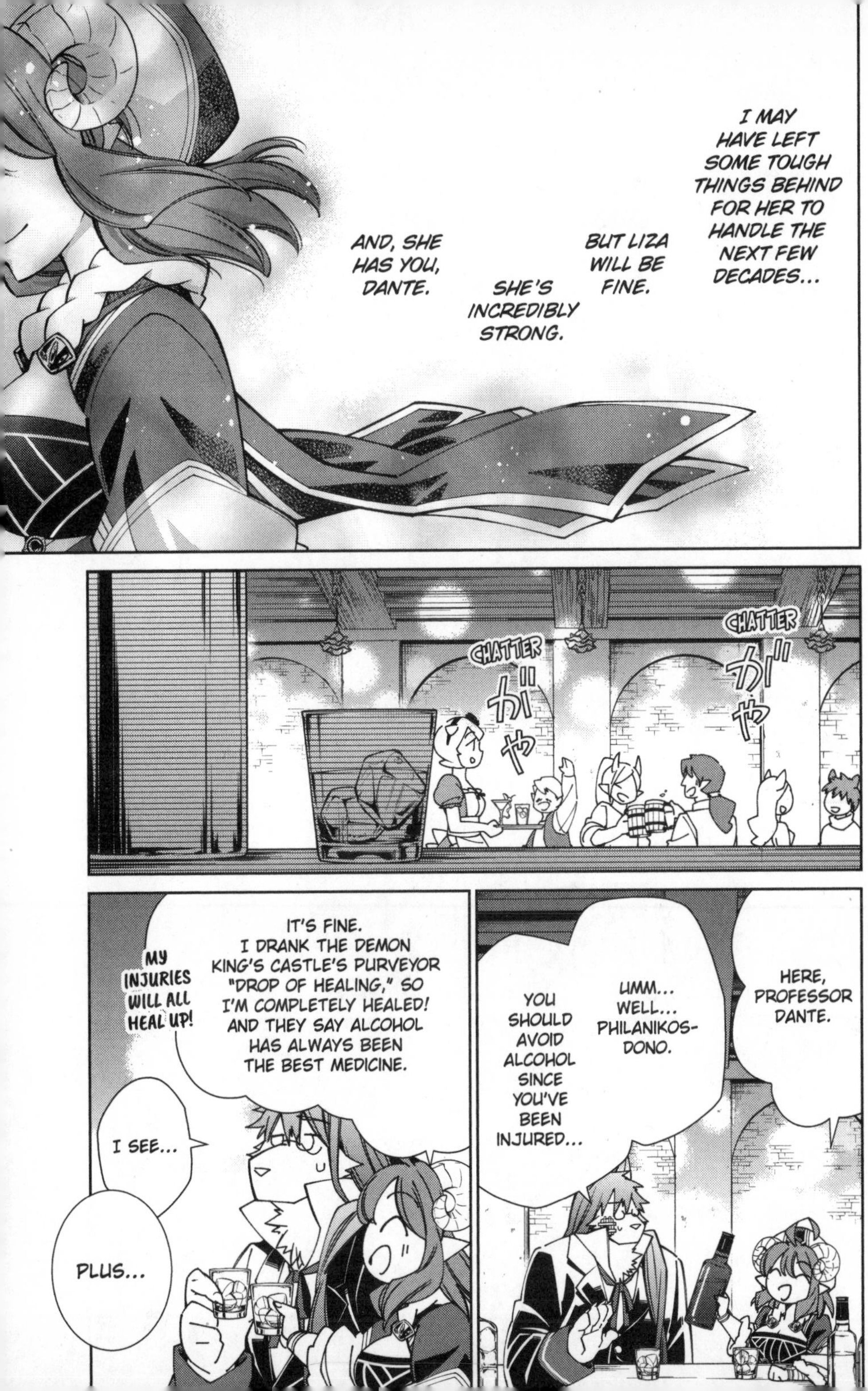

I MAY HAVE LEFT SOME TOUGH THINGS BEHIND FOR HER TO HANDLE THE NEXT FEW DECADES...
BUT LIZA WILL BE FINE.
SHE'S INCREDIBLY STRONG.
AND, SHE HAS YOU, DANTE.
CHATTER
がや
CHATTER
がや
HERE, PROFESSOR DANTE.
UMM... WELL... PHILANIKOS-DONO.
YOU SHOULD AVOID ALCOHOL SINCE YOU'VE BEEN INJURED...
IT'S FINE. I DRANK THE DEMON KING'S CASTLE'S PURVEYOR "DROP OF HEALING," SO I'M COMPLETELY HEALED! AND THEY SAY ALCOHOL HAS ALWAYS BEEN THE BEST MEDICINE.
MY INJURIES WILL ALL HEAL UP!
I SEE...
PLUS...

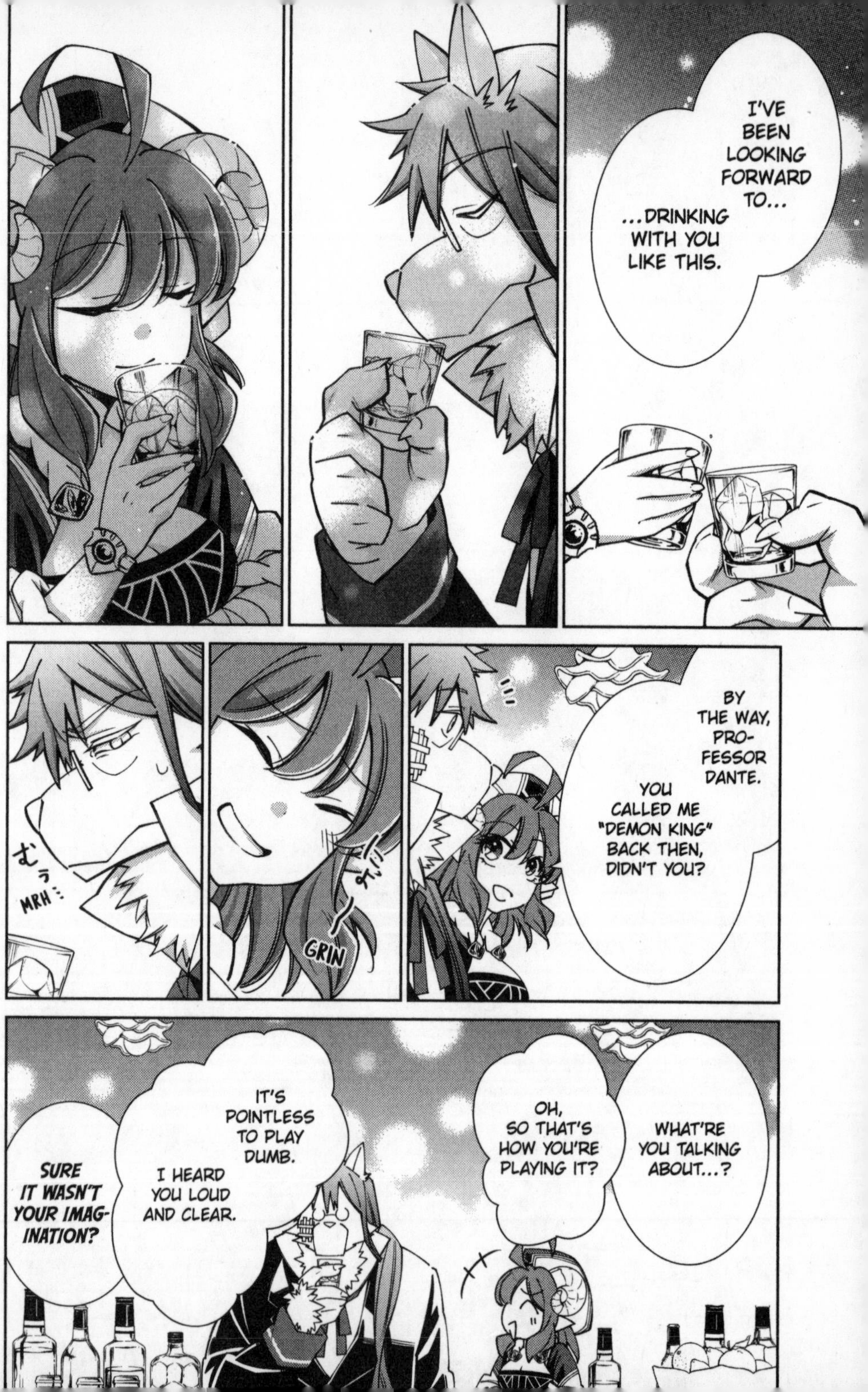
I'VE BEEN LOOKING FORWARD TO...
...DRINKING WITH YOU LIKE THIS.
BY THE WAY, PROFESSOR DANTE.
YOU CALLED ME "DEMON KING" BACK THEN, DIDN'T YOU?
GRIN
MRH...
WHAT'RE YOU TALKING ABOUT...?
OH, SO THAT'S HOW YOU'RE PLAYING IT?
IT'S POINTLESS TO PLAY DUMB.
I HEARD YOU LOUD AND CLEAR.
SURE IT WASN'T YOUR IMAGINATION?

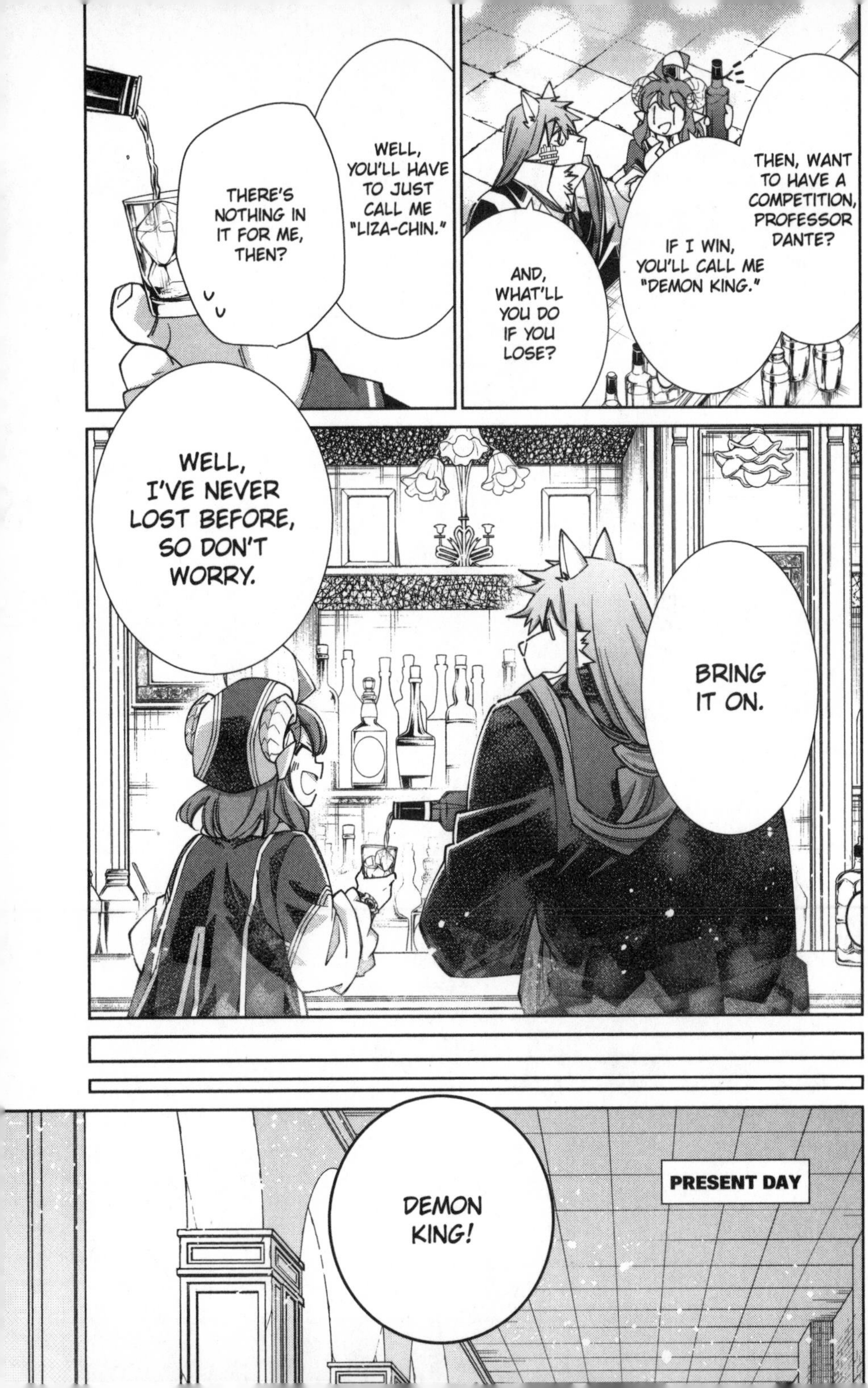
THEN, WANT TO HAVE A COMPETITION, PROFESSOR DANTE?
IF I WIN, YOU'LL CALL ME "DEMON KING."
AND, WHAT'LL YOU DO IF YOU LOSE?
WELL, YOU'LL HAVE TO JUST CALL ME "LIZA-CHIN."
THERE'S NOTHING IN IT FOR ME, THEN?
BRING IT ON.
WELL, I'VE NEVER LOST BEFORE, SO DON'T WORRY.
PRESENT DAY
DEMON KING!

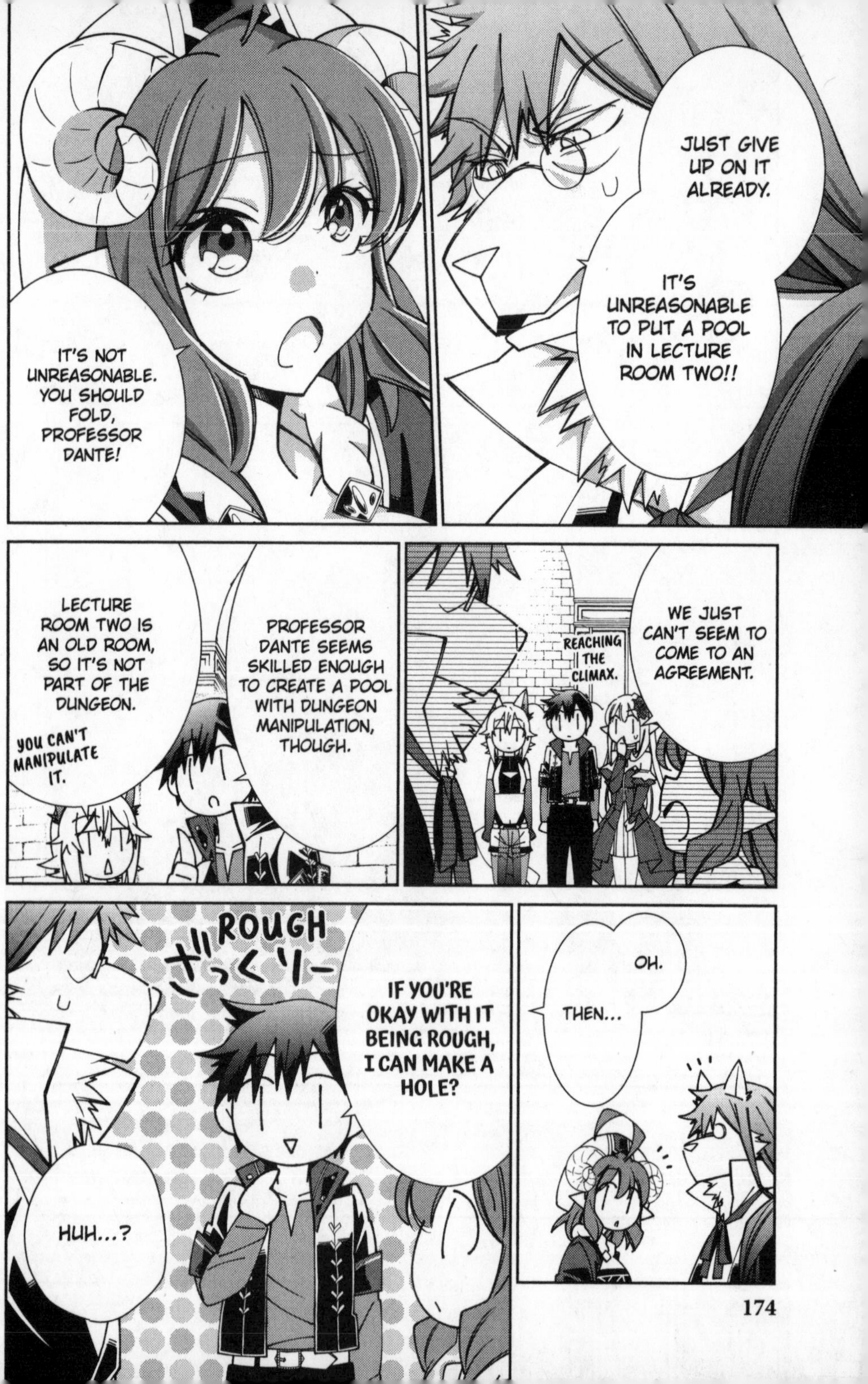
JUST GIVE UP ON IT ALREADY.
IT'S UNREASONABLE TO PUT A POOL IN LECTURE ROOM TWO!!
IT'S NOT UNREASONABLE. YOU SHOULD FOLD, PROFESSOR DANTE!
WE JUST CAN'T SEEM TO COME TO AN AGREEMENT.
REACHING THE CLIMAX.
PROFESSOR DANTE SEEMS SKILLED ENOUGH TO CREATE A POOL WITH DUNGEON MANIPULATION, THOUGH.
LECTURE ROOM TWO IS AN OLD ROOM, SO IT'S NOT PART OF THE DUNGEON.
YOU CAN'T MANIPULATE IT.
OH.
THEN...
ROUGH
ざっくりー
IF YOU'RE OKAY WITH IT BEING ROUGH, I CAN MAKE A HOLE?
HUH...?

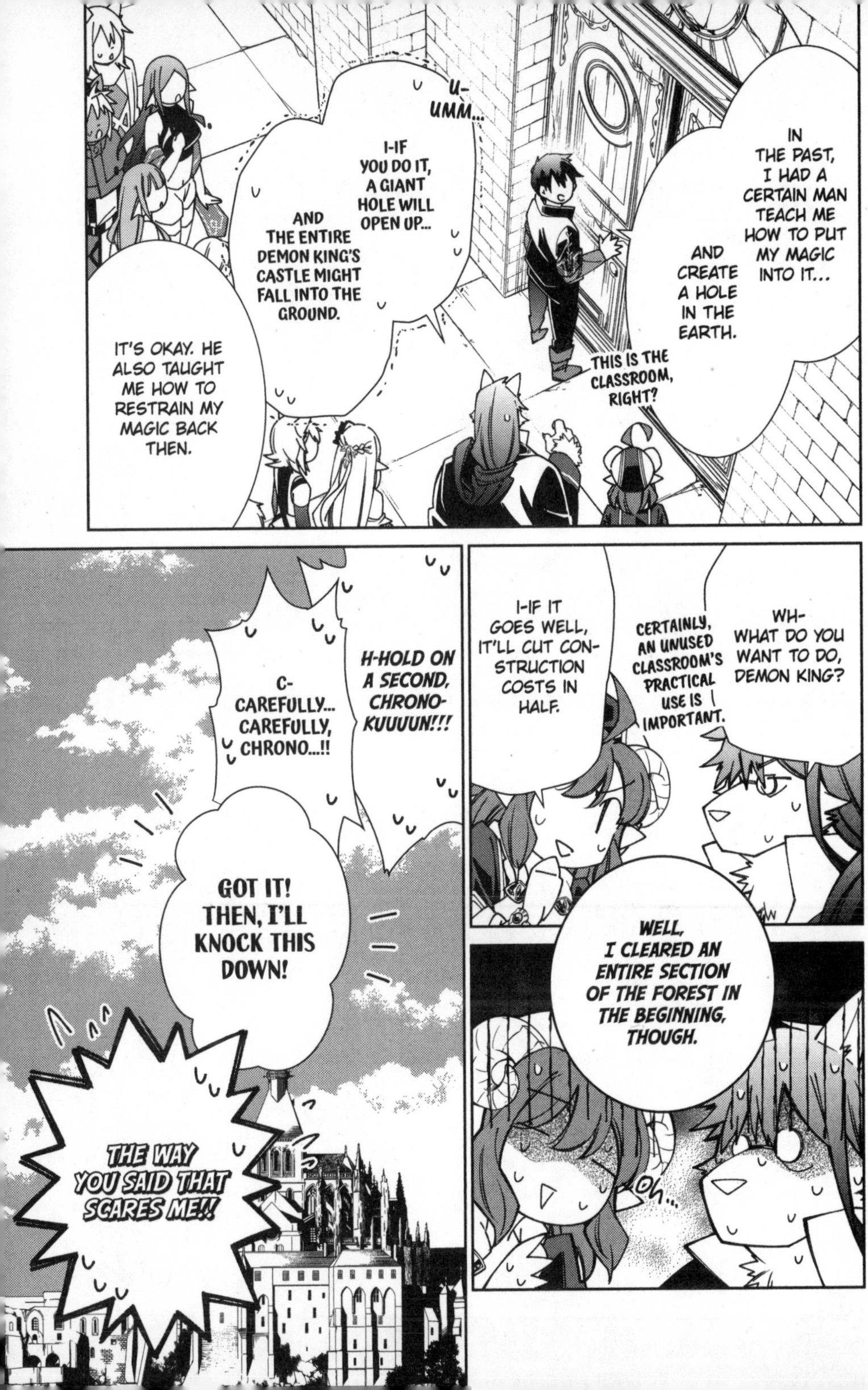
IN THE PAST, I HAD A CERTAIN MAN TEACH ME HOW TO PUT MY MAGIC INTO IT...
AND CREATE A HOLE IN THE EARTH.
THIS IS THE CLASSROOM, RIGHT?
U-UMM...
I-IF YOU DO IT, A GIANT HOLE WILL OPEN UP...
AND THE ENTIRE DEMON KING'S CASTLE MIGHT FALL INTO THE GROUND.
IT'S OKAY. HE ALSO TAUGHT ME HOW TO RESTRAIN MY MAGIC BACK THEN.
WH-WHAT DO YOU WANT TO DO, DEMON KING?
CERTAINLY, AN UNUSED CLASSROOM'S PRACTICAL USE IS IMPORTANT.
I-IF IT GOES WELL, IT'LL CUT CON-STRUCTION COSTS IN HALF.
WELL, I CLEARED AN ENTIRE SECTION OF THE FOREST IN THE BEGINNING, THOUGH.
Oh...
H-HOLD ON A SECOND, CHRONO-KUUUUN!!!
C-CAREFULLY... CAREFULLY, CHRONO...!!
GOT IT! THEN, I'LL KNOCK THIS DOWN!
THE WAY YOU SAID THAT SCARES ME!!

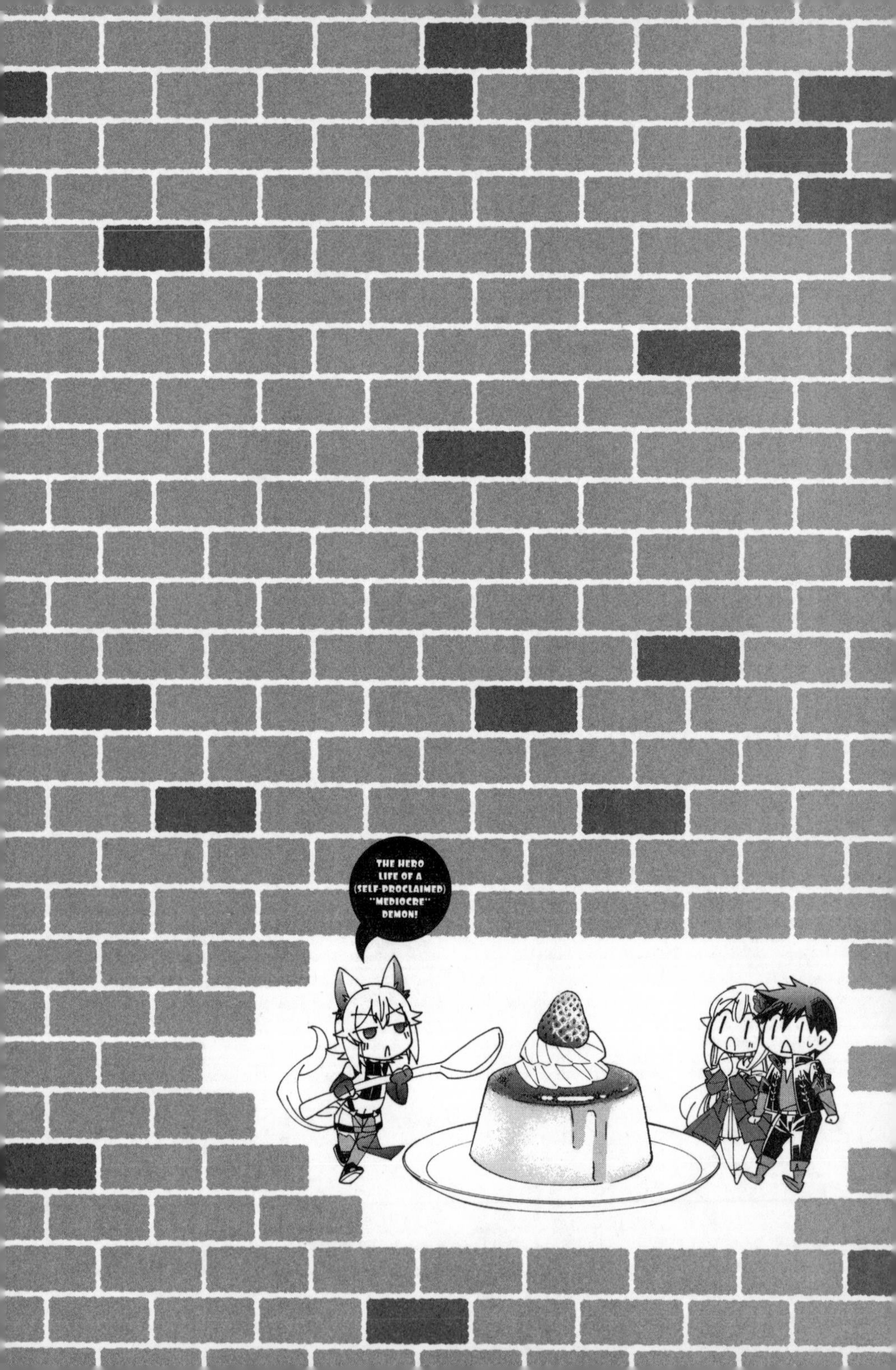
THE HERO LIFE OF A (SELF-PROCLAIMED) "MEDIOCRE" DEMON!

# Even if it's Hard and Busy...

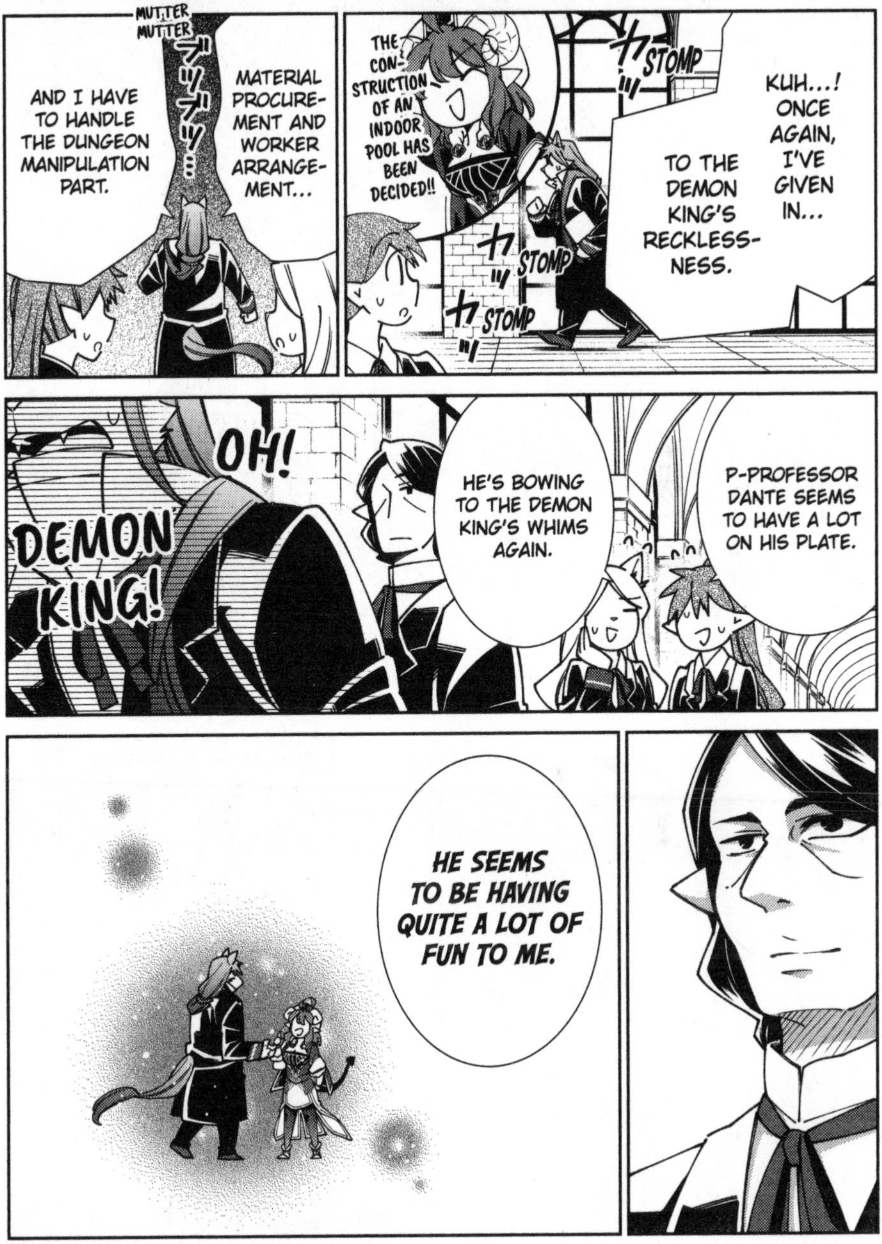
STOMP
KUH...! ONCE AGAIN, I'VE GIVEN IN...
TO THE DEMON KING'S RECKLESSNESS.
THE CONSTRUCTION OF AN INDOOR POOL HAS BEEN DECIDED!!
STOMP
STOMP
MATERIAL PROCUREMENT AND WORKER ARRANGEMENT...
MUTTER MUTTER
ブツブツ…
AND I HAVE TO HANDLE THE DUNGEON MANIPULATION PART.
P-PROFESSOR DANTE SEEMS TO HAVE A LOT ON HIS PLATE.
HE'S BOWING TO THE DEMON KING'S WHIMS AGAIN.
OH!
DEMON KING!
HE SEEMS TO BE HAVING QUITE A LOT OF FUN TO ME.

# The Demon King's Strength

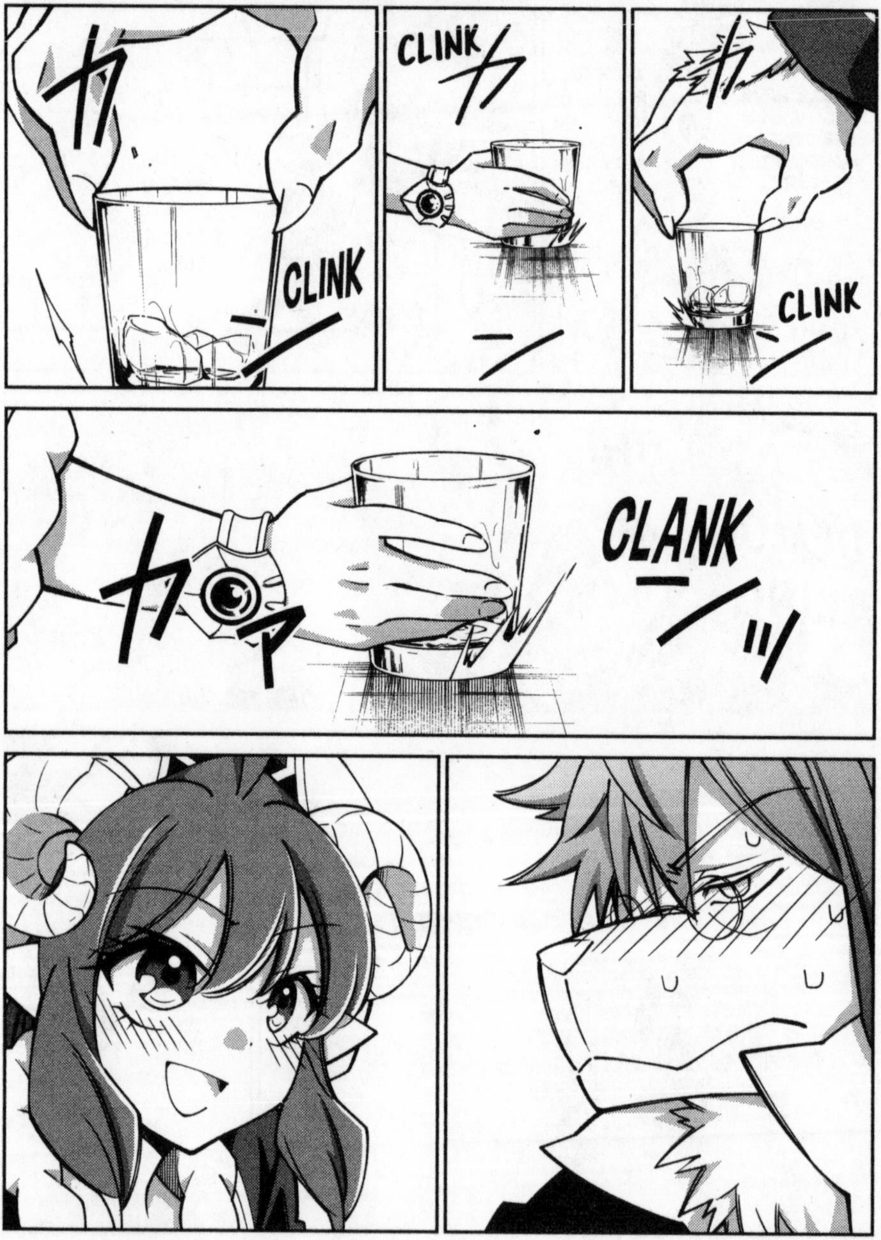
CLINK
CLINK
CLINK
CLANK

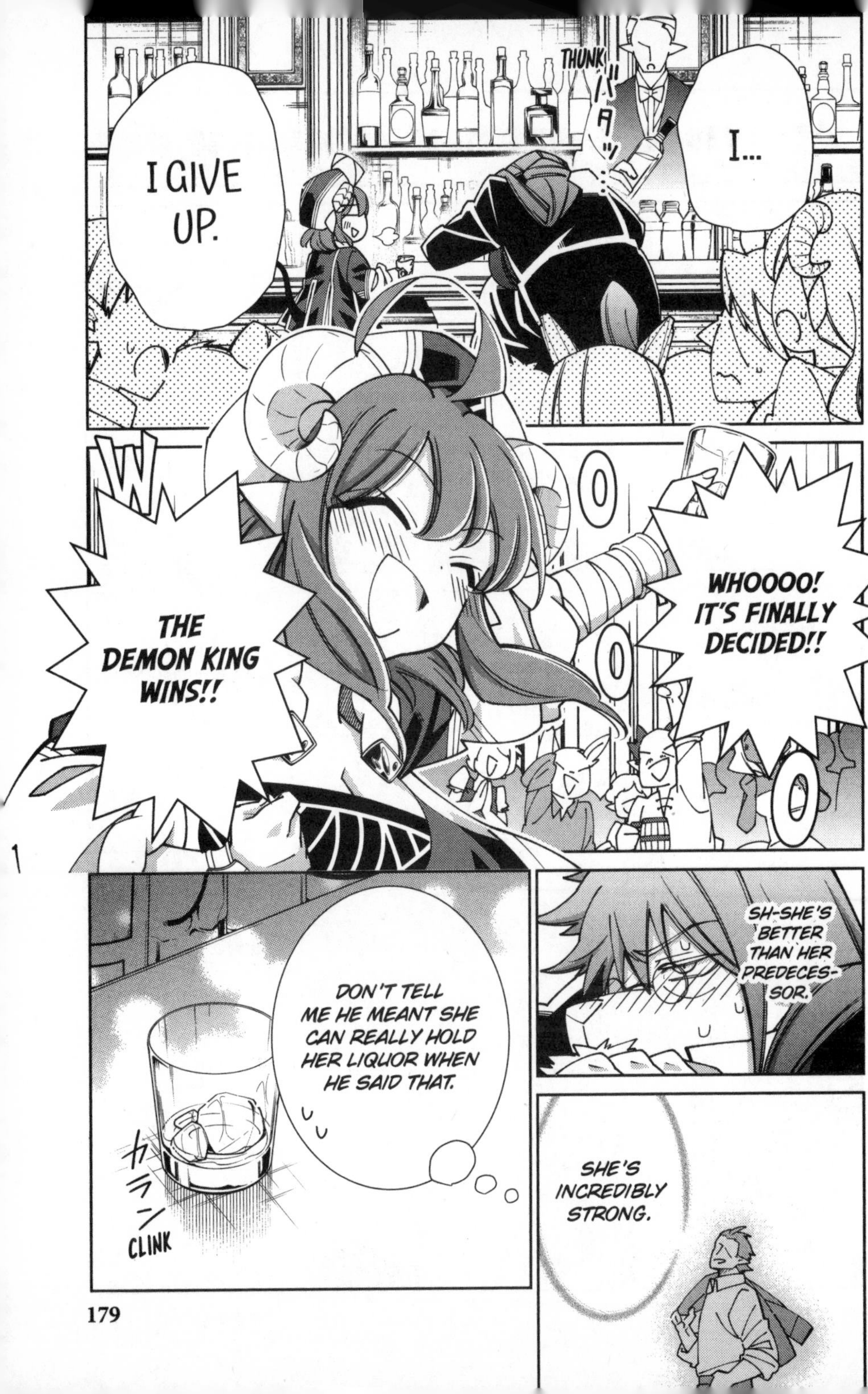
I...
THUNK
I GIVE UP.
WHOOOO! IT'S FINALLY DECIDED!!
THE DEMON KING WINS!!
SH-SHE'S BETTER THAN HER PREDECES-SOR.
SHE'S INCREDIBLY STRONG.
DON'T TELL ME HE MEANT SHE CAN REALLY HOLD HER LIQUOR WHEN HE SAID THAT.
CLINK

# Professor Dante Can't Figure it Out

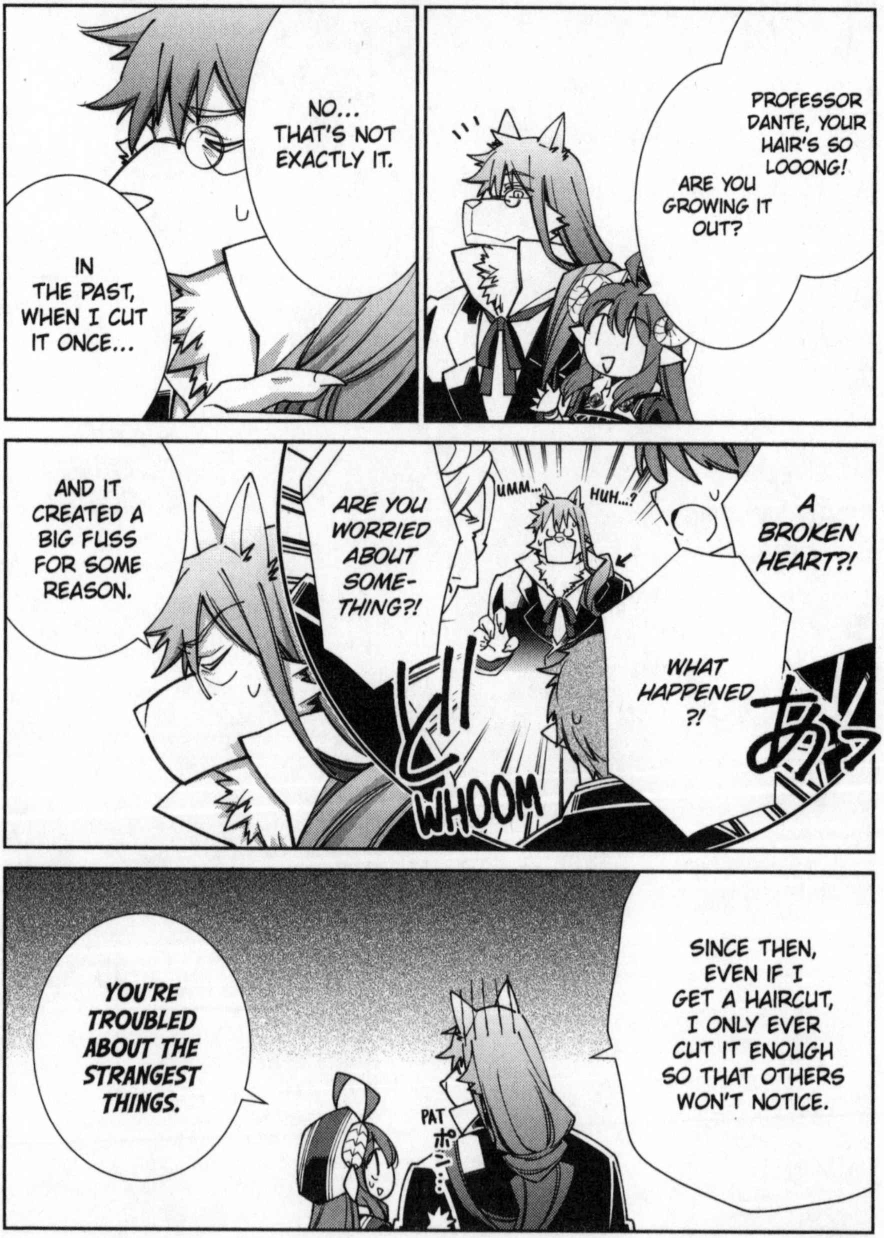
PROFESSOR DANTE, YOUR HAIR'S SO LOOONG!
ARE YOU GROWING IT OUT?
NO... THAT'S NOT EXACTLY IT.
IN THE PAST, WHEN I CUT IT ONCE...
A BROKEN HEART?!
HUH...?
UMM...
ARE YOU WORRIED ABOUT SOME-THING?!
AND IT CREATED A BIG FUSS FOR SOME REASON.
WHAT HAPPENED?!
WHOOM
SINCE THEN, EVEN IF I GET A HAIRCUT, I ONLY EVER CUT IT ENOUGH SO THAT OTHERS WON'T NOTICE.
PAT
YOU'RE TROUBLED ABOUT THE STRANGEST THINGS.

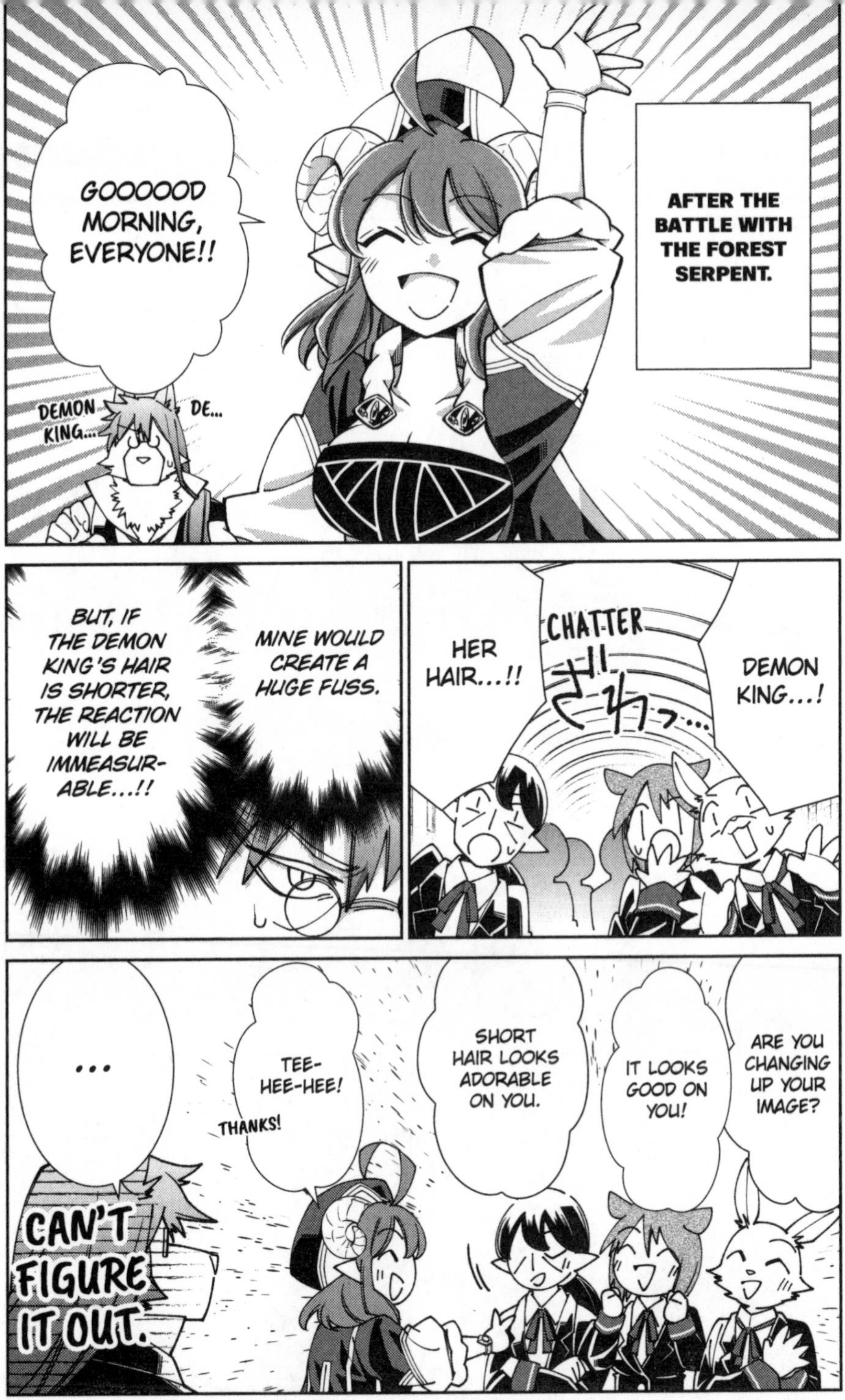
AFTER THE BATTLE WITH THE FOREST SERPENT.
GOOOOOD MORNING, EVERYONE!!
DE...
DEMON KING...
DEMON KING...!
CHATTER
ざわっ…
HER HAIR...!!
MINE WOULD CREATE A HUGE FUSS.
BUT, IF THE DEMON KING'S HAIR IS SHORTER, THE REACTION WILL BE IMMEASUR-ABLE...!!
ARE YOU CHANGING UP YOUR IMAGE?
IT LOOKS GOOD ON YOU!
SHORT HAIR LOOKS ADORABLE ON YOU.
TEE-HEE-HEE!
THANKS!
...
CAN'T FIGURE IT OUT.

# 5 Seconds Before Plunging into the Slime

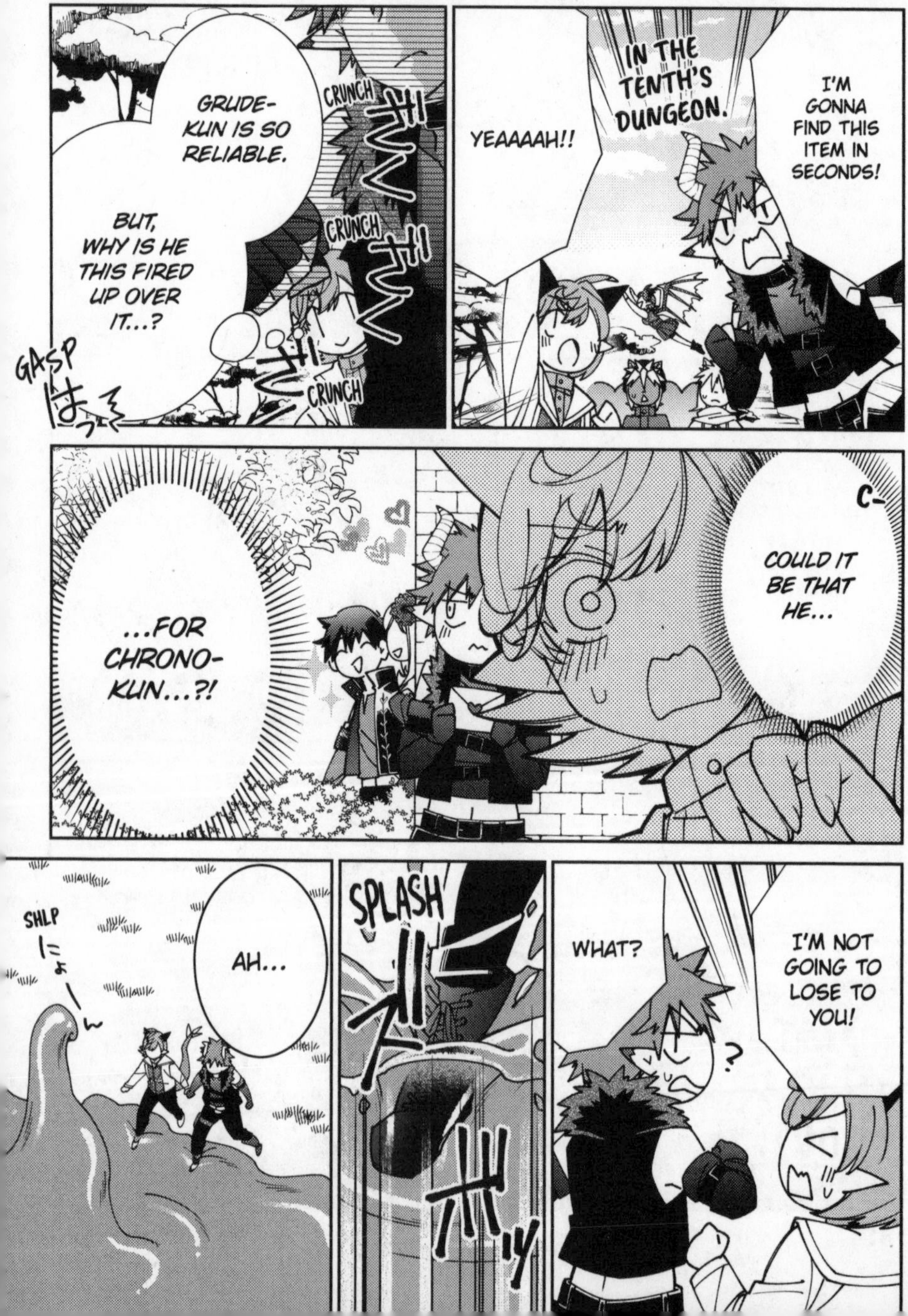
I'M GONNA FIND THIS ITEM IN SECONDS!
IN THE TENTH'S DUNGEON.
YEAAAAH!!
CRUNCH
CRUNCH
GRUDE-KUN IS SO RELIABLE.
BUT, WHY IS HE THIS FIRED UP OVER IT...?
CRUNCH
GASP
C-
COULD IT BE THAT HE...
...FOR CHRONO-KUN...?!
I'M NOT GOING TO LOSE TO YOU!
WHAT?
SPLASH
AH...
SHLP

# Yukino During the Fight With the Kraken

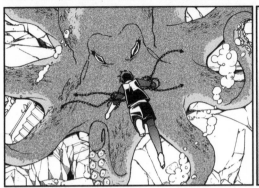

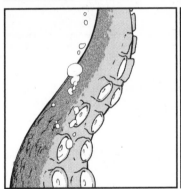

I WANNA EAT...

...TAKOYAKI.

# Curious About Everyone's Pajama Situation

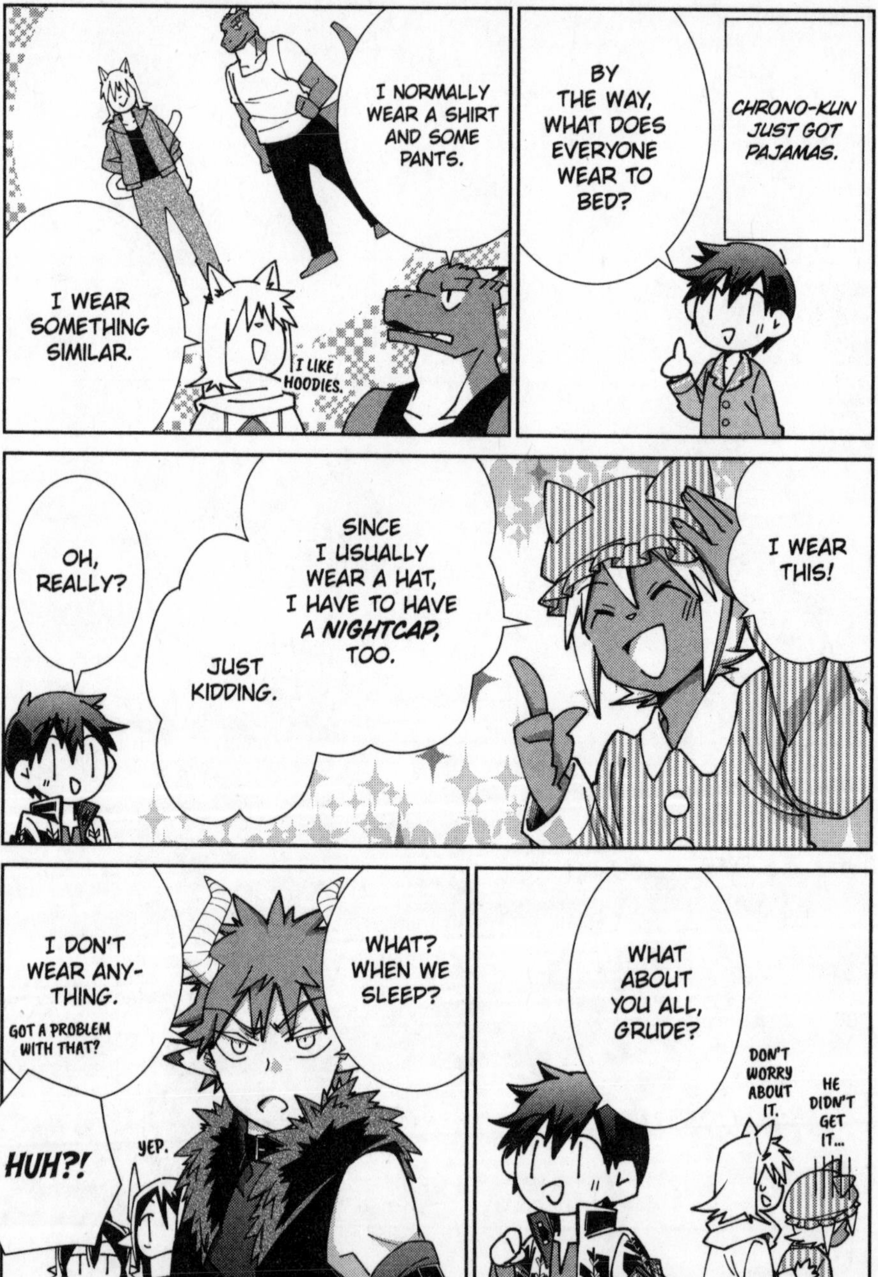
CHRONO-KUN JUST GOT PAJAMAS.
BY THE WAY, WHAT DOES EVERYONE WEAR TO BED?
I NORMALLY WEAR A SHIRT AND SOME PANTS.
I WEAR SOMETHING SIMILAR.
I LIKE HOODIES.
I WEAR THIS!
SINCE I USUALLY WEAR A HAT, I HAVE TO HAVE A *NIGHTCAP*, TOO.
JUST KIDDING.
OH, REALLY?
WHAT ABOUT YOU ALL, GRUDE?
HE DIDN'T GET IT...
DON'T WORRY ABOUT IT.
WHAT? WHEN WE SLEEP?
I DON'T WEAR ANY-THING.
GOT A PROBLEM WITH THAT?
YEP.
HUH?!

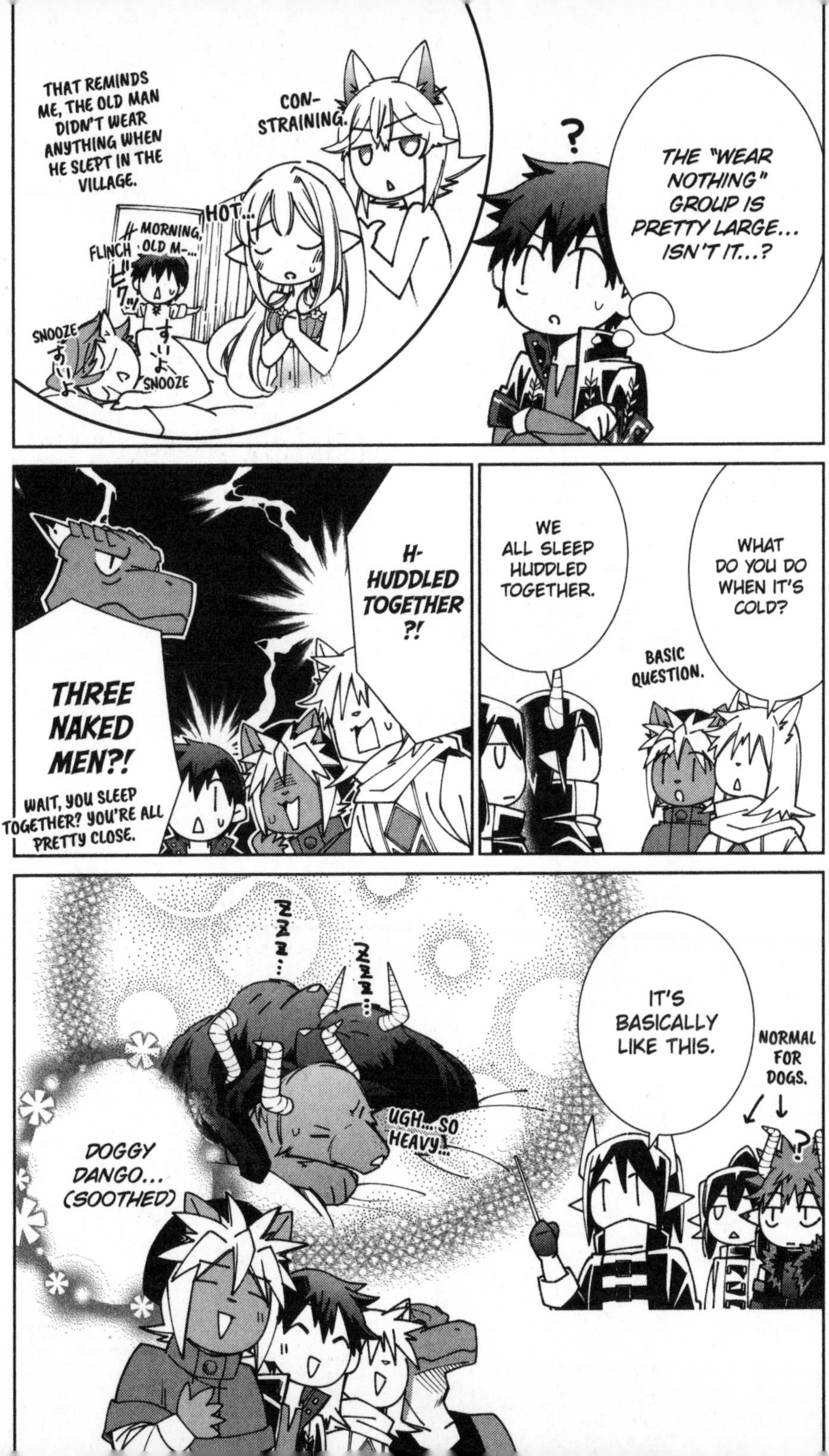
?
THE "WEAR NOTHING" GROUP IS PRETTY LARGE... ISN'T IT...?
CON-STRAINING.
THAT REMINDS ME, THE OLD MAN DIDN'T WEAR ANYTHING WHEN HE SLEPT IN THE VILLAGE.
HOT...
MORNING, OLD M-...
FLINCH
SNOOZE
SNOOZE
WHAT DO YOU DO WHEN IT'S COLD?
BASIC QUESTION.
WE ALL SLEEP HUDDLED TOGETHER.
H-HUDDLED TOGETHER?!
THREE NAKED MEN?!
WAIT, YOU SLEEP TOGETHER? YOU'RE ALL PRETTY CLOSE.
IT'S BASICALLY LIKE THIS.
NORMAL FOR DOGS.
?
ZZZ...
ZZZ...
UGH... SO HEAVY...
DOGGY DANGO... (SOOTHED)

# IDENTITIES OF THE POWERFUL

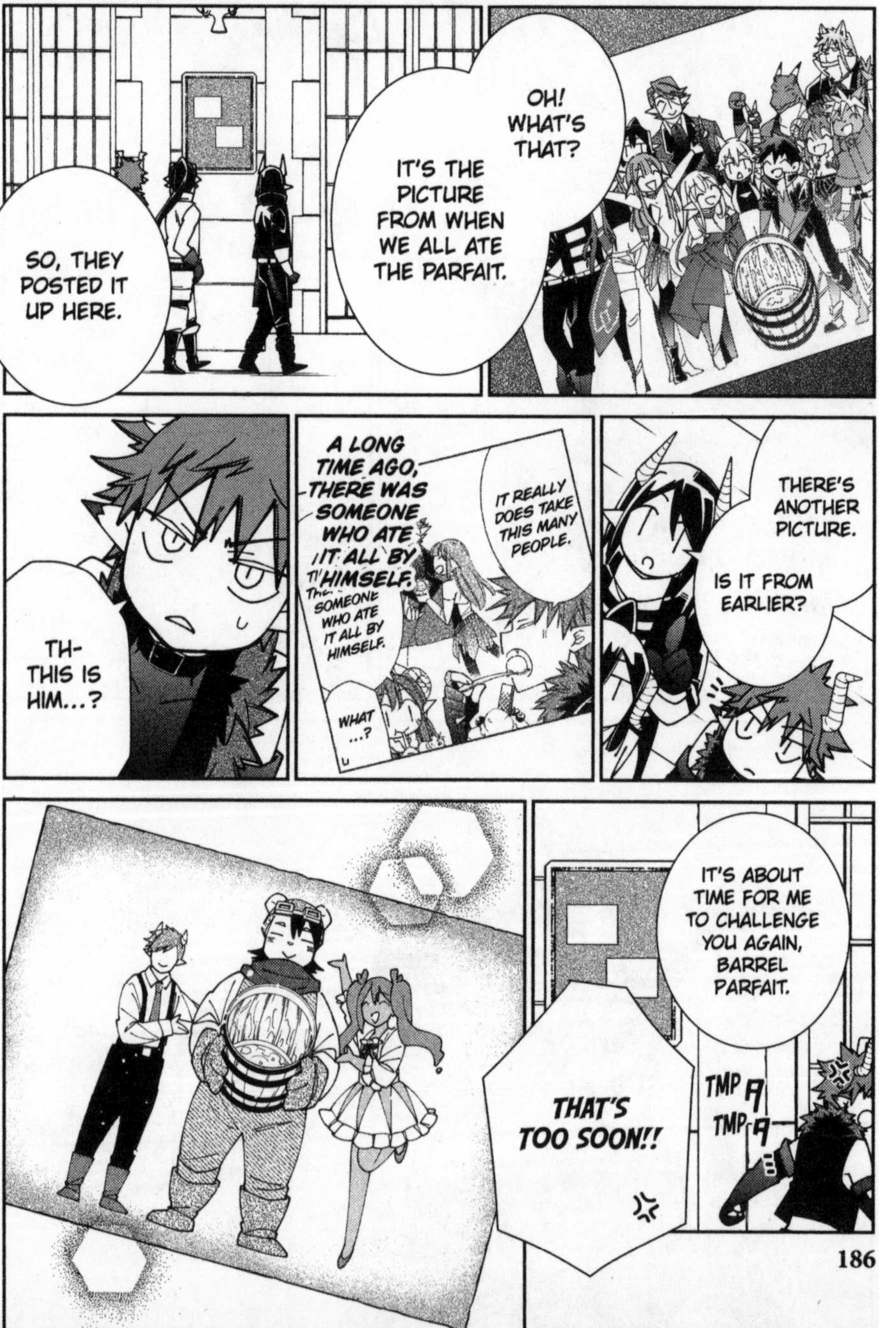
OH! WHAT'S THAT?
IT'S THE PICTURE FROM WHEN WE ALL ATE THE PARFAIT.
SO, THEY POSTED IT UP HERE.
THERE'S ANOTHER PICTURE.
IS IT FROM EARLIER?
IT REALLY DOES TAKE THIS MANY PEOPLE.
A LONG TIME AGO, THERE WAS SOMEONE WHO ATE IT ALL BY HIMSELF.
SOMEONE WHO ATE IT ALL BY HIMSELF.
WHAT ...?
TH- THIS IS HIM...?
IT'S ABOUT TIME FOR ME TO CHALLENGE YOU AGAIN, BARREL PARFAIT.
TMP
TMP
THAT'S TOO SOON!!

# Fifteen Years Since Then

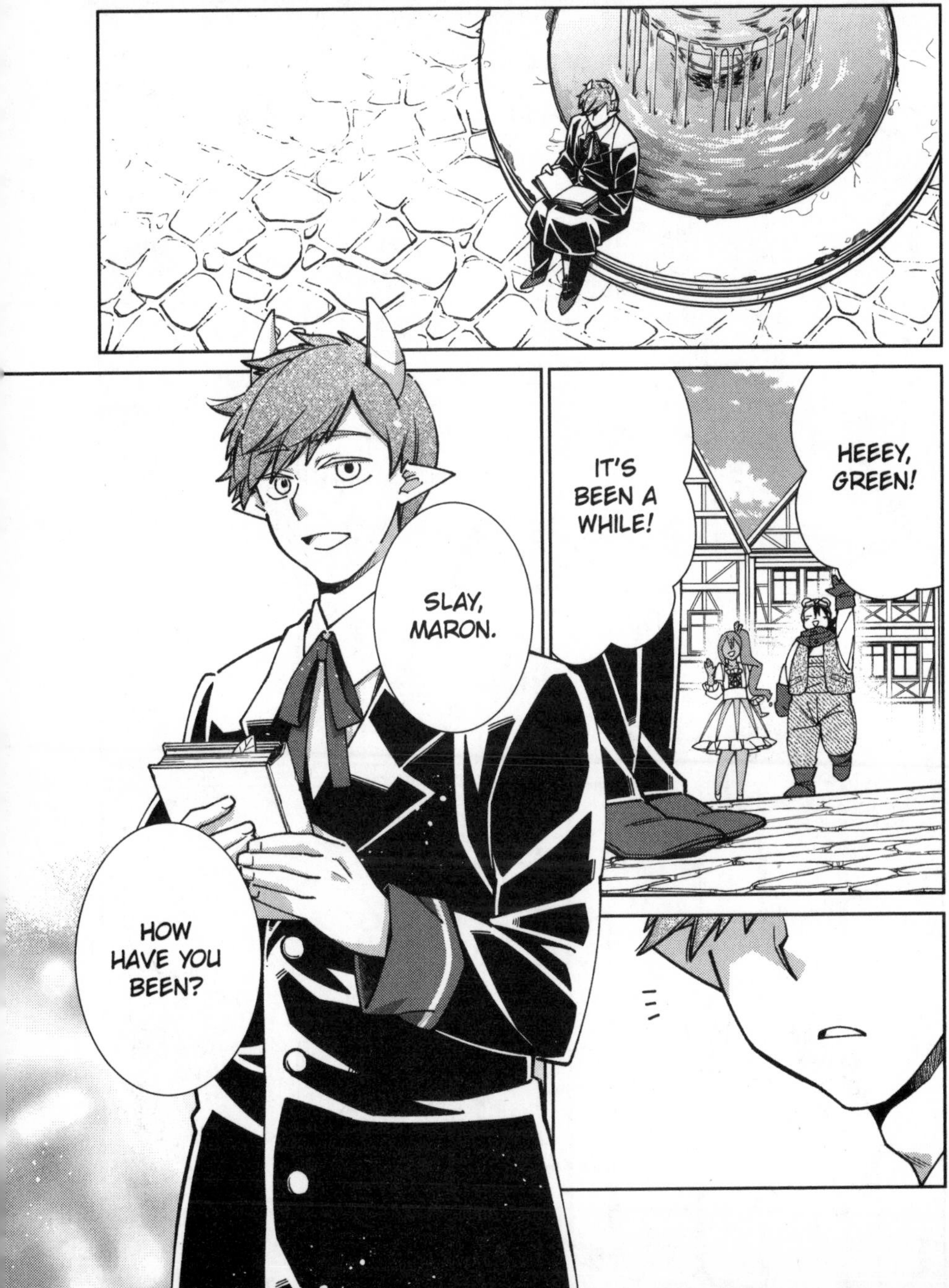
HEEEY, GREEN!
IT'S BEEN A WHILE!
SLAY, MARON.
HOW HAVE YOU BEEN?

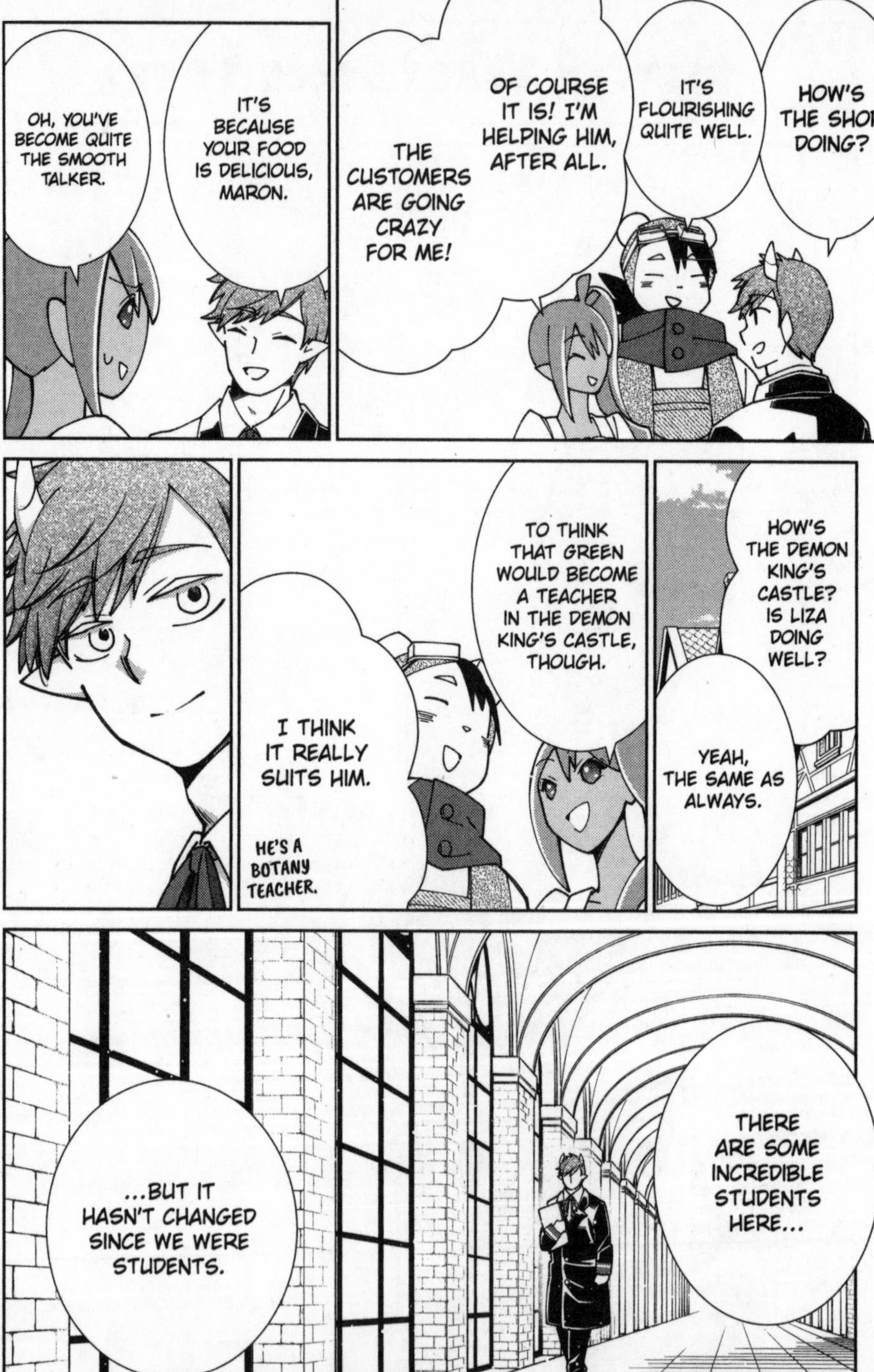
HOW'S THE SHOP DOING?
IT'S FLOURISHING QUITE WELL.
OF COURSE IT IS! I'M HELPING HIM, AFTER ALL.
THE CUSTOMERS ARE GOING CRAZY FOR ME!
IT'S BECAUSE YOUR FOOD IS DELICIOUS, MARON.
OH, YOU'VE BECOME QUITE THE SMOOTH TALKER.
HOW'S THE DEMON KING'S CASTLE? IS LIZA DOING WELL?
YEAH, THE SAME AS ALWAYS.
TO THINK THAT GREEN WOULD BECOME A TEACHER IN THE DEMON KING'S CASTLE, THOUGH.
I THINK IT REALLY SUITS HIM.
HE'S A BOTANY TEACHER.
THERE ARE SOME INCREDIBLE STUDENTS HERE...
...BUT IT HASN'T CHANGED SINCE WE WERE STUDENTS.

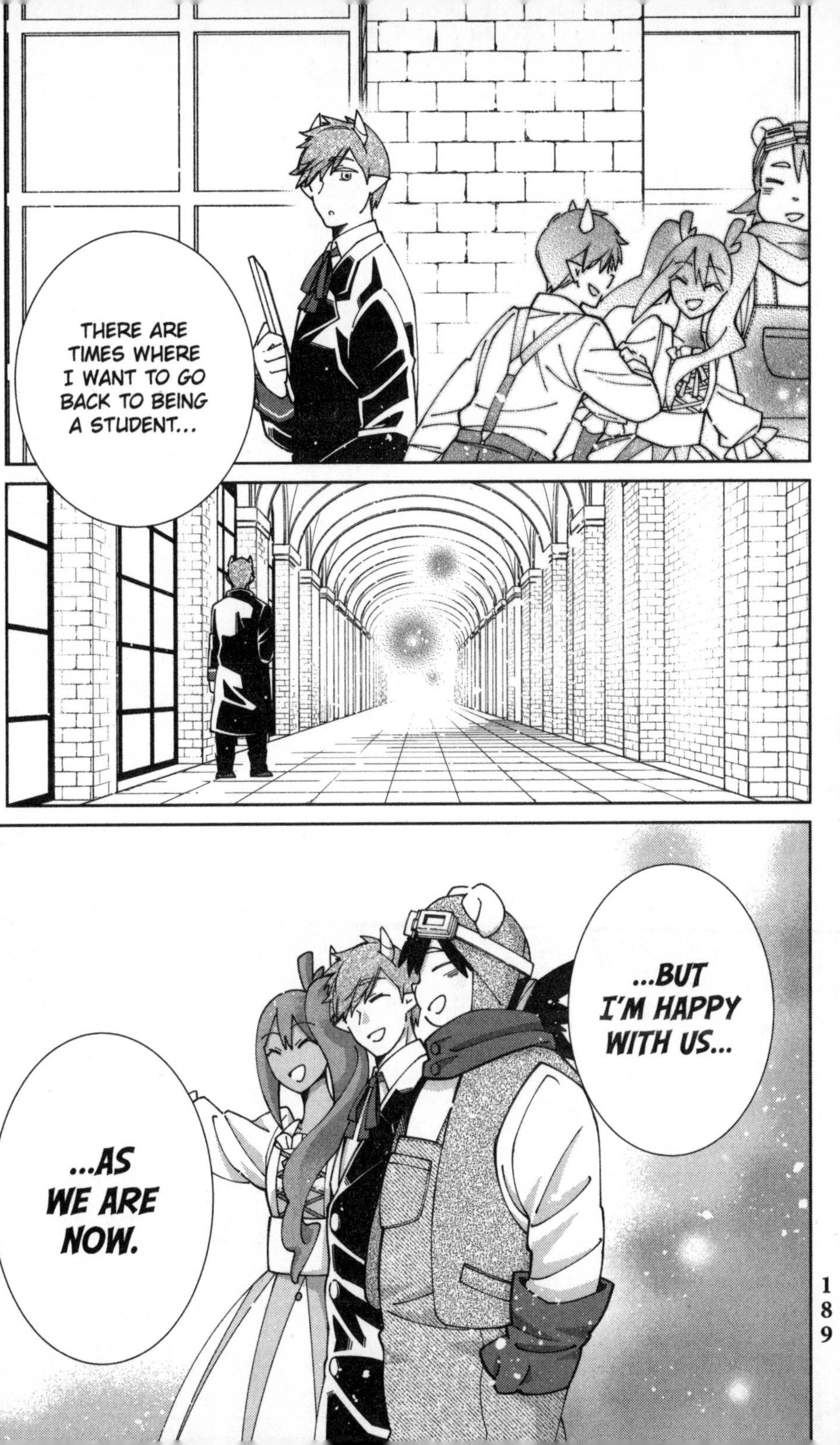
THERE ARE TIMES WHERE I WANT TO GO BACK TO BEING A STUDENT...
...BUT I'M HAPPY WITH US...
...AS WE ARE NOW.

# End of Book Bonus

# Special Release! Volume 7's Cover Rough Drafts

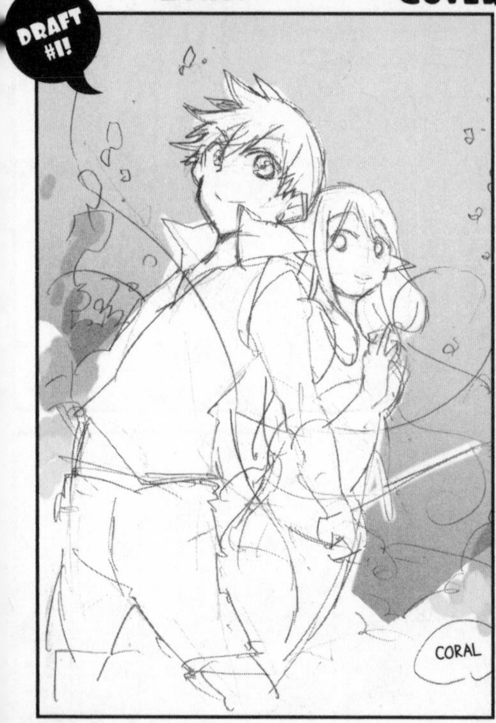
DRAFT #1!
CORAL

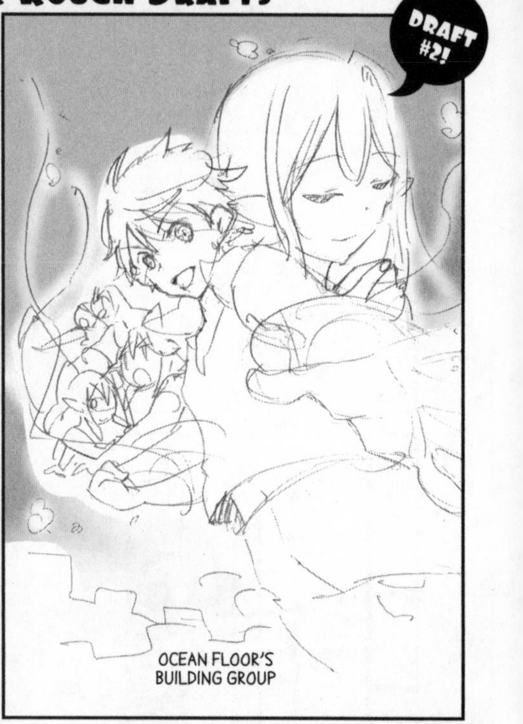
DRAFT #2!
OCEAN FLOOR'S BUILDING GROUP

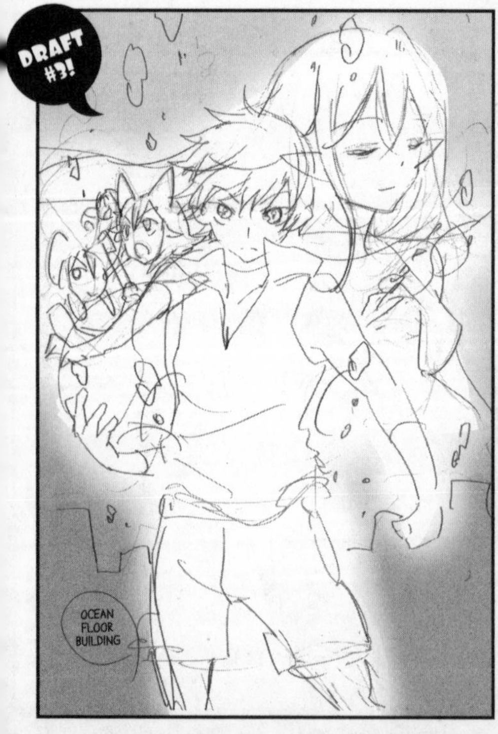
DRAFT #3!
OCEAN FLOOR BUILDING

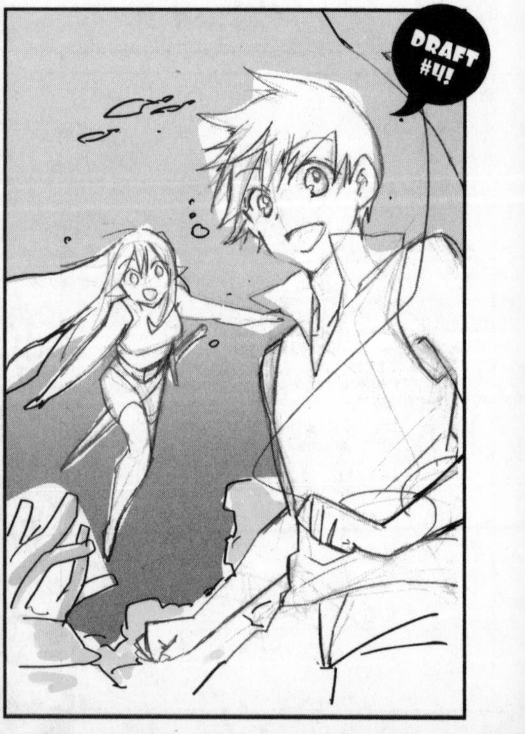
DRAFT #4!

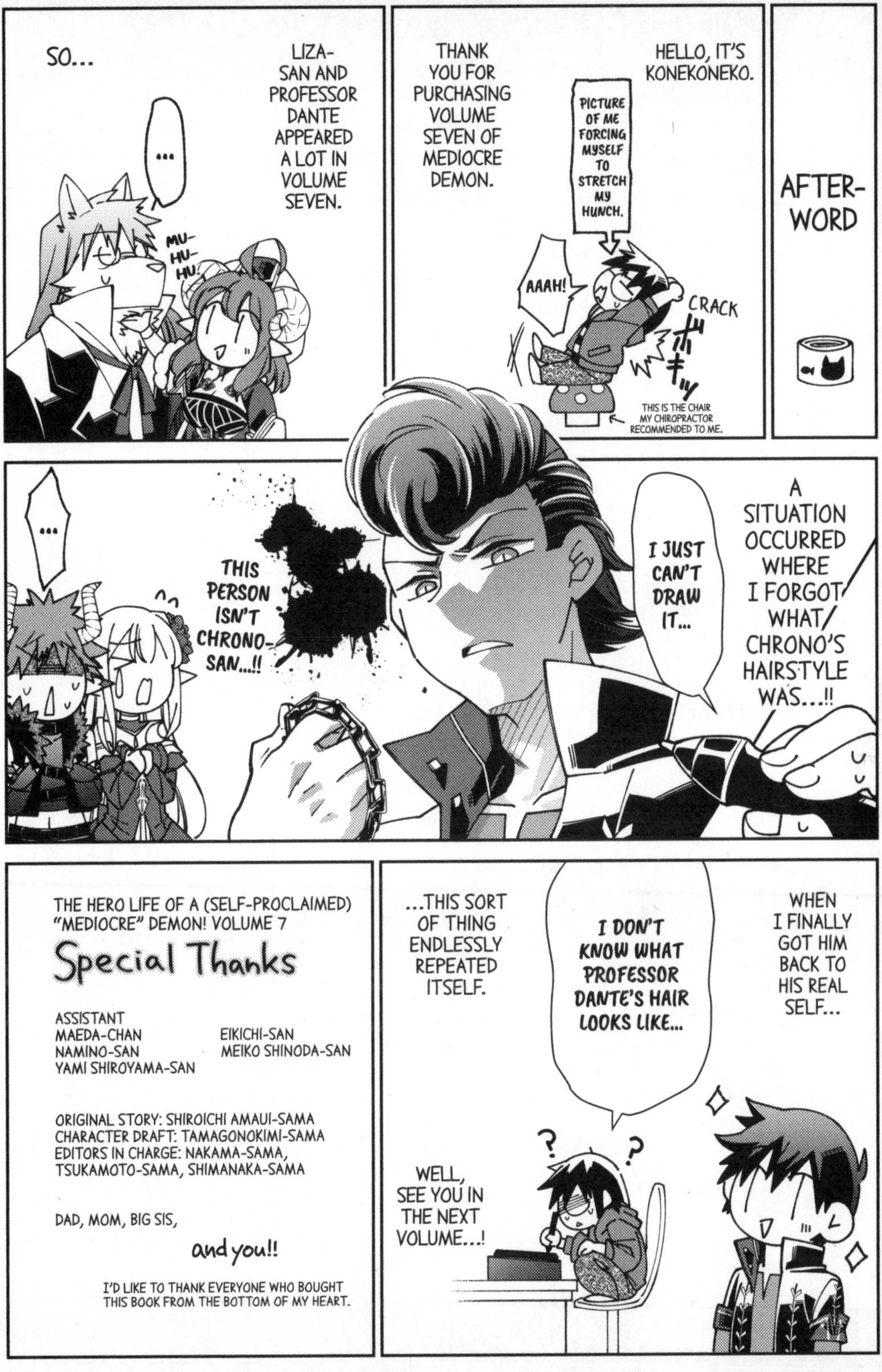
AFTERWORD
HELLO, IT'S KONEKONEKO.
PICTURE OF ME FORCING MYSELF TO STRETCH MY HUNCH.
THANK YOU FOR PURCHASING VOLUME SEVEN OF MEDIOCRE DEMON.
AAAH!
CRACK
THIS IS THE CHAIR MY CHIROPRACTOR RECOMMENDED TO ME.
LIZA-SAN AND PROFESSOR DANTE APPEARED A LOT IN VOLUME SEVEN.
...
SO...
MU-HU-HU
A SITUATION OCCURRED WHERE I FORGOT WHAT CHRONO'S HAIRSTYLE WAS...!!
I JUST CAN'T DRAW IT...
THIS PERSON ISN'T CHRONO-SAN...!!
...
WHEN I FINALLY GOT HIM BACK TO HIS REAL SELF...
I DON'T KNOW WHAT PROFESSOR DANTE'S HAIR LOOKS LIKE...
...THIS SORT OF THING ENDLESSLY REPEATED ITSELF.
WELL, SEE YOU IN THE NEXT VOLUME...!
THE HERO LIFE OF A (SELF-PROCLAIMED) "MEDIOCRE" DEMON! VOLUME 7
Special Thanks
ASSISTANT
MAEDA-CHAN
NAMINO-SAN
YAMI SHIROYAMA-SAN
EIKICHI-SAN
MEIKO SHINODA-SAN
ORIGINAL STORY: SHIROICHI AMAUI-SAMA
CHARACTER DRAFT: TAMAGONOKIMI-SAMA
EDITORS IN CHARGE: NAKAMA-SAMA, TSUKAMOTO-SAMA, SHIMANAKA-SAMA
DAD, MOM, BIG SIS,
and you!!
I'D LIKE TO THANK EVERYONE WHO BOUGHT THIS BOOK FROM THE BOTTOM OF MY HEART.

A Kodansha Trade Paperback Original

Published in the United States by
Kodansha USA Publishing, LLC, New York.

Publication rights for this English edition arranged through
Kodansha Ltd., Tokyo.

First published in Japan in 2021 by Kodansha Ltd., Tokyo as
*Jishō! Heibon mazoku no eiyū raifu 7.*

ISBN 978-1-64651-599-8

Printed in the United States of America.

1st Printing

Translation: Jessica Latherow / amimaru
Lettering: Chris Burgener / amimaru
Additional Lettering: Phil Christie
Editing: David Yoo
Kodansha USA Publishing edition cover design by Matt Akuginow

Publisher: Kiichiro Sugawara

Director of Publishing Services: Ben Applegate
Director of Publishing Operations: Dave Barrett
Associate Director of Publishing Operations: Stephen Pakula
Publishing Services Managing Editors: Madison Salters, Alanna Ruse, with Grace Chen
Production Manager: Jocelyn O'Dowd

KODANSHA.US

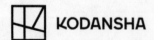

**KODANSHA**